FRENCH MADE SIMPLE

Revised Edition

BY

EUGENE JACKSON, A.B.

Chairman of Foreign Languages (Ret.)
Samuel J. Tilden High School, Brooklyn, N.Y.

AND

ANTONIO RUBIO, Ph.D.

Late Chairman, Dept. of Modern Languages
DePaul University, Chicago, Ill.

REVISED BY

SUSAN DERECSKEY, B.A.

Brevet d'Aptitude à l'Enseignement de Français
Alliance Française, Paris

Certificate in French-English Translation
British Institute, Paris

MADE SIMPLE BOOKS

DOUBLEDAY & COMPANY, INC.
GARDEN CITY, NEW YORK
1987

PRINTED IN THE UNITED STATES OF AMERICA

Library of Congress Cataloging-in-Publication Data

Jackson, Eugene.
French made simple.

1. French language—Text-books for foreign speakers—English. 2. French language—Grammar—1950–
I. Rubio, Antonio, date. II. Derecskey, Susan.
III. Title.
PC2129.E5J33 1986 448.2′421 86-21803
ISBN 0-385-23362-0

ABOUT THIS BOOK

French for Tourist, Traveler, and Businessman

Do you wish to learn rapidly and easily how to pronounce French well, how to engage in day-to-day conversation, how to read simple French texts—in short, do you wish to acquire enough knowledge of French to meet your needs as a tourist, traveler, or businessman in a French-speaking country? Then FRENCH MADE SIMPLE is the book for you.

The bilingual text which eliminates the time-consuming task of looking up words in the dictionary, dialogues dealing with everyday topics, the word-building exercises, French questions with an answer key for self-checking—all these will enable you to attain your goal pleasantly and effectively.

Important words and expressions and cultural facts are easy to remember because they appear naturally in a series of conversations between the French teacher Mr. Picard and his pupil Mr. Potter, a businessman from New York, who like you is about to take a trip to France and wants to be able to get along in French.

French for Students

Do you wish a thorough grounding in the French language for secondary school or college? FRENCH MADE SIMPLE will enable you to attain your goal. The essential grammatical facts of French grow naturally out of the conversation and reading texts. The facts are clearly explained. Non-essentials are omitted. The numerous illustrative drills and exercises and the answer key for self-checking will provide you with a thorough knowledge of the elements of French and lay the foundation for advanced study of the language.

FRENCH MADE SIMPLE thus meets the needs of self-learners, whether their aim is the kind of practical conversation and comprehension ability the tourist, traveler, or businessman needs, or the thorough grounding in the fundamentals of the French language the high school or college student desires. It can also serve as an excellent refresher course for those who have already had some study of the language.

French Text for Classroom Use

Although primarily designed for self-study, FRENCH MADE SIMPLE can serve as a textbook in French classes in secondary schools or college. The material is practical; the conversational approach is simple and interesting; and the cultural aspects are closely integrated with the language elements. The book offers an easy method for acquiring vocabulary, everyday expressions, and even those grammatical facts that are often the student's bête noire. FRENCH MADE SIMPLE is a welcome alternative to conventional textbooks with their academic approach and overemphasis on grammar.

TABLE OF CONTENTS

CHAPITRE 1 (UN)—CHAPTER 1

MEET THE FRENCH LANGUAGE

1. *French is no stranger.*

On beginning your study of the French language you will be surprised to learn that you already know, or you can make a good guess at, the meaning of thousands of French words. There are several thousand words that have the same spelling and meaning in French and English, and thousands more with the same meaning that differ only slightly in spelling. Of course the pronunciation of the French words differs greatly from that of the corresponding English words.

There are also many words borrowed directly from the French without any change in spelling and with little or no change at all in pronunciation.

Here are a few examples of words alike or very similar in French and English:

a. words spelled alike and having the same meaning but different in pronunciation:

vain	**fruit**	**danger**	**nation**	**absent**	**station**	**excellent**
page	**image**	**humble**	**nature**	**avenue**	**question**	**important**
train	**table**	**automobile**	**voyage**	**action**	**original**	**diligent**
place	**index**	**bureau**	**client**	**cousin**	**accident**	**intelligent**

b. words of the same meaning, slightly different in spelling and different in pronunciation:

riche	**oncle**	**balle**	**objet**	**scène**	**hôtel**	**brun**	**bleu**
rich	*uncle*	*ball*	*object*	*scene*	*hotel*	*brown*	blue
salade	**madame**	**touriste**	**sévère**	**rivière**	**parfum**	**mètre**	**poste**
salad	*madam*	*tourist*	*severe*	*river*	*perfume*	*meter*	*post*
difficile	**famille**	**qualité**	**liberté**	**docteur**	**acteur**	**téléphone**	**télévision**
difficult	*family*	*quality*	*liberty*	*doctor*	*actor*	*telephone*	*television*
visiter	**excuser**	**arriver**	**entrer**	**désirer**	**signer**	**dîner**	**inviter**
to visit	*to excuse*	*to arrive*	*to enter*	*to desire*	*to sign*	to dine	*to invite*

c. words borrowed directly from the French with no changes in spelling and only minor changes in pronunciation. These words contain some good clues to French pronunciation:

café	**garage**	**ennui**	**lingerie**	**château**	**coquette**	**nouveau riche**
route	**chauffeur**	**encore**	**ensemble**	**bouquet**	**rendez-vous**	**laissez-faire**
rôle	**liqueur**	**chemise**	**consommé**	**matinée**	**coup d'état**	**savoir-faire**
rouge	**à propos**	**purée**	**à la carte**	**entrée**	**sabotage**	**sauté**

There are some French words whose appearance is deceiving. Thus, **demander** means *to ask* or *ask for,* not *to demand.* Watch out for these **faux amis** (*false friends*).

2. *French and English pronunciation differ greatly.*

The similarities between French and English vocabulary will be of great help to you in learning French. However, French and English pronunciation are very different. You must learn not only to pronounce the French words correctly but to understand them when you hear them. As in English there are many silent letters, and some sounds, particularly the vowel sounds, are spelled in various ways. You will have little difficulty with the spelling if you practice writing as well as saying new words and exercises. The most important words appear many times in this book, and that will also help you to remember pronunciation, meaning, and spelling.

In Chapter 2, the pronunciation of the French sounds and their spelling is explained in detail. The description of the sounds and the pronunciation key should enable you to pronounce them quite well. If possible you should get a French-speaking person to help you with your pronunciation, for it is important for you to hear the sounds spoken correctly and to have your own pronunciation checked.

You can improve your pronunciation and understanding of the spoken word by listening to French recordings and radio broadcasts in French. Commercials are particularly valuable for this purpose, because they contain so much repetition and emphatic expression. Cassettes of interviews and readings can often be borrowed free or for a small fee from university libraries or the Alliance Française in your community. At first a few minutes of listening each day will probably be enough. Then, as you progress in your study of French, you should increase the amount of time you spend listening to the spoken language.

3. *French is spoken by many people.*

French is spoken not only by the nearly 55 million people of France. About half the people of Belgium and a fifth of those of Switzerland have French as their mother tongue, and many more people in those countries speak it as a second language. In the countries of North Africa and West Africa that were once under French or Belgian rule, many people still speak French; in fact, it is often the official language of those countries. In the Western Hemisphere, French is the language of Quebec, Canada, and many English-speaking Canadians are also fluent in French. It is spoken in Haiti, Martinique, and Guadeloupe in the Caribbean, and in French Guyana in South America.

For many years French was the sole language of diplomacy and the preferred foreign language among educated persons in Europe. That is no longer so, but even today French is probably the second most useful language after English for tourists and businessmen traveling in Europe. It is almost indispensable for travel off the beaten track in North Africa and West Africa.

But knowing French is not merely of practical value. It opens the door to a better understanding of France, its people, its rich and colorful past, its cultural life and history, and its unique way of life.

CHAPITRE 2 (DEUX)

FRENCH PRONUNCIATION

In Part 1 of this chapter you will learn the elements of French pronunciation. The words used to illustrate the French sounds need no translation, for they have the same or almost the same spelling as corresponding English words of like meaning, such as you have seen in Chapter 1. As you learn the correct French pronunciation of these words, you are without further effort gradually adding to your French vocabulary.

The description of each French sound is accompanied by a pronunciation key, which indicates the nearest English equivalent of that sound. This key will be used freely throughout the book to ease your way in the pronunciation of new words, phrases, and sentences.

In Part 2 and Part 3 of this chapter you will practice correct French pronunciation in words and expressions useful for the traveler, and in short easy dialogues.

PREMIÈRE PARTIE (FIRST PART)

French Sounds Illustrated in Familiar Words

Pronounce each sound and the words which illustrate it three times. Stress (emphasize) lightly the syllable in heavy type in the pronunciation key of each word. Note well:

The last syllable—and only the last syllable—of French words is stressed.

a(a) **madame** (ma-**dam**) French **a** is generally like *a* in *cat*. Key symbol a. See Diagram 1. Occasionally
a(ah) French **a** is like *a* in *father*. Key symbol ah. Practice:
balle (bal) **place** (plas) **salade** (sa-**lad**) **table** (tabl) **garage** (ga-**razh**) **classe** (klahs)

NOTE: French **r** is trilled as in the telephone operator's *thrrr-ee*.
French **g** before **e** or **i** equals *s* in *measure*. Symbol zh.

i(ee) **difficile** (dee-fee-**seel**) French **i** equals *ee* in *feet*. Symbol ee. See Diagram 2. Practice:
riche (reesh) **image** (ee-**mazh**) **famille** (fa-**meey**) **Paris** (pa-**ree**)

NOTE: French **ch** equals *sh* in *short*. Symbol sh. French **ll** is usually pronounced like *y* in *yes*. Symbol y.

FRENCH VOWEL SOUNDS
With Nearest English Equivalents and Pronunciation Key

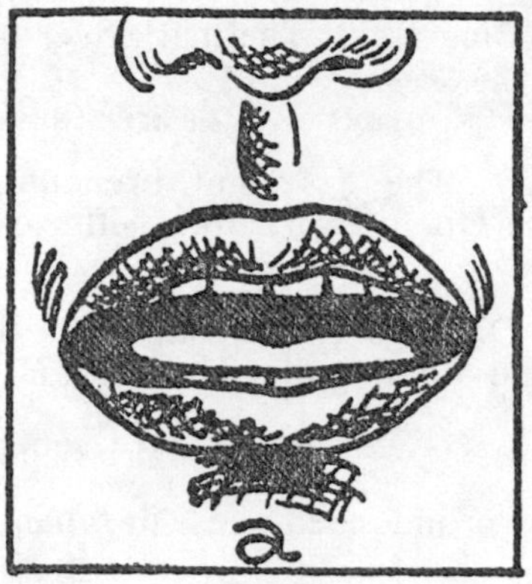

1

a is like *a* in *cat*. Key symbol (a). **balle** (bal). See Note 1 below.

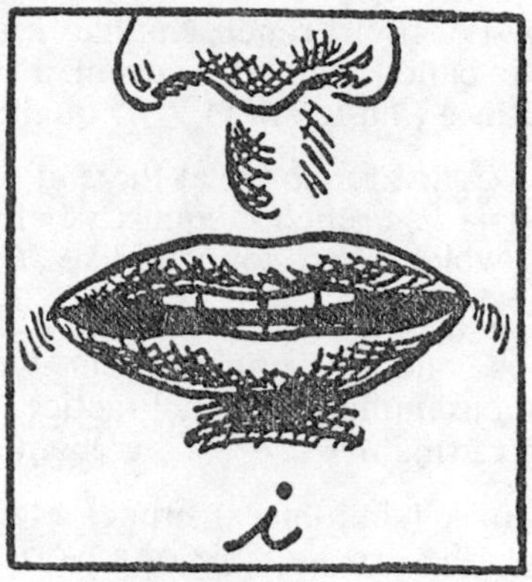

2

i is like *ee* in *feet*. Key Symbol (ee). **riche** (reesh), **Paris** (pa-**ree**). See Note 2.

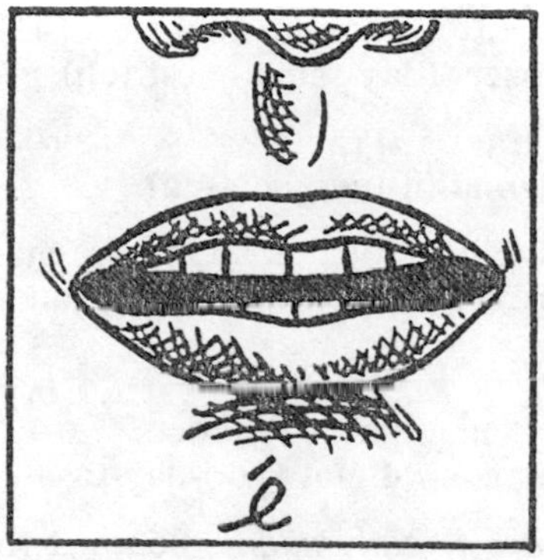

3

é is like *a* in *hate*. Key symbol (ay). **café** (ka-**fay**), **matinée** (ma-tee-**nay**).

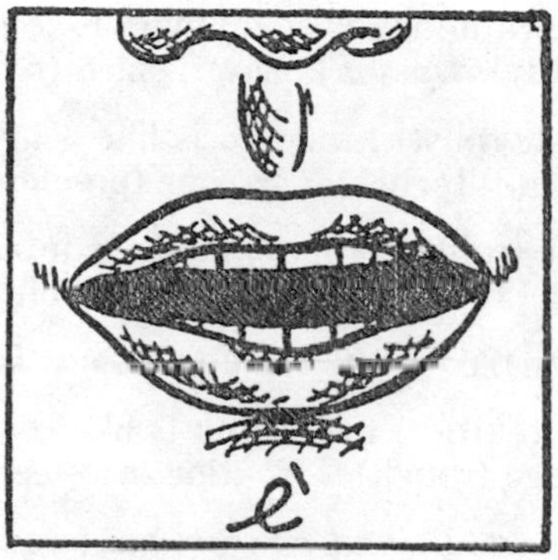

4

è is like *e* in *there*. Key Symbol (eh). **scène** (sehn), **sévère** (say-**vehr**).

5

o is like *u* in *but*. Key Symbol (u). **poste** (pust), **poème** (pu-ehm). See Note 3.

6

ou is like *oo* in *boot*. Key Symbol (oo). **route** (root), **touriste** (too-**reest**).

NOTE 1. French **a** is sometimes like *a* in *father*. Key Symbol (ah). **classe** (klahs).

NOTE 2. Stress (emphasize) slightly the last syllable in French words of more than one syllable. The last syllable is indicated by heavy type in the pronunciation key.

NOTE 3. French **o** is sometimes like *o* in *note*. Key Symbol (oh). **hôtel** (oh-tel).

é(ay) **café** (ka-fay) French **é** is like *a* in *hate*. Symbol ay. See Diagram 3. The mark over this letter (´) is called the acute accent. Practice:
matinée (ma-tee-**nay**) **qualité** (ka-lee-**tay**) **papier** (pa-**pyay**) **désirer** (day-zee-**ray**)

NOTE: French **-er** at the end of a word often equals é (ay). The **-r** is silent. French **qu** always equals *k*. French **c** equals *s* before **i** or **e;** French **c** is like *k* before any other letter except for **ch,** which is pronounced like *sh*, as in **riche** (reesh).

è(eh) **scène** (sehn) French **è** is like *e* in *there*. Symbol eh. See Diagram 4. The mark over this letter (`) is called the grave accent. Other spellings of this sound are **ai** and **ê.** The mark (ˆ) is called the circumflex accent. Practice:
mètre (mehtr) **crème** (krehm) **fête** (feht) **laissez-faire** (leh-say-**fehr**)

e(uh) **chemise** (shuh-**meez**) French **e** without any accent mark is pronounced like *e* in *father*, when it ends the first syllable of a word. Symbol uh. Practice:
menace (muh-**nas**) **cheval** (shuh-**val**) **regard** (ruh-**gar**) **venir** (vuh-**neer**)

At the end of a word, **e** without an accent mark is silent except in words of one syllable. Practice:
le (luh) **je** (zhuh) **me** (muh) **ne** (nuh) **ce** (suh) **de** (duh) **que** (kuh)

e without an accent mark is sometimes pronounced like **é** (ay), sometimes like **è** (eh). Practice:
et (ay) **assez** (a-**say**) **pied** (pyay) **effet** (ay-**feh**) **dessert** (day-**sehr**) **est** (eh) **elle** (ehl)

o(u) **poste** (pust) French **o** is like *u* in *but*. Symbol u. See Diagram 5. Practice:
objet (ub-**zheh**) **poème** (pu-**ehm**) **effort** (ay-**fur**) **original** (u-ree-zhee-**nal**)

ô(oh) **rôle** (rohl) French **ô** is like *o* in *note*. Symbol oh. Other spellings of this sound are **au** and **eau.**
hôtel (oh-**tehl**) **au revoir** (oh-ruh-**vwar**) **rose** (rohz) **chapeau** (sha-**poh**)

NOTE: French **oi** equals *wa*. French **h** is always silent.

ou(oo) **route** (root) French **ou** is like *oo* in *boot*. Symbol oo. See Diagram 6. Practice:
rouge (roozh) **routine** (roo-**teen**) **touriste** (too-**reest**) **coup d'état** (koo-day-**ta**)

NOTE: *Final consonants* (except **c, f, l, r**) *in French are usually silent*. **bouquet** (boo-**keh**), **Paris** (par-**ree**), **regard** (ruh-**gar**); but **chef** (shehf), **hôtel** (oh-**tehl**).

u(ü) **bureau** (bü-**roh**) French **u** is like *ee* spoken with lips held firmly in a small circle as for whistling. Symbol ü. See Diagram 6. Practice:
nature (na-**tür**) **public** (pü-**bleek**) **avenue** (av-**nü**) **excuser** (ehks-kü-**zay**)

eu(eu) **liqueur** (lee-**keur**) French **eu** is like *u* in *urge*. It is the sound eh spoken with lips firmly rounded on a somewhat larger circle than for French **u.** Symbol eu. Practice:
docteur (duk-**teur**) **acteur** (ak-**teur**) **professeur** (pru-feh-**seur**) **monsieur** (muh-**syeu**)

French Nasal Vowel Sounds

In syllables ending in **n** and **m,** the **n** and **m** are not pronounced. Instead the preceding vowel sound is nasalized as described below. There are four nasal vowel sounds in French. As you will note, each of these nasal vowel sounds has a number of spellings. In the pronunciation key **ñ** indicates that the preceding vowel sound is nasalized.

an(ahñ) **piquant** (pee-**kahñ**) Say the English syllable *ahn* as in *want* loudly.

Mouth wide open. Hold the tongue down with a flat stick so that it cannot rise for the **n,** and try to say *ahn*. An excellent French nasal **an,** symbol ahñ, results. Now practice the sound without using stick. Be sure to keep tongue down. Other spellings of the nasal sound **an** (ahñ) are **am, en, em.** Practice:
France (frahñs) **danger** (dahñ-**zhay**) **encore** (ahñ-**kur**) **absent** (ap-**sahñ**)
ensemble (ahñ-**sahñbl**) **rendez-vous** (rahñ-day-**voo**) **enveloppe** (ahñ-vuh-**lup**)

on(awñ) **consomme** (kawñ-su-**may**) Say the English sound *awn* as in *dawn*. Hold the tongue down with a flat stick, so that it cannot rise for the **n** and try to say *awn*. An excellent French nasal **on,**

symbol awñ, results. Practice the sound without using stick. Another spelling of the nasal **on** is **om.** Practice:

oncle (awñkl) **nation** (nah-**syawñ**) **station** (stah-**syawñ**) **question** (kehs-**tyawñ**)

in(añ) **lingerie** (lañ-zhuh-ree) Say *an* as in the English word *ban*. Hold tongue down with flat stick so that it cannot rise for the **n,** and try to say *an*. The French nasal **in,** symbol añ, results. Practice the sound without using stick. Other spellings of the nasal **in** are **im, ain, aim, ein, oin.** Practice:

index (añ-**dehks**) **vain** (vañ) **train** (trañ) **importateur** (añ-pur-ta-**teur**)
intelligent (añ-teh-lee-**zhahñ**) **américain** (a-may-ree-**kañ**) **meringue** (muh-**rañg**)

un(euñ) **brun** (breuñ) Pronounce the nasal sound **in** (añ). For the nasal sound **in** (añ) the corners of the lips are drawn back as in a smile. Round the lips as in Diagram 5 and try to say **in** (añ). The result is a good French nasal **un,** symbol euñ. Another spelling of the nasal **un** (euñ) is **um** (euñ). Practice:

un (euñ) **brun** (breuñ) **parfum** (par-**feuñ**) **humble** (euñbl) **chacun** (sha-**keuñ**)

Summary of French Vowel Sounds

Letters:	**a**	**é**	**è**	**e**	**i**	**o**	**ou**	**u**	**eu**	**au (eau)**	**oi**
Symbols:	a ah	ay	eh	ay eh uh	ee	u oh	oo	ü	eu	oh	wa

NOTE 1. French **a** is generally like *a* in *cat*. Symbol a. Sometimes French **a** is like *a* in *father*. Symbol ah.

NOTE 2. French **e** is sometimes pronounced like **é** (ay), sometimes like **è** (eh). When an **e** without an accent ends the first syllable of a word, it is pronounced like the *e* in *mother*. Symbol uh. The French **e** is silent at the end of a word, except for words of one syllable; then it is also pronounced like the *e* in *mother*.

NOTE 3. French **o** is generally like *u* in *but*. Symbol u. Sometimes it is like *o* in *wrote*. Symbol oh.

Summary of French Nasals

Letters:	**an (am, en, em)**	**in (im, ain, aim, ein, eim)**	**on (om)**	**un (um)**
Symbols:	ahñ	añ	awñ	euñ

French Consonants

Most French consonant sounds are like the corresponding English consonant sounds. The following, however, need special attention:

c before **e** or **i** is like *s* in *see*. **difficile** (dee-fee-**seel**)
c before any other letter (except ch) is like *k*. **café** (ka-**fay**)
ç with cedilla is always like hissing *s*. **français** (frahñ-**seh**)
ch is like English *sh*. **riche** (reesh)
g before **e** or **i** is like *s* in *measure*. **rouge** (roozh)
g before any other letter is like *g* in *goat*. **garage** (ga-**razh**)
h is always silent. **hôtel** (oh-**tehl**)
j is like *s* in *measure*. **je** (zhuh)
ll is usually like *y* in *yes*. **famille** (fa-**meey**)
r is trilled as in *thrrr-ee*. **Paris** (pa-**ree**)
qu is always like *k*. **bouquet** (boo-**keh**)
gn is like *ny* in *canyon*. **espagnol** (ehs-pa-**nyul**)

DEUXIÈME PARTIE (deu-zyehm par-**tee**) SECOND PART

The second and third parts of this chapter contain important words and expressions of common usage. If you follow carefully the instructions for pronunciation practice, you will acquire many of these without difficulty. *Do not try to memorize all of them at this point as they will appear again in later chapters when you will have the opportunity to learn them thoroughly.*

Some Useful Words and Expressions for the Traveler

A. Practice the French aloud. Stress slightly the key syllables in heavy type.

1. **Pardon** (par-**dawñ**) — 1. I beg your pardon.
2. **S'il vous plaît** (seel voo **pleh**) — 2. Please; if you please.
3. **Monsieur** (muh-**syeu**); **Madame** (ma-**dam**) **Mademoiselle** (mad-mwa-**zehl**) — 3. Mr., sir; Mrs., madam. Miss, young lady.
4. **Où est l'hôtel . . . ?** (oo eh loh-**tehl**) — 4. Where is the hotel . . . ?
5. **Combien coûte le livre?** (kawñ-byañ koot luh **leevr**) — 5. How much does the book cost?
6. **Je voudrais . . .** (zhuh voo-**dreh**) — 6. I should like . . .
7. **Merci beaucoup** (mehr-see boh-**koo**) — 7. Thank you very much.
8. **Il n'y a pas de quoi** (eel nee-ya pah duh **kwah**) — 8. Don't mention it. *or* You are welcome.
9. **C'est trop cher** (seh troh **shehr**). **Très cher** (treh **shehr**) — 9. It's too expensive. Very expensive.
10. **bon marché** (bawñ mar-**shay**) **meilleur marché** (meh-yeur mar-**shay**) — 10. cheap, cheaper

Combien coûte . . . ? (kawñ-byañ koot . . . ?)

B. Read each heading aloud, completing it with the words listed under it. Thus:

Combien coûte le chapeau? Combien coûte la chemise? etc.

1. **le chapeau** (luh sha-**poh**) the hat
2. **la chemise** (la shuh-**meez**) the shirt
3. **la blouse** (la **blooz**) the blouse
4. **la robe** (la **rub**) dress
5. **la montre** (la **mawñtr**) the watch
6. **le parapluie** (luh pa-ra-**plüee**) the umbrella
7. **le parfum** (luh par-**feuñ**) the perfume
8. **la cravate** (la kra-**vat**) the necktie
9. **l'automobile** (lu-tu-mu-**beel**) the automobile

Pardon, monsieur. Où est . . . , s'il vous plaît?
(par-dawñ, muh-**syeu**. oo eh . . . , seel voo **pleh?**)

1. **la rue Drouot** (la rü droo-**oh**) Drouot Street
2. **l'avenue de la République** (lav-nü duh la ray-pü-**bleek**) Republic Avenue
3. **la place de la Concorde** (la plas duh la kawñ-**kurd**) Concord Place
4. **la gare du Nord** (la gar dü **Nord**) the North Station
5. **L'Hôtel Albert** (loh-tehl al-**behr**) the Albert Hotel
6. **le boulevard Saint Michel** (luh bool-var sañ mee-**shehl**) Saint Michel Boulevard
7. **le bureau de poste** (luh bü-roh duh **pust**) the post office.
8. **la salle d'attente** (la sal da-**tahñt**) the waiting room
9. **la toilette** (lah twah-**leht**) the washroom

Je voudrais . . . (zhuh voo-dreh . . .)

1. **une chambre avec bain** (ün shahñbr a-vehk **bañ**) a room with bath
2. **de l'eau chaude** (duh loh **shohd**) some hot water
3. **des serviettes de bain** (day sehr-vyeht duh **bañ**) some bath towels
4. **la carte** (la **kart**) the menu
5. **l'addition** (la dee-**syawñ**) the bill
6. **la revue** (la ruh-**vü**) the magazine
7. **le journal** (luh zhoor-**nal**) the newspaper
8. **du savon** (dü sa-**vawñ**) some soap
9. **téléphoner** (tay-lay-fu-**nay**) to telephone
10. **changer de l'argent** (shahñ-zhay duh lar-**zhahñ**) to change money

C. Practice aloud many times the numbers 1 to 21.

1. **un** (euñ), **une** (ün)
2. **deux** (deu)
3. **trois** (trwah)
4. **quatre** (katr)
5. **cinq** (sañk)
6. **six** (sees)
7. **sept** (seht)
8. **huit** (üeet)
9. **neuf** (neuf)
10. **dix** (dees)
11. **onze** (awñz)
12. **douze** (dooz)
13. **treize** (trehz)
14. **quatorze** (ka-**turz**)
15. **quinze** (kañz)
16. **seize** (sehz)
17. **dix-sept** (dee-**seht**)
18. **dix-huit** (deez-**üeet**)
19. **dix-neuf** (deez-**neuf**)
20. **vingt** (vañ)
21. **vingt et un** (vañ tay **euñ**)

TROISIÈME PARTIE (trwah-zyehm par-**tee**) THIRD PART

Liaison (lee-eh-**zawñ**) Linking

The final consonant of a French word is generally silent. However, when the next word begins with a vowel or **h**, the final consonant is usually pronounced and linked to the next word unless there is a natural pause.

Final **s** and **x**, when linked, are pronounced like *z;* final **f** like *v;* and final **d** like *t*.

Comment allez-vous?	**beaux arts**	**trois ans**	**neuf amis**	**le grand homme**
(ku-mahñ ta-lay-**voo**)	(boh **zar**)	(trwah zahñ)	(neu va-**mee**)	(luh grahñ **tum**)
How are you?	fine arts	three years	nine friends	the great man

Élision (ay-lee-**zyawñ**) Elision

The letters **e** and **a** of the words **le, la, je, me, te, se, de, ne, que** are dropped before words beginning with a vowel or an **h** (usually) and are replaced by an apostrophe. This process is called elision. Thus:

le + **oncle** becomes **l'oncle** (lawñkl) the uncle
le + **hôtel** becomes **l'hôtel** (loh-**tehl**) the hotel
la + **école** becomes **l'école** (lay-**kul**) the school
je + **ai** becomes **j'ai** (zhay) I have
que + **est-ce que c'est?** becomes **qu'est-ce que c'est?** (kehs kuh **seh**) What is that?

The Stress in French Words and Sentences

1. In French all the syllables of a word are spoken with equal force except the last. The last syllable of the word is stressed (emphasized) slightly.

général (zhay-nay-**ral**) **madame** (ma-**dam**) **chauffeur** (shoh-**feur**) **répeter** (ray-pay-**tay**)

2. In short sentences all the syllables are spoken with equal force except the last. Only the last syllable of the sentence is stressed.

Le leçon est difficile. (la luh-sawñ eh dee-fee-**seel**) The lesson is difficult.

3. In longer sentences, the last syllable of clauses and other groups of words that make sense together is also stressed.

Dialogue 1 (dya-**lug**)

Directions for Study.

1. Read the French text silently, sentence by sentence, using the English translation to get the meaning.
2. Read the whole French text aloud three or more times, using the pronunciation key as an aid. Stress lightly the key syllables in heavy type.

Comment allez-vous (ku-mahñ ta-lay-**voo**)? How are you?

1. — **Bonjour, monsieur Picard. Comment allez-vous?** (Bawñ-zhoor, muh-syeu pee-**kar**. Ku-mahñ ta-lay-**voo**?)	1. Good day, Mr. Picard. How are you?
2. — **Très bien, merci. Et vous?** (Treh byañ, mehr-**see**. Ay **voo**?)	2. Very well, thank you. And you?
3. — **Très bien, merci.** (Treh **byañ**, mehr-**see**)	3. Very well, thank you.
4. — **Au revoir, monsieur Picard.** (Oh ruh-**vwar**, muh-syeu pee-**kar**)	4. Goodbye, Mr. Picard.
5. — **Au revoir, Philippe.** (Oh ruh-**vwar**, fee-**leep**)	5. Goodbye, Philippe.

Dialogue 2

Parlez-vous français? (par-lay-voo frahñ-**seh**) Do you speak French?

1. — **Parlez-vous français, Marie?** (Par-lay-voo frahñ-**seh**, ma-**ree**?)	1. Do you speak French, Marie?

2. **— Oui, monsieur, je parle français.** (Wee muh-**syeu,** zhuh parl frahñ-**seh**) — 2. Yes, sir, I speak French.
3. **— Est-ce que Charles parle français?** (Ehs-kuh sharl parl frahñ-**seh?**) — 3. Does Charles speak French? (*Literally:* Is it that Charles speaks French?)
4. **— Oui, madame, il parle bien le français.** (Wee, ma-**dam,** eel parl byañ luh frahñ-**seh**) — 4. Yes, madam, he speaks French well.
5. **— Est-ce que Louise parle français?** (Ehs-kuh loo-eez parl frahñ-**seh?**) — 5. Does Louise speak French?
6. **— Non, madame, elle parle anglais.** (Nawñ, ma-**dam,** ehl parl ahñ-**gleh**) — 6. No, madam, she speaks English.

Dialogue 3

Les jours de la semaine (lay zhoor duh la suh-**mehn**) The days of the week

1. **— Écoutez, Thomas! Combien de jours y a-t-il dans une semaine?** (Ay-koo-tay tu-**mah!** Kawñ-byañ duh zhoor ya-teel dahñ zün suh-**mehn?**) — 1. Listen, Thomas! How many days are there in a week?
2. **— Il y a sept jours dans une semaine.** (Eel ya seht zhoor dahñ zün suh-**mehn**) — 2. There are seven days in a week.
3. **— Bien. Donnez-moi les noms des sept jours, s'il vous plaît?** (**Byañ.** Du-nay-mwa lay nawñ day seht zhoor duh la suh-**mehn,** seel voo **pleh**) — 3. Good. Give me the names of the seven days of the week, please.
4. **— Dimanche, lundi, mardi, mercredi, jeudi, vendredi, samedi.** (Dee-**mahñsh,** leuñ-**dee,** mar-**dee,** mehr-kruh-**dee,** zheu-**dee,** vahñ-druh-**dee,** sam-**dee**) — 4. Sunday, Monday, Tuesday, Wednesday, Thursday, Friday, Saturday.
5. **— Très bien. Écoutez, Georges! Quel jour de la semaine sommes-nous?** (Treh **byañ.** Ay-koo-tay **zhurzh!** Kehl zhoor duh la suh-mehn sum-**noo?**) — 5. Very good. Listen, George! What day of the week is it today? (*Lit.* What day of the week are we?)
6. **C'est aujourd'hui lundi.** (Seh toh-zhoor-düee leuñ-**dee**) — 6. Today is Monday.
7. **— Très bien, George.** (Treh byañ **zhurzh**) — 7. Very good, George.

CHAPITRE 3 (TROIS)

QUI EST MONSIEUR POTTER?

WHO IS MR. POTTER?

You now have a good working knowledge of French pronunciation and are ready for a more intimate study of the language. Practice the pronunciation aids after each conversational text and follow all directions for reading aloud and speaking. Remember: the only way you can learn to speak a language is by speaking it.

This chapter will introduce you to Mr. Potter, a New York businessman who is as eager as you are to learn French. You will also meet his congenial teacher, Monsieur Picard, a Frenchman living in New York. As he teaches Mr. Potter he will also teach you in a pleasant and interesting way.

So **Bonne Chance** (good luck) and **Bon Voyage** (a good trip) as you accompany Mr. Potter on the road that leads to a practical knowledge of the French language.

Comment étudier le texte How to study the text

• Read the French text silently, referring to the English only when necessary to get the meaning.
• Cover up the English text and read the French text silently.
• Study the Pronunciation and Spelling Aids and the sections Building Vocabulary and French Expressions which follow the text.

- Then read the French text aloud, pronouncing carefully.
- Do the exercise Completion of Text.
- Proceed to Grammar Notes, etc.
- Follow these instructions with the conversational texts in succeeding chapters.

Qui Est Monsieur Potter?

1. Monsieur Potter est un homme d'affaires américain.

2. Il demeure dans une petite ville dans les environs de New York.

3. Il y a six personnes dans le famille Potter: le père, Monsieur Potter, la mère, Madame Potter, deux fils, et deux filles. Monsieur Potter est un homme de quarante ans. Madame Potter est une femme de trente-cinq ans.

4. Les fils s'appellent[1] Charles et Thomas. Les filles s'appellent Elizabeth et Anne.

5. Monsieur Potter demeure dans une maison particulière.

6. Dans la maison il y a cinq pièces: le salon, la salle à manger, et trois chambres à coucher. Il y a aussi la cuisine et la salle de bain.

7. Le bureau de Monsieur Potter est dans la rue Whitehall.

8. Il est au vingtième étage d'un gratte-ciel.

9. Les lundis, les mardis, les mercredis, les jeudis, et les vendredis, Monsieur Potter prend le train pour arriver à son bureau en ville.

10. Toute la journée il travaille dans son bureau.

Who is Mr. Potter?

1. Mr. Potter is an American businessman.

2. He lives in a small town in the suburbs of New York.

3. There are six persons in the Potter family: the father, Mr. Potter, the mother, Mrs. Potter, two sons, and two daughters. Mr. Potter is a forty-year-old man. Mrs. Potter is a thirty-five-year-old woman.

4. The sons are named[1] Charles and Thomas. The daughters are named Elizabeth and Anne.

5. Mr. Potter lives in a private house.

6. In the house there are five rooms: the living room, the dining room, and three bedrooms. There are also the kichen and the bathroom.

7. Mr. Potter's office is on Whitehall Street.

8. It is on the twentieth floor of a skyscraper.

9. On Mondays, Tuesdays, Wednesdays, Thursdays, and Fridays, Mr. Potter takes the train in order to reach his office in the city.

10. All day long he works in his office.

NOTE 1. **s'appellent** (sa-pehl) *Literally:* call themselves

Pronunciation and Spelling Aids

A. Practice aloud

1. un homme d'affaires américain
   (euñ um da-fehr za-may-ree-**kañ**)
2. dans une petite ville
   (dahñ zün puh-teet **veel**)
3. dans les environs
   (dahñ lay zahñ-vee-**rawñ**)
4. trois chambres à coucher
   (trwah shahñbr za koo-**shay**)
5. il est au vingtième étage
   (eel eh toh vañ-tyehm ay-**tazh**)
6. prend le train
   (prahñ luh **trañ**)

B. Remember: **s**, when linked, becomes **z**. **les environs** (lay zahñ-vee-**rawñ**)

Building Vocabulary

A. La famille (la fa-**meey**) The family

le père (pehr) the father
la mère (mehr) the mother
le fils (fees) the son
la fille (feey) the daughter
le frère (frehr) the brother
la soeur (seur) the sister
l'oncle (lawñkl) the uncle
la tante (tahñt) the aunt
le cousin (koo-**zañ**) the cousin (*m*)
la cousine (koo-**zeen**) the cousin (*f*)
l'enfant (lahñ-**fahñ**) the child
le garçon (gar-**sawñ**) the boy, the waiter
le jeune fille (zheun **feey**) the girl
le monsieur (muh-**syeu**) the gentleman, Mr., Sir
messieurs (may-**syeu**) gentlemen
la dame (dam) the lady
Madame (ma-**dam**) Mrs., Madam
l'homme (lum) the man
la femme (fam) the woman
les parents (lay pa-**rahñ**) the parents

B. Les pièces de la maison (lay pyehs duh la meh-**zawñ**) The rooms of the house

le salon (sa-**lawñ**) living room
la chambre à coucher (shahñbr a koo-**shay**) bedroom
la cuisine (küee-**zeen**) kitchen
la salle à manger (sal a mahñ-**zhay**) dining room
la salle de bain (sal duh **bañ**) bath room

French Expressions

1. **il y a** (eel **ya**) there is, there are
2. **y a-t-il?** (ya-**teel**) is there? are there?
3. **par coeur** (par **keur**) by heart
4. **toute la journée** (toot la zhoor-**nay**) all day long

Exercise No. 1—Completion of Text

For maximum benefit follow these instructions carefully in all Completion of Text exercises.

Complete each sentence by putting the English words into French. Do this from memory where you can.

If you do not remember the words refer to the French text. There you will find the words in the order of their appearance. You have only to reread the text to find them easily.

When you have completed each sentence with the needed words, read the complete sentence aloud in French.

It will be a great help to your memory if you write each completed sentence. This is true for all exercises.

The correct French words for the Completion of Text exercises are in the Answers section at the end of this book, along with the answers to all other exercises. Check all your answers.

Exemple (ehg-**zahñpl**) Example 1. **Qui est Monsieur Potter?**

1. (Who) **est Monsieur Potter?**
2. **Il est un** (businessman) **américain.**
3. **Il demeure** (in) **une petite ville.**
4. (There are) **six personnes dans la famille.**
5. **Monsieur Potter est le** (father).
6. **Madame Potter est la** (mother).
7. **Les** (sons) **s'appellent Charles** (and) **Thomas.**
8. **Les filles** (are named) **Elizabeth** (and) **Anne.**
9. **Il y a** (five rooms) **dans la maison.**
10. **Il y a une** (kitchen) **et une** (bathroom).
11. **Le** (office) **est dans la Whitehall** (street).
12. (It is) **dans un gratte-ciel.**
13. **Il est au** (twentieth) **étage.**
14. **Monsieur Potter travaille** (all day long).

Grammar Notes

1. Definite article

Note the four ways in which the definite article *the* is expressed in French.

With Singular Nouns

Masculine:	**le père**	**le fils**	**le frère**	**l'oncle**	**l'homme**	**l'enfant**
Feminine:	**la mère**	**la fille**	**la soeur**	**la tante**	**la femme**	**l'enfant**

With Plural Nouns

Masculine:	**les pères**	**les fils**	**les frères**	**les oncles**	**les hommes**	**les enfants**
Feminine:	**les mères**	**les filles**	**les soeurs**	**les tantes**	**les femmes**	**les enfants**

The definite article in French is **le** (luh). **la** (la), **l'**, **les** (lay).

Le is used with a masculine singular noun; **la** is used with a feminine singular noun; **l'** is used with any noun that begins with a vowel or **h** (usually); **les** is used with any plural noun, masculine or feminine.

When the **s** of **les** is linked with the following noun, it is pronounced like *z*. Thus:
les enfants (lay zahñ-**fahñ**), **les hommes** (lay **zum**).

2. Gender of nouns

Nouns are either masculine or feminine. This is true for thing-nouns as well as for person-nouns.

Masculine:	**le salon**	**le train**	**le gratte-ciel**	**l'étage**	**le père**
Feminine:	**la chambre**	**la maison**	**la cuisine**	**la ville**	**la mère**

Learn the gender of thing-nouns as they occur.

3. Plural of nouns

Note the singular and plural of the following nouns:

les salon	**la chambre**	**l'enfant**	**le fils**	**le bureau**
les salons	**les chambres**	**les enfants**	**les fils**	**les bureaux**

The plural of nouns is usually formed by adding s to the singular. The added s is not pronounced. If a noun already ends in s in the singular, it remains unchanged in the plural. Learn exceptions as you meet them. Thus:

le bureau **les bureaux** Nouns ending in **eau** add **x** to form their plural.

4. Indefinite article

Note how the indefinite article *a* (*one*) is expressed in French.

Masculine:	**un père**	**un fils**	**un salon**	**un train**	**un homme**
Feminine:	**une mère**	**une fille**	**une ville**	**une rue**	**une femme**

Un (euñ) *a, one* is used with a masculine noun.
Une (ün) *a, one* is used with a feminine noun.

Exercise No. 2. Replace the English words *the* and *a* (*one*) by **le, la, l', les, un** or **une** as appropriate.

Exemple: 1. La famille Potter demeure à New York.

1. (The) **famille Potter demeure à New York.**
2. **New York est** (a) **grande ville.**
3. (The) **gratte-ciel est dans** (the) **Whitehall Street.**
4. (The) **père est Monsieur Potter.**
5. (The) **mère est Madame Potter.**
6. **Anne est** (one) **fille.**
7. **Charles est** (one) **fils.**
8. (The) **chambre à coucher est grande.**
9. (The) **maison est** (a) **maison particulière.**
10. (The) **homme est dans** (the) **salon.**
11. (The) **enfant est dans** (the) **bureau.**
12. **Il y a** (one) **soeur et** (one) **frère.**

Exercise No. 3. Change the following nouns to the plural.

Exemple: la salle les salles

1. **la chambre**
2. **la mère**
3. **la pièce**
4. **le fils**
5. **l'homme**
6. **le salon**
7. **l'Américain**
8. **l'étage**
9. **le bureau**
10. **la personne**
11. **l'oncle**
12. **l'enfant**
13. **la cuisine**
14. **la rue**
15. **l'avenue**

5. Some common verbs

il est (**eel eh**) he is
est-il? (**eh-teel**) is he?
il demeure (**duh-meur**) he lives (dwells)
demeure-t-il? (**duh-meur-teel**) does he live?
il prend (prahñ) he takes
prend-il? (prahñ-teel) does he take?
il travaille (tra-vahy) he works
travaille-t-il? (tra-vahy-teel) does he work?

Exercise No. 4. Translate into French.

1. Mr. Potter is an American businessman.
2. He lives in (à) New York.
3. There are six persons in the family.
4. He lives in a private house.
5. There are five rooms in the house.
6. Mr. Potter is the father.
7. Mrs. Potter is the mother.
8. The office is on Whitehall Street.
9. Mr. Potter takes the train.
10. He works in the office.

Exercise No. 5—Questionnaire

First read each French question and answer silently, noting the English meaning.
Then read each French question and answer aloud twice, without referring to the English.

Questions (kehs-tyawñ) **et Reponses** (ray-pawñs)

1. **Qui est Monsieur Potter?**
Il est homme d'affaires à New-York.

Questions and Answers

1. Who is Mr. Potter?
He is a businessman in New York.

2. **Est-il Américain?**
Oui, monsieur, il est Américain.
3. **Où demeure Monsieur Potter?**
Il demeure dans les environs de New York.
4. **Combien de personnes y a-t-il dans se famille?**
Il y a six personnes dans sa famille.
5. **Comment les fils s'appellent-ils?**
Ils[1] s'appellent Charles et Thomas.
6. **Comment les filles s'appellent-elles?**
Elles[1] s'appellent Elizabeth et Anne.
7. **Combien de pièces y a-t-il dans la maison de Monsieur Potter?**
Il y a cinq pièces.
8. **Y a-t-il aussi une cuisine et une salle de bain?**
Oui, monsieur, il y a aussi une cuisine et une salle de bain.
9. **Dans quelle rue est le bureau de Monsieur Potter?**
Il est dans la rue Whitehall.
10. **Où travaille-t-il?**
Il travaille dans son bureau.

2. Is he an American?
Yes sir, he is an American.
3. Where does Mr. Potter live?
He lives in the suburbs of New York.
4. How many persons are there in his family?
There are six persons in his family.
5. What are the sons' names?
They are called Charles and Thomas.
6. What are the daughters' names?
They are called Elizabeth and Anne.
7. How many rooms are there in Mr. Potter's house?
There are five rooms.
8. Are there also a kitchen and a bathroom?
Yes sir, there are also a kitchen and a bathroom.
9. On what street is Mr. Potter's office?
It is on Whitehall Street.
10. Where does he work?
He works in his office.

NOTE 1. **ils** = they (*masculine*) **elles** = they (*feminine*)

Learn these question words:

qui (kee) who? **comment** (ku-mahñ) how?
où (oo) where? **combien** (kawñ-byañ) how many?

CHAPITRE 4 (QUATRE)

POURQUOI EST-CE QUE M. POTTER ÉTUDIE LE FRANÇAIS?

WHY IS MR. POTTER STUDYING FRENCH?

1. M. Potter est importateur.

2. Il importe des objets d'art et des articles divers de France et du Maroc.

3. Au printemps M. Potter va faire un voyage en France. Il désire rencontrer son représentant à Paris. Il désire parler français avec lui.

4. Il désire aussi visiter des endroits intéressants en France. Il compte aussi aller au Maroc et peut-être en Corse.

5. M. Potter sait lire un peu le français. Mais il ne parle pas français. C'est pourquoi il étudie la langue française.

6. M. Picard est le professeur de M. Potter.

7. M. Picard, un ami de M. Potter, est Français. C'est[1] un homme de quarante-cinq ans.

8. Tous les mardis et jeudis les deux messieurs ont rendez-vous, presque toujours chez M. Potter. Là ils parlent français.

9. M. Picard est un bon professeur.

10. M. Potter est très intelligent et il apprend rapidement.

11. Pendant la première leçon il apprend par coeur ce dialogue:

1. Mr. Potter is an importer.

2. He imports art objects and various articles from France and from Morocco.

3. In the spring Mr. Potter is going to make a trip to France. He wants to meet his agent in Paris. He wants to speak French with him.

4. He also wants to visit some interesting places in France. He also expects to go to Morocco and perhaps to Corsica.

5. Mr. Potter knows how to read French a little. But he does not speak French. That is why he is studying the French language.

6. Mr. Picard is Mr. Potter's teacher.

7. Mr. Picard, a friend of Mr. Potter, is a Frenchman. He is a forty-five-year-old man.

8. The two gentlemen have an appointment every Tuesday and Thursday, almost always at Mr. Potter's house. There they speak French.

9. Mr. Picard is a good teacher.

10. Mr. Potter is very intelligent and he learns quickly.

11. During the first lesson he learns this dialogue by heart:

12. — Bonjour, M. Picard. Comment allez-vous? — Très bien, merci. Et vous? — Très bien, merci.
12. Good day, Mr. Picard. How are you? — Very well, thank you. And you? — Very well, thank you.

13. M. Potter apprend aussi des salutations et des adieux.
13. Mr. Potter also learns some greetings and some farewells.

14. Bonjour.
14. Good day. (*Also* good morning, good afternoon).

15. Bonsoir.
15. Good evening. (*Also* good night).

16. Adieu. Au revoir. À toute à l'heure. À bientôt.
16. Farewell. Goodbye. See you later. So long.

NOTE 1. **C'est** is used instead of **il (elle) est** *he (she) is,* when a modified noun follows. You will learn more later about the use of **C'est.**

Pronunciation and Spelling Aids

A. Practice aloud

1. importateur
(añ-pur-ta-**teur**)
2. représentant
(ruh-pray-zahñ-**tahñ**)
3. des salutations
(day-sa-lü-tah-**syawñ**)
4. messieurs
(may-**syeu**)
5. La France
(lah **frahñs**)
6. Le Maroc
(luh ma-**ruk**)
7. des adieux
(day za-**dyeu**)
8. des objets d'art
(day zub-zhay **dar**)
9. des endroits intéressants
(day zahñ-drwa zañ-tay-reh-**sahñ**)

B. Remember: Accent marks can make a difference in pronunciation or meaning. The cedilla under a *c* (ç) indicates that it is pronounced like an *s*: **français (frahñ-seh).** The word **la** means *the* but **là** means *there;* **ou** means *or* but **où** means *where.*

C. The names of countries, cities, people, are capitalized but languages and adjectives of nationality are not: **l'Amérique, l'Américain; l'Italie, l'Italien** (person), **l'italien** (language). Days of the week and months are written with small letters.

Building Vocabulary

A. Synonyms (words of like meaning)

le professeur professor, teacher in a college or secondary school

le maître (mehtr) **la maîtresse** (meh-trehs) teacher in an elementary school

B. Antonyms (words of opposite meaning)

1. **grand** big **petit** small
2. **bon** good **mauvais** bad
3. **ici** here **là** there
4. **l'homme** man **la femme** woman
5. **rapidement** rapidly **lentement** slowly
6. **l'importateur** importer
l'exportateur exporter

C. **Quelques langues d'Europe** (deu-**rup**) Some languages of Europe

1. **le français** (frahñ-**seh**) French
2. **l'anglais** (ahñ-**gleh**) English
3. **l'espagnol** (ehs-pa-**nyul**) Spanish
4. **l'italien** (ee-ta-**lyañ**) Italian
5. **l'allemand** (lal-**mahñ**) German
6. **le russe** (rüs) Russian

NOTE. The names of languages are always masculine.

French Expressions

1. **bonjour** (bawñ-**zhoor**) good morning (day)
2. **bonsoir** (bawñ-**swar**) good evening
3. **au revoir** (oh ruh-**vwar**) goodbye
4. **adieu** (a-**dyeu**) goodbye

5. **à bientôt** (a byañ-**toh**) see you soon
6. **à toute à l'heure** (a toot a **leur**) see you later
7. **à demain** (a duh-**mañ**) until tomorrow
8. **au printemps** (oh prañ-**tahñ**) in the spring
9. **peut-être** (peu-**tehtr**) perhaps
10. **par coeur** (par **keur**) by heart
11. **c'est pourquoi** (seh poor-**kwa**) that's why
12. **chez** (shay) **M. Potter** at Mr. Potter's house or home
13. **Comment allez-vous?** How are you?
14. **Très bien, merci.** Very well, thank you.

Exercise No. 6—Completion of Text

Follow carefully the instructions given in Exercise No. 1 (page 18).

1. (Who) **est M. Potter?**
2. **Il est** (an importer).
3. **Il importe des** (art objects).
4. (in the spring) **il va faire un voyage.**
5. (He wants) **rencontrer son représentant.**
6. **Il désire** (to speak) **français avec lui.**
7. **Il compte** (also) **aller au Maroc.**
8. (But) **il ne parle pas français.**
9. (That is why) **il étudie la langue.**
10. **M. Picard est** (the teacher) **de M. Potter.**
11. **Il est** (a friend of Mr. Potter).
12. **Les deux messieurs ont** (an appointment).
13. (They speak) **français.**
14. **M. Potter apprend** (rapidly).
15. **Il est** (very intelligent).
16. **M. Picard est** (a good teacher).

Grammar Notes

1. Use of **des** (day) some

des objets d'art (day zub-zhay **dar**) some art objects
des maisons (day meh-**zawñ**) some houses
des endroits (day zahñ-**drwa**) some places
The word *some,* before a plural noun, may be expressed by **des.**

The word *some* may be omitted in English, but **des** is never omitted in French. Thus:
des objets d'art some art objects *or* art objects

Quelques (kehl-**kuh**) is also used for *some,* in the sense of *several* or *a few:* **quelques langues** some (several) languages

2. More common verbs

il sont (eel **sawñ**) they are
sont-ils? (sawñ-**teel**) are they?
il n'est pas (eel neh **pah**) he is not
il va (eel **va**) he goes, is going
va-t-il? (va-**teel**) does he go, is he going?
il parle (eel **parl**) he speaks
parle-t-il? (parl-**teel**) does he speak?
il ne parle pas (eel nuh parl **pah**) he does not speak
il désire (eel day-**zeer**) he wants
il étudie (eel ay-tü-**dee**) he studies
il compte (eel **kawñt**) he expects
il apprend (eel a-**prahñ**) he learns
il sait (eel **seh**) he knows, *or* he knows how
ils ont (eel **zawñ**) they have
ont-ils? (awñ-**teel**) have they?
aller (a-**lay**) to go
parler (par-**lay**) to speak
visiter (vee-zee-**tay**) to visit
lire (leer) to read
faire (fehr) to make

To form the negative of a verb, place **ne** directly before the verb and **pas** directly after the verb:
il *ne* parle *pas* he does not speak **il *ne* sait *pas*** he does not know

Ne becomes **n'** before a verb that begins with a vowel or **h** (usually).
il n'étudie (nay-tü-dee) **pas** **il n'apprend** (na-prahñ) **pas**

3. Question forms

In the simple question form, the verb is inverted and a hyphen is required. Thus:
est-il? is he? **ont-ils?** have they? **sait-il?** does he know?

If the verb ends in **e** or **a** the letter **t** must be inserted between the verb and the subject pronoun. Thus:
parle-t-il? does he speak? **étudie-t-il?** does he study? **va-t-il?** does he go?

Another way of forming a question is by placing **Est-ce que** (ehs **kuh**) literally, Is it that . . . ?, before the subject:
Est-ce qu'il apprend? = Apprend-il? **Est-ce qu'ils ont? = Ont-ils?**

4. Omission of the indefinite article

The indefinite article (**un, une**) is omitted before nouns for professions or nationalities after the verb *to be*. If, however, the noun is modified, the definite article is not omitted.
Il est professeur. He is a teacher. *but*
C'est un bon professeur. He is a good teacher.

Exercise No. 7. Complete the following sentences with the correct verb form.

Exemple 1. Qui est M. Potter?

1. **Qui** (is) **M. Potter?**
2. (Is he) **importateur?**
3. (He does not speak) **français.**
4. (Does he speak) **anglais?**
5. (He learns) **rapidement.**
6. (He wants) **faire un voyage.**
7. (He is not studying) **l'espagnol.**
8. (He knows how) **lire un peu.**
9. (Have they) **rendez-vous?**
10. (He expects) **visiter Paris.**
11. **Il va** (to make) **un voyage.**
12. **Il ne sait pas** (to speak) **français.**

Exercise No. 8. Select from Column II the word groups that best complete the sentences begun in Column I.

Exemple: 1-d. M. Potter désire parler français avec son représentant à Paris.

I	II
1. M. Potter désire parler français	**a. des salutations et des adieux.**
2. Il sait lire	**b. de France et du Maroc.**
3. Il est très intelligent. C'est pourquoi	**c. chez M. Potter.**
4. Il importe des objets d'art	**d. avec son représentant à Paris.**
5. Les deux messieurs ont rendez-vous	**e. de quarante ans.**
6. M. Picard est un homme	**f. un peu le français.**
7. M. Potter apprend aussi	**g. il apprend rapidement.**
8. Le bureau de M. Potter n'est pas	**h. dans la famille de M. Potter.**
9. Il y a cinq personnes	**i. Charles, Thomas, Elizabeth et Anne.**
10. Les enfants de M. Potter s'appellent	**j. dans la Wall Street.**

Exercise No. 9. Find the corresponding French words in the Reading Text or Building Vocabulary. Write them. Say them aloud.

1. French (language)	6. the office	11. a little	16. but	21. some articles
2. the Frenchman	7. almost	12. there	17. where	22. some places
3. thank you	8. always	13. from, of	18. good	23. that is why
4. also	9. very well	14. here	19. bad	24. How are you?
5. perhaps	10. rapidly	15. big	20. with	

Exercise No. 10—Questionnaire

Follow the instructions given in Exercise No. 5 (page 19).

Questions et Réponses

1. **Qui est le professeur?**
   M. Picard est le professeur.
2. **Parle-t-il français?**
   Oui, monsieur, il parle français.

1. Who is the teacher?
   Mr. Picard is the teacher.
2. Does he speak French?
   Yes, sir, he speaks French.

3. **Qui est l'homme d'affaires?**
M. Potter est l'homme d'affaires.
4. **Parle-t-il français?**
Non, monsieur, il ne parle pas français.
5. **Où est le bureau de M. Potter?**
Il est dans la Whitehall Street.
6. **Est-il importateur d'automobiles?**
Non, monsieur, il n'est pas importateur d'automobiles.
7. **Apprend-il rapidement ou lentement?**
Il apprend rapidement.
8. **Quand ces messieurs ont-ils rendez-vous?**
Ils ont rendez-vous tous les mardis et les jeudis.
9. **M. Potter est-il intelligent?**
Il est très intelligent.
10. **Pourquoi étudie-t-il le français?**
Parce qu'il désire faire un voyage en France.

3. Who is the businessman?
Mr. Potter is the businessman.
4. Does he speak French?
No, sir, he does not speak French.
5. Where is Mr. Potter's office?
It is in Whitehall Street.
6. Is he an importer of automobiles?
No, sir, he is not an importer of automobiles.
7. Does he learn rapidly or slowly?
He learns rapidly.
8. When do these gentlemen have an appointment?
They have an appointment every Tuesday and Thursday.
9. Is Mr. Potter intelligent?
He is very intelligent.
10. Why is he studying French?
Because he wants to make a trip to France.

Learn: **quand** (kahñ)? when? **pourquoi** (poor-kwa)? why? **parce que** (pars-kuh) because

---

CHAPITRE 5 (CINQ)

DANS LE SALON DE MONSIEUR POTTER
IN MR. POTTER'S LIVING ROOM

1. **C'est mardi le 7 (sept) janvier, 1986.**
2. **Il est 8 (huit) heures du soir.**
3. **M. Potter est assis dans le salon de sa maison. M. Picard est assis près de lui.**
4. **M. Picard dit à M. Potter, — Autour de nous il y a beaucoup de choses: dans la maison, dans la rue, dans le bureau, dans le parc, dans la ville, et à la campagne.**
5. **Aux États-Unis et en Angleterre il faut savoir les noms des choses en anglais. En France il faut savoir les noms des choses en français.**
6. **Nous sommes dans le salon de votre maison. Dites-moi, s'il vous plaît, qu'est-ce que c'est que ça?**
7. **— C'est un piano. Ma femme joue bien du piano. Elle chante bien aussi.**
8. **— Très bien. Et qu'est-ce qui est sur le piano?**
9. **— Une lampe et un cahier de musique.**
10. **— Et qu'est-ce qui est au mur au-dessus du piano?**
11. **— C'est le portrait de ma femme.**
12. **— Excellent. Dites-moi, s'il vous plaît, les noms d'autres objets dans le salon, et dites-moi où ils sont.**
13. **— Avec plaisir.**

1. It is Tuesday, January 7, 1986.
2. It is 8 o'clock in the evening.
3. Mr. Potter is seated in the living room of his house. Mr. Picard is seated near him.
4. Mr. Picard says to Mr. Potter, "Around us there are many things: in the house, in the street, in the office, in the park, in the city, and in the country."
5. In the United States and in England it is necessary to know the names of things in English. In France it is necessary to know the names of things in French.
6. We are in the living room of your house. Tell me, please, what is that?
7. It is a piano. My wife plays the piano well. She also sings well.
8. Very good. And what is on the piano?
9. A lamp and a music book.
10. And what is on the wall over the piano?
11. It is the portrait of my wife.
12. Excellent. Tell me, please, the names of other objects in the living room and tell me where they are.
13. With pleasure.

14. — La bibliothèque est près d'une fenêtre. Le miroir est entre les fenêtres. Le bureau est près de la porte. Une chaise est devant le bureau. Sur le bureau il y a un crayon, un stylo, des papiers et des lettres. Il y a des livres sur la petite table.

15. — Très bien. C'est assez pour aujourd'hui. Au revoir, M. Potter.

16. — À jeudi, M. Picard.

14. The bookcase is near a window. The mirror is between the windows. The desk is near the door. A chair is in front of the desk. On the desk there are a pencil, a fountain pen, some papers and some letters. There are some books on the little table.

15. Very good. That's enough for today. So long, Mr. Potter.

16. Until Thursday, Mr. Picard.

Pronunciation and Spelling Aids

A. Practice aloud

1. **Monsieur Potter est assis dans le salon de sa maison.**
   (muh-syeu pu-tehr eh ta-see dahñ luh sa-lawñ duh sa meh-zawñ)
   Monsieur Picard est assis près de lui.
   (muh-syeu pee-kar eh ta-see preh duh lüee)
2. **dans la ville** (dahñ la **veel**)
3. **en France** (ahñ **frahñs**)
4. **en Angleterre** (ahñ nahñ-gluh-**tehr**)
5. **autour de nous** (oh-toor duh **noo**)

B. Remember: Final **x** and **s** are linked to the vowel beginning the next word and are pronounced as **z.**

aux États Unis (oh zay-ta zü-**nee**)

Building Vocabulary

A. **Dans le salon** (dahñ luh sa-**lawñ**) In the living room

1. **le bureau** (bü-**roh**) desk, office
2. **la chaise** (shehz) chair
3. **le cahier de musique** (ka-yay duh mü-**zeek**) music book
4. **le crayon** (kreh-**yawñ**) pencil
5. **la fenêtre** (fuh-**nehtr**) window
6. **la lampe** (lahnp) lamp
7. **la lettre** (lehtr) letter
8. **le miroir** (mee-**rwar**) mirror
9. **le papier** (pa-**pyay**) paper
10. **le piano** (pya-**noh**) piano
11. **la porte** (purt) door
12. **le portrait** (pur-**treh**) portrait
13. **le stylo** (stee-**loh**) pen
14. **la table** (tabl) table
15. **la bibliothèque** (bee-blee-u-**tehk**) bookcase

B. Some common prepositions

1. **à** to, at, in, on
2. **en** in, into
3. **de** (duh) of, from
4. **autour de** (oh-toor **duh**) around
5. **avec** (a-**vehk**) with
6. **au-dessus de** (oh-duh-sü **duh**) above, over
7. **près de** (preh **duh**) near
8. **chez** (shay) at the house of
9. **entre** (ahñtr) between
10. **dans** (dahñ) in, inside of
11. **devant** (duh-**vahñ**) before, in front of
12. **derrière** (deh-**ryehr**) behind
13. **sous** (soo) under
14. **sur** (sür) on, upon

French Expressions

1. **le sept janvier**
   (luh set zhahñ-**vyay**) January 7
2. **Il est huit heures**
   (eel eh üee **teur**) It is 8 o'clock
3. **beaucoup de choses**
   (boh-koo duh **shohz**) many things
4. **il faut** (eel **foh**) it is necessary
5. **dites-moi** (deet-**mwa**) tell me
6. **qu'est-ce que c'est que ça?**
   (kehs kuh seh kuh **sa**) what is that?
7. **qu'est-ce qui?** (kehs **kee**) what?
8. **elle joue du piano**
   (ehl zhoo dü pya-**noh**) she plays the piano
9. **C'est assez** (seh ta-**say**) It's enough
10. **pour aujourd'hui**
    (poor oh-zhoor-**düee**) for today

Exercise No. 11—Completion of Text

1. **Le monsieur** (is seated) **dans le salon.**
2. **Il y a** (many things) **dans la rue.**
3. (It is necessary to know) **les noms des choses.**
4. **Dites-moi,** (what is that?)
5. **Ma femme** (plays) **bien du piano et** (sings) **bien.**
6. **Le portrait est** (over the piano).
7. **Un miroir est** (between) **les fenêtres.**
8. **Sur le bureau il y a** (some letters).
9. (That's enough) **pour aujourd'hui.**
10. (Until Thursday), **M. Picard.**

Grammar Notes

1. The contractions **du, des, au, aux**

de (of, from) plus **le** (the) becomes **du** (of, from the)
de (of, from) plus **les** (the) becomes **des** (of, from the)
à (to, at, in, on) plus **le** (the) becomes **au** (to, at, in, on the)
à (to, at, in, on) plus **les** (the) becomes **aux** (to, at, in, on the)

Où est le bureau *du* commerçant?	Where is the office *of the* merchant?
Mme. Picard est une amie *des* enfants.	Mrs. Picard is a friend *of the* children.
M. Picard parle *au* commerçant.	Mr. Picard is speaking *to the* merchant.
Le maître parle *aux* garcons.	The teacher is speaking *to the* boys.

de la, de l', à la and **à l'** never contract. Thus:

Le salon *de la* maison est grand.	The living room *of the* house is large.
Il sait le nom *de l'*hôtel.	He knows the name *of the* hotel.
Charles va *à la* fenêtre.	Charles is going *to the* window.
La mère parle *à l'*enfant.	The mother is speaking *to the* child.

2. Possession

In French possession is indicated by a phrase with **de,** never by an apostrophe:
la maison du professeur the teacher's house, the house of the teacher
l'oncle de Marie Mary's uncle, the uncle of Mary

Possession is also expressed by a phrase with the preposition à:

À qui est ce bureau?	Whose office is this? (*Literally:* To whom is this office?)
Ce bureau est au professeur.	It is the teacher's office. (*Literally:* This office is to the teacher.)

Exercise No. 12. Use **du, de l', de la, des; au, à l', à la, aux,** as required.

Exemple 1. Le salon du professeur est grand.

1. **Le salon** (of the) **professeur est grand.**
2. **M. Potter parle** (to the) **professeur.**
3. **M. Picard est le maître** (of the) **garçons.**
4. **C'est un ami** (of the) **docteur.**
5. **Charles va** (to the) **oncle.**
6. **L'enfant va** (to the) **fenêtre.**
7. **La mère parle** (to the) **enfants.**
8. **Le portrait est** (on the) **mur.**
9. **Il ne parle pas** (to the) **homme.**
10. **Où est la maison** (of the) **tante?**

Exercise No. 13. Complete in French. First review Building Vocabulary B (page 25).

Exemple 1. Au-dessus du piano il y a un portrait.

1. (Above the) **piano il y a un portrait.**
2. **L'automobile est** (near the) **maison.**
3. (On the) **bureau il y a beaucoup de lettres.**
4. **Le miroir est** (above the desk).
5. **Une petite table est** (between the) **fenêtres.**
6. **Il y a des chaises** (around the) **table.**
7. **Qu'est-ce qui**[1] **est** (behind the) **porte?**
8. **Qu'est-ce qui est** (in front of the) **piano.**
9. **Qu'est-ce qui est** (in the) **cuisine?**
10. **M. Potter est** (with) **M. Picard** (in the) **salon.**

NOTE 1. **Qu'est-ce qui** (kehs **kee**) = what? (*subject of a verb*)

Exercise No. 14—Questionnaire

1. Qui est assis dans le salon?
2. Qui est assis près de lui?
3. Y a-t-il beaucoup de choses autour de nous?
4. Est-ce que Madame Potter chante bien?
5. Qui joue bien du piano?
6. Où est le cahier de musique?
7. Où est le portrait de Madame Potter?
8. Qu'est-ce qui est près d'une fenêtre?
9. Où est le miroir?
10. Où est le bureau?
11. Qu'est-ce qui est devant le bureau?
12. Où y a-t-il des livres?

RÉVISION (REVIEW) 1
CHAPITRES 1–5 PREMIÈRE PARTIE

Each Review Chapter will begin with a summary of the most important words and expressions that have occurred in the chapters reviewed. Check yourself as follows:

1. Cover up the English words on the right of the page with a piece of paper. Read one French word at a time aloud and give the English meaning. Uncover the English word of the same number in order to check.

2. Cover up the French words. Say aloud, one at a time, the French for each English word. Uncover the French word to check.

3. Write the words you have difficulty in remembering three or four times.

Review of Words (Révision de Mots)

NOUNS

1. l'ami (m)
2. l'amie (f)
3. le bureau
4. les bureaux[1]
5. la campagne
6. la chaise
7. la chambre à coucher
8. la chose
9. le crayon
10. la cuisine
11. l'enfant
12. la famille
13. la femme
14. la fenêtre
15. la fille
16. la jeune fille
17. le garçon
18. l'homme
19. l'homme d'affaires
20. le jour
21. la lampe
22. la langue
23. la leçon
24. la lettre
25. le livre
26. la dame, madame
27. le monsieur
28. les messieurs
29. la mademoiselle
30. la mère
31. le miroir
32. l'oncle
33. le papier
34. le père
35. la personne
36. la porte
37. la rue
38. la salle à manger
39. la salle de bain
40. le salon
41. la soeur
42. le stylo
43. la tante
44. le voyage
45. la ville

1. friend (m)
2. friend (f)
3. office, desk
4. offices, desks
5. country
6. chair
7. bedroom
8. thing
9. pencil
10. kitchen
11. child
12. family
13. wife, woman
14. window
15. daughter, girl
16. girl
17. boy, waiter
18. man
19. businessman
20. day
21. lamp
22. language
23. lesson
24. letter
25. book
26. lady, madam, Mrs.
27. sir, Mr.
28. gentlemen
29. young lady, Miss
30. mother
31. mirror
32. uncle
33. paper
34. father
35. person
36. door
37. street
38. dining room
39. bathroom
40. living room
41. sister
42. pen
43. aunt
44. voyage
45. city, town

NOTE 1. When the noun has an irregular plural, the plural is given.

VERBS

1. aller
2. apprendre
3. faire
4. lire
5. parler
6. rencontrer
7. savoir
8. il apprend
9. elle chante
10. il compte
11. il demeure
12. il désire
13. il étudie
14. elle joue
15. il parle
16. parle-t-il?
17. il ne parle pas
18. il prend
19. il sait
20. il travaille
21. il va
22. va-t-il?
23. il y a
24. y a-t-il?
25. il faut
26. il est
27. est-il?
28. il n'est pas
29. ils ont
30. dites-moi

1. to go
2. to learn
3. to do, make
4. to read
5. to speak
6. to meet
7. to know
8. he learns
9. she sings
10. he intends
11. he lives
12. he wants
13. he studies
14. she plays
15. he speaks
16. does he speak?
17. he does not speak
18. he takes
19. he knows
20. he works
21. he goes
22. does he go?
23. there is (are)
24. is (are) there?
25. it is necessary
26. he is
27. is he?
28. he is not
29. they have
30. tell me

ADJECTIVES

1. assis
2. autre
3. beaucoup (de)
4. bon
5. divers
6. grand
7. intéressant
8. mauvais
9. petit
10. peu (de)
11. premier
12. tous

1. seated
2. other
3. much, many
4. good
5. various
6. big, large
7. interesting
8. bad
9. little, small
10. little, few
11. first
12. all

ADVERBS

1. aujourd'hui	**5. ici**	**9. presque**	1. today	5. here	9. almost
2. assez	**6. là**	**10. rapidement**	2. enough	6. there	10. rapidly
3. bien	**7. lentement**	**11. très**	3. well	7. slowly	11. very
4. aussi	**8. peut-être**	**12. toujours**	4. also	8. perhaps	12. always

PREPOSITIONS

1. à	**6. dans**	**11. entre**	1. to, at, on	6. in, inside of	11. between
2. au-dessus de	**7. de**	**12. pour**	2. over, above	7. of, from	12. for
3. autour de	**8. derrière**	**13. près de**	3. around	8. behind	13. near
4. avec	**9. devant**	**14. sous**	4. with	9. in front of	14. under
5. chez	**10. en**	**15. sur**	5. at the house of	10. in, on	15. on, upon

QUESTION WORDS

1. qui?	**5. comment?**	**8. quand?**	1. who (*subject*)?	5. how?	8. when?
2. qui est-ce qui?	**6. où?**	**9. qu'est-ce que c'est que ça?**	2. who (*subject*)?	6. where?	9. what is that?
3. qu'est-ce qui?	**7. pourquoi?**		3. what (*subject*)?	7. why?	
4. combien de?			4. how much, many?		

CONJUNCTIONS

1. et	**2. ou**	**3. mais**	**4. parce que**	1. and	2. or	3. but	4. because

FRENCH EXPRESSIONS

1. à demain	**9. au printemps**	1. until tomorrow, goodbye	9. in the spring
2. à bientot	**10. aux États-Unis**	2. see you soon, goodbye	10. in the U.S.
3. à toute à l'heure	**11. c'est assez**	3. so long	11. that's enough
4. au revoir	**12. c'est pourquoi**	4. goodbye	12. that's why
5. Bonjour.	**13. Comment allez-vous?**	5. Good morning (afternoon).	13. How are you?
6. Bonsoir.	**14. par coeur**	6. Good evening (night).	14. by heart
7. à la campagne	**15. s'il vous plaît**	7. in the country	15. please
8. en ville	**16. toute la journée**	8. in (to) the city	16. all day long

DEUXIÈME PARTIE

Exercise 15. Select the antonym (opposite) for each word in Group I from Group II.

I			II		
1. bon	**5. au-dessus de**	**9. Bonjour.**	**a. devant**	**e. non**	**i. là**
2. oui	**6. beaucoup de**	**10. le garçon**	**b. la campagne**	**f. l'homme**	**j. sous**
3. ici	**7. le père**	**11. la ville**	**c. la jeune fille**	**g. mauvais**	**k. peu de**
4. petit	**8. derrière**	**12. la femme**	**d. Bonsoir.**	**h. grand**	**l. la mère**

Exercise 16. Complete the following sentences in French.

1. **M. Potter travaille** (all day).
2. **Dites-moi,** (please).
3. (Perhaps) **il est au bureau.**
4. (Good evening), **monsieur.**
5. **M. Potter va** (to the city).
6. (That is why) **il étudie le français.**
7. How are you?
8. (Where) **demeure-t-il?**
9. What is this?
10. (Who) **est professeur?**
11. (What) **est au mur?**
12. (When) **va-t-il en ville?**

Exercise 17. Select the group of words in Column II which best completes each sentence begun in Column I.

Exemple: 1-d. Dans la famille Potter il y a six personnes.

I	II
1. Dans la famille Potter	**a. il apprend les salutations et les adieux.**
2. La maison de M. Potter	**b. et elle joue bien du piano.**
3. M. Potter prend le train	**c. parce qu'il est très intelligent.**

4. **Il étudie le français**
5. **Il travaille toute la journée**
6. **Il sait lire un peu le français**
7. **Il apprend rapidement**
8. **Pendant la première leçon**
9. **Tous les mardis et jeudis**
10. **La femme de M. Potter chante bien**
11. **M. Potter va faire un voyage**

d. **il y a six personnes.**
e. **en France et peut-être au Maroc.**
f. **est dans les environs de New-York.**
g. **mais il ne parle pas le français.**
h. **dans son bureau.**
i. **pour arriver à son bureau en ville.**
j. **les deux messieurs ont rendez-vous.**
k. **parce qu'il désire voyager en France.**

Exercise 18. Complete these sentences in French.

1. **L'automobile est** (in front of the house).
2. **Les chaises sont** (around the table).
3. **La bibliothèque est** (near the door).
4. **M. Potter est assis** (behind the desk).
5. **La lampe est** (on the piano).
6. (The boy's books) **sont sur la petite table.**
7. (The girl's mother) **est en ville.**
8. (The children's teacher) **est Français.**
9. **Le portrait de Madame Potter est** (on the wall).
10. (To whom) **est l'automobile?**

Exercise 19. Translate into French:

1. Who is Mr. Potter?
2. He is an American businessman.
3. Where does he live?
4. He lives in the suburbs of New York.
5. Why is he learning French?
6. He wants to make a trip to France.
7. Who is his **(son)** teacher?
8. His teacher is Mr. Picard.
9. Why does he learn rapidly?
10. He learns rapidly because he is intelligent.
11. How many children are there in Mr. Potter's family?
12. There are four children.
13. How many rooms are there in Mr. Potter's house?
14. There are five rooms, a bathroom and a kitchen.

Dialogue 1

Read each dialogue silently several times, using the English translation to make certain of the meaning. Practice the French text aloud many times. Follow this procedure with all dialogues.

Où est la rue Scribe? (oo eh la rü **skreeb**?)

1. **Pardon, monsieur, où est la rue Scribe?**
2. **Continuez tout droit, mademoiselle.**
3. **Est-ce que c'est loin?**
4. **Non, mademoiselle, c'est à trois rues d'ici.**
5. **Merci beaucoup, monsieur.**
6. **De rien, mademoiselle.**

Where is the rue Scribe?

1. Pardon me, sir, where is the rue Scribe?
2. Continue straight ahead, Miss.
3. Is it far?
4. No, miss. It's three blocks from here.
5. Thank you very much, sir.
6. Don't mention it, miss.

Dialogue 2

Ou s'arrête l'autobus? (oo sa-reht lu-toh-**boos**?)

1. **S'il vous plaît, monsieur, où s'arrête l'autobus, le 52?**
2. **Il s'arrête au coin là-bas, mademoiselle.**
3. **Merci beaucoup, monsieur.**
4. **Il n'y a pas de quoi.**

Where does the bus stop?

1. Please sir, where does the number 52 bus stop?
2. It stops at the corner over there, miss.
3. Thank you so much, sir.
4. Don't mention it. (You're welcome.)

LECTURE (READING SELECTION)

Exercise No. 20—How to Read the Lectures

1. Read the passage silently from beginning to end to get the meaning as a whole.
2. Reread the passage, looking up any words you may have forgotten in the French-English dictionary at the end of this book. There are a few new words in the reading selections of the review chapters and the meaning of these is given in footnotes.

3. Read the passage silently a third time. Then translate it and check your translation with that given in the answers section of the appendix.
4. Follow this procedure in all succeeding *lectures*.

Monsieur Potter apprend le français

Monsieur Potter est un homme d'affaires américain qui importe des objets d'art de France. C'est pourquoi il désire faire un voyage en France au printemps. Il désire parler avec son représentant. Il désire aussi visiter des endroits intéressants en France. Mais il ne sait pas parler français.

Monsieur Potter a un bon professeur. C'est un Français qui habite New York et qui s'appelle Monsieur Picard. Tous les mardis et jeudis le professeur prend le train pour aller chez son élève.[1] Là les deux messieurs parlent un peu en français. Monsieur Potter est très intelligent et il apprend rapidement. Pendant la première leçon, par exemple, il apprend par coeur les salutations et les adieux. Il sait déjà[2] dire bonjour, comment allez-vous? à bientôt, et à demain. Il sait déjà dire en français les noms de beaucoup de choses qui[3] sont dans son salon, et il sait répondre[4] aux questions, "Qu'est-ce que c'est que ca?" et "Où est. . . . ?" Monsieur Picard est très content des progrès[5] de son élève et il dit, — Très bien. C'est assez pour aujourd'hui. À bientôt.

NOTE 1. **chez son élève** to the home of his pupil
NOTE 2. **déjà** already
NOTE 3. **qui** that, which (*relative pronoun*)
NOTE 4. **répondre (à)** reply, answer
NOTE 5. **très . . . progrès** very satisfied with the progress

---

CHAPITRE 6 (SIX)

LES VERBES SONT IMPORTANTS AUSSI
VERBS ARE IMPORTANT TOO

1. M. Potter et M. Picard sont assis dans le salon chez M. Potter. M. Picard commence à parler. M. Potter l'écoute[1] avec attention.

1. Mr. Potter and Mr. Picard are seated in the living room at Mr. Potter's house. Mr. Picard begins to speak. Mr. Potter listens to him[1] attentively.

2. — Vous savez déjà que les noms des choses et des personnes sont importants. Mais les verbes sont importants aussi. Il n'est pas possible de former une phrase sans les verbes. Il n'est pas possible non plus de causer sans les verbes.

2. "You already know that the names of things and of persons are important. But verbs are important too. It is not possible to make a sentence without verbs. It is not possible to talk without verbs either."

3. — Nous allons étudier des verbes d'usage courant. Je vais vous[2] poser des questions. Vous allez répondre aux questions.

3. "We are going to study some commonly used verbs. I am going to ask you[2] some questions. You are going to reply to the questions."

4. — Si vous ne savez pas la réponse, dites, s'il vous plaît, "Je ne sais pas."

4. "If you don't know the answer, please say, 'I don't know.' "

5. — Très bien, dit M. Potter. Je vais dire, "Je ne sais pas," si je ne sais pas la réponse.

5. "Very good," says Mr. Potter. "I am going to say, 'I don't know,' if I don't know the answer."

6. — Est-ce que vous êtes homme d'affaires?

6. Are you a businessman?

7. — Oui, monsieur, je suis homme d'affaires; je suis importateur d'objets d'art et d'autres articles de France et du Maroc.

7. Yes, sir, I am a businessman; I am an importer of art objects and other articles from France and from Morocco.

8. — Et pourquoi est-ce que vous étudiez le français?

8. And why are you studying French?

9. — J'étudie le français parce que je désire faire un voyage en France pour rendre visite à mon représentant à Paris. Je désire parler en français avec lui. Il ne parle pas anglais.

9. I am studying French because I want to make a trip to France in order to pay a visit to my agent in Paris. I want to speak with him in French. He does not speak English.

10. — Comptez-vous visiter d'autres pays?

10. Do you intend to visit other countries?

11. — Je compte visiter aussi le Maroc et peut-être la Corse.
11. I expect to visit Morocco too and perhaps Corsica.

12. — Quand est-ce que vous partez en voyage?
12. When are you leaving on your trip?

13. — Je pars le 31 (trente et un) mai.
13. I am leaving on the 31st of May.

14. — Est-ce que vous allez voyager en bateau?
14. Are you going to travel by boat?

15. — Non, je vais voyager en avion parce que c'est le plus rapide.
15. I am going to travel by plane because that is the quickest (way).

16. — Combien coûte le voyage?
16. How much does the trip cost?

17. — Je ne sais pas. Je vais prendre des renseignements demain et je vais retenir ma place.
17. I don't know. I am going to get information tomorrow and I'll make a reservation. (*Literally:* I'm going to reserve my seat.)

18. — Excellent, monsieur. Vous apprenez le français rapidement.
18. Excellent, sir. You are learning French rapidly.

19. — Merci. Vous êtes trop aimable.
19. Thank you. You are too kind. (You flatter me.)

20. — Pas du tout. C'est la vérité. Eh, bien, ça suffit pour aujourd'hui. À bientôt.
20. Not at all. It is the truth. Well, that's enough for today. So long.

21. — A jeudi prochain.
21. Until next Thursday.

NOTE 1. **Le (l')**, *him,* is a direct object pronoun. In French, direct object pronouns precede the verb.
NOTE 2. **Vous,** *you,* is an indirect object pronoun. In French, indirect object pronouns also precede the verb.

Pronunciation and Spelling Aids

Practice aloud

1. **attention** (a-tahñ-syawñ)
2. **nous allons étudier** (noo za-lawñ zay-tü-**dyay**)
3. **je ne sais pas** (zhuh nuh seh **pah**)
4. **je suis importateur** (zhuh süee zañ-pur-ta-**teur**)
5. **d'autres articles** (doh-truh zar-**teekl**)
6. **c'est le plus vite** (seh luh plü **veet**)

Building Vocabulary

A. **Quelques pays d'Europe.** (kehl-kuh pay-ee deu-**rup**) Some countries of Europe

1. **l'Angleterre** (lahñ-gluh-**tehr**) England
2. **la Belgique** (behl-**zheek**) Belgium
3. **l'Allemagne** (lal-man-**yuh**) Germany
4. **la France** (frahñs) France
5. **l'Espagne** (leh-span-**yuh**) Spain
6. **l'Italie** (lee-ta-**lee**) Italy
7. **la Suisse** (süees) Switzerland
8. **la Russie** (rü-**see**) Russia

B. **Les pays de l'Amérique du Nord** (la-may-reek dü **nur**) The countries of North America

1. **les États Unis** (leh zay-ta zü-**nee**) the United States
2. **le Mexique** (mehk-**seek**) Mexico
3. **le Canada** (ka-na-**da**) Canada
4. **aux États Unis** (oh zay-ta zü-**nee**) in *or* to the United States
5. **au Mexique** in *or* to Mexico
6. **au Canada** in *or* to Canada

French Expressions

1. **pas . . . non plus** (nawñ **plü**) not . . . either
2. **d'usage courant** (dü-zazh koo-**rahñ**) of common usage, commonly used
3. **poser des questions** to ask questions
4. **rendre visite à** to pay a visit to
5. **en bateau** (ahñ ba-**toh**) by boat
6. **en avion** (ahñ na-**vyawñ**) by airplane
7. **prendre des renseignements** (prahñdr day rahñ-seh-nyuh-**mahñ**) to get information
8. **retenir une place** (ruh-tuh-neer oon **plas**) to reserve a seat
9. **pas du tout** (pah dü **too**) not at all
10. **ça** (*or* **cela**) **suffit** (sah *or* suh-lah sü-**fee**) that's enough

Exercise No. 21—Completion of Text

1. **Les verbes** (are important), **monsieur.**
2. **Nous allons étudier** (some verbs).
3. (Why) **étudiez-vous le français?**
4. (Because) **je désire rendre visite à mon représentant.**
5. **Je désire parler** (with him).
6. **Je compte visiter** (other countries).
7. **Allez-vous voyager** (by boat or by plane)?
8. (How much) **coûte le voyage?**
9. **Vous apprenez** (very rapidly).
10. (That's enough for today.)

Grammar Notes

1. About verb endings

The infinitive is the basic form of the verb. In English it is expressed by *to: to* speak, *to* learn, etc. The infinitive of all French verbs ends in **-er, -ir, -re,** or **-oir.** Thus:

parler to speak **partir** to leave **apprendre** to learn **savoir** to know

That part of the verb which remains after the ending is removed is called the stem. Thus: **parl-, part-, apprend-** and **sav-** are the stems of **parler, partir, apprendre** and **savoir.**

Learn the present tense of the verb **parler,** *to speak.* Note carefully the endings which are added to the stem **parl-.**

2. Present tense of **parler** to speak. Regular **-er** verb.

je	**parle** (parl)	I speak	**nous**	**parlons** (par-lawñ)	we speak
tu	**parles** (parl)	you speak	**vous**	**parlez** (par-lay)	you speak
il	**parle** (parl)	he speaks	**ils**	**parlent** (parl)	they (*m*) speak
elle	**parle** (parl)	she speaks	**elles**	**parlent** (parl)	they (*f*) speak

a. The endings of a regular **-er** verb in the present tense are:

Singular **-e -es -e** Plural **-ons -ez -ent**

The endings are silent except for **-ons** and **-ez.**

b. The pronoun **vous** (voo), like English *you,* is used both in the singular and plural. It is the polite or usual form of address. Thus:

Parlez-vous français, monsieur? Do you speak French, sir?
Vous parlez bien, mesdames. You speak well, ladies.

The pronoun **tu** (tü) is used in addressing a near relative, an intimate friend, or a child. It is the familiar form of address. Thus:

Tu parles trop haut, mon enfant. You speak too loudly, child.

c. The present tense may be translated in three ways:

I speak, I am speaking, I do speak; you speak, you are speaking, you do speak, etc.

3. The imperative or command forms of **parler.**

parle, mon enfant (speak, child), **parlons** (let us speak), **parlez, monsieur** or **messieurs** (speak, sir or gentlemen)

The imperative forms are like the corresponding present tense forms, except that the pronouns are omitted, and the familiar singular is **parle** rather than **parles.**

4. The interrogative

As you have already noted, there are two ways of forming a question: by placing **Est-ce que?** (*Is it that?*) before the subject of the sentence; or by placing the subject after the verb (inverted form of question). The inverted form is rarely used with **je.** There is no difference in meaning between the two forms.

Question with **est-ce que**	*Inverted form of question*	
est-ce que je parle?	———	do I speak?
est-ce que tu parles?	**parles-tu?**	do you (*fam.*) speak?

est-ce qu'il parle?	**parle-t-il?**	does he speak?
est-ce qu'elle parle?	**parle-t-elle?**	does she speak?
est-ce que nous parlons?	**parlons-nous?**	do we speak?
est-ce que vous parlez?	**parlez-vous?**	do you speak?
est-ce qu'ils parlent?	**parlent-ils?**	do they (*m*) speak?
est-ce qu'elles parlent?	**parlent-elles?**	do they (*f*) speak?

Note the two ways of forming a question when there is a noun subject.

Est-ce que M. Potter est professeur?
M. Potter est-il professeur? — Is Mr. Potter a teacher?

5. The negative

The negative is formed by placing **ne** before the verb and **pas** after the verb.

Il *ne* parle *pas* anglais.	He does not speak English.
Est-ce qu'il *ne* parle *pas* anglais? ***Ne* parle-t-il *pas* anglais?**	Does he not speak English?
***Ne* parlez *pas* trop haut.**	Do not speak too loudly.

6. Regular **-er** verbs like **parler**

The vast majority of verbs in French are regular **-er** verbs like **parler.** You are already familiar with the following:

causer to chat	**je cause,** etc.	**écouter** to listen	**j'écoute,** etc.
compter to expect, intend	**je compte,** etc.	**étudier** to study	**j'étudie,** etc.
commencer to begin	**je commence,** etc.	**importer** to import	**j'importe,** etc.
coûter to cost	**il coûte**	**jouer** to play	**je joue,** etc.
demeurer to live	**je demeure,** etc.	**travailler** to work	**je travaille,** etc.
désirer to want	**je désire,** etc.	**visiter** to visit	**je visite,** etc.

Exercise No. 22. Complete each of the following verbs with the correct ending:

Exemple: j'étudie (I study, I am studying)

1. j'étudi___	**5. je travaill___**	**9. nous caus___**	**13. vous commenc___**
2. ils ne parl___ pas	**6. demeur___-vous?**	**10. vous étudi___**	**14. import___-t-il?**
3. nous compt___	**7. il écout___**	**11. elles demeur___**	**15. Qui parl___?**
4. elles désir___	**8. il ne coût___ pas**	**12. elle ne visit___ pas**	**16. Les enfants jou___**

Exercise No. 23. Change the following sentences into the negative:

Exemple: Henri ne joue pas bien du piano.

1. **Henri joue bien du piano.**
2. **Paul étudie le français.**
3. **Nous parlons espagnol.**
4. **Ils écoutent avec attention.**
5. **Mes enfants, jouez dans le salon.**
6. **Elle désire aller en Europe.**
7. **Qui ètudie l'anglais?**
8. **Nous travaillons toute la journée.**
9. **Elle compte aller au Maroc.**
10. **Vous travaillez bien.**

Exercise No. 24. Practice aloud the following brief dialogues:

1. **— Parlez-vous français, Jean?**
— Oui monsieur, je parle français.
— Marie parle-t-elle français?
— Non, monsieur, elle ne parle pas français.

2. **— Qui joue du piano?**
— Annette joue du piano.
— Ne joues-tu pas du piano, Michelle?
— Non, je ne joue pas du piano.

3. **— Est-ce que les garçons étudient la leçon?**
— Non, il n'étudient pas la leçon.
— Est-ce qu'ils jouent dans la rue?
— Oui, ils jouent dans la rue.

4. **— Qui est le professeur de M. Potter?**
— M. Picard est son professeur.
— N'est-il pas Français?
— Si,[1] il est Français.

NOTE 1. Use **si** in answer to a negative question instead of **oui.**

Exercise No. 25—Questionnaire

1. **Où est-ce que les messieurs sont assis?**
2. **Qui commence à parler?**
3. **Qui écoute avec attention?**
4. **Qui pose les questions?**
5. **Qui est-ce qui[1] répond aux questions?**
6. **Est-ce que les verbes sont importants?**
7. **M. Potter importe-t-il des objets d'art?**
8. **Pourquoi étudie-t-il le français?**
9. **Quels pays[2] est-ce qu'il compte visiter?**
10. **Est-ce qu'il va voyager en bateau ou en avion?**
11. **Est-ce que M. Potter apprend rapidement ou lentement?**

NOTE 1. **Qui est-ce qui?**, *who?*, is a longer form of **qui?**, *who?* NOTE 2. What countries.

CHAPITRE 7 (SEPT)

LA FAMILLE DE M. POTTER

MR. POTTER'S FAMILY

1. C'est jeudi, le 17 janvier. Il est 8 (huit) heures du soir.

2. M. Picard sonne à la porte chez M. Potter. La bonne ouvre la porte et dit, — Entrez, monsieur. Passez au salon, s'il vous plaît.

3. Dans le salon M. Potter attend M. Picard. Quand il arrive, M. Potter dit, — Bonsoir. Comment allez-vous?

4. — Comme ci, comme ça. Et vous?

5. — Quant à moi, ça va très bien, mais ma fille Anne est malade. Elle est enrhumée.

6. — Je le[1] regrette beaucoup. Avez-vous d'autres enfants?

7. — Bien sûr. J'ai quatre enfants, deux garçons et deux filles. Nous sommes six dans notre famille.

8. — Comment vos enfants s'appellent-ils?

9. — Ils s'appellent Charles, Thomas, Elizabeth et Anne.

10. — Quel âge ont-ils?

11. — Charles a dix ans. Il est l'aîné. Charles a huit ans. Thomas a six ans. Anne est la plus jeune. Elle a cinq ans.

12. — Ils vont tous à l'école excepté Anne.

13. Les deux messieurs causent un peu plus. Ensuite M. Potter invite M. Picard à visiter son bureau lundi prochain à midi et demi. M. Picard accepte l'invitation avec plaisir.

14. À neuf heures M. Picard dit,—À bientôt.

15. M. Potter répond,—À lundi à midi et demi.

1. It is Thursday, January 17. It is 8 o'clock in the evening.

2. Mr. Picard rings the bell (*Literally:* at the door) of Mr. Potter's house. The maid opens the door and says, "Come in, sir. Please go in to the living room."

3. In the living room Mr. Potter is waiting for Mr. Picard. When he arrives Mr. Potter says, "Good evening. How are you?"

4. "So so. And you?"

5. "As for me, I'm fine, but my daughter Anne is ill. She has a cold."

6. "I'm very sorry.[1] Have you any other children?"

7. "Certainly. I have four children, two boys and two girls. There are six of us in our family."

8. "What are the names of your children?"

9. "Their names are Charles, Thomas, Elizabeth and Anne."

10. "How old are they?"

11. "Charles is ten years old. He is the oldest. Thomas is eight years old. Elizabeth is six years old. Anne is the youngest. She is five years old."

12. "They all go to school except Anne."

13. The two gentlemen chat a while longer. Then Mr. Potter invites Mr. Picard to visit his office the following Monday at half past twelve. Mr. Picard accepts the invitation with pleasure.

14. At 9 o'clock Mr. Picard says, "So long."

15. Mr. Potter answers, "Until Monday at half past twelve."

NOTE 1. *Literally:* I regret it very much. **le** stands for *him* or *it*. **le** is a direct object pronoun, which usually precedes the verb.

Pronunciation and Spelling Aids

A. Practice aloud

1. **passez au salon** (pa-say zoh sa-**lawñ**)
2. **quand il arrive** (kahñ teel a-**reev**)
3. **comme ci comme ça** (kum see kum sa)
4. **elle est enrhumée** (ehl eh tahñ-rü-**may**)
5. **d'autres enfants** (doh-truh zahñ-**fahñ**)
6. **lundi prochain** (leuñ-dee pru-**shañ**)
7. **l'aîné** (leh-**nay**)
8. **la plus jeune** (la plü **zheun**)

B. Final **d** when linked with the next word is pronounced as *t*. Thus:
quand il (kañ **teel**) apprend-il (a-prahñ-**teel**)

C. **sur** = on **sûr** = sure **à** = to, at, on **a** (as in **il a**) = has. The accent marks (ˆ`) here indicate a difference in meaning, *not* in pronunciation.

Building Vocabulary

A. Most French words ending in **-tion** and **-sion** (syawñ) have corresponding English words ending in *-tion* and *-sion*. They are always feminine. They are pronounced somewhat differently in French.

la nation	**l'élection**	**la situation**	**l'observation**
la prononciation	**l'attention**	**l'obligation**	**l'invitation**
la continuation	**la direction**	**l'invention**	**la révolution**
l'expression	**la profession**	**la concession**	**l'obsession**

B. The ending **-ment** (mahñ) is equal to the ending *-ly* in English.

rapidement rapidly
lentement slowly
certainement certainly
probablement probably
généralement generally
facilement easily

French Expressions

1. **comme ci, comme ça** so so
2. **quant à moi** (kahñ ta **mwa**) as for me
3. **Ça va très bien.** I'm fine. (*Literally:* It goes very well)
4. **Elle est enrhumée.** She has a cold.
5. **Je le regrette beaucoup.** I'm sorry.
6. **bien sûr** (byañ sür) surely, certainly
7. **Quel âge avez-vous?** How old are you?
8. **J'ai quinze ans.** I am fifteen years old.
9. **Comment s'appellent-ils?** What are their names?
10. **Ils s'appellent . . .** Their names are . . .

Exercise No. 26—Completion of Text

1. **La bonne** (opens) **la porte.**
2. **Elle dit, —** (Enter, sir.)
3. (Go) **au salon** (please).
4. (My daughter) **Anne est malade.**
5. (Have you) **d'autres enfants?**
6. **Bien sûr.** (I have) **quatre enfants.**
7. (We are) **six dans notre famille.**
8. **Charles est** (the oldest).
9. **Il a** (ten years).
10. **Anne est** (the youngest).
11. (They chat) **un peu plus.**
12. **M. Picard** (accepts) **l'invitation.**

Grammar Notes

1. Present tense of **avoir** to have. Irregular verb.

j'ai (zhay)	I have	**nous avons** (noo za-**vawñ**)	we have
tu as (tü **a**)	you have	**vous avez** (voo za-**vay**)	you have
il a (eel **a**)	he has	**ils ont** (eel **zawñ**)	they have
elle a (ehl **a**)	she has	**elles ont** (ehl **zawñ**)	they have

Interrogative (have I, etc.?)

est-ce que j'ai?	**avons-nous?**
as-tu?	**avez-vous?**
a-t-il?	**ont-ils?**
a-t-elle?	**ont-elles?**

Negative (I have not, etc.)

je n'ai pas	**nous n'avons pas**
tu n'as pas	**vous n'avez pas**
il n'a pas	**ils n'ont pas**
elle n'a pas	**elles n'ont pas**

Negative-Interrogative: **N'a-t-il pas?** Has he not?
N'ont-ils pas? Have they not?

Exercise No. 27. Complete the following in French with the correct form of **avoir:**

1. **Combien d'enfants** (have you)?
2. (I have) **six enfants.**
3. **Combien de filles** (has she)?
4. (She has) **trois filles.**

5. (Do you have) **les livres, Jean?**
6. (We do not have) **les livres.**
7. **Anne,** (have you) **le miroir?**
8. (I do not have) **le miroir.**
9. **Les jeunes filles** (have they) **la balle?**
10. (They do not have) **la balle.**
11. **Qui** (has) **quatre enfants?**
12. **Mme. Picard** (has) **quatre enfants.**
13. **Quel âge** (have) **vous?**
14. (I have) **dix ans.**

2. Present tense of **aller** to go. Irregular verb.

je vais (zhuh **vay**)	I go	**nous allons** (noo za-**lawñ**)	we go
tu vas (tü **va**)	you go	**vous allez** (voo za-**lay**)	you go
il va (eel **va**)	he goes	**ils vont** (eel **vawñ**)	they go
elle va (ehl **va**)	she goes	**elles vont** (ehl **vawñ**)	they go

Interrogative (do I go? etc.)

est-ce que je vais?	**allons-nous?**
vas-tu?	**allez-vous?**
va-t-il?	**vont-ils?**
va-t-elle?	**vont-elles?**

Negative (I do not go, etc.)

je ne vais pas	**nous n'allons pas**
tu ne vas pas	**vous n'allez pas**
il ne va pas	**ils ne vont pas**
elle ne va pas	**elles ne vont pas**

Negative-Interrogative: **Ne va-t-il pas?** Does he not go?
Ne vont-ils pas? Do they not go?

NOTE. The verb aller is frequently used to indicate future time. Thus:

Je vais faire un voyage en France. I am going to (I shall) take a trip to France.
Ils vont apprendre le français. They are going to (will) learn French.

Exercise No. 28. Complete the following in French with the correct form of **aller:**

1. **Où** (is he going)?
2. (He is going) **à l'hôtel.**
3. (Are you going) **à la campagne?**
4. **Non,** (we are going) **en Europe.**
5. **Les enfants** (do they go) **à l'école?**
6. **Qui** (is going) **faire visite à son représentant?**
7. **Où** (are you going), **mon enfant?**
8. **M. Potter** (is going) **faire un voyage en France.**
9. (Are you going) **visiter l'Espagne?**
10. (We are not going) **visiter l'Espagne.**
11. **Où** (are you going), **mes enfants?**
12. (We are going) **au parc.**
13. How are you?
14. I am fine.

3. Present tense of **être** to be. Irregular verb.

je suis (zhuh **süee**)	I am	**nous sommes** (noo **sum**)	we are
tu es (tü **eh**)	you are	**vous êtes** (voo **zeht**)	you are
il est (eel **eh**)	he is	**ils sont** (eel **sawñ**)	they are
elle est (ehl **eh**)	she is	**elles sont** (ehl **sawñ**)	they are

Interrogative (am I, etc.?)

est-ce que je suis?	**sommes-nous?**
es-tu?	**êtes-vous?**
est-il?	**sont-ils?**
est-elle?	**sont-elles?**

Negative (I do not, etc.)

je ne suis pas	**nous ne sommes pas**
tu n'es pas	**vous n'êtes pas**
il n'est pas	**ils ne sont pas**
elle n'est pas	**elles ne sont pas**

Negative-Interrogative: **N'est-il pas?** Is he not?
Ne sommes-nous pas? Are we not?

Exercise No. 29. Complete the following in French with the correct form of **être:**

1. **Qui** (is) **dans le bureau?**
2. **M. Potter** (is) **dans le bureau.**
3. **Où** (is) **Mme. Potter?**
4. **Elle** (is) **dans le salon.**
5. **M. Picard,** (is he) **Anglais?**
6. **Non, il** (is not) **Anglais.**
7. (Are you) **Français?**
8. **Non,** (I am) **Américain.**
9. **Où** (are) **les enfants?**
10. (They are) **dans la rue.**
11. **Les messieurs** (are they) **assis?**
12. (They are) **assis dans le salon.**
13. (Are you) **professeurs, messieurs?**
14. **Non,** (we are not) **professeurs.**

Exercise No. 30—Questionnaire

1. **Qui sonne a la porte?**
2. **Qui est-ce qui ouvre la porte?**
3. **Où est-ce que M. Potter attend M. Picard?**
4. **Qui est malade?**
5. **Est-elle enrhumée?**
6. **Combien d'enfants M. Potter a-t-il?**
7. **Combien de personnes y a-t-il dans sa famille?**
8. **Comment les enfants s'appellent-ils?**
9. **Quel âge a Charles?**
10. **Les enfants vont-ils à l'école?**
11. **Qui est-ce que** (whom) **l'homme d'affaires invite à visiter son bureau?**
12. **Est-ce que le professeur accepte l'invitation?**

NOTE. **qui** *or* **qui est-ce** ***qui?*** = who? (*subject*); **qui** *or* **qui est-ce** ***que?*** = whom? (*object of verb*).

CHAPITRE 8 (HUIT)

AU BUREAU DE M. POTTER

AT MR. POTTER'S OFFICE

1. Le bureau de M. Potter est au vingtième étage d'un gratte-ciel. Il n'est pas grand mais il est commode. Par deux grandes fenêtres on peut voir en bas la Whitehall Street. Aux murs gris il y a des affiches illustrées et une grande carte de la France.

1. Mr. Potter's office is on the twentieth floor of a skyscraper. It is not large but it is comfortable. Through two large windows one can see Whitehall Street below. On the gray walls there are some illustrated posters and a large map of France.

2. Sur le bureau de M. Potter il y a beaucoup de papiers. Près de la porte il y a un petit bureau avec une machine à écrire. Entre les deux fenêtres il y a une longue table. Sur la table il y a des journaux, des revues, et un cendrier.

2. On Mr. Potter's desk there are many papers. Near the door is a small desk with a typewriter. Between the two windows there is a long table. On the table there are some newspapers, magazines, and an ash tray.

3. M. Potter est assis à son bureau quand M. Picard arrive. Il va a la porte pour le[1] saluer.

3. Mr. Potter is seated at his desk when Mr. Picard arrives. He goes to the door to greet him.[1]

4. — Bonjour, M. Picard. Je suis très content de vous[1] voir.

4. Good afternoon, M. Picard. I am very glad to see you.[1]

5. — Bonjour, M. Potter. Comment allez-vous?

5. Good afternoon, Mr. Potter. How are you?

6. — Très bien, merci.

6. Very well, thank you.

7. — Votre bureau est très beau. J'aime bien cette carte de la France, et ces affiches illustrées. Quelles jolies couleurs! À propos, M. Potter, qu'est-ce que vous voyez sur cette affiche là?

7. Your office is very beautiful. I like this map of France and these illustrated posters. What pretty colors! By the way, Mr. Potter, what do you see on that poster?

8. — Je vois le ciel et le soleil, un château blanc sur une colline, avec un toit rouge et beaucoup de cheminées.

8. I see the sky and the sun, a white castle on a hill, with a red roof and many chimneys.

9. — De quelle couleur est le soleil?

9. What color is the sun?

10. — Il est jaune et il est immense.

10. It is yellow and it is immense.

11. — De quelles couleurs sont le ciel, les cheminées et la colline?

11. What colors are the sky, the chimneys and the hill?

12. — Le ciel est bleu. Les cheminées sont noires. La colline est verte. Mon Dieu, il est déjà une heure! C'est assez de couleurs! Je commence à avoir faim. Et vous? N'avez-vous pas faim?

12. The sky is blue. The chimneys are black. The hill is green. My goodness! It's already one o'clock. That's enough of colors! I'm beginning to be hungry. How about you? Aren't you hungry?

13. — Eh, bien, moi aussi, j'ai faim.

13. Well, I am hungry, too.

14. — Bon. Pas loin d'ici il y a un bon restaurant.

14. Good. Not far from here there is a good restaurant.

15. — Tant mieux! Allons-y![2]

15. Good! Let's go there![2]

NOTE 1. **Le,** *him,* and **vous,** *you,* are direct object pronouns. Such pronouns usually precede the verb in French.

NOTE 2. **y** = *there*. It is used to refer to a place already mentioned, in this case, *to a good restaurant*.

Pronunciation and Spelling Aids

Practice aloud

1. **deux grandes fenêtres** (deu grahñd fuh-**nehtr**)
2. **des affiches illustrées** (deh za-feesh zee-lü-**stray**)
3. **une machine à ecrire** (ün ma-sheen a ay-**kreer**)
4. **quelles jolies couleurs** (kehl zhu-lee koo-**leur**)
5. **beaucoup de cheminées** (boh-koo duh shuh-mee-**nay**)
6. **pas loin d'ici** (pah lwañ dee-**see**)

Building Vocabulary

Some common adjectives

blanc (blahñ) white
noir (nwar) black
bleu (bleu) blue
gris (gree) gray
jaune (zhohn) yellow
rouge (roozh) red
vert (vehr) green
bon (bawñ) good
mauvais (mu-**veh**) bad

beau (boh) beautiful
joli (zhu-**lee**) pretty
grand (grahñ) big
petit (puh-**tee**) small
long (lawñ) long
court (koor) short
riche (reesh) rich
haut (oh) high
bas (bah) low

pauvre (pohvr) poor
facile (fa-**seel**) easy
jeune (zheun) young
vieux (vyeu) old
difficile (dee-fee-**seel**) difficult
malade (ma-**lad**) sick
important (añ-pur-**tahñ**) important
intéressant (añ-tay-reh-**sahñ**) interesting
assis (a-**see**) seated

French Expressions

1. **on peut voir** (awñ peu **vwar**) one can see
2. **à propos** (a pru-**poh**) by the way
3. **j'aime bien** (zhehm **byañ**) I like
   j'aime beaucoup (zhehm boh-**koo**) I like very much
4. **de quelle couleur** (duh kehl koo-**leur**) (of) what color
5. **Il est une heure.** (eel eh tü **neur**) It is one o'clock.
6. **tant mieux** (tahñ **myeu**) good; so much the better
7. **avoir faim.** (a-vwar **fañ**) to be hungry. (*Literally:* to have hunger)
8. **J'ai faim.** (zhay **fañ**) I am hungry. (*Literally:* I have hunger)
9. **Mon dieu!** (mawñ **dyeu**) Goodness!
10. **moi aussi** (mwa oh-**see**) I too

Exercise No. 31—Completion of Text

1. **Il y a deux** (large) **fenêtres.**
2. (One can) **voir la rue.**
3. **Sur la table il y a des** (newspapers).
4. **M. Potter** (is seated) **à son bureau.**
5. **Je suis content** (to see you).
6. (I like) **cette carte.**
7. (I see) **un château blanc.**
8. (What color) **est le ciel?**
9. **Le ciel est** (blue).
10. (Goodness!) **Il est une heure.**
11. (Not far from here) **il y a un restaurant.**
12. (Good! Let's go there.)

Grammar Notes

1. Agreement of adjectives

Adjectives have masculine, feminine and plural forms, and agree in number and gender with the nouns they accompany. Study the following examples which illustrate such agreement, noting especially the feminine and plural forms of adjectives.

le père intelligent
la mère intelligent*e*
les pères intelligent*s*
les mères intelligent*es*

le crayon noir
la table noir*e*
les crayons noir*s*
les tables noir*es*

le stylo bleu
la carte bleu*e*
les stylos bleu*s*
les cartes bleu*es*

un exemple facile
une question facile
les exemples facile*s*
les questions facile*s*

l'homme riche
la femme riche
les hommes riche*s*
les femmes riche*s*

le mur gris
la carte gris*e*
les murs gris
les cartes gris*es*

a. To make an adjective feminine, add a silent **e** to the masculine, unless the masculine already ends in **e. (riche, facile, rouge, jaune)**

b. To make an adjective plural, add **-s** to the singular, unless the singular adjective already ends in **-s. (gris, assis)**

2. Position of adjectives.

In general, adjectives come *after* the nouns they modify, in French. A few common adjectives, however, usually come *before* the noun:

bon good	**grand** big, tall	**jeune** young	**long** long
meilleur better	**petit** small	**vieux** old	**haut** high, loud
mauvais bad	**beau** beautiful	**joli** pretty	**gros** big, thick

un bon livre	**le mauvais garçon**	**les hautes collines**
une jolie femme	**la grande station**	**les petites jeunes filles**

3. If the adjective is used after some form of the verb **être,** *to be,* the adjective must agree with the subject of the sentence. For example:

Anne est très jolie. Charles est très beau.

Exercise No. 32. Complete in French with the correct form of the adjective:

Exemple: 1. Madame Potter est assise dans le salon.

1. **Mme. Potter est** (seated) **dans le salon.**
2. **Les** (little) **enfants jouent dans le parc.**
3. **Mme. Potter est une femme** (intelligent).
4. **J'aime bien les** (pretty) **couleurs.**
5. **M. Potter a un bureau** (comfortable).
6. **Le château est situé sur une** (high) **colline.**
7. **Les murs du bureau sont** (gray).
8. **Tous les élèves sont** (intelligent).
9. **Avez-vous un** (good) **stylo?**
10. **Anne et Elizabeth sont très** (pretty).
11. **Il y a beaucoup de** (big) **parcs à Paris.**
12. **Où sont les affiches** (illustrated)?
13. **Il y a une** (large) **carte au mur.**
14. **Le ciel est-il** (red) **ou** (blue)?
15. **Les cheminées sont-elles** (black)?
16. **Son grand-père est très** (old).

NOTE. Some plural nouns may include both masculine and feminine persons, such as **élèves,** *pupils;* **étudiants,** *students;* **enfants,** *children.* In that case the agreeing adjective is in the masculine plural.

3. Some irregular adjectives.

a. Note the feminine forms.

le bon livre	**le long crayon**	**le beau bureau**	**le papier blanc**
la *bonne* fille	**la *longue* table**	**la *belle* maison**	**la chaise *blanche***
les bons livres	**les longs crayons**	**les beaux bureaux**	**les papiers blancs**
les *bonnes* filles	**les *longues* tables**	**les *belles* maisons**	**les chaises *blanches***

b. Note carefully the forms and meanings of the adjective **tout,** and of the question adjective **quel.**

tout le livre the whole book	**quel frère?** which, what brother?
toute la salle the whole room	**quelle soeur?** which, what, sister?
tous les livres all the books	**quels frères?** which, what brothers?
toutes les salles all the rooms	**quelles soeurs?** which, what sisters?

Exercise No. 33. Complete in French with the correct form of the adjective:

Exemple: 1. Madame Picard est une belle femme.

1. **Madame Picard est une** (beautiful) **femme.**
2. **Marie est une** (good) **fille.**
3. **Les filles de M. Potter sont très** (beautiful).
4. **Elles ont beaucoup de** (good) **amies.**
5. **Voyez-vous les maisons** (white)?
6. **Où est la** (long) **table?**
7. (Which) **homme parle français?**
8. (What) **jolies jeunes filles!**
9. **De** (what) **couleur est la colline?**
10. (Which) **cendriers avez-vous?**
11. **M. Potter travaille** (all) **la journée.**
12. **Où sont** (all) **les journaux?**

Exercise No. 34. Translate into French:

1. Mr. Potter's office is very comfortable.
2. The windows of the office are large.
3. There are some illustrated posters on the walls.
4. There are some French newspapers on the table.
5. The sky on the poster is blue.
6. The sun is yellow.
7. How are you, Mr. Potter?
8. Very well, thank you.
9. I am hungry.
10. I too.

Exercise No. 35—Questionnaire

1. **Où est la bureau de M. Potter?**
2. **Est-ce que[1] le bureau est grand?**
3. **Est-ce qu'il est commode?**
4. **Où est-ce qu'il y a des affiches illustrées?**
5. **Où est-ce qu'il y a beaucoup de papiers?**
6. **Où est-ce qu'il y a un petit bureau?**
7. **Où est-ce qu'il y a une longue table?**
8. **De quelle couleur est le soleil sur l'affiche?**
9. **De quelle couleur sont les cheminées?**
10. **De quelle couleur est la colline?**
11. **Est-ce que le ciel est bleu?**
12. **De quelle couleur est le château?**
13. **Est-ce que le toit est rouge ou jaune?**
14. **Est-ce que M. Potter a faim?**

NOTE 1. Remember: In any question with **est-ce que** the word order is subject first, then the verb.

CHAPITRE 9 (NEUF)

M. POTTER SALUE UN AMI À SON BUREAU
MR. POTTER GREETS A FRIEND IN HIS OFFICE

1. M. Dupont, un ami de M. Potter, demeure à New York. Cependant il parle bien le français parce que ses parents sont Canadiens.

1. Mr. Dupont, a friend of Mr. Potter, lives in New York. However, he speaks French well because his parents are Canadian.

2. Il sait que son ami M. Potter apprend le français. Il désire voir si son ami fait des progrès dans ses études. Donc il entre un jour dans le bureau de M. Potter et le salue en français.

2. He knows that his friend Mr. Potter is learning French. He wants to see if his friend is making progress in his studies. Therefore he enters Mr. Potter's office one day and greets him in French.

3. — Comment ça va?

3. How's it going?

4. — Très bien merci. Et vous?

4. Very well thank you. And you?

5. — Comme ci, comme ça. À propos, vous apprenez le français, n'est-ce pas?

5. So so. By the way, you are learning French, aren't you?

6. — Bien sûr. J'apprends à[1] parler, à lire et à écrire le français.

6. Of course. I am learning to[1] speak, read and write French.

7. — Est-ce que le français est difficile à[1] apprendre?

7. Is French difficult to learn?

8. — Eh bien, non. Le français n'est pas difficile à apprendre. J'aime beaucoup la langue française et je l'étudie[2] avec plaisir.

8. Well, no. French is not difficult to learn. I like the French language very much and I study it[2] with pleasure.

9. — Qui est votre professeur de français?

9. Who is your French teacher?

10. — M. Picard. C'est un très bon professeur, et de jour en jour je parle, je lis, et j'écris le français de mieux en mieux. J'apprends les mots et les expressions de la vie quotidienne. Je comprends M. Picard quand il parle français, et il me comprend quand je le[2] parle. Le français me plaît beaucoup.

10. Mr. Picard. He is a very good teacher, and day by day I speak, read, and write better and better. I learn the words and expressions of daily life. I understand Mr. Picard when he speaks French and he understands me when I speak it. I like French very much.

11. — Mon ami, vous parlez français à merveille.

11. My friend, you speak French wonderfully.

12. — Merci. Vous êtres trop aimable.

12. Thanks. You are too kind.

13. — Pas du tout. C'est la vérité. Mes amis me disent que vous allez faire un voyage en France cet été. C'est vrai?

13. Not at all. It is the truth. My friends tell me that you are going to make a trip to France this summer. Is that true?

14. — Oui. J'espère partir au printemps, le 31 mai. Je vais voyager en avion. Je désire arriver en France le plus tôt possible.
15. — Bon voyage! Et bonne chance! Au revoir.
16. — À bientôt.

14. Yes. I hope to go in the spring, the 31st of May. I am going to travel by plane. I want to arrive in France as soon as possible.
15. Have a good trip. And good luck! Goodbye.
16. So long.

NOTE 1. The *to* of infinitives (*to* read, *to* write, etc.) is often not expressed in French. However, after some verbs, including **apprendre,** to learn, **enseigner**, to teach, **commencer**, to begin, the *to* is translated by **à**. Similarly, the infinitive is introduced by **à** after certain adjectives, for example **difficile,** *difficult,* and **facile,** *easy*. Sometimes *to* is translated by **de** after a verb or adjective, as in:

Il refuse *de* parler. He refuses *to* speak.
Il est content *de* le faire. He is happy *to* do it.

NOTE 2. **le (l'),** *him, it,* **la (l')** *her, it,* and **me,** *me,* are direct object pronouns. They usually precede the verb.

Pronunciation and Spelling Aids

Practice aloud

1. **Cependant il parle bien le français.** (suh-pahñ-dahñ eel parl byañ luh frahñ-seh)
2. **Ses parents sont Canadiens.** (say pa-rahñ sawñ ka-na-**dyañ**)
3. **Dupont** (dü-**pawñ**)
4. **donc** (dawñk)
5. **C'est un très bon professeur.** (seh teuñ treh bawñ pru-feh-**seur**)
6. **je prends** (prahñ), **ils prennent** (prehn)

Building Vocabulary

Antonyms

1. **apprendre** to learn, **enseigner** to teach
2. **partir** to leave, **arriver** to arrive
3. **beaucoup de choses** many things
   peu de choses few things
4. **poser une question** to ask a question
   répondre à une question to answer a question
5. **loin d'ici** far from here **près d'ici** near here
6. **le professeur** the professor
   l'étudiant the student
7. **le maître, la maîtresse** the teacher
   l'élève the pupil
8. **il est assis** he is seated
   il est debout he is standing
9. **voici** here is (are) **voilà** there is (are)

French Expressions

1. **faire des progrès** (fehr day pru-**greh**) to make progress, to progress
2. **voici** (vwa-**see**) here is, are
3. **n'est-ce pas** (nehs **pah**) is it not true? Translated in various ways: isn't he, she, it? aren't you? don't you? etc.
4. **de jour en jour** (duh zhoor ahñ **zhoor**) day by day
5. **de mieux en mieux** (duh myeu zahñ **myeu**) better and better
6. **à merveille** (a mehr-**vehy**) wonderfully
7. **pas du tout** (pah dü **too**) not at all
8. **le plus tôt possible** (luh plü toh pu-**seeble**) as soon as possible
9. **bon voyage** (bawñ vwa-**yazh**) happy voyage
10. **bonne chance** (bun **shahñs**) good luck

Exercise No. 36—Completion of Text

1. (His parents) **sont Canadiens.**
2. (His friend) **fait des progrès.**
3. (Here is) **leur conversation.**
4. **Vous apprenez le français,** (aren't you)?
5. (I am learning) **à parler français.**
6. **Le français** (is not difficult) **à apprendre.**
7. (I am studying it) **diligemment.**
8. (I like French) (*Literally:* French pleases me) **beaucoup.**
9. **Vous parlez français** (wonderfully well).
10. I understand Mr. Picard.
11. (You are) **trop aimable.**
12. (Not at all). **C'est** (the truth).

Grammar Notes

1. Present tense of **vendre** to sell. Regular **-re** verb.

I sell, you sell, etc.

je vends (vahñ)	**nous vendons** (vahñ-dawñ)
tu vends (vahñ)	**vous vendez** (vahñ-day)
il, elle vend (vahñ)	**ils, elles vendent** (vahñd)

Imperative: **vends** sell **vendons** let us sell **vendez** sell

The endings of regular **-re** verbs in the present tense are:

Singular **-s -s —** Plural **-ons -ez -ent**

Other regular **-re** verbs are:

attendre *to wait for,* **j'attends,** etc.	**perdre** *to lose,* **je perds,** etc.
entendre *to hear,* **j'entends,** etc.	**rendre** *to give back,* **je rends,** etc.
descendre *to go down,* **je descends,** etc.	**répondre** *to answer* **je réponds,** etc.

2. Present tense of **prendre,** *to take,* **lire,** *to read,* **écrire,** *to write*. Irregular **-re** verbs.

I take, you take, etc.		*I read, you read, etc.*		*I write, you write, etc.*	
je prends	**nous prenons**	**je lis**	**nous lisons**	**j'écris**	**nous écrivons**
tu prends	**vous prenez**	**tu lis**	**vous lisez**	**tu écris**	**vous écrivez**
il prend	**ils prennent**	**il lit**	**ils lisent**	**il écrit**	**ils écrivent**
elle prend	**elles prennent**	**elle lit**	**elles lisent**	**elle écrit**	**elles écrivent**
Imperative		*Imperative*		*Imperative*	
prends prenons prenez		**lis lisons lisez**		**écris écrivons écrivez**	

Other verbs like **prendre** are:

apprendre *to learn* **j'apprends, nous apprenons, ils apprennent**
comprendre *to understand* **je comprends, nous comprenons, ils comprennent**

Other verbs like **lire** are: **élire,** *elect;* **relire,** *reread.*

Other verbs like **écrire** are: **décrire,** *describe;* **inscrire,** *to register.*

The most common irregular verbs will appear gradually in the conversation texts and Grammar Notes. You will learn them as you meet them. A summary of common irregular verbs can be found in the Appendix.

Exercise No. 37. Translate these short dialogues. Then practice them aloud. They will help you to get a feel for the correct use of the verbs.

1. **— Apprenez-vous le français?**
   — Oui monsieur, j'apprends le français.
   — Est-ce que Charles apprend le français?
   — Non, il n'apprend pas le français.
2. **— Écrivez-vous une lettre?**
   — Je n'écris pas une lettre.
   — Qu'est-ce que vous écrivez?
   — J'écris la leçon de français.
3. **— Que lisez-vous?**
   — Je lis un journal français.
   — Qu'est-ce qu'Anne lit?
   — Elle lit une revue française.
4. **— Comprenez-vous votre professeur quand il parle rapidement?**
   — Non madame, mais nous le comprenons bien quand il parle lentement.
5. **— Qu'est-ce que M. Potter vend?**
   — Il vend des objets d'art.
   — Vend-il en gros (wholesale) **ou en détail** (retail)?
   — Il vend seulement (only) **en gros.**
6. **— Qui est-ce que M. Potter attend?**
   — Il attend M. Picard.
   — Où est-ce qu'il l'attend?
   — Il l'attend dans le salon.

Exercise No. 38. Complete these sentences in French with the correct form of the verb indicated:

Exemple: 1. Nous vendons notre automobile.

1. (We are selling) **notre automobile.**
2. (We are learning) **à parler français.**
3. (I understand) **le professeur.**
4. (They read) **les journaux français.**
5. (Are you writing) **les exercices?**
6. (I take) **le train en ville.**
7. (They are not taking) **de train.**
8. (We answer) **à toutes les questions.**
9. **Qui** (is learning) **l'espagnol?**
10. (They do not understand) **la leçon.**
11. **Mais** (we do not write) **bien le français.**
12. (Let us write) **les lettres.**
13. **Que** (do they sell)?
14. (Read) **cette lettre, s'il vous plaît.**
15. (We are waiting for) **nos amis.**
16. (Do you hear) **le maître?**

Exercise No. 39—Questionnaire

1. **Qui demeure à New-York?**
2. **Est-ce que M. Dupont parle bien le français?**
3. **Est-ce que ses parents sont Américains?**
4. **Qu'est-ce que M. Dupont sait?**
5. **Où est-ce qu'il entre un jour?**
6. **Qui est-ce que** (whom) **M. Dupont salue en français?**
7. **Qui apprend à parler, à lire et à écrire le français?**
8. **Comment M. Potter étudie-t-il?**
9. **Qui est son professeur de français?**
10. **Est-ce un bon professeur?**
11. **Est-ce que M. Potter comprend quand M. Picard parle français?**
12. **Quels mots et quelles expressions M. Potter apprend-il?**
13. **Qui va faire un voyage en France?**
14. **Quand est-ce qu'il espère partir?**

RÉVISION 2
CHAPITRES 6–9 PREMIÈRE PARTIE

Review of Words (Révision de Mots)

NOUNS

1. **l'an**	11. **la couleur**	21. **le nom**	1. year	11. color	21. name
2. **l'avion**	12. **l'élève**	22. **la revue**	2. airplane	12. pupil	22. magazine
3. **le bateau**	13. **l'endroit**	23. **le plaisir**	3. boat	13. place	23. pleasure
4. **les bateaux**	14. **les environs**	24. **le soleil**	4. boats	14. suburbs	24. sun
5. **la bonne**	15. **l'étage**	25. **le printemps**	5. maid	15. story, floor	25. spring
6. **la carte**	16. **l'été**	26. **le toit**	6. map	16. summer	26. roof
7. **le cendrier**	17. **l'étudiant**	27. **le travail**	7. ash tray	17. student	27. work
8. **le château**	18. **le journal**	28. **le voyage**	8. castle	18. newspaper	28. trip
9. **les châteaux**	19. **les journaux**	29. **la vie**	9. castles	19. newspapers	29. life
10. **le ciel**	20. **le mot**	30. **la vérité**	10. sky	20. word	30. truth

VERBS

1. **aimer**	11. **écouter**	21. **voyager**	1. to like, love	11. to listen	21. to travel
2. **s'appeler**	12. **entrer (dans)**	22. **répondre**	2. to be named	12. to enter	22. to answer
3. **il s'appelle**	13. **espérer**	23. **vendre**	3. his name is	13. to hope	23. to sell
4. **causer**	14. **étudier**	24. **dire**	4. to chat, talk	14. to study	24. to say, tell
5. **commencer**	15. **jouer**	25. **écrire**	5. to begin	15. to play	25. to write
6. **coûter**	16. **poser**	26. **voir**	6. to cost	16. to ask (question)	26. to see
7. **chanter**	17. **regretter**	27. **partir**	7. to sing	17. to regret, to be sorry	27. to leave
8. **demeurer**	18. **saluer**	28. **je sais**	8. to live, dwell	18. to greet	28. I know
9. **demander**	19. **sonner**	29. **ils prennent**	9. to ask	19. to ring	29. they take
10. **desirer**	20. **travailler**	30. **je vais dire**	10. to want	20. to work	30. I am going to say

ADJECTIVES

1. **blanc**	4. **gris**	7. **vert**	1. white	4. gray	7. green
2. **blanche (*f*)**[1]	5. **jaune**	8. **beau (bel)**[2]	2. white (*f*)	5. yellow	8. beautiful
3. **bleu**	6. **rouge**	9. **belle (*f*)**	3. blue	6. red	9. beautiful (*f*)

10. **bon**	10. good
11. **bonne (*f*)**	11. good (*f*)
12. **commode**	12. comfortable
13. **difficile**	13. difficult
14. **facile**	14. easy
15. **joli**	15. pretty
16. **jeune**	16. young
17. **long**	17. long
18. **longue (*f*)**	18. long (*f*)
19. **malade**	19. sick
20. **pauvre**	20. poor
21. **prochain**	21. next
22. **riche**	22. rich
23. **quel homme**	23. which man
24. **quelle femme**	24. which woman
25. **quels garçons**	25. which boys
26. **quelles filles (*f*)**	26. which girls
27. **tout le mur**	27. the whole wall
28. **toute la cuisine**	28. the whole kitchen
29. **tous les journaux**	29. all the newspapers
30. **toutes les revues**	30. all the magazines

NOTE 1. If adjectives are irregular, the masculine and feminine forms are given.

NOTE 2. **Bel** is used only before a masculine noun beginning with a vowel or **h** (usually).
un beau portrait un bel ami un bel hôtel une belle amie

ADVERBS

1. **déjà**	1. already
2. **ensuite**	2. then
3. **trop**	3. too much, too many
4. **demain**	4. tomorrow
5. **vite**	5. quickly, fast
6. **le plus vite**	6. most quickly, fastest

PREPOSITIONS

1. **après**	1. after
2. **par**	2. by, through
3. **pour**	3. for, in order to
4. **loin de**	4. far from

CONJUNCTIONS

1. **cependant**	1. however
2. **donc**	2. therefore
3. **si**	3. if, whether
4. **que**	4. that

FRENCH EXPRESSIONS

1. **à propos**	1. by the way
2. **à merveille**	2. wonderfully
3. **bien sûr**	3. surely
4. **bon voyage**	4. happy voyage
5. **bonne chance**	5. good luck
6. **comme ci comme ça**	6. so so
7. **eh bien**	7. well
8. **mon Dieu!**	8. goodness!
9. **De quelle couleur est-il?**	9. What color is it?
10. **de jour en jour**	10. day by day
11. **de mieux en mieux**	11. better and better
12. **tant mieux**	12. so much the better
13. **en avion**	13. by plane
14. **moi aussi**	14. I too, me too
15. **pas du tout**	15. not at all
16. **demander des renseignements**	16. to ask for information
17. **poser des questions**	17. to ask questions
18. **répondre aux questions**	18. to answer questions
19. **partir en voyage**	19. to leave on a trip
20. **le plus tôt possible**	20. as soon as possible
21. **quant à moi**	21. as for me
22. **Elle est enrhumée.**	22. She has a cold.
23. **voici**	23. here is (are)
24. **J'ai faim.**	24. I am hungry.
25. **Quel âge avez-vous?**	25. How old are you?
26. **n'est-ce pas?**	26. is it not so; isn't it? etc.

Exercise No. 40. Select the words in Column II which best complete each sentence begun in Column I:

Exemple: l-c Je suis importateur d'objets d'art de la France et du Maroc.

I	II
1. **Je suis importateur d'objets d'art**	a. **dites, "Je ne sais pas."**
2. **Je ne comprends pas bien**	b. **nous allons faire des progrès de jour en jour.**
3. **Si vous ne savez pas la réponse**	c. **de la France et du Maroc.**
4. **M. Picard dit, "Je le regrette beaucoup,"**	d. **pas loin d'ici.**
5. **Ils vont en avion parce que**	e. **quand le professeur parle rapidement.**
6. **Si nous étudions diligemment**	f. **du voyage.**
7. **Quand j'ai faim**	g. **parce que l'enfant est enrhumée.**
8. **Il y a un bon restaurant**	h. **"Comment ça va?"**
9. **Son ami salue M. Potter et dit,**	i. **c'est le plus vite.**
10. **Je ne sais pas le prix**	j. **je vais au restaurant.**

Exercise No. 41. Answer each of the following questions in complete sentences, using the suggested words in the answer. Make the adjectives agree with their nouns in number and gender.

Exemple: De quelle couleur sont les toits? (blanc) Ils sont blancs.

1. **Quelle langue parlez-vous? (français)**
2. **Où demeurent-ils? (aux États-Unis)**
3. **Qui a faim? (Nous)**
4. **De quelles couleurs est la revue? (blanc et noir)**
5. **De quelle couleur sont les maisons? (rouge)**
6. **Quel age avez-vous? (quinze ans)**
7. **Qui pose des questions? (les professeurs)**
8. **Qui répond aux questions? (nous)**
9. **Qui est-ce que M. Potter attend? (son ami)**
10. **Qu'est-ce que vous écrivez? (des lettres)**

Exercise No. 42. Complete each verb with the correct ending:

1. **nous travaill_____**
2. **elles apprenn_____**
3. **vous ne sav_____ pas**
4. **tu écri_____**
5. **ils lis_____**
6. **je ne comprend_____ pas**
7. **il étudi_____**
8. **vous pren_____**
9. **elles attend_____**
10. **vous ne répond_____ pas**
11. **Lis_____!**
12. **N'attend_____ pas, M. Picard.**

Exercise No. 43. Answer each of the following questions in the affirmative and negative singular:

Exemple: 1. Oui, monsieur, j'ai faim. Non, madame, je n'ai pas faim.

1. **Avez-vous faim?**
2. **Êtes-vous enrhumé?**
3. **Étudiez-vous la leçon?**
4. **Attendez-vous le professeur?**
5. **Comptez-vous voyager en France?**
6. **Apprenez-vous à écrire le français?**
7. **Lisez-vous la revue?**
8. **Écrivez-vous la lettre?**
9. **Comprenez-vous les questions?**
10. **Acceptez-vous l'invitation?**
11. **Commencez-vous à lire?**
12. **Répondez-vous à la question?**

Exercise No. 44. You have met the following question pronouns:

1. **qui** *or* **qui est-ce qui?** who? (*subject of verb*)
2. **qui** *or* **qui est-ce que?** whom? (*object of verb or with a preposition*)
3. **qu'est-ce qui?** what? (*subject of verb*)
4. **que** *or* **qu'est-ce que?** what? (*object of verb*)

Supply the correct question pronouns in the French sentences which follow. Remember: **que** becomes **qu'** if the next word begins with a vowel or **h** (usually).

Question pronouns containing **est-ce que** are followed by the regular word order (*subject — verb*).

1. (Who) **sait parler français?**
2. (Whom) **voyez-vous tous les jours?**
3. (Whom) **M. Picard voit le mardi et le jeudi?**
4. **Avec** (whom) **Madame Potter parle-t-elle?**
5. **À** (whom) **parlez-vous?**
6. (What) **M. Potter apprend?**
7. (What) **apprenez-vous?**
8. (Who) **va faire un voyage en France?**
9. (What) **est sur le toit de la maison?**
10. (What) **lisez-vous?**
11. (What) **les enfants lisent?**
12. (What) **est au mur au-dessus du piano?**

Dialogue 1

Quel autobus faut-il prendre?[1]

1. **Excusez-moi, monsieur, quel autobus faut-il prendre pour l'Étoile? (pour le Quai Voltaire)? (pour la Place Vendôme)?**
2. **Prenez l'Autobus 52**[2]**, etc. Il s'arrête ici-même, au coin.**
3. **Merci beaucoup, monsieur.**
4. **De rien, monsieur.**

What bus should I take?

1. Excuse me sir, which bus do I take for the Etoile? (for the Quai Voltaire)? (for the Place Vendôme)?
2. Take the 52 bus, etc. It stops right here at the corner.
3. Thank you very much, sir.
4. Don't mention it, sir.

NOTE 1. *Lit.* What bus is it necessary to take? 2. **cinquante-deux.**

Dialogue 2

Quel autobus va à . . . ?

1. **Excusez-moi, monsieur, pouvez-vous me dire quel autobus va à l'Opéra? (au Jardin du Luxembourg)? (au Louvre)?**
2. **Je regrette. Je ne suis pas d'ici, monsieur. Je ne sais pas. Mais cet agent au coin va certainement vous le dire.**

Which bus goes to . . . ?

1. Excuse me sir, can you tell me which bus goes to the Opera? (the Luxembourg Gardens)? (the Louvre)?
2. I'm sorry. I am not from here, sir. I don't know. But that policeman at the corner will certainly tell you.

3. Merci beaucoup, monsieur. Je vais lui[1] demander.

3. Thank you very much, sir. I am going to ask him.

NOTE 1. **Lui,** *him,* is an indirect object pronoun; it usually precedes the verb.

Exercise No. 45—Lecture 1

Deux amis de M. Potter

M. Potter sait déjà les noms de tous les objets dans sa maison. Maintenant il commence à étudier les verbes parce qu'il désire apprendre à lire, à écrire et à parler en français. Il désire aussi apprendre les nombres en français. Comme[1] il désire rendre visite à[2] son représentant à Paris, qui ne parle pas anglais, il désire apprendre à parler français le plus tôt possible. Donc il lui faut[3] beaucoup de pratique avec des personnes qui parlent bien le français. Heureusement, il a deux amis français qui sont dans les affaires[4] près de son bureau dans la rue Whitehall.

Un jour M. Potter rend visite à ces messieurs français. Les deux messieurs écoutent avec attention pendant que[5] M. Potter cause avec eux[6] en français. Après dix minutes de conversation, les messieurs posent beaucoup de questions à leur[7] ami, et ils sont très contents de ses[8] progrès.

NOTE 1. **comme** as 2. **rendre visite à** to pay a visit to 3. Therefore he needs (*Lit*. It is necessary to him.) 4. **être dans les affaires** to be in business 5. **pendant que** while 6. **eux** them 7. **leur** their 8. **ses** his

Exercise No. 46—Lecture 2

M. Potter est malade

Jeudi le vingt-deux avril à neuf heures du soir M. Picard arrive à la maison de son élève, M. Potter. Le fils aîné,[1] un garçon de dix ans, ouvre la porte, et salue le professeur poliment. Ils entrent dans le salon où d'habitude[2] M. Potter attend son professeur.

Mais ce soir il n'est pas là. Mme. Potter n'est pas là non plus. M. Picard est très surpris, et il demande au garçon,—Où est ton papa? Le fils répond tristement[3]—Papa est malade. Il est au lit[4] parce qu'il est très enrhumé.

Le professeur est un peu ennuyé[5], mais il dit seulement—Quel dommage![6] Eh bien, la semaine prochaine nous allons étudier deux heures. A mardi prochain, alors. Au revoir, mon petit. Le garçon répond,—Au revoir, monsieur.

NOTE 1. **le fils ainé** the oldest son 2. **d'habitude** usually 3. **tristement** sadly 4. **au lit** in bed 5. **ennuyé** annoyed 6. **Quel dommage!** What a pity!

CHAPITRE 10 (DIX)

DANS LA SALLE À MANGER
IN THE DINING ROOM

1. M. Potter et M. Picard sont assis dans la salle à manger chez M. Potter. Sur la table il y a deux tasses et soucoupes, deux verres, des cuillers[1] à thé, des fourchettes, un couteau, un pot à lait, un sucrier, et un plat avec une tarte aux fruits. Les deux messieurs prennent du café avec des gâteaux.

1. Mr. Potter and Mr. Picard are seated in the dining room at Mr. Potter's house. On the table there are two cups and saucers, two glasses, some teaspoons, some forks, a knife, a milk pitcher, a sugar bowl, and a plate with a fruit tart. The two gentlemen are having coffee with some cakes.

2. M. Potter dit, — Comment trouvez-vous ces tasses et ces soucoupes?

2. Mr. Potter says, "How do you like (*Lit*. find) these cups and saucers?"

3. — Je les[2] trouve charmantes, répond M. Picard. Cette tasse blanche ornée de fleurs bleues est de Limoges, n'est-ce pas?

3. "I find them charming," answers Mr. Picard. "This white cup decorated with blue flowers is from Limoges, isn't it?"

4. — Mais oui. La porcelaine fine de Limoges est célèbre. Il y a plusieurs régions en France connues pour leurs produits céramiques et chaque région a son style individuel.

5. — Et ce gai petit pot à lait jaune avec des dessins verts, d'où vient-il?

6. — Ce pot à lait est de Vallauris, en Provence. C'est une ville célèbre pour sa poterie. La petite ville de Biot, près de Vallauris, est aussi un centre de l'industrie céramique.

7. — Il y a d'autres régions en France connues pour leurs produits céramiques, n'est-ce pas?

8. — Bien sûr. Il y a surtout la Bretagne. La poterie bretonne est très jolie. La poterie de Normandie est prèsque aussi jolie.

9. — Je vois que vous connaissez bien votre métier, dit M. Picard.

10. — Mais oui, il le faut, dit M. Potter.

11. — C'est vrai, répond M. Picard. En tout cas, je vois ici beaucoup de beaux échantillons de l'industrie céramique français.

12. — Naturellement. Comme vous dites, c'est mon métier. J'ai aussi des échantillons de poterie ordinaire pour la cuisine. Cette poterie est généralement très simple en couleur unie, tout en marron, comme ce plat-là près de vous.

13. — C'est un plat simple, mais beau.

14. — Voulez-vous encore une tasse de café? Un peu de cette tarte aux fruits?

15. — Merci bien. Tout est délicieux.

4. "Yes, indeed. The fine porcelain of Limoges is famous. There are several districts in France known for their ceramic products and each district has its individual style."

5. "And this bright little milk pitcher, yellow with green designs, where does that come from?"

6. "This milk pitcher is from Vallauris, in Provence. It is a town famous for its pottery. The little town of Biot, near Vallauris, is also a center of the ceramic industry."

7. "There are other regions in France known for their ceramic products, aren't there?"

8. "Certainly. There is above all Brittany. Breton pottery is very lovely. The pottery of Normandy is almost as pretty."

9. "I see that you know your trade very well," says Mr. Picard.

10. "Yes indeed; it is necessary," says Mr. Potter.

11. "That's true," answers Mr. Picard. "At any rate, I see here many fine samples of the French ceramic industry."

12. "Naturally. As you say, it's my trade. I also have some samples of ordinary pottery for kitchen use. This pottery is usually very simple and in one color, all in brown, like this dish near you."

13. "It is a simple dish, but it is handsome."

14. "Do you want another cup of coffee? A little of this fruit tart?"

15. "Thanks very much. Everything is delicious."

NOTE 1. **Cuiller,** *spoon,* is often spelled **cuillère.** Both are correct. 2. **les,** *them,* is an object pronoun. Object pronouns usually precede the verb.

Pronunciation and Spelling Aids

Practice aloud

1. **Limoges** (lee-**muzh**)
2. **Vallauris** (va-loh-**rees**)
3. **Provence** (pruh-**vahñs**)
4. **Normandie** (nur-mahñ-**dee**)
5. **Bretagne** (bruh-tahn-**yuh**)
6. **bretonne** (bruh-**tun**)
7. **l'industrie céramique** (lañ-dü-stree say-ra-**meek**)
8. **leurs produits** (leur pru-**düee**)
9. **son style individuel** (sawñ steel añ-dee-vee-dü-**ehl**)
10. **tout est délicieux** (too teh day-lee-**syeu**)

Building Vocabulary

Dans la salle à manger (dahñ la sal a mahñ-**zhay**)

1. **le plat** (pla) plate
2. **la tasse** (tas) cup
3. **la soucoupe** (soo-**koop**) saucer
4. **le couteau** (koo-**toh**) knife
5. **la fourchette** (foor-**sheht**) fork
6. **la cuiller** (küee-**yehr**) spoon
7. **la cuiller à soupe** (soop) soup spoon
8. **la cuiller à thé** (tay) teaspoon
9. **le pot à lait** (pu ta **leh**) milk pitcher
10. **le sucrier** (sü-kree-**ay**) sugar bowl
11. **le verre** (vehr) the glass
12. **manger** (mahñ-**zhay**) to eat; **on mange** (awñ **mahñzh**) one eats

French Expressions

1. **c'est vrai** (seh **vray**) certainly
2. **comment trouvez-vous?** (ku-mahñ troo-vay-**voo**) How do you like (*Lit.* find)?
3. **surtout** (sur-**too**) above all, especially
4. **en tout cas** (ahñ too **kah**) at any rate
5. **Il le faut** (eel luh **foh**) it is necessary

6. **d'ordinaire** (dur-dee-**nehr**) usually
7. **encore une tasse** (akñ-kur ün tas) another, i.e., one more cup
8. **autre** (oh-**tr** *or* oh-**truh**) another, i.e., a different one

Exercise No. 47—Completion of Text

1. (They are having) **du café avec des gâteaux.**
2. **Comment trouvez-vous** (these cups)?
3. **Cette tasse est ornée de** (blue flowers).
4. **La poterie fine de Limoges est** (famous).
5. (Each region) **a son style individuel.**
6. **La poterie bretonne est** (very pretty).
7. **La poterie de Normandie est** (almost as pretty).
8. (You know) **bien votre métier.**
9. — (That's true), **répond M. Picard.**
10. **Je vois** (many) **beaux échantillons.**
11. (As you say), **c'est mon métier.**
12. — (It's a simple dish), **dit M. Picard.**
13. **Voulez-vous** (another cup) **de café?**
14. **Merci bien.** (Everything) **est délicieux.**

Grammar Notes

1. The verbs **dire** *to say,* **voir** *to see*

I say, you say, etc.		*I see, you see, etc.*	
je dis (dee)	**nous disons** (dee-sawñ)	**je vois** (vwa)	**nous voyons** (vwa-yawñ)
tu dis (dee)	**vous dites** (deet)	**tu vois** (vwa)	**vous voyez** (vwa-yay)
il dit (dee)	**ils disent** (deez)	**il voit** (vwa)	**ils voient** (vwa)
elle dit (dee)	**elles disent** (deez)	**elle voit** (vwa)	**elles voient** (vwa)

Imperative

dis disons dites

Imperative

vois voyons voyez

Exercise No. 48. Practice these questions and answers:

1. **Que dites-vous? Je dis: — Non.**
2. **Que dit-il? Il dit: — Oui.**
3. **Que dit-elle? Elle dit: — C'est vrai.**
4. **Que disent-elles? Elles disent: — Ce n'est pas vrai.**
5. **Dites-moi où vous demeurez. Je demeure dans cette rue.**
6. **Qu'est-ce que vous voyez au mur? Je vois une carte de France.**
7. **Voyez-vous le château sur une colline? Nous le voyons.**
8. **Voit-il son ami Jean le dimanche? Non, il ne le voit pas le dimanche; il le voit le samedi.**

Exercise No. 49. Translate into French:

1. we say
2. I see.
3. he does not say
4. he says
5. does he say?
6. What do you say?
7. What do you see?
8. they see
9. do you (**tu**) see?
10. I do not see.
11. they are saying
12. What are they saying?
13. she does not see
14. Let's see.
15. Tell me.

2. The demonstrative adjective **ce, cet, cette, ces,** *this* or *that, these* or *those.*

a. **ce** (*this, that*) is used before masculine singular nouns.
cet is used instead of **ce** before masculine singular nouns beginning with a vowel or **h** (usually).
cette (*this, that*) is used before feminine singular nouns.
ces (*these, those*) is used before all nouns in the plural.

Study the following sentences. They show the various forms of the demonstrative adjective **ce.**

***Ce* garçon apprend le français.**	*This* (*that*) boy is learning French.
***Cet* article est de la France.**	*This* (*that*) article is from France.
***Cet* homme est professeur.**	*This* (*that*) man is a teacher.

***Cette* jeune fille est ma soeur.**	*This* (*that*) girl is my sister.
***Ces* garçons apprennent le français.**	*These* (*those*) boys are learning French.
***Ces* jeunes filles sont mes soeurs.**	*These* (*those*) girls are my sisters.

b. **-ci** (contraction of **ici** *here*) and **-là** (*there*) are added to the noun to distinguish between *this* and *that*, and *these* and *those*, if the meaning is not clear without them. Thus:

ce pot-ci	this pot	**cette tasse-ci**	this cup	**ces plats-ci**	these dishes
ce pot-là	that pot	**cette tasse-là**	that cup	**ces plats-là**	those dishes

Exercise No. 50. Complete the following expressions in French:

1. (this) **soir**
2. (these) **couteaux-ci**
3. (that) **portrait-là**
4. (those) **plats-là**
5. (this) **tasse-ci**
6. (that) **étudiant-là**
7. (this) **mot-ci**
8. (that) **fleur-là**
9. (these) **échantillons-ci**
10. (that) **homme-là**
11. (these) **revues-ci**
12. (that) **ami-là**

3. When to use **c'est,** *this is* or *it is,* instead of **il est, elle est.**

a. **c'est** is used before an adjective when the adjective refers to a thought already expressed in a sentence, and not to a single noun. Thus:

M. Potter étudie le français. C'est vrai. It's (That's) true.

b. **c'est** is used for **il (elle) est** and **ce sont** for **ils (elles) sont,** when a modified noun or a proper noun follows. Thus:

C'est une ville célèbre. It is (This is) a famous town.
Ce sont des portraits de mes enfants. They are portraits of my children.
C'est M. Picard. It's Mr. Picard.

Exercise No. 51. Practice these common **c'est** expressions aloud:

1. **C'est assez.** It's enough.
2. **C'est bon.** It's good.
3. **C'est mal.** It's bad.
4. **C'est bien.** It's (That's) all right.
5. **C'est ça (cela).** That's it. That's right. O.K.
6. **C'est ceci.** This is it.
7. **Ce n'est rien.** It's nothing.
8. **C'est facile.** It's easy.
9. **C'est difficile.** It's hard.
10. **C'est ici.** It's here.
11. **C'est là.** It's there.
12. **C'est près d'ici.** It's near here.
13. **C'est loin d'ici.** It's far from here.
14. **Ce n'est pas loin.** It's not far.

Exercise No. 52—Questions

1. **Où M. Picard et M. Potter sont-ils assis?**
2. **Qu'est-ce qu'ils prennent?**
3. **Que dit M. Potter?**
4. **D'où est la tasse blanche?**
5. **Quelle porcelaine est célèbre?**
6. **D'où est le petit pot à lait?**
7. **Pourquoi la ville de Vallauris est-elle célèbre?**
8. **Où est la ville de Vallauris?**
9. **Est-ce que la poterie de la Bretagne est jolie?**
10. **Qui connaît bien son métier?**
11. **Qu'est-ce que M. Potter a pour la cuisine?**
12. **La poterie ordinaire, est-elle simple ou ornée?**
13. **Est-ce que M. Picard accepte encore une tasse de café?**
14. **Qu'est-ce qu'il dit?**

CHAPITRE 11 (ONZE)

LES NOMBRES, TOUJOURS LES NOMBRES
NUMBERS, ALWAYS NUMBERS

1. — M. Potter, vous savez déjà que les noms des choses et des personnes sont importants. Vous savez qu'il n'est pas possible de former une phrase sans les verbes.	1. Mr. Potter, you already know that the names of things and of persons are important. You know that it is not possible to make a sentence without verbs.

2. — C'est vrai, M. Picard.

2. That's true, Mr. Picard.

3. — Eh bien, monsieur, il y a une catégorie de mots qui est tout aussi importante que les noms et les verbes. En effet, il est difficile d'imaginer notre civilisation moderne sans ces mots. Pouvez-vous devinez à quoi je pense?

3. Well sir, there is a class of words that is just as important as nouns and verbs. In fact, it is difficult to imagine our modern civilization without these words. Can you guess what I am thinking of?

4. — Je crois que oui. Vous voulez dire les nombres.

4. I think so. You mean numbers.

5. — Vous avez raison. Pouvez-vous expliquer comment les nombres sont indispensables pour la vie moderne?

5. You are right. Can you explain how numbers are indispensable to modern life?

6. — Certainement, rien de plus facile. Nous avons besoin des nombres pour le commerce.

6. Certainly. Nothing easier. We need numbers for business.

7. — Ha, Ha! L'homme d'affaires pense tout de suite au commerce. Cependant, sans argent les nombres ne valent pas grand'chose, n'est-ce pas?

7. Ha, ha! The businessman thinks immediately of business. However, without money, numbers are not worth much, are they?

8. — Évidemment. Eh bien, nous avons besoin de nombres pour désigner les dates, les heures, la température; pour exprimer les quantités et les mesures; pour téléphoner; pour la radio; pour toutes les sciences, et pour des milliers d'autres choses.

8. Of course. Well, we need numbers to indicate dates, the hours (of the day), the temperature; to express quantities; to telephone; for the radio; for all the sciences, and for thousands of other things.

9. — Les nombres, toujours les nombres. Oui, M. Potter, les nombres sont essentiels. Cependant, il est nécessaire non seulement connaître les nombres mais aussi savoir les employer correctement et rapidement dans la vie quotidienne.

9. Numbers, always numbers. Yes, Mr. Potter, numbers are essential. However, it is necessary not only to know the numbers, but also to know how to use them correctly and rapidly in daily life.

10. — Vous avez raison. Je vais faire tout mon possible pour les comprendre et les employer correctement.

10. You are right. I am going to do all I can to understand and use them correctly.

11. — En attendant, je veux vous dire que vous avancez rapidement dans vos études.

11. Meanwhile, I want to tell you that you are progressing rapidly in your studies.

12. — Vous êtes trop aimable, M. Picard.

12. You are too kind, Mr. Picard.

13. — Pas du tout. C'est la vérité. Eh bien, c'est assez pour aujour d'hui. Au revoir.

13. Not at all. It's the truth. Well, enough for today. Goodbye.

14. — Au revoir, monsieur. À jeudi prochain.

14. Goodbye, sir. Until next Thursday.

Pronunciation and Spelling Aids

Practice aloud. Stress slightly only the key syllables in heavy type.

Il y a une catégorie de mots
qui est tout aussi importante
que les noms et les verbes.

(Eel ya ün ka-tay-gu-ree duh **moh**
kee eh too toh-see añ-pur-**tahñt**
kuh lay nawñ zay lay **vehrb**)

Building Vocabulary

Related words

1. **vrai** true **la vérité** the truth
2. **répondre** to answer **la réponse** the answer
3. **étudier** to study **l'étude** the study
4. **savoir** to know
   le savant the scientist, scholar
5. **connaître** to know
   la connaissance knowledge
6. **le commerce** the commerce
   le commerçant the merchant
7. **civiliser** to civilize
   la civilisation the civilization
8. **le jour** the day
   le journal the daily newspaper

Locutions Françaises

1. **aussi bien que** (oh-see bjañ **kuh**) as well as
2. **en effet** (ahñ nay-**feh**) in fact
3. **penser à** (pahñ-say **a**) to think of
   À quoi[1] **pensez-vous?** (a kwa pahñ-say **voo**) What are you thinking about?
4. **Je crois que oui.** (zhuh krwa kuh **wee**) I think so.
   Je crois que non. I think not.
5. **Vous voulez dire** (voo voo-lay **deer**) You mean (*Lit.* You wish to say)
6. **avoir raison** (a-vwah reh-**sawñ**) to be right (*Lit.* to have right)
   Vous avez raison You are right.
7. **avoir besoin de** (a-vwar buh-zwañ **duh**) to need (*Lit.* to have need of)
   Vous avez besoin d'argent. You need money.
8. **tout de suite** (too duh süeet) at once
9. **pas du tout** (pah dü **too**) not at all
10. **rien de plus facile** (ryañ duh plü fa-**seel**) nothing easier
11. **d'ailleurs** (dah-jeur) besides
12. **d'accord** (da-kur) okay, agreed
13. **entendu** (ahñ-tahñ-dü) understood, agreed
14. **bien entendu** (bjañ ahñ-tahñ-dü) of course

NOTE 1. The interrogative pronoun **quoi,** *what?* is used after prepositions: **à quoi? de quoi? dans quoi? avec quoi?**, etc.

Exercise No. 53—Completion of Text

1. (You know) **déjà les noms des choses.**
2. **Cette catégorie de mots est tout** (as important as) **les noms et les verbes.**
3. **Pouvez-vous deviner** (of what) **je pense?**
4. (I think so). **Vous** (mean) **les nombres.**
5. (You are right). **Les nombres** (are indispensable).
6. (We need) **de nombres pour le commerce.**
7. (Without money) **les nombres ne valent pas** (much).
8. (In the meantime), **je veux vous dire que** (you are progressing rapidly) **dans vos études.**
9. (It is) **la vérité.**
10. Until next Thursday.

Grammar Notes

1. Present tense of the verbs **vouloir** *to wish, want* — **pouvoir** *to be able*

I wish, want, you wish, want, etc.	*I can (am able) you can, etc.*
je veux (veu)	**je peux** (peu) or **je puis**
tu veux (veu)	**tu peux** (peu)
il, elle veut (veu)	**il, elle peut** (peu)
nous voulons (voo-lawñ)	**nous pouvons** (poo-vawñ)
vous voulez (voo-lay)	**vous pouvez** (poo-vay)
ils, elles veulent (veul)	**ils, elles peuvent** (peuv)

Exercise No. 54. Translate into French

1. (I want) **savoir.**
2. (I am able) **deviner.**
3. (Do you want) **manger?**
4. (Can you) **jouer?**
5. (We wish) **étudier.**
6. (We are not able) **attendre.**
7. (They do not want) **travailler.**
8. (Are you able) **travailler?**
9. (Does he wish) **comprendre?**
10. (Is she able) **apprendre?**

2. **Les nombres de 1 (un) à 69 (soixante-neuf)**

1 **un** (euñ) **une** (ün)	10 **dix** (dees)	19 **dix-neuf** (deez-neuf)
2 **deux** (deu)	11 **onze** (awñz)	20 **vingt** (vañ)
3 **trois** (trwah)	12 **douze** (dooz)	21 **vingt et un** (vañ tay **eun**)
4 **quatre** (katr)	13 **treize** (trehz)	22 **vingt-deux** (vañt-**deu**)
5 **cinq** (sañk)	14 **quatorze** (ka-turz)	23 **vingt-trois** (vañ-**trwah**)
6 **six** (sees)	15 **quinze** (kañz)	24 **vingt-quatre** (vañt-**katr**)
7 **sept** (seht)	16 **seize** (sehz)	25 **vingt-cinq** (vañt-**sank**)
8 **huit** (üeet)	17 **dix-sept** (dee-seht)	26 **vingt-six** (vañt-sees)
9 **neuf** (neuf)	18 **dix-huit** (dee-züeet)	27 **vingt-sept** (vañt-seht)

28 **vingt-huit** (vañt-üeet)
29 **vingt-neuf** (vañt-neuf)
30 **trente** (trahñt)
31 **trente et un**
32 **trente-deux**
40 **quarante** (ka-rahnt)
41 **quarante et un**
50 **cinquante** (sañ-kahnt)
51 **cinquante et un**
60 **soixante** (swa-sahnt)
65 **soixante-cinq**
69 **soixante-neuf**

NOTE: The final consonants of 5, 6, 7, 8, 9, 10 are silent before words beginning with a consonant.
cinq livres (sañ leevr) **sept plumes** (seh plüm) **dix choses** (dee shohz)

Exercise No. 55. Write the numbers in French. Then read each expression aloud saying the numbers in French.

Exemple: a. (30) trente mots français

a. 30 mots français
b. 10 leçons faciles
c. 50 bonnes phrases
d. 49 affiches françaises
e. 16 maisons blanches
f. 38 femmes anglaises
g. 17 belles filles
h. 15 tables longues
i. 62 papiers verts
j. 68 hommes riches
k. 24 grandes villes
l. 13 plumes noires

Exercise No. 56. Write each arithmetical expression in French. Then read each expression aloud.

NOTE: + = **et** − = **moins** × = **fois** ÷ = **divisé par** make = **font**

Exemples: 4 + 6 = 10 **quatre et six font dix**
20 ÷ 5 = 4 **vingt divisé par cinq font quatre**

a. 2 + 6 = 8
b. 10 + 7 = 17
c. 7 × 8 = 56
d. 9 × 7 = 63
e. 19 − 8 = 11
f. 18 − 6 = 12
g. 60 ÷ 10 = 6
h. 69 ÷ 3 = 23

Exercise No. 57. Read each question aloud in French. Answer it aloud in a complete French sentence.

Exemple: 1. Il y a sept jours dans une semaine.

1. **Combien de jours y a-t-il dans une semaine?**
2. **Combien de mois y a-t-il dans une année?**
3. **Combien d'heures y a-t-il dans une journée?**
4. **Combien de minutes y a-t-il dans une heure?**
5. **Combien de secondes y a-t-il dans une minute?**
6. **Combien de jours y a-t-il dans le mois de septembre?**
7. **Combien d'étudiants y a-t-il dans la classe? (36 étudiants)**
8. **Quel âge avez-vous? (17 ans)**
9. **Quel âge a Louis? (19 ans)**
10. **Combien d'automobiles y a-t-il dans le garage? (15 automobiles)**

Exercise No. 58—Questionnaire

1. **Qu'est-ce que M. Potter sait déjà?**
2. **Quelle catégorie de mots est aussi importante que les noms et les verbes?**
3. **De quoi avons-nous besoin pour le commerce?**
4. **À quoi est-ce que l'homme d'affaires pense tout de suite?**
5. **Avons-nous besoin des nombres pour téléphoner?**
6. **Qui veut comprendre et employer les nombres correctement?**
7. **Comment est-ce que M. Potter avance dans ses études?**
8. **Dites à haute voix (*aloud*) en français les nombres 10, 20, 30, 40, 50, 60.**

CHAPITRE 12 (DOUZE)

LE SYSTÈME MONÉTAIRE DE LA FRANCE
FRENCH MONEY

1. — Dans notre dernière conversation nous avons dit qu'il est difficile d'imaginer notre civilisation moderne sans les nombres, c'est à dire, sans les mathématiques. Il est difficile également d'imaginer faire un voyage sans les mathématiques.

1. In our last conversation we said that it is difficult to imagine our modern civilization without numbers, that is to say, without mathematics. It is equally difficult to imagine making a trip without mathematics.

2. — Savez-vous combien de fois on fait usage des mathématiques en voyage?

2. Do you know how many times one makes use of mathematics on a trip?

3. — Je crois que oui. On en[1] fait usage pour changer de l'argent, pour acheter des billets, pour payer ses repas et sa note d'hôtel, pour faire peser ses bagages, pour estimer les distances, pour faire des achats dans les grands magasins, dans les boutiques et aux marchés.

3. I think so. One makes use of it[1] in order to change money, to buy tickets, to pay for one's meals and hotel bill, to weigh luggage, to estimate distances, to make purchases in department stores, in shops, and at the markets.

4. — Connaissez-vous le système monétaire de la France?

4. Are you familiar with the monetary system of France?

5. — Par exemple! Je le connais à fond. Je suis importateur d'articles français, n'est-ce pas? Le franc est l'unité monétaire de la France. Le dollar américain vaut à peu près 5 (cinq) francs.[2]

5. What an idea! I know it thoroughly. I am an importer of French things, am I not? The franc is the monetary unit in France. The American dollar is worth about 5 francs.

6. — Si vous voulez changer 10 (dix) dollars en francs, combien de francs allez-vous recevoir?

6. If you want to change 10 dollars into francs, how many francs are you going to receive?

7. — Je vais recevoir à peu près 50 (cinquante) francs.

7. I will receive about 50 francs.

8. — Si vous voulez changer 100 (cent) dollars en francs, combien de francs allez-vous recevoir?

8. If you want to change 100 dollars into francs, how many francs will you receive?

9. — Je vais recevoir à peu près 500 (cinq cents) francs.

9. I am going to receive about 500 francs.

10. — C'est ça. Encore: vous allez à la gare. Vous voulez acheter deux billets de chemin de fer. Chaque billet coûte 40 (quarante) francs et vous donner 100 (cent) francs à l'employé du guichet. Combien de francs est-ce qu'il vous rend en monnale?

10. That's right. Another example. You go to the railroad station. You want to buy two railroad tickets. Each ticket costs 40 francs and you give the ticket agent 100 francs. How much does he give you back in change?

11. — Il me rend 20 (vingt) francs. Deux fois 40 font 80; et 100 francs moins 80 francs égalent 20 francs.

11. He gives me back twenty francs. Twice 40 is 80; and 100 francs minus 80 francs equals 20 francs.

12. — C'est ça. Dans notre prochaine conversation, continuons ce sujet important. Usage rend maître.

12. Right. In our next conversation let us continue this important subject. Practice makes perfect. (*Lit.* Practice makes the master.)

NOTE 1. **en** before a verb means *of it* or *of them.* You will learn more about this form later.

NOTE 2. The relative value of the U.S. dollar and the French franc often changes. The following examples are for purpose of language study, not economics.

Pronunciation and Spelling Aids

Practice aloud

1. **l'unité monétaire** (lü-nee-tay mu-nay-**tehr**)
2. **civilisation** (see-vee-lee-zah-**syawñ**)
3. **mathématiques** (ma-tay-ma-**teek**)
4. **boutiques** (boo-**teek**)
5. **les billets** (leh bee-**yeh**)
6. **un million** (añ meel-**yawñ**)
7. **chemin de fer** (shuh-mañ duh **fehr**)
8. **le guichet** (luh gee-**shay**)

Building Vocabulary

A. **Le système monétaire de la France** (luh see-stehm mu-nay-**tehr**)

The monetary unit of France is the franc. The ratio of the franc to the dollar has undergone many changes through the years.

The word **l'argent,** *money* (it also means *silver*), is used for any kind of money. **Les billets** are *bills* (or *tickets*) and **la monnaie** means *coins.* **En monnaie** means *in change;* **le porte-monnaie** is the *changepurse.*

B. Antonyms and related words

1. **vendre** to sell **acheter** to buy
   je vends I sell **j'achète** I buy
2. **le vendeur, la vendeuse** (*f*) salesperson
   l'acheteur, l'acheteuse (*f*) buyer

3. **donner** to give **recevoir** to receive
4. **emprunter** to borrow **rendre** to give back
   prêter to loan **rembourser** to pay back
5. **vrai** true **faux** false
6. **Vous avez raison.** You are right.
   Vous avez tort. You are wrong.

French Expressions

1. **c'est à dire** (seh ta **deer**) that is to say
2. **combien de fois** (kawñ-byañ duh **fwa**) how many times
3. **changer de l'argent** (shahñ-zhay duh lar-**zhahñ**) to change money
4. **par exemple!** (par eg-**zahñpl**) the idea!
5. **payer ses repas** (pay-jay seh ruh-**pa**) to pay for one's meals
6. **faire peser les bagages** (fehr puh-zay lay ba-**gazh**) to have the baggage weighed
7. **faire des achats** (deh za-**sha**) to go shopping
8. **c'est ça** (seh **sa**) that's right
9. **Usage rend maître** (ü-zazh rahñ **mehtr**). Practice makes perfect.
10. **à peu près** (a peu-**preh**) about, nearly

Exercise No. 59—Completion of Text

1. (How many times) **fait-on usage des mathématiques** (on a trip)?
2. (One) **en fait usage** (in order to buy tickets).
3. **Nous faisons des achats** (in the big department stores).
4. (Are you familiar with) **le système monétaire de la France?**
5. (I know it) **à fond.**
6. **Le dollar** (is worth) **à peu près 5 francs.**
7. **Je vais recevoir** (about) **3500 francs.**
8. (You want to purchase) **deux billets de chemin de fer.**
9. (You give) **80 francs à l'employé du guichet.**
10. (He gives me back) **20 francs en monnaie.**

Grammar Notes

1. Present tense of **faire,** *to make, to do*

I make, do, you make, do, etc.

je fais (feh)
tu fais (feh)
il, elle fait (feh)
nous faisons (fuh-zawñ)
vous faites (feht)
ils, elles font (fawñ)

Imperative
fais faisons faites

croire, *to believe, to think*

I believe, think, you believe, etc.

je crois (krwah)
tu crois (krwah)
il, elle croit (krwah)
nous croyons (krwah-yawñ)
vous croyez (krwah-yay)
ils, elles croient (krwah)

Imperative
crois croyons croyez

Exercise No. 60. Translate into English. Then practice aloud in French.

1. **Que faites vous?**
   J'écris une lettre.
2. **Qu'est-ce que Jean fait?**
   Il joue du piano.
3. **Qu'est-ce que Marie fait?**
   Elle étudie la leçon de français.
4. **Qu'est-ce que les jeunes filles font?**
   Elles font des achats.
5. **Que fait-tu, mon enfant?**
   Je joue à la balle.
6. **Qu'est-ce que M. Martin fait?**
   Il fait peser les bagages.
7. **Croyez-vous cette histoire** (story)?
   Je ne la crois pas.
8. **Est-ce que votre ami la croit?**
   Il ne la croit pas non plus.

2. **Les nombres de 70 (soixante-dix)**[1] **à 1000 (mille)**

70 **soixante-dix**[1]
71 **soixante et onze**
72 **soixante-douze**
73 **soixante-treize**
74 **soixante-quatorze**
75 **soixante-quinze**
76 **soixante-seize**
77 **soixante-dix-sept**
78 **soixante-dix-huit**
79 **soixante-dix-neuf**
80 **quatre-vingts** (katr-vañ)
81 **quatre-vingt-un**
89 **quatre-vingt-neuf**
90 **quatre-vingt-dix**[1]
91 **quatre-vingt-onze**
92 **quatre-vingt-douze**
93 **quatre-vingt-treize**
94 **quatre-vingt-quatorze**
95 **quatre-vingt-quinze**
96 **quatre-vingt-seize**
97 **quatre-vingt-dix-sept**
98 **quatre-vingt-dix-huit**
99 **quatre-vingt-dix-neuf**
100 **cent** (sahñ)
101 **cent un** (sahñ euñ)
102 **cent deux** (sahñ deu)
200 **deux cents** (deu sahñ)
345 **trois cent quarante-cinq**
1000 **mille** (meel)
2000 **deux mille**

NOTE 1. In some French-speaking countries, Belgium for example, the numbers 70 and 90 are called **septante** and **nonante.** There 71 is **septante et un,** 72 is **septante-deux,** etc.; 91 is **nonante et un,** 92 is **nonante-deux;** 70th and 90th are **septantième** and **nonantième,** respectively.

a. Numbers between 1000 (**mille**) and one million (**un million**) are formed as in English. Thus:

987,896 **neuf cent quatre-vingt-sept mille huit cent quatre-vingt-seize**

b. **et** is used in 21, 31, 41, 51, 61, 71; never in 81, 91, 101.

c. **quatre-vingts** and **cents** (**deux cents**) drop the **s** if another number follows them. Thus:
(83) **quatre-vingt-trois** (945) **neuf cent quarante-cinq**

d. **mille** never takes an **s.**
deux mille 2000

Exercise No. 61. Write out the numbers in French:

Exemple: 18,942 **dix-huit mille neuf cent quarante-deux**

a. 400	c. 753	e. 95	g. 86	i. 670
b. 1000	d. 1,974	f. 77	h. 71	j. 14,586

Exercise No. 62. Practice the following table aloud:

$1.00	**Un dollar américain vaut**	**5 (cinq) francs**
$2.00	**Deux dollars américains valent**	**10 (dix) francs**
$3.00	**Trois dollars américains valent**	**15 (quinze) francs**
$4.00	**Quatre dollars américains valent**	**20 (vingt) francs**
$5.00	**Cinq dollars américains valent**	**25 (vingt-cinq) francs**
$6.00	**Six dollars américains valent**	**30 (trente) francs**
$7.00	**Sept dollars américains valent**	**35 (trente-cinq) francs**
$8.00	**Huit dollars américains valent**	**40 (quarante) francs**
$9.00	**Neuf dollars américains valent**	**45 (quarante-cinq) francs**
$10.00	**Dix dollars américains valent**	**50 (cinquante) francs**
$100.00	**Cent dollars américains valent**	**500 (cinq cents) francs**

Exercise No. 63—Questionnaire

1. **Si une chose coûte 400 (quatre cents) francs et vous donnez un billet de 1000 (mille) francs, combien recevez-vous en monnaie?**
2. **Si un billet de train coûte 750 (sept cent cinquante) francs, combien payez-vous pour deux billets?**
3. **Si une revue coûte 5 (cinq) francs, combien payez-vous pour quatre revues?**
4. **Si un journal coûte 12 (douze) francs et vous donnez au vendeur un billet de cent francs, combien recevez-vous en monnaie?**
5. **Si vous avez un billet de cinquante francs, deux billets de cent francs, et trois billets de mille francs, combien d'argent avez-vous en poche** (*in your pocket*)?
6. **Si un homme a un million de dollars, est-il millionaire?**
7. **Qu'est-ce qui a plus de valeur** (*more value*), **un billet de mille francs, ou un billet de cinq dollars?**
8. **Savez-vous combien d'argent il y a dans la banque de France?**

CHAPITRE 13 (TREIZE)

LES PROBLÈMES D'ARITHMÉTIQUE AU RESTAURANT, À LA GARE, DANS UNE BOUTIQUE

ARITHMETIC PROBLEMS IN THE RESTAURANT, AT THE STATION, IN A SHOP

1. — Continuons notre étude de l'usage des mathématiques en voyage.

1. Let us continue our study of the uses of mathematics on a trip.

2. — Nous dînons au restaurant. Nous sommes quatre. Les repas coûtent: 50 (cinquante) francs, 75 (soixante-quinze) francs, 80 (quatre-vingts) francs et 65 (soixante-cinq) francs. Nous laissons dix pour cent comme pourboire. Combien est l'addition pour tout le monde? Et combien le pourboire?

2. We are dining in the restaurant. We are four. The meals cost: 50 francs, 75 francs, 80 francs, and 65 francs. We leave 10% for a tip. What is the total bill for everybody? And how much is the tip?

3. — L'addition pour tout le monde monte à 270 (deux cent soixante-dix) francs, le pourboire à 27 (vingt-sept) francs.

3. The bill for everybody amounts to 270 francs, the tip to 27 francs.

4. — Très bien. Continuons. Je suis à la gare et je porte une valise très lourde. Je la fais peser. Elle pèse 30 (trente) kilos. Comment est-ce que je peux calculer le poids de la valise en livres?

4. Very good. Let us continue. I am at the railroad station and I am carrying a very heavy suitcase. I have it weighed. It weighs 30 kilos. How can I calculate the weight of the suitcase in pounds?

5. — Ce n'est pas difficile. Un kilo equivaut à 2,2 (deux virgule deux) livres. On multiplie 30 (trente) par 2,2. La valise pèse 66 (soixante-six) livres.

5. It is not difficult. One kilo is equal to 2.2 pounds. You multiply 30 by 2.2. The suitcase weighs 66 pounds.

6. — Correct. En France et dans les autres pays de l'Europe continentale on ne compte pas les distances en milles mais en kilomètres. Savez-vous changer les kilomètres en milles?

6. Correct. In France and in the other countries of continental Europe one does not figure distance in miles but in kilometers. Do you know how to change kilometers into miles?

7. — Certainement. Je divise par huit et je multiplie par cinq. Ainsi, quatre-vingts kilomètres équivalent à cinquante milles. C'est facile, n'est-ce pas?

7. Certainly. I divide by eight and I multiply by five. Thus 80 kilometers are equal to 50 miles. It's easy, isn't it?

8. — Vous calculez vite et bien. Encore un problème, le dernier: vous entrez dans une boutique. Vous achetez une paire de chaussures pour vous-même à 1200 (douze cents) francs; deux paires de chaussures pour votre femme à 1500 (quinze cents) francs chacune; et une ceinture en cuir pour chacun de vos quatre enfants à 500 (cinq cents) francs chacune. Quel est le montant de tous vos achats?

8. You figure fast and well. One more problem, the last one: you go into a shop. You buy a pair of shoes for yourself at 1200 francs; two pairs of shoes for your wife at 1500 francs each; and a leather belt for each of your four children at 500 francs each. What is the total price of all your purchases?

9. — 6200 (six mille deux cents) francs. Si je donne à la vendeuse sept billets de mille francs je vais recevoir 800 (huit cents) francs en monnaie.

9. 6200 francs. If I give the salesgirl seven 1000 franc notes, I am going to receive 800 francs in change.

10. — Parfait. Assez de mathématiques pour aujourd'hui. Jeudi nous allons parler des heures de la journée. C'est un sujet très important.

10. Perfect. Enough mathematics for today. On Thursday we are going to talk about the time of day. It is a very important subject.

11. —Bien sûr. Je compte sur une conversation intéressante.

11. Certainly. I am expecting an interesting conversation.

12. — À propos, M. Potter, je ne peux pas arriver avant huit heures et demie jeudi prochain.

12. By the way, Mr. Potter, I cannot arrive before 8:30 next Thursday.

13. — C'est bien. Mieux vaut tard que jamais.

13. That's all right. Better late than never.

14. — Bien dit! Au revoir, M. Potter.

14. Well said. Goodbye, Mr. Potter.

15. — Au revoir. A jeudi, M. Picard.

15. Goodbye. Until Thursday, Mr. Picard.

Pronunciation and Spelling Aids

A. Practice aloud

1. **les problèmes d'arithmétique** (pru-blehm da-reet-may-**teek**)
2. **les autres pays** (lay zoh-truh pay-**yee**)
3. **l'addition** (la-dee-**syawñ**)
4. **le restaurant** (rehs-toh-**rahñ**)
5. **la ceinture** (sañ-**tür**)
6. **parfait** (par-**feh**)
7. **la virgule** (veer-**gül**)
8. **je multiplie** (mül-tee-**plee**)

B. In French a comma is used instead of a period to set off decimals. Thus: 2,2 **(deux virgule deux)** instead of 2.2.

Building Vocabulary

Weights and measures

In France and in Europe generally, the decimal system of weights and measures is used. Instead of the yard and inch, the meter (39.4 inches) and centimeter (2.54 cms equal 1 inch) are used; instead of pounds, the kilogram or kilo (2.2 pounds) is used.

NOTE: **la livre** = pound, **le livre** = book

French Expressions

1. **comme pourboire** (poor-bwar) as a tip
2. **tout le monde** (too luh **mawñd**) everybody
3. **en monnaie** (ahñ mu-**neh**) in change
4. **Mieux vaut tard que jamais.** (myeu voh tar kuh zha-**meh**) Better late than never.

Grammar Notes

1. Present tense of **savoir,** *to know (how)*

I know (how), you know (how) etc.

je sais (seh) **nous savons** (sa-vawñ)
tu sais (seh) **vous savez** (sa-vay)
il sait (seh) **ils savent** (sav)
elle sait (seh) **elles savent** (sav)

connaître, *to know, to be acquainted, familiar with*

I know (am acquainted with, etc.)

je connais (ku-**neh**) **nous connaissons** (ku-nehs-**sawñ**)
tu connais (ku-**neh**) **vous connaissez** (ku-nehs-say)
il connaît (ku-**neh**) **ils connaissent** (ku-nehs)
elle connaît (ku-**neh**) **elles connaissent** (ku-nehs)

a. **savoir,** *to know* or *to know how* (with or without **comment**) means to know facts, rules, etc. In general this verb implies mental action, memory.

b. **connaître** means *to know* in the sense of to be acquainted with, to be familiar with persons or things. In general this verb implies knowing through the senses—hearing, seeing, etc.

Vous savez les noms des choses. You know the names of things.
Il sait lire le français. He knows how to read French.
Je sais où cet homme travaille. I know where that man works.
Je connais cet homme. I know (am acquainted with) that man.
Nous connaissons cette rue. We know (are familiar with) this street.

Exercise No. 64. Complete these sentences with the correct form of **savoir** or **connaître** as appropriate.

1. (Do you know) **les noms de ces choses?**
2. (We know) **cet homme.**
3. (We do not know) **où il demeure.**
4. (He knows how) **écrire le français.**
5. (I know) **qui est ici.**
6. (They do not know) **cette région de la France.**
7. (I know) **les enfants de M. Picard.**
8. (Do you know how) **changer kilomètres en milles?**
9. (Do they know) **les musées de Paris?**
10. **Que veulent-elles** (to know)?

2. Possessive adjectives. You are already familiar with most of the possessive adjectives. Here is a summary of the forms and meanings of all of them.

	Mas. Singular	Fem. Singular	Mas. Plural	Fem. Plural
my	**mon frère**	**ma soeur**	**mes frères**	**mes soeurs**
your	**ton oncle**	**ta tante**	**tes oncles**	**tes tantes**
his, her	**son fils**	**sa fille**	**ses fils**	**ses filles**
our	**notre salon**	**notre rue**	**nos salons**	**nos rues**
your	**votre crayon**	**votre plume**	**vos crayons**	**vos plumes**
their	**leur bureau**	**leur maison**	**leurs bureaux**	**leurs maisons**

a. Possessive adjectives agree in number and gender with the nouns they precede.

b. **ton, ta, tes** (*your*) like **tu** (*you*) are used only in addressing children, relatives or close friends.

c. **son, sa, ses** mean either *his* or *her,* according to the sense of the sentence.

d. **mon, ton, son** are used instead of **ma, ta, sa,** before feminine nouns beginning with a vowel or **h** (usually). Thus:

mon amie (*f*) **ton école** (*f*) **son histoire** (*f*)

Exercise No. 65. Complete these sentences with the correct form of **mon, (ma, mes), ton, (ta, tes), etc.:**

1. (Our) **conversations sont très intéressantes.**
2. **Je vais payer** (my) **note d'hôtel.**
3. **Continuons** (our) **étude des numéros.**
4. (Their) **valises sont très lourdes.**
5. **M. Potter est un de** (his) **amis.**
6. **Où sont** (your) **bagages, monsieur?**
7. **Achetez-vous une paire de gants pour** (your) **femme?**
8. (His) **professeur est M. Picard.**
9. (His) **femme joue du piano.**
10. (Their) **enfants vont à l'école.**
11. **Nous sommes six dans** (our) **famille.**
12. **Qui est** (her) **professeur?**
13. **Aimes-tu** (your) **maître,** (my) **enfant?**
14. **Où est** (his) **bureau?**
15. **Je ne connais pas** (their) **professeur.**

Exercise No. 66. Write out in French the numbers in the following table. Then read the table aloud.

Exemples: Dix kilos èquivalent (ay-kee-val) **à 22 (vingt-deux) livres.**
Seize kilomètres équivalent à dix milles.

10 kilos = 22 livres	**40 kilos = 88 livres**	**16 kilomètres = 10 milles**	**64 kilomètres = 40 milles**
20 kilos = 44 livres	**50 kilos = 110 livres**	**32 kilomètres = 20 milles**	**80 kilomètres = 50 milles**
30 kilos = 66 livres	**100 kilos = 220 livres**	**48 kilomètres = 30 milles**	**160 kilomètres = 100 milles**

Exercise No. 67—Questionnaire

1. **Où est-ce que vous dînez?**
2. **Combien est l'addition pour tout le monde?**
3. **Qu'est-ce que vous laissez comme pourboire dans un bon restaurant?**
4. **Où portez-vous une valise très lourde?**
5. **Combien de kilos pèse-t-elle? Combien de livres pèse-t-elle?**
6. **Comment est-ce qu'on compte les distances en France, en milles ou en kilomètres?**
7. **Qui sait changer les kilomètres en milles?**
8. **Combien de paires de chaussures est-ce que M. Potter achète dans une boutique?**
9. **Quel est le sujet de la prochaine conversation?**
10. **De quel proverbe M. Potter fait-il usage?**

CHAPITRE 14 (QUATORZE)

QUELLE HEURE EST-IL?—I
WHAT TIME IS IT?—I

1. — L'heure! Tout le monde veut savoir, — Quelle heure est-il? À quelle heure est-ce que l'avion arrive? À quelle heure est-ce que le train part? À quelle heure est-ce que les examens commencent? À quelle heure est-ce que le film commence? À quelle heure est-ce que la séance commence? et des milliers d'autres questions.

1. The time! Everyone wants to know: "What time is it? At what time does the plane arrive? At what time does the train leave? At what time do the examinations begin? At what time does the film begin? At what time does the performance begin?" And thousands of other questions.

2. M. Potter, je vais jouer le rôle de l'employé du guichet à la gare. Vous allez jouer le rôle d'un voyageur qui désire acheter un billet et qui demande des renseignements. Commençons.

2. Mr. Potter, I am going to play the role of the ticket agent at the railroad station. You are going to play the role of a traveler who wants to buy a ticket and is asking for information. Let us begin.

3. —Bonjour, monsieur. Un billet pour Chartres, s'il vous plaît.

3. Good day, sir. One ticket to Chartres, please.

4. — Oui, monsieur. Première ou deuxième classe?
5. — Première classe, s'il vous plaît. Quel est le prix de la place?
6. — Soixante-dix-sept francs pour un billet d'aller.
7. Donnez-moi un billet d'aller et retour, s'il vous plaît. Je désire partir lundi.
8. — Voici votre billet. Ça fait cent cinquante-quatre francs.
9. — Merci, monsieur. A quelle heure est-ce que le train part et à quelle heure arrive-t-il à Chartres?
10. — Il y a plusieurs trains par jour pour Chartres. Vous avez un bon train à quatre heures moins le quart, qui arrive à cinq heures moins cinq.
11. — Merci beaucoup, monsieur.
12. —À votre service, monsieur.
13. — Excellent, M. Potter. Vous jouez votre rôle à merveille.

4. Yes sir. First or second class?
5. First class, please. How much is the fare?
6. For a one-way ticket, 77 francs.
7. Please give me a round trip ticket. I wish to leave on Monday.
8. Here is your ticket. That is 154 francs.
9. Thank you sir. At what time does the train leave, and when does it arrive at Chartres?
10. There are several trains a day for Chartres. You have a good train at 3:45 (a quarter to four), which arrives at 4:55 (five minutes to 5).
11. Thank you very much, sir.
12. At your service, sir.
13. Excellent Mr. Potter. You play your part wonderfully.

Quelle Heure Est-Il?—II

1. — Maintenant, je joue le rôle de l'employé au cinéma. Vous demandez des renseignements sur les séances. Voulez-vous commencer, s'il vous plaît?
2. — Dites-moi, s'il vous plaît, à quelles heures est-ce que les séances commencent?
3. — Il y a trois séances. La première commence à quatre heures vingt de l'après midi, la deuxième à six heures cinquante, et la troisième à neuf heures dix du soir.
4. — Y a-t-il des actualités?
5. — Mais oui. Vingt minutes avant le film.
6. — Quel est le prix des billets?
7. — Les billets coûtent vingt francs. Si vous arrivez de bonne heure vous allez avoir de bonnes places.
8. — Donnez-moi deux billets pour la troisième séance, s'il vous plaît.
9. — Les voici. Merci bien.
10. — Admirable. Je répète: vous jouez votre rôle à merveille.

1. Now I am playing the role of the ticket seller at the movies. You are asking for information about the performances. Will you begin, please?
2. Please tell me at what time do the shows begin?
3. There are three showings. The first one begins at 4:20 in the afternoon, the second at 6:50 and the third at 9:10 in the evening.
4. Is there a newsreel?
5. Of course. Twenty minutes before the picture.
6. What is the price of the tickets?
7. The tickets cost 20 francs. If you come early you will get good seats.
8. Please give me two tickets for the third showing.
9. Here they are. Thank you very much.
10. Admirable. I repeat: you play your part wonderfully.

Pronunciation and Spelling Aids

A. Practice aloud

1. **L'heure! Tout le monde veut savoir, — Quelle heure est-il?**
2. **Vous demandez des renseignements sur les séances.**
3. **des milliers d'autres questions.**

1. (**Leur!** Too luh mawñd veu sa-**vwar**, kehl leur eht-**teel?**)
2. (Voo duhmahñ-day day rahñ-sehn-yuh-mahñ sür lay say-**ahñs**)
3. (day mee-lyay dohtr kehs-**tyawñ**)

B. Remember: **ll** is usually pronounced like y:

fille (feey) **billet** (bee-yay) **merveille** (mehr-**vehy**) **Marseille** (mar-**sehy**)

Exceptions: 1. **ll** is pronounced like ly in **million** (mee-**lyawñ**), **milliers** (mee-**lyay**)
2. **ll** is pronounced like l in **mille** (meel), **ville** (veel), **tranquille** (trahñ-**keel**)

Building Vocabulary

A. Expressions of approval and praise

1. **admirable** (ad-mee-**rabl**) splendid
2. **excellent** (ehk-seh-**lahñ**) excellent
3. **très bien** (treh **byañ**) very good
4. **c'est ça** (seh **sa**) right, that's right
5. **correct** (ku-**rehkt**) correct
6. **parfait** (par-**feh**) perfect
7. **c'est bien** (seh **byañ**) that's good
8. **c'est exact** (seh tayg-**zakt**) that's so
9. **c'est vrai** (seh **vray**) that's true
10. **à merveille** (a mehr-**vehy**) wonderfully

B. Railroad travel terms

1. **la gare** the railroad station
2. **À quelle heure est-ce que le train part pour ....?** At what time does the train leave for ....?
3. **À quelle heure est-ce que le train arrive à (de) ....?** At what time does the train arrive at (from) ....?
4. **Le train arrive (part) à sept heures du matin.** The train arrives (leaves) at 7 a.m.
5. **un billet de première (deuxième) classe** a first (second) class ticket
6. **un billet d'aller** (*or* **billet simple**) a one-way ticket
7. **un billet d'aller et retour** a round trip ticket
8. **Quel est le prix de la place?** *or* **Combien coûte la place?** What is the fare?
9. **plusieurs trains par jour** several trains a day
10. **payer les billets** to pay for the tickets
11. **En voiture!** All aboard!
12. **la salle de bagages** baggage room
13. **un wagon-lit** sleeping car
14. **un wagon-restaurant** dining car

French Expressions

1. **demander des renseignements** to ask for information
2. **jouer le rôle** to play the role
3. **mais oui** (meh **wee**) yes indeed, of course
4. **mais non** indeed no, of course not
5. **de bonne heure** (duh bu-**neur**) early
6. **les voici** (lay vwa-**see**) here they are
7. **les voilà** there they are

Exercise No. 68—Completion of Text

1. (At what time) **est-ce que le film commence?**
2. (The first showing) **commence à** (4:30 p.m.).
3. **Il y a des milliers** (of other questions).
4. **Où est** (the railroad station)?
5. **Vous êtes un voyageur qui** (asks for information).
6. **Donnez-moi** (a round trip ticket).
7. **À quelle heure** (does the train leave)?
8. (Does it arrive) **à neuf heures du matin?**
9. **Venez** (early) **si vous désirez de bonnes places.**
10. (Here they are).
11. (Many thanks, sir).
12. (At your service), **monsieur.**

Grammar Notes

1. Present tense of **partir,** *to leave*

I leave, you leave, etc.

je pars (par)	**nous partons** (par-tawñ)
tu pars (par)	**vous partez** (par-tay)
il part (par)	**ils partent** (part)
elle part (par)	**elles partent** (part)

Imperative

pars **partons** **partez**

sortir, *to go out*

I go out, you go out, etc.

je sors (sur)	**nous sortons** (sur-tawñ)
tu sors (sur)	**vous sortez** (sur-tay)
il sort (sur)	**ils sortent** (surt)
elle sort (sur)	**elles sortent** (surt)

Imperative

sors **sortons** **sortez**

Other verbs like **partir** and **sortir** are:

servir to serve **je sers, tu sers, il sert, nous servons, vous servez, ils servent**
sentir to feel, smell **je sens, tu sens, il sent, nous sentons, vous sentez, ils sentent**
dormir to sleep, **je dors, tu dors, il dort, nous dormons, vous dormez, ils dorment**

Exercise No. 69. Complete these sentences by writing the correct forms of **partir, sortir, dormir, sentir, servir.** Then read the completed sentences aloud:

1. **Le train** (leaves) **à sept heures.**
2. **À quelle heure** (do you leave)?
3. (We sleep) **jusqu'à** (*until*) **huit heures.**
4. **Elle** (does not sleep) **bien.**
5. **Madame Potter** (serves) **le café.**
6. (Do you smell) **le parfum?**
7. (I do not smell) **le parfum.**
8. **À quelle heure** (do they go out) **de la maison?**
9. (I go out) **du bureau à cinq heures.**
10. (Do not sleep) **jusqu'à neuf heures.**

2. Time of day

Quelle heure est-il? What time is it?
Il est midi. It is noon.
Il est une heure. It is 1 o'clock.
Il est deux heures. It is 2 o'clock.
Il est trois heures. It is 3 o'clock.
Il est minuit. It is midnight.
Il est une heure et demie. It is half-past one.
Il est deux heures et quart.
It is a quarter past two.
Il est trois heures moins le (un) quart.
It is a quarter to three.
Il est quatre heures dix (minutes).
It is ten minutes past four.
Il est quatre heures moins dix.
It is ten minutes to four.

NOTE: **et,** *and,* is used for time after the hour; **moins,** *less* or *minus,* is used for time before the hour; the word **minutes** may be omitted; **heures** is never omitted.

Time expressions after the half hour are based on the hour which follows. Thus: **6:40 Il est sept heures moins vingt.** It is twenty minutes to seven. However, as in English, you may say: **six heures quarante** (*six forty*).

France uses the 24-hour clock. In timetables and schedules, and sometimes in conversation, time is indicated by 24 hours beginning with midnight. The hours 24.00 (midnight) through 11.59 are a.m. The hours 12.00 (noon) through 23.59 are p.m. Thus:

24.20 **(vingt-quatre heures vingt)** = 12.20 a.m. **(douze heures vingt du matin)**
12.20 **(douze heures vingt)** = 12.20 p.m. **(douze heures vingt de l'après-midi)**
15.20 **(quinze heures vingt)** = 3.20 p.m. **(trois heures vingt de l'après-midi)**

Usually in conversation the following expressions are used to distinguish a.m. from p.m.:

du matin in the morning **de l'après-midi** in the afternoon **du soir** in the evening

Exercise No. 70. Write out the time expressions. Then read the sentences aloud giving the time in French.

Exemple: 1. Le train de Lyons arrive à sept heures et demie du soir

1. **Le train de Lyon arrive à** (7.30 p.m.)
2. **Le train arrive à Paris à** (10.15 p.m.)
3. **Le train pour Marseille part à** (6.30 a.m.)
4. **Le train pour Rouen part à** (noon)
5. **La première séance commence à** (4.30 p.m.)
6. **La deuxieme séance commence à** (6.40 p.m.)
7. **La troisième séance commence à** (9 p.m.)
8. **Les actualités commencent à** (4.10 p.m.)
9. **M. Potter prend le train en ville à** (7.45 a.m.) **précises.**
10. **Il arrive en ville à** (8.40 a.m.)

Exercise No. 71—Questionnaire

1. **Qu'est-ce que tout le monde veut savoir?**
2. **Qui joue le rôle du voyageur?**
3. **Qui joue le rôle de l'employé du guichet?**
4. **Quelle classe de billet est-ce que M. Potter désire?**
5. **Combien coûte un billet d'aller et retour?**
6. **Qui joue le rôle de l'employé au cinéma?**
7. **Qui demande des renseignements?**
8. **Combien de séances y a-t-il à ce ciné (cinéma)?**
9. **Pour quelle séance est-ce que M. Potter achète deux billets?**
10. **Combien paye-t-il pour ces billets?**

RÉVISION 3
CHAPITRES 10–14 PREMIÈRE PARTIE

Révision de Mots

NOUNS

1. l'acheteur	**15. la fourchette**	**29. le pot au lait**	1. buyer	15. fork	29. milk pitcher
2. l'addition	**16. le gant**	**30. le porte-monnaie**	2. bill (restaurant)	16. glove	30. purse
3. l'argent	**17. la gare**	**31. le prix**	3. money, silver	17. station	31. price, prize
4. les bagages	**18. le gâteau**	**32. la radio**	4. baggage	18. cake	32. radio
5. le billet	**19. le guichet**	**33. le repas**	5. ticket	19. ticket window	33. meal
6. la boutique	**20. l'heure**	**34. la séance**	6. shop	20. hour	34. performance
7. la chaussure	**21. la livre**	**35. la soucoupe**	7. shoe	21. pound	35. saucer
8. le chemin de fer	**22. le magasin**	**36. le style**	8. railroad	22. store	36. style
9. le couteau	**23. le maître**	**37. le sujet**	9. knife	23. teacher, master	37. subject
10. le cuiller	**24. le marché**	**38. la tarte**	10. spoon	24. market	38. tart
11. l'échantillon	**25. la note**	**39. la tasse**	11. sample	25. bill (hotel), etc.	39. cup
12. l'employé	**26. le pays**	**40. le verre**	12. employee	26. country (nation)	40. glass
13. la fleur	**27. le plat**	**41. le vendeur**	13. flower	27. dish	41. seller
14. une fois	**28. la poche**	**42. le voyageur**	14. one time, once	28. pocket	42. traveller

VERBS

1. acheter	**14. trouver**	**27. sentir**	1. to buy	14. to find	27. to feel
2. avancer	**15. connaître**	**28. sortir (de)**	2. to progress	15. to know	28. to go out (of)
3. changer	**16. n. connaissons**	**29. venir**	3. to change	16. we know	29. to come
4. continuer	**17. croire**	**30. pouvoir**	4. to continue	17. to believe	30. to be able
5. dîner	**18. perdre**	**31. je peux**	5. to dine	18. to lose	31. I can
6. donner	**19. rendre**	**32. recevoir**	6. to give	19. to give back	32. to receive
7. laisser	**20. faire**	**33. je reçois**	7. to let	20. to make, do	33. I receive
8. manger	**21. je fais**	**34. savoir**	8. to eat	21. I make, do	34. to know (how)
9. payer	**22. dire**	**35. je sais**	9. to pay for	22. to say	35. I know (how)
10. penser(à)	**23. nous disons**	**36. valoir**	10. to think (of)	23. we say	36. to be worth
11. peser	**24. dormir**	**37. il vaut**	11. to weigh	24. to sleep	37. it is worth
12. porter	**25. partir**	**38. vouloir**	12. to carry, wear	25. to leave	38. to want
13. téléphoner	**26. je pars**	**39. je veux**	13. to telephone	26. I leave	39. I want

ADJECTIVES

1. célèbre	**6. délicieuse (*f*)**	**11. plusieurs**	1. famous	6. delicious (*f*)	11. several
2. chaque	**7. gai**	**12. précis**	2. each	7. gay, bright	12. exact
3. charmant	**8. lourd**	**13. premier**	3. charming	8. heavy	13. first
4. connu	**9. ordinaire**	**14. première (*f*)**	4. known	9. ordinary	14. first (*f*)
5. délicieux	**10. parfait**	**15. vrai**	5. delicious	10. perfect	15. true

ADVERBS

1. à peu près	**5. encore**	**9. naturellement**	1. more or less	5. again	9. naturally
2. comme	**6. encore un**	**10. presque**	2. as, like, how	6. one more	10. almost, nearly
3. correctement	**7. maintenant**	**11. surtout**	3. correctly	7. now	11. especially
4. d'ordinaire	**8. moins**	**12. tout de suite**	4. generally	8. less	12. at once

PREPOSITIONS

1. avant	**3. devant**	**5. pour**	1. before	3. in front of	5. for, in order to
2. après	**4. derrière**	**6. vers**	2. after	4. behind	6. towards, about

FRENCH EXPRESSIONS

1. j'ai besoin de	**8. Combien de fois?**	1. I need	8. How many times?
2. j'ai raison	**9. je crois que oui**	2. I am right	9. I think so
3. vous avez tort	**10. je crois que non**	3. you are wrong	10. I think not
4. c'est ça	**11. en tout cas**	4. that's correct	11. in any case
5. c'est vrai	**12. en effet**	5. that's true	12. in fact
6. c'est à dire	**13. en monnaie**	6. that is to say	13. in change
7. changer de l'argent	**14. il le faut**	7. to change money	14. it is necessary

15. **faire des achats**
16. **faire peser**
17. **mais oui (non)**
18. **payer ses repas**
19. **Par exemple!**
20. **comme pourboire**
21. **merci bien**
22. **rien de plus facile**
23. **tout le monde**
24. **Que veut dire . . . ?**
25. **il veut dire . . .**
26. **les voici**
27. **il n'y a pas de quoi** *ou*
28. **de rien**

15. to go shopping
16. to have weighed
17. indeed yes (no)
18. to pay for one's meals
19. The idea!
20. as a tip
21. many thanks
22. nothing easier
23. everybody
24. What does . . . mean?
25. it means . . .
26. here they are
27. you're welcome, *or*
28. don't mention it

Deuxième Partie

Exercise No. 72. Select the group of words in Column II which best completes each sentence begun in Column I:

Exemple: 1-f Cette région en France est connue pour ses produits céramiques.

I	II
1. Cette région en France est connue	**a. tout de suite au commerce?**
2. De quelle région sont	**b. que jamais.**
3. Est-ce que le commerçant pense	**c. dans les grands magasins.**
4. Vous savez que l'usage	**d. le système monétaire de la France.**
5. Mieux vaut tard	**e. d'aller et retour.**
6. Le voyageur a besoin d'argent	**f. pour ses produits céramiques.**
7. Nous faisons des achats	**g. à quatre heures de l'après-midi.**
8. Ils ne connaissent pas	**h. ces tasses et ces soucoupes?**
9. Donnez-moi un billet	**i. pour acheter des billets.**
10. La première séance commence	**j. rend maître.**

Exercise No. 73. Complete these sentences by choosing the correct expression from those listed below. Be sure to use the correct form of the verb.

Exemple: 1. Le touriste demande des renseignements.

1. **Le touriste** (asks for information).
2. (We need) **un porte-monnaie.**
3. **M. Potter** (knows his trade).
4. **Ils veulent** (to change some money).
5. **À quoi** (are you thinking)?
6. (Do you like) **bien ce portrait?**
7. **Je mange quand** (I am hungry).
8. **Que** (do you mean)?
9. (We pay for our meals) **en francs.**
10. (You are right) **M. Potter.**
11. **J'ai raison, mais** (you are wrong).
12. **De quoi** (do you need)?

demander des renseignements	**payer nos repas**	**aimer bien**
avoir raison (tort)	**connaître son métier**	**vouloir dire**
avoir faim	**penser à**	**aimer bien**
avoir besoin de	**changer de l'argent**	

Exercise No. 74. From Group II select antonyms for each word in Group I:

I		II	
1. arriver	**7. vendre**	**a. moins**	**g. perdre**
2. donner	**8. apprendre**	**b. acheter**	**h. recevoir**
3. plus	**9. avant**	**c. partir**	**i. peu de**
4. devant	**10. le vendeur**	**d. derrière**	**j. j'ai tort**
5. trouver	**11. beaucoup de**	**e. enseigner**	**k. écouter**
6. parler	**12. j'ai raison**	**f. l'acheteur**	**l. après**

Exercise No. 75. Answer these questions in the affirmative in complete sentences. Use the pronoun **je** in the answers.

Exemple: 1. Oui, monsieur, je pense à mon ami.

1. **Pensez-vous à votre ami?**
2. **Voulez-vous faire un voyage en France?**
3. **Pouvez-vous acheter une automobile?**
4. **Portez-vous les bagages à la gare?**
5. **Partez-vous demain de la ville?**
6. **Comptez-vous toujours la monnaie?**
7. **Dites-vous les mots deux fois?**
8. **Connaissez-vous cet homme-là?**
9. **Donnez-vous un pourboire au garçon?**
10. **Savez-vous compter en français?**

Exercise No. 76. Answer these questions in the negative in complete sentences. Use **nous** in the answers.

Exemple: 1. Non, madame, nous ne posons pas beaucoup de questions.

1. **Posez-vous beaucoup de questions?**
2. **Calculez-vous rapidement en français?**
3. **Trouvez-vous cette revue intéressante?**
4. **Lisez-vous les journaux français?**
5. **Écrivez-vous bien en français?**
6. **Dînez-vous au restaurant?**
7. **Connaissez-vous la ville de Biot?**
8. **Achetez-vous beaucoup de parfum?**
9. **Avez-vous besoin d'une valise?**
10. **Savez-vous l'adresse de M. Picard?**

Dialogue

Un touriste prend des renseignements sur la poterie française

1. — Dites-moi, s'il vous plaît, monsieur, dans quelles régions de la France peut-on trouver de jolie poterie? Je désire acheter un service à thé: tasses, soucoupes, et assiettes.

2. — Eh bien, chaque région a son style individuel: Limoges, la Bretagne et la Provence sont toutes connues pour leurs produits céramiques.

3. — Est-ce qu'il faut aller dans ces régions pour trouver de la poterie régionale?

4. — Pas du tout. Vous pouvez acheter de la poterie de toutes les régions ici même à Paris.

5. — Est-que ça coûte plus cher ici?

6. — Naturellement, ça coûte plus cher. Mais vous avez un assortiment bien choisi.

7. — Voulez-vous bien me dire où est-ce qu'on peut acheter de la poterie à Paris?

8. — Vous allez trouver le meilleur assortiment dans les grands magasins—aux Galeries Lafayette, au Printemps, et surtout au Bazar de l'Hôtel de Ville—et dans les boutiques dans la rue du Paradis.

9. — Merci infiniment, monsieur.

10. — De rien, mademoiselle.

1. Please tell me, sir, in what districts of France can one find beautiful pottery? I want to buy a tea service: cups, saucers and plates.

2. Well, each district has its own individual style: Limoges, Brittany and Provence are all well known for their ceramic products.

3. Does one have to go to these regions to find regional pottery?

4. Not at all. You can buy pottery from all regions right here in Paris.

5. Does it cost more here?

6. Of course it costs more. But you have a well chosen assortment.

7. Will you tell me, please, where one can buy pottery in Paris?

8. You will find the best assortment in the department stores—Galeries Lafayette, Printemps and especially at BHV—and in the shops on the rue du Paradis.

9. Thank you ever so much, sir.

10. Don't mention it, miss.

Exercise No. 77—Lecture 1

La famille Potter fait une petite visite à papa

C'est la première fois que la famille Potter vient voir Monsieur Potter à son bureau. Madame Potter et ses quatre enfants entrent dans un gratte-ciel et ils montent par ascenseur au vingtième étage. Anne, la plus jeune, qui n'a que cinq ans,[1] est très curieuse. Elle pose beaucoup de questions à sa maman au sujet du bureau.

Quand ils arrivent au bureau, le père se lève[2] et dit, — Quelle bonne surprise! Que je suis content de vous voir!

Les enfants admirent tous les objets qu'ils voient dans le bureau: la machine à écrire, l'ordinateur[3], les articles de Paris, les échantillons de la céramique française, les revues françaises et surtout les affiches illustrées aux murs. Tout le monde est très content.

Charles, l'aîné, regarde par la grande fenêtre, et il voit le ciel bleu et le soleil qui brille. Il voit en bas les automobiles qui passent dans la rue. Du vingtième étage elles paraissent[4] toutes petites.

La visite terminée, toute la famille entre dans un restaurant qui n'est pas loin du bureau. Ils mangent tous de bon appétit, surtout les garçons, parce qu'ils ont bien faim.

NOTE 1. **qui . . . ans** who is *only* five years old; **ne** *verb* **que** is one way of saying *only*.

NOTE 2. **se lever,** *to get up:* **je me lève, tu te lève, il, elle se lève, nous nous levons, vous vous levez, ils se lèvent.** 3. computer. 4. **paraître,** *to seem:* **il, elle paraît, ils, elles paraissent.**

Exercise No. 78—Lecture 2
Le percheron[1] et l'automobile
Une fable moderne

Anne, la plus jeune des enfants de M. Potter, aime beaucoup les fables anciennes d'Ésope. Elle aime bien aussi cette fable moderne que M. Picard a écrite[2] pour elle. Voici la fable, "Le percheron et l'automobile."

Une automobile passe sur la route et elle voit un percheron. Le percheron est un cheval français, grand et fort. Cependant ce percheron paraît très fatigué. Il est attelé[3] à une charrette bien lourde.[4]

L'automobile s'arrête et dit au percheron, — Bonjour. Vous allez bien lentement. Ne désirez-vous pas aller rapidement comme moi?

— Oh oui, madame! Mais dites-moi comment est-ce possible?

— Ce n'est pas difficile, dit l'automobile. Mon réservoir à essence[5] est plein. Buvez-en[6] et vous allez voir ça.

Alors le percheron boit de l'essence. Maintenant, il ne va plus lentement. Il ne va pas rapidement non plus. En effet il ne va pas du tout. Il a mal à l'estomac.[7]

Ce pauvre cheval! Il n'est pas très intelligent, n'est-ce pas? Il ne sait pas que l'essence est bonne pour les automobiles, mais qu'elle ne vaut rien pour les chevaux.[8]

NOTE 1. **le percheron,** *draft horse;* **le cheval,** *horse;* **les chevaux,** *the horses* 2. has written 3. harnessed 4. a very heavy cart 5. gasoline tank 6. drink some. **boire,** *to drink:* **je bois, tu bois, il, elle boit; nous buvons, vous buvez, ils, elles boivent.** 7. **Il a mal à l'estomac (mal à la tête, mal aux dents);** he has a stomach ache (headache, toothache) 8. **qu'elle ne vaut rien,** that it is not worth anything.

CHAPITRE 15 (QUINZE)

LE CINÉMA
THE MOVIES

1. — M. Potter, vous savez déjà demander des renseignements sur les séances des cinémas. Mais dites-moi, êtes-vous amateur du ciné?

1. Mr. Potter, you already know how to ask for information about the show-times of the movies. But tell me, are you a movie fan?

2. — J'aime voir un bon film quelquefois, mais pour la plupart, les films ne m'intéressent pas.

2. Well, I like to see a good picture sometimes, but for the most part films do not interest me.

3. — Alors vous préférez le théâtre?

3. Then you prefer the theater?

4. — Mais oui. Ma femme et moi nous le préférons. Nous y[1] allons souvent voir une bonne pièce ou une opérette.

4. Oh yes. My wife and I prefer it. We go there[1] often to see a good play or a musical comedy.

5. — Et vos enfants? Est-ce qu'ils préfèrent le théâtre?

5. And your children? Do they prefer the theater?

6. — Pas du tout! Ils adorent les films policiers et les opérettes qui nous[2] ennuient à mourir.

6. Not at all! They love detective stories and musicals which bore us[2] to death.

7. — Ils connaissent toutes les vedettes de l'écran, n'est-ce pas?

7. They know all the stars of the screen, don't they?

8. — Naturellement. Ils les[2] connaissent bien. Ils connaissent aussi les vedettes de la télévision.

8. Of course. They know them[2] well. They also know the stars of television.

9. — Vous habitez une petite ville dans les environs de New-York. Y a-t-il un ciné près de chez vous?

9. You live in a small town on the outskirts of New York. Is there a movie theater near your house?

10. — Oui monsieur, pas loin. Nous y allons à pied dans un quart d'heure à peu près.

10. Yes sir, not far away. We walk there (*Lit.* go on foot) in fifteen minutes more or less.

11. — Quelles places préférez-vous, les places des premiers rangs, ou les places du fond?

11. Which seats do you prefer, the seats in the first rows or the seats in the back?

12. — Nous préférons les places du quatorzième ou du quinzième rang. De là, on peut bien voir et entendre. De là, la lumière et les mouvements sur l'ècran ne font pas mal aux yeux.

12. We prefer the seats in the fourteenth or fifteenth row. From there, one can see and hear well. From there, the light and the movements on the screen do not hurt the eyes.

13. — Que faites-vous si la plupart des places sont ocupées?

13. What do you do if most of the seats are occupied?

14. — Alors, nous prenons n'importe quelles places libres, devant, au fond, aux côtés. Mais nous n'aimons pas ces places. Donc nous arrivons de bonne heure.

14. Then we take any vacant seats whatsoever, in front, in back, or at the side. But we do not like those seats. Therefore we come early.

15. — Merveilleux, M. Potter! Vous avancez très rapidement.

15. Splendid, Mr. Potter! You are progressing very fast.

16. — Grâce à vous, M. Picard.

16. Thanks to you, Mr. Picard.

NOTE 1. **y** = *there*. It usually precedes the verb.
NOTE 2. **nous,** *us,* and **les,** *them,* are object pronouns. They also usually precede the verb.

Pronunciation and Spelling Aids

A. Practice aloud

1. **Vous savez demander des renseignements sur les séances des cinémas.**
2. **Êtes-vous amateur du ciné?**
3. **Ils adorent les films policiers et les opérettes en couleurs.**

1. (Voo sa-vay duh-mahñ-day day rahñ-seh-nyuh-**mahñ** sür lay say-ahñs day see-nay-**ma**)
2. (Eht-voo za-ma-teur dü see-**nay**?)
3. (Eel za-dur lay feelm pu-lee-**syay** ay lay zu-pay-reht ahñ koo-**leur**)

B. Remember **â** = ah, **ô** = oh, **ê** = eh. Thus:
rôle (rohl) **grâce** (grahs) **êtes-vous** (eht-voo)

Building Vocabulary

Words dealing with the movies

1. **le cinéma** (see-nay-ma) movies, movie theater
2. **le ciné** (short for **cinéma**)
3. **le film** (feelm) film
4. **la séance** (say-ahñs) showing, show-time
5. **l'écran** (lay-**krahñ**) screen
6. **le vedette** (vuh-**deht**) star actor
7. **la pièce** (pyehs) play
8. **les actualités** (lay zak-tü-a-lee-**tay**) newsreel
9. **le rôle** (rohl) role
10. **le rang** (rahñ) row
11. **la place** (plas) seat

French Expressions

1. **pour la plupart** for the most part
2. **Ils nous ennuient à mourir.** They bore us to death.
3. **près de chez vous** near your home
4. **à pied** (a **pyay**) on foot
5. **faire mal aux yeux** (oh-**zyeu**) to hurt the eyes
6. **la plupart des places** most of the seats
7. **N'importe** (nañ-**purt**). It doesn't matter.
8. **Grâce à vous.** Thanks to you.
9. **Je vous remercie.** I thank you.

Exercise No. 79—Completion of Text

1. (I like very much to see) **un bon film.**
2. **Les films** (do not interest me).
3. (They adore) **les films policiers.**
4. **Connaissent-ils** (all the screen stars)?
5. (They know them) **bien.**
6. **Y a-t-il un ciné** (near your home)?
7. **Nous y allons** (on foot).
8. (We prefer) **les places des premiers rangs.**
9. (Therefore) **nous arrivons** (early).

Grammar Notes

1. Present tense of **venir,** *to come*

I come, I am coming, you come, you are coming, etc.

je viens (vyañ)	**nous venons** (vuh-nawñ)
tu viens (vyañ)	**vous venez** (vuh-nay)
il, elle vient (vyañ)	**ils, elles viennent** (vyehn)

Imperative: **viens,** come **venons,** let's come **venez,** come

Like **venir: revenir,** *to come back,* **devenir,** *to become*

Exercise No. 80. Translate each verb into French. Read each sentence aloud.

1. (I am coming) **aujourd'hui.**
2. (They do not come) **de bonne heure.**
3. **Qui** (is coming) **avec vous?**
4. **Les petits garçons** (come) **avec leurs pères.**
5. (Come) **ici, mes enfants.**
6. (Are you coming) **à sept heures?**
7. (We are coming back) **de bonne heure ce soir.**
8. **Quand** (is he coming back)?
9. (She is not coming) **ici ce matin.**
10. **M. Martin, à quelle heure** (are you coming)?
11. **Que voulez-vous** (to become)?
12. (I want to become) **professeur.**

2. Direct object pronouns

Study the following sentences. They illustrate the direct object pronouns. You are already familiar with most of them.

1. M. Picard *me* connaît.	1. Mr. Picard knows *me.*
2. Il *te* connaît aussi, Anne.	2. He knows *you* also, Anne.
3. Qui *vous* apprend à parler français?	3. Who is teaching *you* to speak French?
4. M. Picard *nous* apprend à parler français.	4. Mr. Picard is teaching *us* to speak French.
5. Qui salue M. Picard?	5. Who greets Mr. Picard?
M. Potter *le* salue.	Mr. Potter greets *him.*
6. Connaissez-vous Mlle. Picard?	6. Do you know Miss Picard?
Je ne *la* connais pas.	I do not know *her.*
7. Avez-vous le journal français?	7. Have you the French newspaper?
Nous ne *l'*avons pas.	We do not have *it.*
8. Connaissent-ils les vedettes de l'écran?	8. Do they know the screen stars?
Oui, ils *les* connaissent bien.	Yes, they know *them* well.

a. The direct object pronouns are:

me (m') me	**nous** us	**le (l')** him, it	**les** them
te (t') you (*fam.*)	**vous** you	**la (l')** her, it	

b. **me** and **te** become **m'** and **t'**, and **le** and **la** become **l'**, when they precede a verb beginning with a vowel or **h** (usually).

c. Object pronouns precede the verb *except* in the affirmative imperative when they follow the verb and are joined to it by a hyphen. In the negative imperative the object pronouns precede the verb:

Prenez la fleur. Prenez-*la*. Take the flower. Take *it*.
Ne prenez pas la fleur. Ne *la* prenez pas. Do not take the flower. Do not take *it*.

d. **me** when used after the verb in the imperative becomes **moi.**
Dites-moi. Écoutez-moi. Tell *me*. Listen to *me*.

3. The use of **y,** *there*

The word **y,** *there,* is used to indicate a place already mentioned. Like the object pronouns it always precedes the verb, except in the affirmative imperative.

Quand est-ce que M. Potter va en France?	When is Mr. Potter going to France?
Il *y* va au printemps.	He is going *there* in the spring.
Allons-*y* avec lui.	Let's go *there* with him.

Exercise No. 81. Read each question. Write each answer filling in the correct object pronoun in French. Finally read the questions and complete answers aloud.

1. **Achetez-vous les billets?**
2. **Connaissez-vous cette rue?**
3. **Est-ce que Jean attend son ami, Louis?**
4. **Les enfants adorent-ils les vedettes de l'écran?**
5. **Préfèrent-ils le premier rang?**
6. **Comment trouvez-vous cette tasse?**
7. **Allez-vous visiter M. Potter?**
8. **Est-ce que le professeur m'attend?**
9. **Qui vous attend au ciné?**
10. **Qui vous apprend à parler français?**
11. **Vont-ils au ciné à pied ou en autobus?**
12. **Demeure-t-il dans cette maison-là?**
13. **Quand allez-vous nous aider?**
14. **Est-ce que les films vous intéressent?**
15. **Est-ce que tu m'aimes, maman?**

1. **Oui, je** (them) **achète.**
2. **Non, nous ne** (it) **connaissons pas.**
3. **Oui, il** (him) **attend dans le salon.**
4. **Certainement! Ils** (them) **adorent.**
5. **Non, ils ne** (it) **préfèrent pas.**
6. **Je** (it) **trouve charmante.**
7. **Nous allons** (him) **visiter ce soir.**
8. **Bien sûr, il** (you) **attend.**
9. **Notre ami** (us) **attend.**
10. **M. Picard** (us) **apprend à parler français.**
11. **Ils** (there) **vont en autobus.**
12. **Oui, il** (there) **demeure.**
13. **Nous allons** (you) **aider demain.**
14. **Non, ils ne** (me) **intéressent pas.**
15. **Je** (you) **aime beaucoup, mon enfant.**

Exercise No. 82—Questionnaire

1. **Qui sait demander des renseignements?**
2. **Qu'est-ce que M. et Mme. Potter préfèrent, le théâtre ou le cinéma?**
3. **Qu'est-ce que les enfants préfèrent?**
4. **Est-ce que les enfants connaissent les vedettes de l'écran?**
5. **Le ciné est-il près de la maison de M. Potter ou loin de sa maison?**
6. **Quelles places préfèrent-ils au ciné?**
7. **Est-il possible de bien voir et entendre de là?**
8. **Est-ce qu'ils arrivent de bonne heure ou en retard** (late)?

CHAPITRE 16 (SEIZE)

QUELQUES DATES DE L'HISTOIRE DE FRANCE
SOME DATES IN FRENCH HISTORY

1. —M. Potter, vous connaissez bien les nombres. Je vois que vous savez les employer correctement et rapidement. Voyons si vous connaissez les nombres en forme de dates.

2. — Avec plaisir, M. Picard. J'aime bien les questionnaires en français.

3. — C'est pourquoi vous apprenez vite. Je vais citer quelques dates de l'histoire de France et vous allez citer un événement important pour chacune.

4. — Bon. Commençons.

5. — Le quatorze juillet, 1789. (mil[1] sept cent quatre-vingt-neuf)

6. — Comme vous êtes gentil! C'est facile: la prise de la Bastille pendant la Révolution française.

7. — Très bien. 1815. (mil huit cent quinze)

8. — C'est sans doute Napoléon. Voyons. C'est la bataille de Waterloo, n'est-ce pas?

9. — Correct. 1870. (mil huit cent soixante-dix)

10. — Ah, c'est une date triste pour la France: la défaite de l'armée dans la guerre franco-allemande.

11. — Voici une date victorieuse: 1918. (mil neuf cent dix-huit.)

1. Mr. Potter, you know the numbers well. I see that you know how to use them correctly and rapidly. Let us see if you know the numbers in the form of dates.

2. With pleasure, Mr. Picard. I like quizzes in French.

3. That's why you learn quickly. I am going to mention some dates in the history of France and you will mention an important event for each one.

4. Good. Let's begin.

5. July 14, 1789.

6. How nice you are! That's easy: the capture of the Bastille during the French Revolution.

7. Very good. 1815.

8. That's Napoleon, no doubt. Let's see. It's the battle of Waterloo, isn't it?

9. Correct. 1870.

10. Ah, that's a sad date for France: the defeat of the army in the Franço-Prussian war.

11. Here is a victory date: 1918.

12. **— La victoire des Alliés à la fin de la première guerre mondiale.**
13. **— Finissons le questionnaire. Encore une date, la dernière: 1944. (mil neuf cent quarante-quatre.)**
14. **— C'est une date glorieuse pour les Parisiens: la libération de Paris à la fin de l'occupation Nazi.**
15. **— Merveilleux, M. Potter. Je vois que vous connaissez l'histoire de France aussi bien que son système monétaire.**
16. **— Mais, M. Picard, je n'ai pas passé**[2] **seize ans en classe pour rien. D'ailleurs, j'ai un professeur qui m'apprend à aimer la France.**
17. **— C'est vous maintenant qui êtes trop aimable.**
18. **— Pas du tout. C'est la vérité.**

12. The victory of the Allies at the end of World War I.
13. Let us finish the quiz. One more date, the last: 1944.
14. That is a glorious date for Parisians: the liberation of Paris at the end of the Nazi occupation.
15. Marvellous, Mr. Potter. I see that you know the history of France as well as its monetary system.
16. Well, Mr. Picard, I didn't spend sixteen years in school for nothing. Besides I have a teacher who teaches me to love France.
17. Now it is you who flatter me.
18. Not at all. It's the truth.

NOTE 1. **Mille,** *thousand,* is shortened to **mil** in dates. 2. **je n'ai pas passé** means I have not spent or did not spend. This is the conversational past tense. You will learn more about this tense later.

Pronunciation and Spelling Aids

Practice aloud

1. **Voyons si vous connaissez les nombres en forme de dates.**
2. **Avec plaisir, Monsieur Picard.**
3. **J'aime bien les questionnaires en français.**

1. (Vwa-yawñ see voo ku-neh-say lay nawñ-br ahñ furm duh **dat**)
2. (A-vehk pleh-**zeer**, muh-syeu pee-**kar**)
3. (Zhehm byañ lay kehs-tyu-nehr ahñ frahñ-**seh**)

Vocabulary Building

A. **Les mois de l'année** (lay mwah duh la-**nay**) The months of the year

janvier (zhañ-**vyay**) January
février (fay-vree-**ay**) February
mars (mars) March
avril (a-**vreel**) April
mai (meh) May
juin (zhwañ) June
juillet (zhüee-**yeh**) July
août (oo) August
septembre (sehp-**tahñbr**) September
octobre (uk-**tubr**) October
novembre (nu-**vahñbr**) November
décembre (day-**sahñbr**) December

B. **l'an, l'année, le jour, la journée**

l'année and **la journée** are used instead of **l'an** and **le jour** when one has in mind the events that take place during the year or during the day. Thus:

J'étudie toute la journée (toute l'année). I study all day (all year) long.
But: **Je vais rester trois jours (ans) à Paris.** I am going to stay in Paris for three days (years).

Exercise No. 83—Completion of Text

1. (You know how) **employer correctement les nombres.**
2. **Vous allez citer** (an important event).
3. Let's begin.
4. (How) **vous êtes gentil!**
5. **L'an 1870 est** (a sad date) **pour la France.**
6. **Voici** (a victorious date).
7. (Let us finish) **le questionnaire.**
8. **Vous connaissez l'histoire de France** (as well as) **son système monétaire.**
9. (Besides), **j'ai un bon professeur.**
10. (He teaches me) **à aimer la France.**
11. (It is you) **qui êtes trop aimable.**
12. (Not at all.) **C'est la vérité.**

French Expressions

1. **Comme vous-êtes gentil!** How nice you are!
2. **sans doute** (sahñ **doot**) without doubt
3. **en classe** (ahñ **klahs**) in school, in class
4. **Il m'apprend à aimer la France.** He teaches me to love France. **Apprendre** may mean either *to learn* or *to teach.*

Grammar Notes

1. Present tense of **finir,** *to finish.* Regular **-ir** verb.

I finish, am finishing, do finish, you finish, etc.

je finis (fee-nee)	**nous finissons** (fee-nee-sawñ)
tu finis (fee-nee)	**vous finissez** (fee-nee-say)
il, elle finit (fee-nee)	**ils, elles finissent** (fe-nees)

Imperative: **finis** finish **finissons** let us finish **finissez** finish
Interrogative: **finit-il?** does he finish?
Negative: **il ne finit pas** he does not finish.
Negative Interrogative: **ne finit-il pas?** is he not finishing?

2. Some common regular **-ir** verbs like **finir** are:

bâtir	to build	**je bâtis**	**tu bâtis**	**il bâtit**	**nous bâtissons,** etc.
choisir	to choose	**je choisis**	**tu choisis**	**il choisit**	**nous choisissons,** etc.
obéir	to obey	**j'obéis**	**tu obéis**	**il obéit**	**nous obéissons,** etc.
punir	to punish	**je punis**	**tu punis**	**il punit**	**nous punissons,** etc.
remplir	to fill	**je remplis**	**tu remplis**	**il remplit**	**nous remplissons,** etc.
saisir	to seize	**je saisis**	**tu saisis**	**il saisit**	**nous saisissons,** etc.

Exercise No. 84. Write the correct form of the verbs indicated. Read each completed sentence aloud in French.

1. **À quelle heure** (do you finish) **le dîner?**
2. (We finish) **notre dîner à sept heures.**
3. **Quelle place** (do you choose)?
4. (I choose) **une place dans le premier rang.**
5. **Pourquoi est-ce que le maître** (punishes) **Jacques?**
6. **Parce qu'** (he does not obey).
7. **Les enfants** (are building) **une petite maison.**
8. (Fill) **ma tasse de café, s'il vous plaît.**
9. (They are not finishing) **leurs exercises.**
10. **Elle** (is filling) **son stylo d'encre** (ink) **bleue.**
11. (Let us choose) **nos places maintenant.**

3. Ordinal numbers

1st **premier** (*m*) (pruh-myay)	6th **sixième** (see-zyehm)
1st **première** (*f*) (pruh-myehr)	7th **septième** (seh-tyehm)
2nd **deuxième** (deu-zyehm)	8th **huitième** (üee-tyehm)
3d **troisième** (trwa-zyehm)	9th **neuvième** (neu-vyehm)
4th **quatrième** (ka-tryehm)	10th **dixième** (dee-zyehm)
5th **cinquième** (sañ-kyehm)	last **dernier** (*m*) **dernière** (*f*)

Ordinal numbers are formed by adding **-ième** to the cardinals with the exception of **premier,** *first.* Final e is dropped before adding **-ième (quatrième); u** is added after **q (cinquième)** and **f** becomes **v (neuvième); second** (suh-gawñ) is used instead of **deuxième** for the *second* of only two.

Exercise No. 85. Complete in French. Read the completed expressions aloud.

1. **la** (first) **leçon**
2. **la** (third) **place**
3. **le** (fourteenth) **chapitre**
4. **la** (fifth) **semaine**
5. **le** (twelfth) **jour**
6. **le** (first) **mois**
7. **la** (last) **classe**
8. **la** (ninth) **rue**
9. **les** (last) **rangs**

4. Dates

a. **Quel jour du mois sommes-nous aujourd'hui?** *or* **Quel jour du mois est-ce aujourd'hui?**
What is today's date?
C'est aujourd'hui le vingt mai.
Today is May 20.

b. **le 1er (premier) janvier 1987 (mil neuf cent quatre-vingt-sept)** January 1, 1987
le 2 (deux) juin 1926 (dix-neuf cent vingt-six) June 2, 1926
le 14 (quartorze) juillet 1789 (mil sept cent quatre-vingt-neuf) July 14, 1789

premier is used for the first day of the month. For the other days the cardinal numbers **deux, trois,** etc., are used.

In dates **mil** is used instead of **mille** for thousand. As in English dates, **dix-neuf cent** (nineteen hundred), etc., may be used instead of **mil neuf cent** (one thousand nine hundred), etc.

Exercise No. 86. Write out the following dates in full. Read each date aloud in French.

Exemple: le 4 juillet 1776 — le quatre juillet, mil sept cent (*or* dix-sept cent) soixante-seize

1. **le 18 avril 1775**
2. **le 12 octobre 1492**
3. **le 22 février 1809**
4. **le 1er mai 1956**

Exercise No. 87—Questionnaire

1. **Pourquoi est-ce que M. Potter apprend vite?**
2. **Qu'est-ce que M. Picard va citer?**
3. **Qu'est-ce que M. Potter va citer?**
4. **Quel événement important M. Potter cite-t-il pour 1789?**
5. **Quel événement important cite-t-il pour 1815?**
6. **Est-ce que 1870 est une date triste ou une date glorieuse pour la France?**
7. **Quel événement est-ce que M. Potter cite pour 1918?**
8. **Est-ce que 1944 est une date glorieuse ou une date triste pour les Parisiens?**

CHAPITRE 17 (DIX-SEPT)

QUESTIONS SUR LA GÉOGRAPHIE DE FRANCE
QUESTIONS ABOUT FRENCH GEOGRAPHY

1. — M. Potter, aujourd'hui voyons si vous connaissez la géographie de France aussi bien que son histoire. Vous permettez que je vous pose quelques questions?

1. Mr. Potter, today let us see if you know French geography as well as its history. Will you permit me to ask you a few questions?

2. — Certainement. Est-ce que je vais recevoir un prix si mes réponses sont correctes?

2. Certainly. Shall I receive a prize if my answers are correct?

3. — Non, M. Potter. Ce n'est pas un programme de TV. Commençons avec la question la plus facile. Sur quel grand fleuve est-ce que la ville de Paris est située?

3. No, Mr. Potter. This is not a TV program. Let us begin with the easiest question. On what great river is the city of Paris situated?

4. — C'est vraiment trop facile. Sur la Seine.

4. That is really too easy. On the Seine.

5. — Et quel port très important est situé à l'embouchure de la Seine?

5. And what very important port is situated at the mouth of the Seine?

6. — C'est Le Havre, grand marché de café, coton, et sucre. La plus grande partie du commerce entre la France et l'Amérique du Nord passe par ce port.

6. It is Le Havre, an important market for coffee, cotton, and sugar. Most of the trade between France and North America passes through this port.

7. — Quel est le fleuve le plus long de France?

7. What is the longest river in France?

8. — Voyons. Est-ce le Rhône?

8. Let's see. Is it the Rhône?

9. — Non, pas tout à fait exact. La Loire est le fleuve le plus long de France. Il n'est pas beaucoup plus long que le Rhône, une centaine de kilomètres plus ou moins.

9. No, not quite right. The Loire is the longest river in France. It is not very much longer than the Rhône, one hundred kilometers, more or less.

10. — En tout cas, il est bien plus petit que notre Mississippi.

10. In any case, it is much smaller than our Mississippi.

11. — O décidément. Le Mississippi est plus long et plus large que la Loire. Savez-vous quelle est la plus haute montagne de France?

11. Oh definitely. The Mississippi is longer and wider than the Loire. Do you know which is the highest mountain in France?

12. — Ça oui, je sais bien, le Mont Blanc.

12. That I do know, Mont Blanc.

13. — Savez-vous s'il y a une montagne aussi haute que le Mont Blanc ici aux États-Unis?

13. Do you know if there is a mountain as high as Mont Blanc here in the United States?

14. — Je sais bien que le Mont Blanc n'est pas plus haut que le Mount McKinley, qui est la montagne la plus haute des États-Unis, mais je ne sais pas exactement sa hauteur.

14. I do know that Mont Blanc is not higher than Mount McKinley, which is the highest mountain in the United States, but I don't know its height exactly.

15. — Ni moi non plus, M. Potter; mais je sais bien que vous avez raison. Alors, voilà: l'examen est terminé. Je vous en[1] félicite.

15. Neither do I, Mr. Potter, but I know that you're right. Well, there you are, the examination is over. I congratulate you.

16. — Merci. J'attends mon diplôme la semaine prochaine.

16. Thank you. I will expect my diploma next week.

17. — O non, M. Potter. Pas encore. Ce n'est que[2] la partie élémentaire du cours.

17. Oh no, Mr. Potter. Not yet. This is only[2] the elementary portion of the course.

18. — Eh bien, nous pouvons entreprendre la deuxième partie plus tard.

18. Well, we can undertake the second part later.

NOTE 1. **en** is not translated here. It means *on it*. 2. **ne** *verb* **que** is one way of saying *only*. Another way of saying this sentence is: **C'est seulement** (only) **la première partie,** etc.

Pronunciation and Spelling Aids

A. Practice aloud

1. Voyons si vous connaissez la géographie de France aussi bien que son histoire.

1. Vwa-yawñ see voo ku-neh-say la zhay-u-gra-fee duh **frahñs** oh-see byañ kuh sawñ nees-**twar.**

2. Vous permettez que je vous pose quelques questions?

2. Voo pehr-meh-tay kuh zhuh voo pohz kehl-kuh kehs-**tyawñ?**

B. Elision

1. **le** and **la** become **l'** before words beginning with a vowel and usually before h. Thus:
   l'hôtel **l'homme** **l'histoire** **l'heure** **l'habitude**
   But **la hauteur** **la haute montagne** **le huitième jour** **le Havre** **le héros**

2. **si** (if) plus **il** becomes **s'il.**

Building Vocabulary

Related words

1. **grand** great **la grandeur** greatness
2. **haut** high **la hauteur** height
3. **long** long **la longueur** length
4. **large** wide **la largeur** width
5. **visiter** to visit **le visiteur** visitor
6. **porter** to carry **le porteur** porter
7. **compter** to count **le compteur** accountant
8. **vendre** to sell **le vendeur** seller

French Expressions

1. **pas tout à fait** (pah too ta **feh**) not quite
2. **en tout cas** (ahñ too **kah**) in any case
3. **ni moi non plus** (nee mwa nawñ **plü**) neither do I
4. **pas encore** (pah zahñ-**kur**) not yet
5. **alors** (a-**lur**) well, then, in that case, and so.
6. **voilà** (vwa-**la**) is used in the sense of *there is* or *there are* (pointing); also as an exclamation translated in various ways: *there! there now! that's that! behold!* etc.

Exercise No. 88—Completion of Text

1. (Let us see) **si vous connaissez** (French geography).
2. **Vous permettez** (that I ask you) **quelques questions?**

3. **Vous n'allez pas** (to receive a prize).
4. **Le Havre** (is situated) **à l'embouchure de la Seine.**
5. **C'est un grand marché de** (coffee, cotton and sugar).
6. **Quelle est** (the longest river) **de France.**
7. **Elle n'est pas** (much longer than) **le Rhône.**
8. **Elle est** (smaller than) **le Mississippi.**
9. **Le Mont Blanc est** (the highest mountain) **de France.**
10. **Le Mont Blanc n'est pas** (higher than) **le Mount McKinley.**
11. **Je sais** (that you are right).
12. **L'examen** (is finished).

Grammar Notes

1. Present tense of **mettre,** *to put*

I put, you put, etc.

je mets (meh)
tu mets (meh)
il, elle met (meh)
nous mettons (meh-tawñ)
vous mettez (meh-tay)
ils, elles mettent (meht)

Imperative: **mets** put **mettons** let us put **mettez** put

Like **mettre** are: **permettre,** *to permit* **admettre,** *to admit* **remettre,** *to put back*

Exercise No. 89. Translate into French:

1. I am putting
2. Who puts?
3. Why do you put?
4. What do you (**tu**) put?
5. We are putting
6. They do not put
7. I do not permit
8. Does he permit?
9. Why do you permit?
10. We permit
11. Does he not permit?
12. Permit me

2. Comparison of adjectives and adverbs

Observe the positive, comparative, and superlative forms of the adjectives **grand** and **diligent,** and of the adverb **vite:**

La Seine est un *grand* fleuve.	The Seine is a *large* river.
Le Rhin est *plus grand* que la Seine.	The Rhine is *larger* than the Seine.
Le Volga est *le plus grand* fleuve d'Europe.	The Volga is *the largest* river in Europe.
Louise est très *diligente*.	Louise is very *diligent*.
Marie est *moins diligente* qu'Louise.	Marie is *less diligent* than Louise.
Anne est l'élève *la moins diligente* de cette classe.	Anne is *the least diligent* pupil in this class.
Le vélo marche *vite*.	The bicycle travels *fast*.
Le scooter marche *plus vite* que le vélo.	The scooter travels *faster* than the bicycle.
La moto marche *le plus vite* de tous.	The motorcycle travels *fastest* of all.

Positive	Comparative	Superlative
grand tall, big, great	**plus grand** taller	**le plus grand** tallest
diligent diligent	**moins diligent** less diligent	**le moins diligent** least diligent
vite fast	**plus vite** faster	**le plus vite** fastest

a. The comparative of an adjective or adverb is formed by placing **plus** (*more*) or **moins** (*less*) before the positive. The superlative of an adjective is formed by placing the definite article (**le, la,** or **les**) before the comparative. Only **le** is used to form the superlative of an adverb.

See above: ***La* moto marche *le* plus vite.**

b. The superlative of the adjective may be preceded by the possessive instead of the definite article.

le meilleur ami, mon meilleur ami, the best friend, my best friend

c. As in English, the superlative of an adjective may stand alone as a noun: **le meilleur des amis,** the best of friends.

d. After a superlative use **de** not **dans** for *in*.

la montagne la plus haute d'Europe the highest mountain *in* Europe.

3. Expressions of comparison

a. When unequals are compared **que** is used for *than*, except with numbers; then **de** is used.

La Loire est *plus longue que* le Rhône.	The Loire is *longer than* the Rhone.
Ce tour coûte *plus (moins) de* cent dollars.	This tour costs *more (less) than* $100.

b. When equals are compared **aussi . . . que** (*as . . . as*) is used. After a negative **si . . . que** is used instead of **aussi . . . que.**

M. Potter connaît l'histoire de France *aussi bien que* sa géographie.	Mr. Potter knows the history of France *as well as* its geography.
Bernard n'est *pas si grand que* Robert.	Bernard is *not as tall as* Robert.

4. Some irregular comparisons

Adjectives	Adverbs
bon (bonne) good	**bien** well
meilleur better	**mieux** better
le meilleur the best	**le mieux** best
mauvais bad	**mal** badly
pire (or **plus mauvais**) worse	**pis (plus mal)** worse
le pire (or **le plus mauvais**) the worst	**le pis (le plus mal)** worst

Exercise No. 90. Translate the following sentences. Read them aloud three times.

1. **Les films français sont-ils *meilleurs* que les films américains?**
2. **Quelques-uns sont *meilleurs*, d'autres sont *pires* (*plus mauvais*). En France et aux États Unis on peut voir *les meilleurs* et aussi *les pires* (*plus mauvais*) films. En général j'aime *mieux* les films français.**
3. **Robert chante *mal*. Richard chante *pis* (*plus mal*) que Robert. Mais Bernard chante *le pis* (*le plus mal*) de tous.**
4. **Herbert écrit *bien*, mais vous écrivez *mieux* que lui. Renée écrit *le mieux* de tous.**
5. **Où fait-on *la meilleure* porcelaine? — On la fait à Limoges.**
6. ***Mieux* vaut tard que jamais.**

Exercise No. 91. Complete the French sentences so that they correspond fully to the English. Read each completed French sentence aloud.

Exemple: 1. Les verbes sont aussi importants que les noms.

1. The verbs are as important as the nouns.	**1. Les verbes sont _____ importants _____ les noms.**
2. Marguerite is nicer than Suzanne.	**2. Marie est _____ aimable _____ Suzanne.**
3. I have the best pen.	**3. J'ai _____ plume.**
4. The black ink is not as good as the blue.	**4. L'encre noire n'est pas _____ bonne _____ la bleue.**
5. Isabel is taller than Julie.	**5. Isabel est _____ que Julie.**
6. John is the most diligent boy in the class.	**6. Richard est l'élève _____ de la classe.**
7. Anne is the youngest child in the family.	**7. Anne est la _____ enfant de la famille.**
8. I find French more interesting than Spanish.	**8. Je trouve le français _____ l'espagnol.**
9. Which is the longest river in France?	**9. Quel est le fleuve _____ de France?**
10. London is the largest city in the world.	**10. Londres est _____ du monde.**
11. The Rhine is longer and wider than the Loire.	**11. Le Rhin est _____ long et _____ large _____ la Loire.**
12. Why do you answer so badly?	**12. Pourquoi répondez-vous si _____?**
13. We like the best films.	**13. Nous aimons les _____ films.**
14. I have the worst pen.	**14. J'ai la _____ plume.**
15. This watch costs more than fifty dollars.	**15. Cette montre coûte _____ cinquante dollars.**

Exercise No. 92—Questionnaire

1. **Avec quelle question facile est-ce que M. Picard commence?**
2. **Où est-ce que le port du Havre est situé?**

3. Le port du Havre est-il un grand marché?
4. Quel fleuve est plus long et plus large que la Loire?
5. Quelle montagne est plus haute, le Mont Blanc ou le Mount McKinley?
6. M. Dupont est un homme de quarante-cinq ans. Il a $100,000 (cent mille dollars).
M. Millet est un homme de cinquante ans. Il a $80,000 (quatre-vingt mille dollars).
M. Arnaud est un homme de soixante ans. Il a $50,000 (cinquante mille dollars).

a. Lequel[1] est le plus jeune des trois?
b. Lequel est le plus âgé des trois?
c. Est-ce que M. Millet est plus âgé que M. Dupont?
d. Lequel est le plus riche?
e. Lequel est le moins riche?
f. Est-ce que M. Millet est aussi riche que M. Dupont?

NOTE 1. **lequel, laquelle** (*f*)? *which one?* **lequels, lesquelles** (*f*)? *which ones?*

CHAPITRE 18 (DIX-HUIT)

LA JOURNÉE DE M. POTTER
MR. POTTER'S DAY

1. — M. Potter, vous permettez que je vous demande comment vous passez une journée typique?

1. Mr. Potter, may I ask you how you spend a typical day?

2. — Certainement. Quand je vais à mon bureau je me lève à six heures et demie. Vous voyez que je suis matinal. Je me lave et je m'habille dans une demi-heure, plus ou moins. Vers sept heures je me mets à table pour prendre mon petit déjeuner.

2. Certainly. When I go to my office I get up at six-thirty. You see that I am an early riser. I wash and dress in half an hour, more or less. At about seven, I sit down at the table to have my breakfast.

Ma femme, qui est matinale aussi, se lève de bonne heure et nous déjeunons ensemble. Naturellement cela me plaît beaucoup. Nous avons une belle occasion pour parler des enfants et d'autres choses qui nous intéressent.

My wife, who is also an early riser, gets up early and we have breakfast together. Naturally that pleases me very much. We have a fine opportunity to talk about the children and other things that interest us.

3. — Que prenez-vous au petit déjeuner?

3. What do you eat for breakfast?

4. — Je prends du[1] jus d'orange, du café, des petits pains et des oeufs. Parfois je mange des crêpes au lieu des oeufs.

4. I have (some)[1] orange juice, coffee, rolls, and eggs. Sometimes I eat pancakes instead of eggs.

5. — Je vois que vous aimez le déjeuner à la fourchette. Et ensuite?

5. I see that you like a substantial breakfast. And afterward?

6. — A sept heures et demie je suis prêt à partir pour prendre le train. Parfois les enfants se lèvent de bonne heure pour m'embrasser avant mon départ.

6. At seven-thirty I am ready to leave to take the train. Sometimes the children get up early to kiss me before my departure.

7. — À quelle heure arrivez-vous au bureau?

7. At what time do you arrive at the office?

8. — J'arrive à neuf heures à peu près. Au bureau je lis mon courrier, je dicte les réponses à la sténo, je parle au téléphone avec certains clients et je fais les choses qu'un homme d'affaires doit faire.

8. I arrive at about nine o'clock. In the office I read my mail, dictate answers to the stenographer, talk on the telephone to various clients, and do the things that a businessman has to do.

9. — Et quand est-ce que vous déjeunez?

9. And when do you have lunch?

10. — Presque toujours à une heure. Il me faut à peu près vingt minutes pour manger.

10. Almost always at one. I need about twenty minutes to eat.

11. — C'est très peu de temps. En France vous allez voir que les habitudes de manger sont tout autres. Le Français passe beaucoup plus de temps à table. Mais parlons de cela une autre fois. Qu'est-ce que vous mangez au déjeuner?

11. It is very little time. In France you will see that eating habits are very different. The Frenchman spends much more time at meals. But let us speak about that some other time. What do you have for lunch?

12. **— D'habitude je prends un sandwich, un café et un dessert quelconque—une pomme cuite ou une tarte.**

12. Usually I have a sandwich, coffee, and some dessert or other—a baked apple or a piece of pie.

13. **— Que faites-vous après le déjeuner?**

13. What do you do after lunch?

14. **— Il y a souvent des clients qui viennent me voir et de temps en temps je sors pour voir d'autres clients.**

14. Often some clients come to see me and from time to time I go out to see other clients.

15. **— A quelle heure finissez-vous votre journée?**

15. At what time do you finish your day's work?

16. **— A cinq heures précises je quitte le bureau. J'arrive chez moi à sept heures moins le quart à peu près. Je fais un bout de toilette, je joue un peu avec les enfants et puis nous nous mettons à table pour dîner.**

16. At five o'clock sharp I leave the office. I arrive home at about a quarter to seven. I wash up a bit, play a little with the children, and then we sit down at the table to have dinner.

17. **— Vous devez être fatigué après une journée pareille.**

17. You must be tired after such a day.

18. **— Je pense bien que oui, répond M. Potter.**

18. "I think so," answers Mr. Potter.

NOTE 1. The idea *some* is expressed in French by **de la, du, de l'** and **des.** This usage is fully treated in the next chapter.

Pronunciation and Spelling Aids

Practice aloud

1. **je me lève** (zhuh muh **lehv**)
2. **je me lave** (zhuh muh **lav**)
3. **je m'habille** (zhuh ma-**beey**)
4. **je me mets à table** (zhuh muh meh za **tabl**)
5. **Je prends du café** (zhuh prahñ dü ka-**fay**)
6. **des petits pains** (day puh-tee **pañ**)
7. **des oranges** (day zu-**rahñzh**)
8. **des oeufs** (day **zeu**)

Building Vocabulary

A. **Les repas** (lay ruh-**pah**) Meals

1. **le déjeuner** (day-zheu-**nay**) lunch
2. **déjeuner ou prendre le déjeuner** to have lunch
3. **le petit déjeuner** breakfast (usually coffee, tea, or hot chocolate with bread or croissants)
4. **le dîner** dinner; **dîner** to dine
5. **le souper** supper

B. **Quelques vivres** (veevr) Some foods

1. **le pain** bread; **du pain** some bread
2. **l'oeuf** (leuf) egg, **des oeufs** (day **zeu**) some eggs
3. **le petit pain** roll
4. **le café** coffee; **du café** some coffee
5. **la crêpe** pancake
6. **le beurre** butter; **du beurre** some butter
7. **le lait** milk; **du lait** some milk
8. **la pomme** apple
9. **le gâteau (les gâteaux)** the cake(s)
10. **la crème** cream; **de la crème** some cream
11. **la viande** meat; **de la viande** some meat
12. **le jus d'orange** orange juice
13. **la soupe** soup
14. **le légume** vegetable

French Expressions

1. **Cela me plaît.** That pleases me.
2. **Il me faut 20 minutes.** I need 20 minutes.
3. **de temps en temps** at times, from time to time
4. **Je fais un bout de toilette.** I wash up a bit.
5. **Je pense bien que oui.** I think so.
6. **se mettre à table** to sit down at table
7. **le déjeuner à la fourchette** substantial breakfast (*Lit.* breakfast with a fork)

Exercise No. 93—Completion of Text

1. **Comment passez-vous** (a typical day)?
2. **Je me lève** (at six-thirty).
3. **Je suis** (an early riser).
4. **Ma femme se lève** (early).
5. (What do you eat) **au petit déjeuner?**
6. **Je prends** (coffee, rolls, and eggs).

7. (At times) **les enfants se lèvent de bonne heure.**
8. **J'arrive** (at the office) **à neuf heures.**
9. **Je lis** (my mail) **et je dicte** (the answers).
10. (What do you do) **après le déjeuner?**
11. **Des clients viennent souvent** (to see me).
12. **À quelle heure** (do you finish) **votre journée?**
13. (I leave) **le bureau à cinq heures.**
14. (We sit down) **à table.**

Grammar Notes

1. Present tense of the reflexive verb **se laver,** *to wash oneself, to get washed*

je me lave (lav)	I wash myself	**nous nous lavons** (la-vawñ)	we wash ourselves
tu te laves (lav)	you wash yourself	**vous vous lavez** (la-vay)	you wash yourselves
il se lave (lav)	he washes himself	**ils se lavent** (lav)	they wash themselves
elle se lave (lav)	she washes herself	**elles se lavent** (lav)	they wash themselves

Interrogative: **Vous lavez-vous?** or **Est-ce que vous vous lavez?** Do you wash yourself? Are you getting washed?

Negative: **Je ne me lave pas.** I am not washing myself.

a. The reflexive pronouns are: **me,** *myself;* **te,** *yourself;* **nous,** *ourselves;* **vous,** *yourself, yourselves;* **se,** *himself, herself, itself, oneself* and *themselves.*

b. Like all object pronouns the reflexive pronouns always precede the verb except in the affirmative imperative when they follow it. Note that **te** becomes **toi** when it comes after the verb.

Imperative (Affirmative)		Imperative (Negative)	
lave-toi (*fam.*)	wash yourself	**ne te lave pas**	do not wash yourself
lavons-nous	let's wash ourselves	**ne nous lavons pas**	let's not wash ourselves
lavez-vous	wash yourself (yourselves)	**ne vous lavez pas**	do not wash yourself (yourselves)

2. Some common reflexive verbs

Note that the French reflexive verb is not always translated by a reflexive verb in English.

1. **s'appeler** *to be called, named*
2. **s'amuser** *to have a good time*
3. **se lever** *to get up*
4. **s'asseoir** (sa-swar) *to sit down*
5. **se mettre à** *to sit down at*
6. **se mettre debout** *to stand up*
7. **se porter** *to feel (health)*
8. **se coucher** *to go to bed*
9. **s'habiller** *to get dressed*
10. **se promener** *to go for a walk, ride*
11. **se souvenir de** *to remember*
12. **se demander** *to wonder*
13. **se dépêcher** *to hurry*
14. **s'ennuyer** *to be bored*

Exercise No. 94. Complete each French sentence by inserting the correct reflexive pronoun. Read the completed sentences aloud.

Exemple: 1. M. Potter va se mettre à table.

1. Mr. Potter is going to sit down at the table.
2. He gets up at seven o'clock.
3. He washes (himself) and dresses (himself).
4. At what time do you go to bed?
5. How do you feel? (How are you?)
6. She is feeling well.
7. My mother is feeling better today.
8. We have a good time at the movies.
9. What is your name? (How do you call yourself?)
10. What are their names?
11. My name is Albert.
12. Dress yourself quickly, Anne.
13. Do not get up late, children.
14. I do not go to bed before 10 o'clock.
15. The children do not want to get up.

1. **M. Potter va _____ mettre à table.**
2. **Il _____ lève à sept heures.**
3. **Il _____ lave et _____ habille.**
4. **A quelle heure _____ couchez-vous?**
5. **Comment _____ portez-vous?**
6. **Elle _____ porte bien.**
7. **Ma mère _____ porte mieux aujourd'hui.**
8. **Nous _____ amusons au ciné.**
9. **Comment _____ appelez-vous?**
10. **Comment _____ appellent-ils?**
11. **Je _____ appelle Albert.**
12. **Habille _____ vite, Anne.**
13. **Ne _____ levez pas tard, mes enfants.**
14. **Je ne _____ couche pas avant dix heures.**
15. **Les enfants ne veulent pas _____ lever.**

Exercise No. 95. Translate the questions and answers. Read the questions and answers aloud several times.

1. — Comment vous appelez-vous?
— Je m'appelle Albert.
2. — À quelle heure est-ce que vous vous levez?
— Je me lève à sept heures du matin.
3. — À quelle heure est-ce que vous vous couchez?
— Je me couche à onze heures du soir.
4. — Est-ce que vous vous habillez vite?
— Je m'habille très vite.
5. — Comment vous portez-vous?
— Je me porte bien, merci.
6. — Comment est-ce que votre père se porte?
— Il ne se porte pas bien. Il est enrhumé.
7. — À quelle heure est-ce que M. Potter se met à table?
— Il se met à table à sept heures du soir.
8. — Est-ce que les garçons s'amusent bien en jouant au baseball?
— Ils s'amusent très bien.

Exercise No. 96—Questionnaire

1. À quelle heure est-ce que M. Potter se lève?
2. Ensuite que fait-il?
3. En combien de temps s'habille-t-il?
4. Que fait-il à sept heures à peu près?
5. Est-ce que sa femme se lève de bonne heure?
6. Est-ce qu'ils déjeunent ensemble?
7. Qu'est-ce qu'il mange au petit déjeuner?
8. Qu'est-ce qu'il mange parfois au lieu des oeufs?
9. A quelle heure est-il prêt à partir?
10. A quelle heure arrive-t-il à son bureau?
11. A quelle heure prend-il son déjeuner?
12. Qu'est-ce qu'il mange au déjeuner?
13. Quelles personnes viennent le voir dans l'après-midi?
14. A quelle heure est-ce qu'il finit sa journée?

CHAPITRE 19 (DIX-NEUF)

LA VIE DANS LA BANLIEUE
LIFE IN THE SUBURBS

1. — Maintenant je suis bien renseigné sur votre journée en ville. Mais je suis toujours curieux. Dites-moi, M. Potter, comment passez-vous le temps chez vous dans la banlieue où vous demeurez?

1. Now I am well informed about your day in town. But I am still curious. Tell me, Mr. Potter, how do you pass the time at home in the suburbs where you live?

2. — Comment je passe mon temps? Mais, c'est bien simple. Vous savez déjà que je rentre assez tard. Nous ne terminons pas notre dîner beaucoup avant huit heures et demie. Alors il ne nous reste pas trop de temps pour de grandes entreprises.

2. How do I pass the time? Well, it's very simple. You know already that I get home rather late. We don't finish our dinner much before 8:30. There is not too much time left for big projects.

3. — Tout de même, vous vous permettez quelques distractions, le cinéma, par exemple.

3. All the same, you do allow yourselves some entertainment, the movies for example.

4. — Évidemment. Mais, d'habitude nous restons sagement chez nous, en famille. Mais nous ne restons pas des heures devant la télévision. Nous causons, nous lisons et nous faisons la guerre aux enfants quand ils ne veulent pas se coucher.

4. Of course. But generally, we stay quietly at home with the family. But we don't spend hours in front of the television. We talk, we read, and we do battle with the children when they don't want to go to bed.

5. — Et quant aux achats, est-ce que Madame peut faire son marché commodément?

5. And as for shopping, can Mrs. Potter do her marketing conveniently?

6. — Oh, tout à fait. Tout près de chez nous il y a un supermarché où on peut acheter non seulement des fruits, des légumes, du lait, du fromage, du beurre, du café, des conserves de toutes sortes, de la viande, des bonbons et des gâteaux mais aussi des bas et des casseroles.

6. Oh, entirely. Very near us there is a supermarket where you can buy not only fruit, vegetables, milk, cheese, butter, coffee, all sorts of canned goods, meat, candy and cakes, but also stockings and saucepans.

7. — Tout de même, vous n'y trouvez pas de pardessus.

7. All the same, you don't find overcoats there.

8. — Pas encore. Mais nous avons un quartier commerçant très important. Plusieurs des grands magasins de New-York ont des succursales qui peuvent nous fournir presque tout ce qu'il nous faut.

8. Not yet. But we have a very large business section. Several of the New York department stores have branches which can furnish us with nearly everything we need.

9. — Vous avez de la chance.

9. You're lucky.

10. — Et le plus beau de l'affaire c'est qu'on peut toujours stationner, on n'est pas bousculé, et on peut causer à son aise avec les vendeurs.

10. And the best part of it is that one can always park, one is not pushed around, and one can talk comfortably with the salesmen.

11. — Et les enfants, sont-ils contents à l'école?

11. And the children, are they happy at school?

12. — Si on peut jamais dire qu'un enfant est content à l'école, alors oui, ils sont contents. Ils aiment bien leurs maîtres d'école, ils ont de bons camarades.

12. If one can ever say that a child is happy at school, then yes, they are happy. They like their teachers, they have good friends.

13. — Vous faites si bien la propagande pour la banlieue que j'ai envie de déménager!

13. You make life in the suburbs sound so attractive that I feel like moving.

14. — Venez donc! Vous serez le bienvenu!

14. Come on, then. You will be very welcome.

Pronunciation and Spelling Aids

Practice aloud

Maintenant je suis bien renseigné sur votre journée en ville.

(Mañt-nahñ zhuh süee byañ rahñ-seh-**nyay** sur vutr zhoor-nay ahñ **veel**.)

Mais je suis toujours curieux.

(Meh zhuh süee too-zhoor kür-**yeu.**)

Dites-moi, Monsieur Potter, comment passez-vous le temps chez vous dans le banlieue où vous demeurez?

(Deet-mwa muh-syeu pu-**tehr**, ku-mawñ pah-say voo luh **tahñ** shay voo dahñ la bahñ-**lyeu** oo voo duh-meu-**ray**?)

Building Vocabulary

Quelques fruits et légumes

Some fruits and vegetables

la banane (ba-**nan**) banana
le citron (see-**trawñ**) lemon
l'orange (*f*) (lu-**rahñzh**) orange
la poire (pwar) pear
la pêche (pehsh) peach
la pomme (pum) apple
la tomate (tu-**mat**) tomato
les raisins (*m*) (reh-**zañ**) grapes

la betterave (beh-**trahv**) beet
la carotte (ka-**rut**) carrot
le chou (shoo) cabbage
les épinards (*m*) (lay zay pee-**nar**) spinach
les petits pois (pwa) green peas
les haricots (lay a-ree-**koh**) beans
l'oignon (*f*) (lu-**nyawñ**) onion
la pomme de terre (pum duh **tehr**) potato

French Expressions

1. **tout de même** (too duh **mehm**) all the same, nevertheless
2. **en famille** (ahñ fa-**meey**) with the family
3. **faire son marché** to do one's marketing
4. **le plus beau de l'affaire** the best part of it
5. **être à son aise** to be at one's ease, comfortable
6. **j'ai envie de** (zhay ahñ-vee duh) I desire, have a mind to
7. **être le bienvenu** (byañ-vuh-**nü**) to be welcome

Exercise No. 97—Completion of Text

1. **Je suis** (well informed).
2. (All the same) **vous vous permettez quelques distractions.**
3. (We remain) **sagement chez nous.**
4. **Mme. Potter peut faire** (her marketing) **commodément.**
5. **On achète au supermarché** (fruits, vegetables, milk, butter, cheese and coffee).
6. **On y achète aussi** (stockings and saucepans).
7. **On peut toujours** (park).
8. **On peut causer** (at one's ease).
9. **Les enfants ont** (good friends).
10. I feel like moving.

Grammar Notes

1. Some or any

Observe in the following sentences how *some* or *any* is expressed in French.

1. Je prends *du* jus d'orange.	1. I take (*some*) orange juice.
2. J'achète *de la* crème.	2. I buy (*some*) cream.
3. Avez-vous *de l'*argent?	3. Have you (*any*) money?
4. M. Potter importe *des* objets d'art.	4. Mr. Potter imports (*some*) art objects.

a. The idea *some* or *any* preceding a noun is usually expressed in French by **de** plus the definite article, that is: **du, de l', de la** or **des.** This construction is called the *partitive* because it indicates *part* but not all of the thing or things.

b. The words *some* and *any* are often omitted in English but the corresponding words in French are almost never omitted.

2. Omissions of the definite article in the partitive

The partitive (*some* or *any*) is usually expressed by **de** without the definite article a) after a negative verb; b) when an adjective precedes the noun.

a. **Je n'achète pas *de* café, *de* crème ou *d'*oeufs.**	a. I am not buying (*any*) coffee, (*any*) cream or (*any*) eggs.
b. **M. Potter importe *de* beaux objets d'art.**	b. Mr. Potter imports (*some*) beautiful art objects.

Exercise No. 98. In these sentences substitute the French words for *some* or *any* **(du, de l', de la, des** or **de)**:

1. **Comme déjeuner je prends** (some) **café et** (some) **jus d'orange.**
2. **Voulez-vous** (some) **lait,** (some) **beurre et** (some) **oeufs?**
3. **N'avez-vous pas** (any) **porcelaine de Limoges?**
4. **Les enfants mangent** (some) **gâteaux.**
5. **Préférez-vous** (some) **crêpes au lieu des oeufs?**
6. **M. Potter ne vend pas** (any) **automobiles.**
7. **Comme dîner M. Potter prend** (some) **soupe,** (some) **viande et** (some) **légumes.**
8. **Est-ce qu'il y a** (any) **bons restaurants près d'ici?**
9. **Je veux acheter** (some) **encre rouge.**
10. **Les enfants ont** (some) **bons camarades.**

3. The partitive pronoun **en** (some of it, any of it, etc.)

You are familiar with the word **en** as a preposition. Thus:

En été il fait chaud.	It is warm in summer.
Ils voyagent en France.	They are traveling in France.
Répétez ces mots en français.	Repeat these words in French.

Study the use of the pronoun **en** in the following sentences:

Voulez-vous de la crème?	Do you want any cream?
Merci. J'*en* ai déjà.	Thanks. I have *some* (*of it*) already.
Avez-vous des stylos?	Have you any fountain pens?
Moi, je n'*en* ai pas. Louis *en* a trois.	I haven't *any* (*of them*). Louis has three (*of them*).
Achetez-vous des oeufs?	Are you buying any eggs?
Oui, j'*en* achète deux douzaines.	Yes, I am buying two dozen (*of them*).
A-t-il beaucoup d'argent?	Has he a great deal of money?
Non. Il n'*en* a qu'un peu.	He has only a little (*of it*).

a. **en** is used as a pronoun meaning *some* or *any;* **en** may be translated as *some, any, some of it, any of it, some of them, any of them.*

b. In English the above words may be expressed or understood. In French the **en** must not be omitted. Thus:

Voici des gâteaux.	Here are some cakes.
N'*en* prenez pas trop.	Do not take too many (*of them*).

c. Like the object pronouns, **en** precedes the verb except in the affirmative imperative.

Voici des gâteaux.	Here are some cakes.
Prenez-*en*. N'*en* prenez pas.	Take *some*. Do not take *any* (*of them*).

Exercise No. 99. Read each question. Then give the indicated answer in French.

Exemple: 1. Oui, nous en vendons beaucoup.

1. Vendez-vous beaucoup de porcelaine?	1. Yes, we sell a good deal of it.
2. Achète-t-elle des conserves?	2. Yes, she is buying some.
3. Avez-vous un pardessus?	3. No, I haven't any.
4. Voici de la soupe.	4. Take some.
5. Les pommes ne sont pas mûres (ripe).	5. Do not eat any (of them).
6. Combien d'élèves a-t-il?	6. He has thirty (of them).
7. Prenez quelques poires.	7. Thanks. I don't want any.
8. Ont-ils assez de livres?	8. Yes, they have enough (of them).

Exercise No. 100—Questionnaire

1. **Qui est toujours curieux?**
2. **Qu'est-ce M. Picard sait déjà?**
3. **À quelle heure est-ce que la famille Potter termine son dîner?**
4. **Pourquoi les parents font-ils la guerre aux enfants?**
5. **Où est-ce que Madame Potter fait ses achats?**
6. **Qu'est-ce qu'on achète au supermarché?**
7. **Qu'est-ce qu'on ne trouve pas au supermarché?**
8. **Est-ce que les grands magasins de New York ont des succursales dans la banlieue?**
9. **Qui est-ce que les enfants aiment?**
10. **Qui a envie de déménager à la banlieue?**

RÉVISION 4
CHAPITRES 15–19 PREMIÈRE PARTIE

NOUNS

1. l'amateur	**11. le dîner**	**21. la pomme**	1. lover (of things)	11. dinner	21. apple
2. le beurre	**12. le film**	**22. le porteur**	2. butter	12. film	22. porter
3. le ciné	**13. la glace**	**23. le programme**	3. movies (slang)	13. ice-cream	23. program
4. le cinéma	**14. l'histoire**	**24. le rang**	4. movies	14. history	24. row
5. le côté	**15. la lumière**	**25. le fleuve**	5. side	15. light	25. river
6. le cours	**16. la montagne**	**26. la sténo**	6. course	16. mountain	26. stenographer
7. la date	**17. l'oeil (les yeux)**	**27. le téléphone**	7. date	17. eye (eyes)	27. telephone
8. le départ	**18. l'oeuf**	**28. la télévision**	8. departure	18. egg	28. television
9. le petit déjeuner	**19. le pain**	**29. la viande**	9. breakfast	19. bread	29. meat
10. le déjeuner	**20. le petit pain**	**30. la voiture**	10. lunch	20. roll	30. car, carriage

VERBS

1. adorer	**13. permettre**	**25. devenir**	1. to adore	13. to permit	25. to become
2. aider	**14. finir**	**26. revenir**	2. to help	14. to finish	26. to come back
3. déjeuner	**15. nous finissons**	**27. s'amuser**	3. to breakfast	15. we finish	27. to enjoy oneself
4. embrasser	**16. bâtir**	**28. je m'amuse**	4. to kiss	16. to build	28. I enjoy myself
5. ennuyer	**17. choisir**	**29. s'appeler**	5. to bore, annoy	17. to choose	29. to be called
6. féliciter	**18. obéir**	**30. il s'appelle**	6. to congratulate	18. to obey	30. his name is
7. intéresser	**19. punir**	**31. se coucher**	7. to interest	19. to punish	31. to go to bed
8. remercier	**20. remplir**	**32. s'habiller**	8. to thank	20. to fill	32. to dress oneself
9. préférer	**21. saisir**	**33. se laver**	9. to prefer	21. to seize	33. to wash oneself
10. rester	**22. mourir**	**34. se lever**	10. to remain, stay	22. to die	34. to get up
11. mettre	**23. venir**	**35. levez-vous**	11. to put	23. to come	35. get up
12. je mets	**24. il vient**	**36. se reposer**	12. I put	24. he comes	36. to rest

ADJECTIVES

1. fatigué	**4. occupé**	**7. quelconque**	1. tired	4. busy	7. any whatsoever
2. gentil (ille *f.*)	**5. pareil (eille *f.*)**	**8. terminé**	2. kind, nice	5. like, such	8. finished
3. glorieux (ieuse *f.*)	**6. la plupart de**	**9. triste**	3. glorious	6. the majority of	9. sad

ADVERBS

1. **alors**	1. well, then
2. **ensemble**	2. together
3. **d'ailleurs**	3. besides
4. **exactement**	4. exactly
5. **parfois**	5. at times
6. **puis**	6. then
7. **seulement**	7. only
8. **souvent**	8. often
9. **toujours**	9. always

PREPOSITIONS

1. **au lieu de**	1. instead of
2. **jusqu'à**	2. up to, until
3. **pendant**	3. during
4. **sans**	4. without

FRENCH EXPRESSIONS

1. **attraper un rhume**	1. to catch cold
2. **être le bienvenu**	2. to be welcome
3. **bien entendu**	3. of course
4. **à l'heure**	4. on time
5. **de bonne heure**	5. early
6. **n'importe**	6. it doesn't matter
7. **se mettre à table**	7. to sit down at the table
8. **ni moi non plus**	8. neither do I
9. **pas encore**	9. not yet
10. **cela me plaît**	10. that pleases me
11. **rester (être) debout**	11. to stand
12. **de temps en temps**	12. from time to time
13. **(pas) tout à fait**	13. (not) quite
14. **tout de même**	14. all the same
15. **voilà**	15. there is (are)
16. **en tout cas**	16. in any case

Exercise No. 101. Select the group of words in Column II which best completes each sentence begun in Column I:

I	II
1. **Les enfants de M. Potter connaissent**	a. **que je me lève de bonne heure.**
2. **Du quatorzième rang**	b. **M. Potter prend du jus d'orange.**
3. **Le quatorze juillet 1789 est la date**	c. **à sept heures du soir.**
4. **M. Potter connaît l'histoire de France**	d. **et moi nous déjeunons ensemble.**
5. **La Loire est le fleuve**	e. **on peut bien voir et entendre.**
6. **"Je suis matinal" veut dire**	f. **de la prise de la Bastille.**
7. **Toute la famille se met à table**	g. **le plus long de la France.**
8. **Pour arriver à son bureau M. Potter voyage**	h. **aussi bien que son système monétaire.**
9. **Pour commencer le déjeuner**	i. **tous les vedettes de l'écran.**
10. **Il me plaît beaucoup que ma femme**	j. **en voiture, par train et par le métro** (subway).

Exercise No. 102. Complete these sentences in French:

1. **La Loire est** (the longest river) **de la France.**
2. **Londres est** (bigger than) **Paris.**
3. **Philippe est** (more tired than) **moi.**
4. **Je ne suis pas** (as tall as) **mon frère.**
5. **Le Mont Blanc n'est pas** (higher than) **le Mount McKinley.**
6. **Le Mont Everest est** (the highest mountain) **du monde.**
7. **Dimanche est** (the first day) **de la semaine.**
8. **January 30, 1988.**
9. **Annette est la plus jeune** (in the family).
10. **Georges est** (my best friend).

Exercise No. 103. Translate the following brief dialogues. Practice them aloud. Note the various examples of the partitive.

1. **— Pour votre déjeuner prenez-vous du café ou du chocolat? — Je ne prends ni l'un ni l'autre. Je bois un verre d'eau.**
2. **— Désirez-vous de la crème et du sucre dans votre café? — Je désire de la crème mais je ne désire pas de sucre.**
3. **— Qu'est-ce qu'on mange comme petit déjeuner en France? — On mange très peu; en général des petits pains**[1] **et du café.**
4. **— Que mange-t-on le matin comme déjeuner aux États-Unis? — D'ordinaire on commence avec du jus d'orange. Puis on mange une céréale quelconque, une tranche de pain grillé ou des oeufs. Les Américains sont aussi très friands** (fond) **de crêpes avec du sirop. Bien entendu il y a aussi du café, du thé ou du lait à boire.**

NOTE 1. **des** (not **de**) **petits pains,** because **petits pains,** like **petits pois,** is considered to be a single noun, not an adjective plus noun.

Exercise No. 104. Read each French question. Then make your answer in French correspond to the English answer that follows the question.

Exemple: 1. Oui, je les invite.

1. **Invitez-vous vos amis à dîner chez vous?** — 1. Yes, I am inviting them.
2. **Préférez-vous le ciné?** — 2. No, I do not prefer it.
3. **Est-ce que les enfants connaissent les vedettes du ciné?** — 3. Yes, they know them well.
4. **Est-ce que vous nous attendez?** — 4. Yes, we are waiting for you.
5. **Vous levez-vous de bonne heure?** — 5. No, I get up late.
6. **À quelle heure est-ce que vous vous couchez?** — 6. We go to bed at 11 o'clock.
7. **Les enfants s'habillent-ils rapidement le matin?** — 7. Yes, they dress themselves very quickly.
8. **Comment vous appelez-vous?** — 8. My name is Albert Martin.
9. **À quelle heure finissez-vous vos examens?** — 9. We finish them at 4 o'clock in the afternoon.
10. **Finissent-ils maintenant le travail?** — 10. Yes, they are finishing it now.

Exercise No. 105. Complete these sentences by choosing the correct expression from those listed below. Be sure to use the correct form of the verbs and adjectives.

1. **Elle doit être** (tired) **après une journée** (such).
2. (They sit down at table) **à sept heures.**
3. (They are standing) **devant la maison.**
4. **Les messieurs** (are seated) **dans le salon.**
5. (From time to time) **nous prenons du chocolat** (instead of) **café.**
6. **Nous ne voulons pas** (to catch cold).
7. **Je vois** (the majority of) **mes clients le matin.**
8. **Le train arrive rarement** (on time).
9. (We are) **toujours** (welcome) **chez M. Potter.**
10. **Nous nous levons** (early); **ils se lèvent** (late).

a. au lieu de
b. pareil (eille *f.*)
c. tard; à l'heure
d. fatigué
e. la plupart de
f. de bonne heure
g. de temps en temps
h. attraper un rhume
i. se mettre à table
j. être le bienvenu
k. être debout
l. être assis

Dialogue
Au marché aux puces

Nous sommes près d'un étalage de couvertures de lit.

We are near a display of bedspreads.

L'Acheteur: **Combien coûte cette couverture blanche brodée en bleu?**

Customer: What is the price of this white bedspread embroidered in blue?

Le Vendeur: **Elle coûte cinq cent francs.**

Salesman: It costs five hundred francs.

L'Acheteur: **C'est beaucoup trop. Je vais vous donner trois cent.**

Customer: That's much too much. I'll give you three hundred francs.

Le Vendeur: **Mais monsieur, vous n'y pensez pas! Regardez ce travail, comme il est fin. Regardez la qualité du drap. Enfin, ça va doucement aujourd'hui. Je vous la laisse à quatre cent cinquante.**

Salesman: But sir, you don't mean it! Look at this fine work. Look at the quality of the cloth. Well, things are slow today. I'll let you have it for four hundred fifty.

L'Acheteur: **C'est toujours beaucoup. Je vous donne trois cent cinquante.**

Customer: It's still high. I'll give you three fifty.

Le Vendeur: **Mais regardez, monsieur, comme elle est grande. Elle est assez grande pour un lit à deux places. Donnez-moi quatre cent vingt.**

Salesman: But look, sir, how big it is. It is big enough for a double bed. Make it four hundred twenty.

L'Acheteur: **Je dors dans un lit à une place. Je suis célibataire. Je ne vais pas me marier. Je vous donne trois cent soixante-dix.**

Customer: I sleep in a single bed. I am a bachelor. I am not going to get married. I'll give you three hundred seventy.

Le Vendeur: **Impossible, monsieur. Je suis marié, moi, et j'ai des enfants à nourrir. Quatre cent francs. C'est mon dernier prix.**

Salesman: Can't be done, sir. I am married and I have children to feed. Four hundred francs. That's my final price.

***L'Acheteur:* Bon, d'accord. Voici, monsieur.**
Il donne au vendeur quatre cent francs et il s'en va[1] avec la couverture blanche brodée en bleu. C'est le coutume de marchander au marché aux puces, et tous les deux sont contents.

Customer: Good, agreed. Here you are sir.
He gives the salesman four hundred francs and he goes away with the white bedspread embroidered in blue. It is the custom to bargain at the flea market, and they are both pleased.

NOTE 1. **s'en aller** means to go away: **je m'en vais, tu t'en vas, ils'en va, nous nous en allons, vous vous en allez, ils s'en vont.**

LECTURE

Exercise No. 106—Une visite au paquebot[1] Queen Elizabeth 2

C'est samedi. M. Potter se lève à huit heures, et il regarde par la fenêtre. Le ciel est bleu. Le soleil brille. Il dit à sa femme, — Aujourd'hui allons visiter le paquebot Queen Elizabeth 2 qui est arrivé ce matin. J'ai de la marchandise à bord. Nous allons avoir une belle occasion pour visiter le bateau.

— Très bien, dit Mme. Potter.

A neuf heures ils partent en voiture et dans à peu près une heure ils arrivent au quai. A l'entrée ils voient un groupe de garçons qui mangent des glaces et qui causent en français.

M. Potter dit bonjour aux garçons et il cause un peu avec le plus proche. Voici la conversation.

— Bonjour, jeune homme! Êtes-vous Français?

— Non, monsieur, je suis Américain.

— Mais vous parlez très bien le français.

— Eh bien, ces garçons qui travaillent sur le paquebot sont mes amis, et ils m'apprennent à parler correctement. Ils sont mes professeurs. D'ailleurs, j'étudie le français au lycée[2] et tous les jours je lis quelques pages de français. À propos, êtes-vous Français?

— Merci pour le compliment. Non, mon petit, je suis Américain comme vous, et comme vous j'étudie le français. Mais moi je n'ai qu'un professeur.

— Ah bon. Mais vous parlez très bien.

— Merci encore une fois. Au revoir et bonne chance.

— Au revoir monsieur.

M. Potter rejoint sa femme qui l'attend en souriant, et ils se remettent en route[3] pour la visite au paquebot.

— Il est sympathique, ce garçon, dit M. Potter à sa femme. Et puis il traduit[4] la phrase, parce qu'elle ne comprend pas le français, "He's a likeable boy."

NOTE 1. steamship, liner 2. **le lycée** is the equivalent of academic high school in the United States 3. **ils . . . route** they continue on their way 4. **traduire,** *to translate:* **il traduit, nous traduisons.**

CHAPITRE 20 (VINGT)

QUEL SALE TEMPS!
WHAT NASTY WEATHER!

1. Il pleut à verse. La bonne ouvre la porte de la maison de M. et Mme. Potter. M. Picard entre.

1. It is raining buckets. The maid opens the door of the house of Mr. and Mrs. Potter. Mr. Picard enters.

2. La bonne dit, — Bonsoir, M. Picard. Quel sale temps! Entrez, entrez. Vous êtes trempé. Donnez-moi votre imperméable et votre chapeau, s'il vous plaît. Mettez votre parapluie dans le porte-parapluies. Vous pouvez laisser vos caoutchoucs ici à l'entrée.

2. The maid says, "Good evening, Mr. Picard. What nasty weather! Come in, come in. You are soaking wet. Give me your raincoat and hat. Put your umbrella in the umbrella stand. You can leave your rubbers here in the hall."

3. M. Picard répond, — Merci. Maintenant ça va mieux. Il pleut à verse, mais il ne fait pas froid. Je suis sûr que je ne vais pas attraper un rhume. Est-ce que M. Potter est là?

3. Mr. Picard answers, "Thank you. Now I feel better. It is raining buckets, but it is not cold. I am sure that I shall not catch cold. Is Mr. Potter at home?"

4. — Oui, oui, monsieur. Il vous attend dans le salon. Le voilà lui-même.

5. — Bonsoir, M. Picard. Je suis très content de vous voir, mais par un sale temps pareil on ne doit pas sortir. Venez dans la salle à manger et prenez une tasse de thé au rhum pour vous réchauffer un peu.

6. — Merci infiniment, M. Potter. J'ai un peu froid. Une tasse de thé au rhum fera mon affaire, et pendant que nous prenons le thé nous allons causer du temps qu'il fait. C'est un sujet de conversation très courant et tout à fait à propos.

7. Les messieurs entrent dans la salle à manger en causant d'un ton animé. Ils s'assoient et la bonne leur[1] apporte un plateau chargé de deux tasses et de deux soucoupes, une théière pleine de thé chaud, un sucrier, et des cuillers à thé. Elle met le plateau sur la table avec une bouteille de rhum qu'elle va chercher au buffet. Puis elle sort de la salle à manger.

8. — Permettez-moi de vous servir, M. Picard, dit M. Potter. Il verse le thé dans les tasses avec une portion libérale de rhum pour chacun.

9. Pendant qu'ils prennent le thé au rhum les messieurs causent toujours d'un ton animé.

10. Dehors il pleut toujours.

4. "Yes sir, yes. He is waiting for you in the living room. There he is himself."

5. "Good evening, Mr. Picard. I am very glad to see you, but in nasty weather like this one should not go out. Come to the dining room and drink a cup of tea with rum to warm yourself a bit."

6. "Thank you very much, Mr. Potter. I am a little cold. A cup of tea with rum will suit me fine, and while we drink the tea with rum we will chat about the weather. It is a very common topic of conversation and quite appropriate."

7. The gentlemen go into the dining room chatting in animated voices. They sit down and the maid brings them[1] a tray with two cups and saucers, a teapot full of hot tea, a sugar bowl and some teaspoons. She puts the tray on the table together with a bottle of rum which she goes and gets from the sideboard. Then she leaves the dining room.

8. "Allow me to serve you, Mr. Picard," says Mr. Potter. He pours tea into the cups, with a generous portion of rum for each.

9. While they are drinking the tea with rum the gentlemen continue chatting in animated voices.

10. Outside it continues raining.

NOTE 1. **leur** means (*to*) *them*. It is an indirect object pronoun.

Pronunciation and Spelling Aids

Practice aloud

Bonsoir, M. Picard. Je suis très content de vous voir; mais par un sale temps pareil on ne doit pas sortir.

(Bawñ-swar, muh-syeu pee-**kar.** zhuh süee treh kawñ-tahñ duh voo **vwar;** may par euñ sal tahñ pa-**ray** awñ nuh dwa pah sur-**teer.**)

Venez dans la salle à manger et prenez une tasse de thé au rhum pour vous réchauffer.

(Vuh-nay dahñ la sal a mahñ-**zhay** ay pruh-nay zün tahs duh tay oh **rum** poor voo ray-shoh-**fay.**)

Building Vocabulary

A. **Quel temps fait-il?** (kehl tahñ feh-**teel?**) What is the weather?

1. **Il fait beau.** (eel feh **boh**) — It is nice (weather).
2. **Il fait mauvais.** (mu-**veh**) — It is bad (weather).
3. **Il fait (très) chaud.** (shoh) — It is (very) hot.
4. **Il fait (très) froid, frais.** (frwah, freh) — It is (very) cold, cool.
5. **Il fait du vent.** (dü **vahñ**) — It is windy.
6. **Il pleut. Il neige. Le soleil brille.** (eel **pleu.** eel **nehzh.** luh su-ley **breey**) — It is raining. It is snowing. The sun is shining.
7. **La pluie (la neige) tombe.** (la plüee, la nehzh **tawñb**) — The rain (the snow) is falling.
8. **Il pleut à verse.** (eel pleu ta **vehrs**) — It is raining buckets.
9. **Avez-vous froid? J'ai froid.** — Are you cold? I am cold.
10. **Avez-vous chaud? Je n'ai pas chaud.** — Are you warm? I am not warm.

NOTE: The French say: What weather does it *make?* not, What *is* the weather? It *makes* **(fait)** warm, cold, etc. not, It *is* warm, cold, etc. They say: I *have* warm, I *have* cold, etc. not I *am* warm, I *am* cold, etc.

B. Clothing for various kinds of weather

le pardessus (par-duh-**sü**) overcoat
l'imperméable (lañ-pehr-may-**abl**) raincoat
le chandail (shahñ-**dahy**), **le pull-over** sweater
le gilet (zhee-**lay**) cardigan sweater
le parapluie (pa-ra-**plüee**) umbrella
les caoutchoucs (kow-**tchoo**) rubbers, galoshes

French Expressions

1. **Quel sale temps!** (kehl sal **tahñ**) What nasty weather!
2. **attraper un rhume** (a-tra-pay euñ **rüm**) to catch cold
3. **le voilà** there he (it) is
4. **Une tasse de thé fera mon affaire.** A cup of tea will suit me.
5. **en causant** while chatting
6. **lui-même** he himself
7. **elle-même** she herself
8. **moi-même** I myself

Exercise No. 107—Completion of Text

1. **La bonne dit, —** (What nasty weather!)
2. (Come in, come in.) **Vous êtes** (soaking wet).
3. **Donnez-moi** (your raincoat)
4. (Put) **votre parapluie dans le porte-parapluies.**
5. **Maintenant,** (I feel better).
6. **Je ne vais pas** (to catch cold).
7. **Par un sale temps pareil** (one should not go out).
8. (Come) **à la salle à manger.**
9. **La bonne** (brings them) **un plateau.**
10. (Drink) **une tasse de thé au rhum.**
11. (Permit me) **de vous servir.**
12. **Dehors,** (it continues to rain).

Grammar Notes

1. The present tense of **ouvrir,** *to open.*

I open, you open, etc.

j'ouvre (zhoovr)
tu ouvres (oovr)
il, elle ouvre (oovr)
nous ouvrons (oo-vrawñ)
vous ouvrez (oo-vray)
ils, elles ouvrent (oovr)

Like **ouvrir** are: **couvrir,** *to cover,* **découvrir,** *to discover,* **offrir,** *to offer*

2. Indirect object pronouns

The indirect object indicates the person *to* or *for* whom the action is performed. Thus:

He writes a letter *to* his agent. He writes (*to*) him a letter. Observe carefully the indirect object pronouns in the following sentences:

1. **Charles** ***me*** **donne un cadeau.**
2. **Ton père** ***t'*****achète un chandail.**
3. **Qui** ***vous*** **apprend le français?**
4. **M. Picard** ***nous*** **apprend le français.**
5. **Voilà M. Potter. Qui** ***lui*** **parle?**
6. **Voilà Mme. Potter. Qui** ***lui*** **parle?**
7. **Nous** ***leur*** **apportons les parapluies.**

1. Charles is giving *me* a gift.
2. Your father is buying (*for*) *you* a sweater.
3. Who is teaching *you* French?
4. Mr. Picard is teaching *us* French.
5. There is Mr. Potter. Who is speaking *to him?*
6. There is Mrs. Potter. Who is speaking *to her?*
7. We are bringing *them* the umbrellas.

Compare the *direct object* pronouns with the *indirect object* pronouns.

Direct		*Indirect*	
me, m' me	**nous** us	**me, m'** (to) me	**nous** (to) us
te, t' you (*fam.*)	**vous** you	**te, t'** (to) you (*fam.*)	**vous** (to) you
le, l' him, it			
la, l' her, it	**les** them	**lui** (to) him, (to) her	**leur** (to) them

a. The direct and indirect objects are alike except in the third person. Direct: **le** (*him*), **la** (*her*), **les** (*them*). Indirect: **lui** (*to him, to her*), **leur** (*to them*).

b. Like the direct object, the indirect object precedes the verb except in the affirmative imperative.

Donnez-*lui* le livre. Give *him* the book.
Ne *lui* donnez pas le livre. Do not give *him* the book.

3. Some common verbs which may take indirect objects

apporter to bring	**prêter** to lend	**rendre** to give back
acheter to buy	**présenter** to present	**répéter** to repeat
dire to say	**montrer** to show	**apporter** to bring
donner to give	**envoyer** to send	**rapporter** to bring back
demander[1] to ask	**écrire** to write	**servir** to serve
parler to speak	**lire** to read	**vendre** to sell

NOTE 1. **demander** means to ask or ask for something. The person asked is the indirect object. The thing asked or asked for is the direct object. Thus:

M. Picard demande à M. Potter (lui demande) le nom de son représentant.

Mr. Picard asks Mr. Potter (asks him) the name of his agent.

demander does not mean *to demand;* the French verb for *demand* is **exiger.** The French verb for *ask (a question)* is **poser. Je lui pose une question** means: I ask him (indirect object) a question (direct object).

Exercise No. 108. Complete the French sentences with the missing indirect objects. Read aloud. Remember **lui** means *to him, to her;* **leur** means *to them.*

Exemple: 1. Je ne lui prête pas d'argent.

1. I am not lending *him* any money.
2. They are bringing *us* some candy.
3. We are teaching *her* French.
4. The maid is serving *them* some tea.
5. He is showing *them* the samples.
6. Are you sending *her* a gift?
7. She is buying *me* a pair of rubbers.
8. Do not speak *to her.*
9. Bring the umbrella back *to him.*
10. They are asking *us* for our tickets.
11. Give *us* more time.
12. Return my fountain pen *to me,* please.
13. You may repeat my words *to them.*
14. I am going to introduce my friend *to her.*
15. Do not sell *him* your bicycle.

1. **Je ne ____ prête pas d'argent.**
2. **Ils ____ apportent des bonbons.**
3. **Nous ____ enseignons (*or* apprenons) le français.**
4. **La bonne ____ sert du thé.**
5. **Il ____ montre les échantillons.**
6. **____ envoyez-vous un cadeau?**
7. **Elle ____ achète une paire de caoutchoucs.**
8. **Ne ____ parlez pas.**
9. **Rapportez-____ le parapluie.**
10. **Ils ____ demandent nos billets.**
11. **Donnez-____ plus de temps.**
12. **Rendez-____ mon stylo, s'il vous plaît.**
13. **Vous pouvez ____ répéter mes mots.**
14. **Je vais ____ présenter mon ami.**
15. **Ne ____ vendez pas votre bicyclette.**

Exercise No. 109—Questionnaire

1. **Quel temps fait-il quand M. Picard arrive chez M. Potter?**
2. **Qui ouvre la porte?**
3. **Où est-ce que M. Picard met son parapluie?**
4. **Où est-ce qu'il laisse ses caoutchoucs?**
5. **Où est-ce que les deux messieurs entrent?**
6. **Qu'est-ce qu'ils prennent dans la salle à manger?**
7. **Qu'est-ce que la bonne met sur la table?**
8. **Et après** (afterwards) **que fait-elle?**

CHAPITRE 21 (VINGT ET UN)

LE CLIMAT DE LA FRANCE
THE CLIMATE OF FRANCE

1. Les deux messieurs sont toujours assis dans la salle à manger. Ils causent toujours en prenant le thé au rhum. Dehors il continue à pleuvoir. M. Picard n'a plus froid.

1. The two men are still sitting in the dining room. They are still chatting while drinking the tea with rum. Outside it continues to rain. Mr. Picard is no longer cold.

2. M. Picard dit, — Le climat des États-Unis et celui de la France sont quelque peu différents. Ici à New-York nous avons un climat qui va d'un extrême à l'autre.

3. — C'est vrai. En été il fait chaud; quelquefois il fait très chaud. En hiver il fait froid; parfois il fait très froid, de temps en temps il neige. Au printemps il commence à faire beau, mais il pleut souvent comme ce soir. Parfois il fait froid pendant des semaines quand tout à coup il fait chaud. Quelle saison préférez-vous, M. Picard?

4. — Je préfère l'automne. L'air est frais et vif. Le ciel est lumineux. Le soleil brille de tout son éclat. Et vous, M. Potter, quelle saison préférez-vous?

5. — Je préfère le printemps quand petit à petit tout devient vert. Mais parlons plutôt du climat de la France. Y a-t-il en France une différence marquée entre les saisons?

6. — Pour la plupart, oui, assez marquée; mais nous n'avons pas des extrêmes de chaleur et de froid.

7. — Cela doit être beaucoup plus agréable.

8. — Pas tout à fait. Il est vrai qu'à Paris par exemple il fait rarement très très froid en hiver. Mais par contre, il pleut beaucoup, il fait du vent, le ciel est gris pâle, et on commence à se demander, — Le printemps ne revient-il jamais?

9. — Ah oui, le printemps à Paris est célèbre.

10. — Vous qui préférez le printemps, vous allez être heureux à Paris. Au printemps il fait presque toujours beau. Le ciel est bleu clair avec de gros nuages blancs; les grands platanes des boulevards commencent à se feuiller; l'air est doux, embaumé. Toute la ville sourit.

11. — Mais vous faites un poème, M. Picard!

12. — Ce n'est pas pour rien que le printemps à Paris est célèbre.

13. — Tant mieux pour moi, car je compte partir au mois de mai. Et les autres saisons?

14. — Il est déjà tard. Laissons le reste pour la semaine prochaine.

2. Mr. Picard says, "The climate of the United States and that of France are somewhat different. Here in New York we have a climate that goes from one extreme to the other."

3. That's true. In summer it is hot; sometimes it is very hot. In winter it is cold; at times it is very cold, and it snows now and then. In spring it begins to be nice, but it often rains like tonight. Sometimes it stays cold for weeks when suddenly it gets hot. Which season do you prefer, Mr. Picard?

4. I prefer the autumn. The air is cool and crisp. The sky is clear. The sun shines brilliantly. And you, Mr. Potter, which season do you prefer?

5. I prefer the spring when little by little everything becomes green. But let us talk rather about the climate of France. Is there a marked difference in France among the seasons?

6. For the most part, yes, quite marked; but we don't have extremes of heat and cold.

7. That must be much nicer.

8. Not quite. It is true that in Paris for example it is rarely extremely cold in winter. But on the other hand, it rains a great deal, it is windy, the sky is a pale gray and one begins to wonder, "Is spring never coming again?"

9. Ah yes, spring in Paris is famous.

10. You who prefer the spring will be happy in Paris. In spring the weather is almost always nice. The sky is blue with thick white clouds; the big sycamores on the boulevards begin to leaf out, the air is mild and balmy. The whole city smiles.

11. But you're composing a poem, Mr. Picard!

12. It's not for nothing that spring in Paris is famous.

13. All the better for me, as I expect to leave in May. And the other seasons?

14. It is already late. Let us leave the rest for next week.

Pronunciation and Spelling Aids

Practice aloud

Les deux messieurs sont toujours assis dans la salle à manger.
(Lay deu may-syeu sawñ too-zhoor **za-see** dahñ la sal a mahñ-**zhay.**)

Ils causent toujours en prenant le thé au rhum.
(Eel kohz too-zhoor ahñ pruh-nahñ luh tay oh **rum.**)

Dehors il continue à pleuvoir.
(Duh-ur eel kawñ-tee-nü a pleu-**vwar.**)

Monsieur Picard n'a plus froid.
(Muh-syeu pee-kar na plü **frwah.**)

Building Vocabulary

A. **Les quatre saisons**

le printemps (prañ-**tahñ**) spring
l'été (lay-**tay**) summer
l'automne (loh-**tun**) autumn
l'hiver (lee-**vehr**) winter

au printemps in spring
en été in summer
en automne in autumn
en hiver in winter

B. Related words

1. **différent, la différence**
2. **intelligent, l'intelligence** (*f*)
3. **diligent, la diligence**
4. **évident, l'évidence** (*f*)
5. **content, le contentement**
6. **intéressant, l'intérêt** (*m*)

French Expressions

1. **tout à coup** (toot ta **koo**) all of a sudden
2. **de tout son éclat** (ay-**kla**) in all its brilliance
3. **petit à petit** little by little
4. **pour la plupart** for the most part
5. **par contre** (par **kawñtr**) on the other hand
6. **se demander** to wonder *Lit.* to ask oneself

Exercise No. 110—Completion of Text

1. **Ils causent** (while drinking) **le thé au rhum.**
2. **Dehors il continue** (to rain).
3. **En été** (it is hot).
4. **En hiver** (it is very cold).
5. **Au printemps** (it often rains).
6. (I prefer) **l'automne.**
7. **Quelle saison** (do you prefer)?
8. **Mais** (let us talk rather) **du climat de la France.**
9. **Nous n'avons pas ces extrêmes** (of heat and of cold).
10. **Cela** (ought) **être plus agréable.**
11. **Au printemps** (the weather is fine) **à Paris.**

Grammar Notes

1. Present tense of **devoir,** *to owe, to be obliged to, to have to;* **recevoir,** *to receive.*

I owe, am obliged to, have to, etc.		*I receive, you receive, etc.*	
je dois (dwa)	**nous devons** (duh-vawñ)	**je reçois**	**nous recevons**
tu dois (dwa)	**vous devez** (duh-vay)	**tu reçois**	**vous recevez**
il doit (dwa)	**ils doivent** (dwav)	**il reçoit**	**ils reçoivent**
elle doit (dwa)	**elles doivent** (dwav)	**elle reçoit**	**elles reçoivent**

Like **recevoir: apercevoir,** *to perceive,* **décevoir,** *to deceive*

The verb **devoir** is a very important verb with various shades of meaning. It expresses the idea of *must, ought, should,* in the sense of duty or obligation, as well as *must* in the sense of *is supposed to, is probably.*

Exercise No. 111. In the following sentences note the various meanings of **devoir.** Repeat each French sentence aloud five times.

1. **Nous leur devons vingt dollars.**
2. **M. Potter doit à M. Picard ses grands progrès dans l'étude du français.**
3. **Les élèves doivent faire leurs devoirs tous les jours.**
4. **Le train doit arriver à six heures.**
5. **Le climat de France doit être plus agréable que celui de notre pays.**
6. **Cela doit être vraiment beau.**
7. **Par un sale temps pareil on ne doit pas sortir.**
8. **Vous devez être fatigué après une journée pareille.**

1. We owe them twenty dollars.
2. Mr. Potter owes his great progress in the study of French to Mr. Picard.
3. The pupils must (ought to, have to) do their homework every day.
4. The train should arrive (is due) at six o'clock.
5. The climate of France must be (is probably) more agreeable than that of our country.
6. That must be really beautiful.
7. One should not go out in such nasty weather.
8. You must be tired after such a day.

2. Some negative expressions

You have learned that the negative *not* is expressed in French by **ne** before the verb and **pas** after the verb. Thus:

Je *ne* sais *pas*. Est-ce que vous *ne* savez *pas*? *Ne* savez-vous *pas*?

Study in the following sentences other negative expressions which also have two parts:

1. **Le professeur *n'*est *pas encore* ici.** — 1. The teacher is *not yet* here.
2. **Ces élèves *ne* sont *jamais* en retard.** — 2. These pupils are *never* late.
3. **M. Martin *ne* me doit *rien*.** — 3. Mr. Martin owes me *nothing*.
4. **Nous *ne* pouvons *pas* aller *non plus*.** — 4. We can *not* go *either*.
5. **Est-ce que vous *n'*avez *que* cinq dollars?** — 5. Do you have *only* five dollars?
6. **Ils *ne* viennent *plus* ici.** — 6. They do *not* come here *any more*.
7. **Il *ne* sait *ni* parler *ni* écrire le français.** — 7. He can *neither* speak *nor* write French.
8. **Il *ne* connaît *personne* à Paris.** — 8. He does *not* know anybody in Paris. (He knows *nobody* in Paris.)

Negative expressions usually have two parts, **ne** before the verb and the rest of each expression after it. Learn:

1. **ne . . . pas encore** not yet
2. **ne . . . jamais**[1] never, not ever
3. **ne . . . rien** nothing, not anything
4. **ne . . . pas . . . non plus** not . . . either
5. **ne . . . que** only
6. **ne . . . plus** no longer, not any more
7. **ne . . . ni . . . ni** neither . . . nor
8. **ne . . . personne** nobody, not anybody

NOTE 1. The word **jamais** used without **ne** means *ever*. For example:

Lisez-vous *jamais* les journaux français? — Do you *ever* read the French newspapers?

Negatives drop the **ne** when used without a verb.

Que faites-vous? *Rien*. — What are you doing? *Nothing*.
Quand le voyez-vous? *Jamais*. — When do you see him? *Never*.
Est-ce que Jean est ici? *Pas encore*. — Is John here? *Not yet*.
Je ne l'aime pas. *Ni moi non plus*. — I don't like him. *Neither* do I.
Qui est là? *Personne*. — Who is there? *Nobody*.

Exercise No. 112. Complete each French sentence with the correct negative. Read each sentence aloud twice.

Exemple: 1. Je ne sais rien de cette affaire.

1. I know nothing about that matter. — **1. Je _____ sais _____ de cette affaire.**
2. The examination is not yet finished. — **2. L'examen _____ est _____ terminé.**
3. We never travel in winter. — **3. Nous _____ voyageons _____ en hiver.**
4. They do not like the detective films either. — **4. Ils _____ aiment _____ les films policiers _____.**
5. He says nothing and he does nothing. — **5. Il _____ dit _____ et il _____ fait _____.**
6. Don't you want to take a trip to France? — **6. _____ voulez-vous _____ faire un voyage en France?**
7. She is no longer satisfied with her TV set. — **7. Elle _____ est _____ contente de sa télévision.**
8. I am not working either. — **8. Je _____ travaille _____.**
9. We have nothing to say to you. — **9. Nous _____ avons _____ à vous dire.**
10. I have only one notebook. — **10. Je _____ ai _____ un cahier.**
11. What you are bringing me? Nothing. — **11. Qu'est-ce que vous m'apportez? _____.**
12. Is the lesson finished? Not yet. — **12. La leçon est-elle finie? _____.**
13. Is spring never coming? — **13. Le printemps _____ vient-il _____?**
14. We have neither the time nor the money. — **14. Nous _____ avons _____ le temps _____ l'argent.**

Exercise No. 113—Questionnaire

1. **De quoi les messieurs parlent-ils?**
2. **Est-ce que le climat de la France est pareil à** (similar to, like) **celui des États-Unis?**
3. **Quel temps fait-il en été à New-York?**
4. **Quelle saison M. Picard préfère-t-il?**
5. **Et M. Potter quelle saison préfère-t-il?**
6. **Y a-t-il une différence marquée entre les saisons en France?**
7. **Comment est l'hiver à Paris?**
8. **Comment est le printemps à Paris?**

CHAPITRE 22 (VINGT DEUX)

LE CLIMAT DE LA FRANCE (SUITE)
THE CLIMATE OF FRANCE (CONT'D)

1. — Ce soir nous allons continuer à parler du climat de la France.

2. — Vous savez maintenant que le climat de Paris est très désagréable en hiver. C'est pour cela que ceux qui ont les moyens quittent Paris en hiver pour aller en Suisse ou à la Côte d'Azur.

3. — Est-ce que le climat de la Suisse en hiver est moins sévère que celui de Paris?

4. — Au contraire, il est plus sévère, mais il est beaucoup plus agréable.

5. — N'y a-t-il pas d'hiver sur la Côte d'Azur?

6. — L'hiver est doux. Presque tous les jours le soleil brille. Il fait bon. En été il fait plus chaud, mais il y a toujours une jolie brise de mer. Au fait, ce climat ressemble un peu à celui de Floride.

7. — Ah bon. Mais ne fait-il jamais froid?

8. — Il fait frais pendant la nuit. Il faut se mettre un lainage quelconque. Mais il ne fait jamais très froid sauf dans les montagnes.

9. — Est-ce vrai qu'on[1] peut nager le matin et faire du ski l'après-midi sur la Côte d'Azur?

10. — Mais oui. Ceux qui sont jeunes et forts le font tout le temps. De la plage on[1] peut voir les grandes montagnes des Alpes Maritimes couvertes de neige. Elles sont à une distance de quatre-vingts kilomètres à peu près.

11. — Ah, cela doit être vraiment beau!

12. — C'est un coin délicieux. Si vous avez le temps de faire un saut jusqu'à Nice ou Cannes vous allez être enchanté de votre visite.

13. — Merci bien pour le bon conseil. Je vais tâcher de faire ce petit voyage au mois du juin.

14. — Vous n'allez pas le regretter, je vous assure.

1. This evening we are going to continue to talk about the climate of France.

2. Now you know that the climate of Paris in winter is very disagreeable. That is why those who can afford it (*Lit.* have the means) leave Paris in winter to go to Switzerland or to the Riviera.

3. Is the climate of Switzerland in winter less severe than that of Paris?

4. On the contrary, it is more severe, but it is much more agreeable.

5. Is there no winter on the Riviera?

6. The winter is mild. Nearly every day the sun shines. The weather is fine. In summer it's warmer, but there is always a good sea breeze. In fact, this climate resembles somewhat that of Florida.

7. Oh, I see. But isn't it ever cold?

8. It is cool during the night. One must put on some woolen garment or other. But it is never very cold except in the mountains.

9. Is it true that you can go swimming in the morning and skiing in the afternoon on the Riviera?

10. Yes, indeed. Those who are young and strong do it all the time. From the beach you can see the high mountains of the Maritime Alps covered with snow. They are at a distance of about eighty kilometers.

11. That must be really beautiful.

12. It is a delightful spot. If you have the time for a short hop (*Lit.* to take a jump, hop) to Nice or Cannes you will be delighted with your visit.

13. Thank you for the good advice. I shall try to make that little trip in the month of June.

14. You won't be sorry, I assure you.

NOTE 1. **on** is an indefinite personal pronoun that takes the third person singular form of the verb (like **il** and **elle**). It can be translated as *one, you, we,* or *they*, depending on the context. It is very commonly used, especially in the spoken language.

Pronunciation and Spelling Aids

Practice aloud

L'hiver est doux. Presque tous les jours le soleil brille. Il fait bon.
(Lee-vehr eh **doo**. Prehsk too lay zhoor luh sulehy **breey**. Eel feh **bawñ**.)

En été il fait plus chaud, mais il y a toujours une jolie brise de mer.
(Ahñ nay-tay eel feh plü **shoh,** meh zeel ya toozhoor zün zhu-lee breez duh **mehr**.)

Building Vocabulary

Antonyms

1. **agréable** agreeable
   désagréable disagreeable
2. **doux** mild, soft
   sévère severe, harsh

3. **toujours** always
   ne . . . jamais never
4. **souvent** often
   rarement rarely
5. **devant** in front of
   derrière behind
6. **avant** before
   après after
7. **entrer dans** to enter
   sortir de to leave
8. **l'entrée** entrance
   la sortie exit

French Expressions

1. **au contraire** on the contrary
2. **au fait** in fact
3. **faire du ski** to go skiing
4. **être enchanté de** to be delighted with
5. **tâcher de faire** to try to do
6. **il faut partir** one must (it is necessary to) leave
7. **il faut avoir** one must (it is necessary) to have

Exercise No. 114—Completion of Text

1. **Ce soir** (we are going to continue) **à parler du climat de la France.**
2. **Le climat en hiver à Paris est** (very disagreeable).
3. **Ceux** (who have the means) **quittent Paris en hiver.**
4. (Isn't there any winter) **sur la Côte d'Azur?**
5. (It is never cold) **sauf dans les montagnes.**
6. (It is necessary to put on) **un lainage quelconque.**
7. **On peut** (swim in the morning).
8. (One can see) **les grandes montagnes.**
9. **Cela** (must be) **vraiment beau.**
10. (If you have the time) **faites un saut jusq'à Nice.**

Grammar Notes

1. Demonstrative pronouns

Compare the demonstrative pronouns (**celui, celle, ceux, celles**) with the demonstrative adjectives (**ce, cette, ces**) in the following sentences:

Demonstrative adjectives	Demonstrative pronouns
Ce (this) **docteur-ci est Français.**	**Celui-ci** (this one) **est Anglais.**
Ce (that) **docteur-là est Américain.**	**Celui-là** (that one) **est Italien.**
Cette (this) **fleur-ci est pour Louise.**	**Celle-ci** (this one) **est pour Marie.**
Cette (that) **fleur-là est pour Anne.**	**Celle-là** (that one) **est pour Jeanne.**
Ces (these) **docteurs-ci sont Français.**	**Ceux-ci** (these) **sont Anglais.**
Ces (those) **docteurs-là sont Américains.**	**Ceux-là** (those) **sont Italiens.**
Ces (these) **fleurs-ci sont pour Louise.**	**Celles-ci** (these) **sont pour Marie.**
Ces (those) **fleurs-là sont pour Anne.**	**Celles-là** (those) **sont pour Jeanne.**

The Demonstrative Pronoun Chart

	Singular		*Plural*	
masc.	**celui**	this (one), that (one)	**ceux**	these, those
fem.	**celle**	this (one), that (one)	**celles**	these, those

a. The demonstrative adjectives (**ce, cet, cette, ces**) are always followed by a noun. The demonstrative pronouns (**celui, celle, ceux, celles**) are never followed by a noun.

b. The demonstrative pronouns have the same gender and number as the nouns for which they stand.

Le climat de la France, et *celui* de l'Italie. The climate of France and *that* of Italy.
***Ceux* qui ont les moyens quittent Paris en hiver.** *Those* who have the means leave Paris in winter.

c. **-ci** and **-là** are used for emphasis or clarity. Omit **-ci** and **-là** before **de** and before a relative pronoun (**qui** or **que**).

2. **ceci, cela (ça)** this, that

ceci and **cela** (often shortened to **ça**) mean *this thing* or *that thing* or they may refer to whole ideas or statements.

Ceci est un rasoir électrique. This is an electric razor.

Cela est un rasoir de sûreté. That is a safety razor.
Cela est vrai (faux). That is true (false).
Ça ne fait rien. That doesn't matter.
N'oubliez pas ceci: Le commerçant français n'est pas pressé. Do not forget this: The French merchant is not in a hurry.

Exercise No. 115. Translate these brief dialogues. Practice them aloud.

1. **— Quelle poterie préférez-vous, celle de Vallauris ou celle de Biot? — Je préfère celle de Biot.**
2. **— Quel chapeau aimez-vous mieux, celui-ci ou celui-là? — J'aime mieux celui-là.**
3. **— Quel climat est plus doux, celui de la France ou celui du Canada? — Celui de la France est plus doux.**
4. **— Comment trouvez-vous ces robes? — J'aime bien celle-ci. Je trouve les couleurs de celle-là trop éclatantes.**
5. **— Quelles places préfèrez-vous, celles des premiers rangs ou celles du fond? — Nous préférons celles des premiers rangs.**
6. **— Quelle sorte de mouchoirs allez-vous acheter? — Je vais acheter ceux qui sont les meilleurs marchés.**

Exercise No. 116. Complete with the correct form of the demonstrative pronoun:

Exemple: 1. Les montagnes du Canada sont plus hautes que *celles* de l'Europe.

1. **Les montagnes du Canada sont plus hautes que** (those) **de l'Europe.**
2. **Les fleuves de l'Amérique du Sud sont plus longs que** (those) **de l'Europe.**
3. **Ce pot au lait-ci est de Limoges,** (that one) **est de Biot.**
4. **Ces tasses et ces soucoupes-ci sont de la France,** (those) **sont du Mexique.**
5. **Ces robes-ci sont meilleur marché que** (those).
6. **Ces problèmes-ci** (*m*) **sont plus difficiles que** (those).
7. **Lequel**[1] **est votre parapluie,** (this one) **ou** (that one)?
8. **Laquelle**[1] **est votre place,** (this one) **ou** (that)?
9. **Le climat de la France est plus doux que** (that) **de la Suisse.**
10. **Ma femme et moi, nous déjeunons ensemble.** (That) **me plaît beaucoup.**

NOTE 1. **lequel (laquelle** *f.***)** which one.

Exercise No. 117—Questionnaire

1. **Pourquoi est-ce que ceux qui ont les moyens quittent Paris en hiver?**
2. **Où vont-ils?**
3. **Comment est l'hiver sur la Côte d'Azur?**
4. **Comment est l'été sur la Côte d'Azur?**
5. **Où est-ce qu'on peut nager le matin et faire du ski l'après-midi?**
6. **Qu'est-ce qu'on peut voir de la plage?**
7. **Quel temps fait-il pendant la nuit?**
8. **Où fait-il très froid?**
9. **À quelle distance les montagnes sont-elles de la plage?**
10. **Quand est-ce que M. Potter va tâcher de faire ce petit voyage?**

CHAPITRE 23 (VINGT-TROIS)

LA BONNE CUISINE FRANÇAISE
GOOD FRENCH COOKING

1. — Vous savez, sans doute, M. Potter, que la bonne cuisine française est un des plus grands plaisirs du touriste en France.

1. No doubt, you know, Mr. Potter, that good French cooking is one of the greatest pleasures of the tourist in France.

2. — Je le sais bien, M. Picard. Je peux même dire que je la connais un peu, la cuisine française. Quand j'ai un client important, je l'invite à déjeuner dans un des bons restaurants français ici à New-York. Et cela arrive assez souvent.

2. I know that well, Mr. Picard. I can even say that I know something about French cooking. When I have an important customer, I invite him out to lunch at one of the good French restaurants here in New York. And this happens quite often.

3. — La cuisine française nous fait cadeau de beaucoup d'expressions d'usage courant en anglais; par exemple: à la carte, bouillon, consommé, purée, sauté, au gratin, café, petits fours, hors d'oeuvres, soufflé, et sans doute beaucoup d'autres. À propos, M. Potter, vous êtes dans l'importation. À Paris, faites une liste de vos plats préférés, et envoyez à votre femme un bon livre sur la cuisine française, en anglais, bien entendu.

3. French cooking gives us (*Lit.* makes us a gift of) many expressions commonly used in English; for example: à la carte, bouillon, consommé, purée, sauté, au gratin, café, petits fours, hors d'oeuvres, soufflé, and no doubt many others. By the way, Mr. Potter, you are in the import business. In Paris make a list of your favorite dishes and send your wife a good French cookbook, in English of course.

4. — Quelle bonne idée! Mais la cuisine française n'est-elle pas compliquée?

4. What a good idea! But isn't French cooking complicated?

5. — Vraiment, non. Il y a certainement des plats célèbres qui sont très compliqués, mais il n'y a rien de mystérieux dans la bonne cuisine française. Je vais vous dire les trois secrets, gratis.

5. Not really. There are certainly some famous dishes which are very complicated but there is nothing mysterious in good French cooking. I am going to tell you the three secrets, free.

6. — Pour commencer, tout ce qui entre dans un plat doit être de bonne qualité: le beurre, les oeufs, la viande, les légumes, tout, enfin; ensuite, il faut avoir le goût et l'amour de la cuisine; et après, du beurre, du beurre, et encore du beurre.

6. First, everything that goes into a dish must be of good quality; the butter, the eggs, the meat, the vegetables, everything, in short; then, one must have a taste for and a love of cooking; then, butter, butter, and more butter.

7. — Merci pour les trois secrets. Je vais les raconter tout de suite à ma femme.

7. Thank you for the three secrets. I am going to tell them at once to my wife.

8. — Voilà un mari modèle!

8. There's a model husband!

9. — M. Picard, j'ai un appétit de loup! Voulez-vous casser la croûte avec moi?

9. Mr. Picard, I'm as hungry as a wolf! Will you have a bite (*Lit.* break the crust) with me?

10. — Avec plaisir, M. Potter.

10. With pleasure, Mr. Potter.

Pronunciation and Spelling Aids

Practice aloud

Vous savez, sans doute, Monsieur Potter, que la bonne cuisine française est un des plus grands plaisirs du touriste en France.

(Voo sa-vay, sahñ doot, muh-syeu pu-**tehr** kuh la bun küee-zeen frahñ-**seh** zeh teuñ day plü grahñ pleh-zeer dü too-reest ahñ **frahñs.**)

Building Vocabulary

A. Some French cooking expressions adopted in English

1. **le bouillon** (boo-yawñ) broth
2. **le consommé** (kawñ-su-may) clear soup
3. **la purée** (pü-ray) mashed vegetables
4. **sauté** (soh-tay) fried
5. **au gratin** (oh gra-tañ) dressed with bread crumbs or cheese, and browned in the oven
6. **les petits fours** (puh-tee-**foor**) small cakes
7. **hors d'oeuvres** (ur-**deuvr**) appetizers served at the beginning of a meal

B. Some French dishes that are not difficult to prepare

1. **la soupe à l'oignon** (soop a lu-**nyawñ**) onion soup
2. **le poulet Marengo** (poo-leh ma-rañ-**goh**) chicken Marengo
3. **le boeuf bourguignon** (beuf boor-gee-**nyawñ**) beef stew Burgundy style
4. **la blanquette de veau** (blahñ-keht duh **voh**) veal stew in cream sauce
5. **les haricots verts** (lay a-ree-koh **vehr**) green beans
6. **les épinards à la crème** (lay zay-pee-nar a la **krehm**) creamed spinach
7. **les petits pois à la française** (puh-tee pwa a la frahñ-**sehz**) peas with lettuce and onions
8. **la poire Hélène** (pawr ay-**lehn**) poached pear with chocolate sauce
9. **les fraises Chantilly** (frehz shahñ-tee-**yee**) strawberries with whipped cream
10. **la crème Chantilly** (krehm shahñ-tee-**yee**) whipped cream

French Expressions

1. **cela arrive** that happens
2. **assez souvent** quite often
3. **bien entendu** of course
4. **faire cadeau de** to make a gift of, to give
5. **beaucoup d'autres** many others
6. **Quelle bonne idée!** What a good idea!
7. **rien de mystérieux** nothing mysterious
8. **tout ce qui** everything that

Exercise No. 118—Completion of Text

1. **Je connais un peu la** (good French cooking).
2. **C'est** (one of the greatest pleasures) **du touriste.**
3. **J'invite un client important** (to lunch).
4. (That happens) **assez souvent.**
5. **La cuisine française** (makes us a gift) **de beaucoup d'expressions.**
6. (Send your wife) **un bon livre sur la cuisine française.**
7. (I am going to tell you) **les trois secrets.**
8. (All that) **entre dans un plat doit être** (of good quality).
9. (One must have) **l'amour de la cuisine.**
10. **Et après** (butter, butter, and more butter).

Grammar Notes

1. Present tense of **envoyer,** *to send*

I send, you send, etc.

j'envoie (zhahñ-vwa)	**nous envoyons** (noo zahñ-vwa-**yawñ**)
tu envoies (tü ahñ-**vwa**)	**vous envoyez** (voo zahñ-vwa-yay)
il envoie (eel ahñ-**vwa**)	**ils envoient** (eel zahñ-**vwa**)
elle envoie (ehl ahñ-**vwa**)	**elles envoient** (ehl zahñ-**vwa**)

Imperative: **envoie** send **envoyons** let us send **envoyez** send
Like **envoyer:** **renvoyer,** *to send back*

2. Independent pronouns used after prepositions

a. Note carefully the personal pronouns used after prepositions. They are called *independent* pronouns because they are usually independent of the verb. They are sometimes called *emphatic* pronouns.

après *moi* after *me*	**près de *nous*** near *us*
sans *toi* without *you*	**loin de *vous*** far from *you*
avec *lui* with *him*	**excepté *eux*** except *them* (*m*)
pour *elle* for *her*	**derrière *elles*** behind *them* (*f*)

b. Note the independent pronouns with the preposition **chez**:

chez moi at my house (home)	**chez nous** at our house (home)
chez toi at your house (home)	**chez vous** at your house (home)
chez lui at his house (home)	**chez eux** (*m*) at their house (home)
chez elle at her house (home)	**chez elles** (*f*) at their house (home)

c. The independent pronouns with the preposition **à** after **est** and **sont** indicate possession.

Ce chapeau est à moi (à toi, à lui, à elle)	This hat is mine (belongs to me) (yours, his, hers)
Ces chaises sont à nous (à vous, à eux, à elles)	These chairs are ours (yours, theirs, *m*, theirs, *f*)

Exercise No. 119. Complete the following in French:

1. **Voulez-vous aller** (with me)?
2. **Cette carte est** (for you), **mon enfant.**
3. **Ils vont dîner** (at my house).
4. **Nous restons** (at home) **en famille.**
5. **Mlle. Martin n'est pas** (at her house).
6. **L'avion va partir** (without them, *m*).
7. **Il est assis** (near her).
8. **Il y a beaucoup de choses** (around us).
9. **Ces places-ci sont** (ours).
10. **Ces places-là sont** (theirs, *f*).

3. Other uses of the independent pronouns

a. When the pronoun stands alone (without a verb):

Qui a un appétit de loup?	Who is as hungry as a wolf?
Moi. Toi. Lui. Elle.	I. You. He. She.
Nous. Vous. Eux. Elles.	We. You. They (*m*). They (*f*).

b. For emphasis and in double pronoun subjects:

Moi, j'aime le théâtre.	I like the theatre.
Lui et moi, nous étudions le français.	He and I (we) are studying French.

c. With **c'est** and **ce sont:**

C'est moi. It is I.
C'est toi. It is you.
C'est lui (elle). It is he (she).
C'est nous. It is we.
C'est vous. It is you.
Ce sont eux (elles). It is they.

NOTE: **Ce sont** is used with **eux** and **elles.**

d. In the affirmative imperative, **me** becomes **moi** and **te** becomes **toi.**

Dites-moi où vous demeurez. Tell me where you live.
Lève-toi, mon enfant. Get up, child.
But: **Ne me dites pas. Ne te lève pas.** Do not tell me. Do not get up.

Exercise No. 120. Complete the following in French:

1. **Qui fait de grands progrès dans ses études?** (He). (She).
2. (I) **j'aime le français; elle aime l'anglais.**
3. **Qui frappe** (knocks) **à la porte? C'est** (me). **C'est** (we). **Ce sont** (they, *m*).
4. **Habille-**(yourself), **Louise.**
5. **Envoyez-**(me) **les fleurs.**
6. **Vous venez plus tard que** (he).
7. (She and I), **nous allons au théâtre.**
8. **Qui étudie diligemment?** (I).
9. **Est-ce que ce stylo-ci est** (yours)?
10. **Non, c'est** (his).

Exercise No. 121—Questionnaire

1. **Quel est un des plus grands plaisirs du touriste en France?**
2. **Est-ce que M. Potter connaît la cuisine française?**
3. **De quoi la cuisine française nous fait-elle cadeau?**
4. **Qu'est-ce que M. Potter doit faire à Paris?**
5. **Est-ce que la cuisine française est compliquée?**
6. **Quel est le troisième secret de la bonne cuisine?**
7. **Est-ce que M. Potter va les raconter à sa femme?**
8. **Qui est un mari modèle?**
9. **Qui a un appétit de loup?**
10. **Qui va casser la croûte avec M. Potter?**

RÉVISION 5
CHAPITRES 20–23 PREMIÈRE PARTIE

NOUNS

1. **l'amour**	11. **les haricots verts**	21. **la pluie**	1. love	11. green beans	21. rain
2. **l'appétit**	12. **l'hiver**	22. **la poire**	2. appetite	12. winter	22. pear
3. **le boeuf**	13. **l'imperméable**	23. **le poulet**	3. beef	13. raincoat	23. chicken
4. **le cadeau**	14. **le légume**	24. **le reste**	4. gift	14. vegetable	24. remainder
5. **le climat**	15. **la mer**	25. **la saison**	5. climate	15. sea	25. season
6. **le coin**	16. **la neige**	26. **la sortie**	6. corner	16. snow	26. exit
7. **le conseil**	17. **les moyens**	27. **la soupe**	7. advice	17. means	27. soup
8. **le dessert**	18. **le parapluie**	28. **le thé**	8. dessert	18. umbrella	28. tea
9. **les épinards**	19. **le pardessus**	29. **le veau**	9. spinach	19. overcoat	29. veal
10. **les fraises**	20. **le plateau**	30. **la visite**	10. strawberries	20. tray	30. visit

VERBS

1. **apporter**	9. **neiger**	17. **couvrir**	1. to bring	9. to snow	17. to cover
2. **briller**	10. **oublier**	18. **je couvre**	2. to shine	10. to forget	18. I cover
3. **casser**	11. **quitter**	19. **devenir**	3. to break	11. to leave, quit	19. to become
4. **chercher**	12. **raconter**	20. **je deviens**	4. to look for	12. to tell about	20. I become
5. **envoyer**	13. **réchauffer**	21. **pleuvoir**	5. to send	13. to warm	21. to rain
6. **j'envoie**	14. **tomber**	22. **il pleut**	6. I send	14. to fall	22. it is raining
7. **frapper**	15. **tâcher**	23. **sourire**	7. to knock	15. to try	23. to smile
8. **nager**	16. **verser**	24. **je souris**	8. to swim	16. to pour, spend	24. I smile

ADJECTIVES

1. **agréable**	6. **faux (fausse *f*)**	11. **pressé**	1. agreeable	6. false	11. in a hurry
2. **chaud**	7. **froid**	12. **sale**	2. hot	7. cold	12. nasty, dirty
3. **clair**	8. **plein**	13. **trempé**	3. clear	8. full	13. soaked
4. **couvert**	9. **pâle**	14. **sûr**	4. covered	9. pale	14. sure
5. **enchanté**	10. **préféré**	15. **vif**	5. delighted	10. preferred	15. brisk, lively

ADVERBS

1. dehors	**3. tôt**	**5. plus tôt**	1. outside	3. soon	5. sooner
2. plutôt	**4. tard**	**6. plus tard**	2. rather	4. late	6. later

PREPOSITIONS

1. à côté de	**2. au lieu de**	**3. sauf**	1. at the side of	2. instead of	3. except

NEGATIVES

1. ne–pas	**3. ne–pas encore**	**5. ne–rien**	1. not	3. not yet	5. nothing
2. ne–jamais	**4. ne—plus**	**6. ne—que**	2. never	4. no longer, no more	6. only
		7. ne–personne			7. nobody

FRENCH EXPRESSIONS

1. cela arrive	**7. ça va mieux**	1. that happens	7. I feel better
2. assez souvent	**8. tout à coup**	2. quite often	8. all of a sudden
3. par contre	**9. moi-même**	3. on the contrary	9. myself
4. petit à petit	**10. lui-même**	4. little by little	10. himself
5. il pleut à verse	**11. elle-même**	5. it is raining buckets	11. herself
6. quel sale temps!	**12. le voilà**	6. what nasty weather!	12. there he (it) is

DEUXIÈME PARTIE

Exercise No. 122. From Group II select the opposite of each word in Group I:

I		II	
1. tôt, bientôt	**7. agréable**	**a. beaucoup de temps**	**g. libre**
2. vieux, ancien	**8. toujours**	**b. ne—jamais**	**h. rarement**
3. peu de temps	**9. faux**	**c. tard**	**i. recevoir**
4. chercher	**10. quelque chose**	**d. vrai**	**j. pas encore**
5. occupé	**11. souvent**	**e. trouver**	**k. désagréable**
6. envoyer	**12. déjà**	**f. jeune, nouveau**	**l. rien**

Exercise No. 123. Complete the following sentences in French:

1. **Quand il fait froid** (I am cold).
2. **Quand il fait chaud** (I am warm).
3. **En été** (it is warm).
4. **Au printemps** (it rains a great deal).
5. **En automne** (it is cool).
6. **En hiver** (it is cold).
7. **Quand il pleut je porte** (a raincoat).
8. **Quand il neige** (I wear an overcoat).
9. **La pluie** (is falling).
10. **J'aime bien** (all the seasons).

Exercise No. 124. Select the group of words in Column II which best completes each sentence begun in Column I:

I	II
1. Moi, je préfère le climat de la France,	**a. quelque chose du climat de la France.**
2. Prenez du thé au rhum	**b. préparer quelques bons plats français.**
3. Je vais vous dire	**c. arriver à cinq heures de l'après-midi.**
4. C'est vrai que l'hiver	**d. mais elle préfère celui de la Suisse.**
5. Prenez un parapluie	**e. mais celles-là sont libres.**
6. Le deux messieurs entrent dans le salon	**f. pour vous réchauffer.**
7. Ces places-ci sont occupées,	**g. à Paris est souvent désagréable.**
8. Il n'est pas difficile de	**h. en causant d'un ton animé.**
9. Je vais faire cadeau à ma femme	**i. parce qu'il pleut à verse.**
10. Le train de Lyon doit	**j. d'un bon livre sur la cuisine française.**

Exercise No. 125. Complete the answer to each question with the correct direct or indirect object pronoun in French:

1. Qu'est-ce que la bonne dit à M. Potter?	**1. Elle** (to him) **dit: — Quel sale temps!**
2. Qu'est-ce que M. Picard donne à la bonne?	**2. Il** (to her) **donne son parapluie.**

3. **Est-ce que M. Potter attend M. Picard?**
4. **Est-il content de voir M. Picard?**
5. **Pourquoi est-ce que M. Picard prend une tasse de thé?**
6. **Qu'est-ce que M. Potter dit à M. Picard?**
7. **Préférez-vous les films policiers?**
8. **Quand allez-vous quitter la ville?**
9. **Qui vous invite à déjeuner?**
10. **Qu'est-ce que vous donnez aux enfants?**

3. **Oui, il** (him) **attend.**
4. **Il est content de** (him) **voir.**
5. **Il** (it) **prend pour** (himself) **réchauffer.**
6. **Il dit: — Permettez-**(me) **de** (you) **servir.**
7. **Nous ne** (them) **préférons pas.**
8. **Je vais** (it) **quitter l'été prochain.**
9. **Mon ami Charles** (me) **invite à déjeuner.**
10. **Je** (to them) **donne un ballon du football.**

Exercise No. 126. Translate the English sentences using the negative indicated. **ne** must precede the verb.

1. (**ne ___ personne**) I do not know anybody.
2. (**ne ___ jamais**) We never eat meat.
3. (**ne ___ que**) I have only one teacher.
4. (**ne ___ plus**) She no longer wants that hat.
5. (**ne ___ pas encore**) Joan does not go to school yet.
6. (**ne ___ pas ___ non plus**) I am not tired either.
7. (**ne ___ plus**) We have no more (**de**) time.
8. (**ne ___ rien**) Why do you say nothing?
9. (**ne ___ ni ___ ni**) We have neither the time nor the money.

Dialogue
Au Restaurant

1. **— Bonjour monsieur. Voici la carte.**	1. Good day, sir. Here is the menu.
2. **— Merci. Qu'est-ce qu'il y a de bon aujourd'hui?**	2. Thank you. What is there that's good today?
3. **Nous avons un très bon dîner à prix fixe aujourd'hui: soupe à l'oignon, entrecôte aux pommes, tomates farcies, salade, fromage et une belle tarte aux pêches.**	3. We have a very good fixed-price dinner today: onion soup, steak with potatoes, stuffed tomatoes, salad, cheese, and a fine peach tart.
4. **— Qu'y a-t-il de bon à la carte?**	4. What is there that's good à la carte?
5. **— Je vous recommande le canard. C'est de l'extra.**	5. I recommend the duck. It is especially good.
6. **— Très bien. J'aime beaucoup le canard. Apportez-moi pour commencer la soupe à l'oignon.**	6. Very good. I like duck very much. Bring me the onion soup to begin with.
7. **— Très bien, monsieur. Voulez-vous un légume? Le canard est garni de pommes sautées.**	7. Very good, sir. Do you want a vegetable? The duck is garnished with sautéed potatoes.
8. **— Non merci. Pas de légumes. Une salade, c'est tout.**	8. No thank you. No vegetables. A salad, that's all.
9. **— Bien, monsieur. Voulez-vous un fromage?**	9. Good, sir. Do you want cheese?
10. **— Ça oui. Comment est le camembert? Est-il bien fait?**	10. That, yes. How is the camembert? Is it ripe?
11. **— Il est au point, monsieur, un délice!**	11. It is just right, sir, a treat!
12. **— Très bien. Avec ça un café bien fort.**	12. Very good. With that, a cup of good strong coffee.
13. **— Et comme boisson?**	13. And what will you drink? (*Lit.* and as a beverage?)
14. **— Une demi-bouteille de Pommard.**	14. A half bottle of Pommard.
15. **— Très bien, monsieur. Tout de suite.**	15. Very good, sir. Right away.
16. **— Le repas terminé M. Potter dit: — Garçon, l'addition, s'il vous plaît.**	16. At the end of the meal Mr. Potter says: "Waiter, the check, please."
17. **— Voici, monsieur.**	17. Here you are, sir.
18. **— Est-ce que le service est compris?**	18. Is the service charge included?
19. **— Oui monsieur, voyez-vous, là, en bas.**	19. Yes sir, see, there, at the bottom.
20. **— Merci.**	20. Thank you.
21. **— Merci bien, monsieur.**	21. Thank you very much, sir.

Exercise No. 127—Lecture
Gérard N'Aime Pas Étudier L'Arithmétique

Un jour, en rentrant de l'école, Gérard dit à sa mère, — Je n'aime pas étudier l'arithmétique. C'est si difficile. Pourquoi avons-nous besoin de tant d'exercices et de tant de problèmes? Nous avons des machines à calculer, n'est-ce pas? Alors!

Mme. Davis regarde son fils et dit, — Tu as tort, mon petit. On ne peut pas se passer de[1] nombres. Par exemple, on a toujours besoin de verser de l'argent, de faire des achats, d'estimer les distances, et puis, et puis. La mère s'arrête en voyant que Gérard ne fait pas attention à ce qu'elle dit.

— A propos, continue-t-elle en souriant, le baseball ne t'intéresse pas non plus, mon petit?

— Par exemple! Tu veux rire.[2]

— Alors, si les Dodgers ont gagné quatre-vingts parties,[3] et ils en ont perdu[4] vingt, sais-tu quel pourcentage de parties ils ont gagné?

En entendant cela Gérard s'écrie, — Tu as raison, maman. Les nombres, l'arithmétique et les mathématiques sont très importants. Je crois que maintenant je vais étudier beaucoup plus.

NOTE 1. **se passer de,** *to do without* 2. You are joking (*Lit.* You want to laugh) 3. games 4. have lost, **perdre,** to lose

---

CHAPITRE 24 (VINGT-QUATRE)

LES FRANÇAIS
THE FRENCH PEOPLE

1. — M. Picard, je vais vous poser quelques questions sur les Français. Êtes-vous prêt? Voulez-vous encore un cigare? Voici les allumettes et le cendrier.

2. — Merci, M. Potter. Je suis bien à mon aise. Continuez, s'il vous plaît.

3. — Pour commencer, est-ce que les Français se ressemblent plus ou moins,[1] ou est-ce qu'ils diffèrent en caractère selon la géographie du pays?

4. — Je vais vous dire tout de suite, M. Potter, qu'un Français est un Français partout. Il est vrai qu'il y a de très grandes différences entre tous les Français, non seulement à cause de la géographie, mais aussi à cause de leurs métiers.

5. — Dites moi, M. Picard, quelles sont quelques-unes de ces différences?

6. — Eh bien, pour commencer, au nord-ouest, nous avons les pêcheurs et les marins de la Bretagne, plus souvent en mer que chez eux; très dévots, et très dévoués à leur eau de vie, le Calvados. Ensuite, les fermiers de la Normandie, ronds et railleurs. Et après, les ouvriers des mines et des usines du nord-est, débrouillards et syndiqués.

7. — Tout cela, seulement pour commencer? Mais, M. Picard, nous allons rester ici toute la nuit!

8. — Je crois que nous n'avons pas besoin de continuer. Vous comprenez par exemple, que l'homme du Midi,[2] bavard et blagueur, ne ressemble pas trop au montagnard taciturne de l'Auvergne.

9. — Sans connaître trop les détails je le comprends bien.

10. — Mais, malgré toutes ces différences, ils sont tous Français; c'est à dire, qu'ils aiment beaucoup discuter, surtout les questions politiques; qu'ils n'ont pas peur des idées; qu'ils sont fiers de leur tradition de démocratie, de belles-lettres, de philosophie et de science; et finalement qu'ils aiment tous la bonne cuisine et le bon vin.

11. — Je les aime déjà sans les connaître.

1. Mr. Picard, I am going to ask you a few questions about the French people. Are you ready? Do you want another cigar? Here are the matches and the ash tray.

2. Thank you, Mr. Potter. I am very comfortable. Continue, please.

3. To begin with, are the French people more or less alike,[1] or do they differ in character according to the geography of the country?

4. I'll tell you at once, Mr. Potter, that a Frenchman is a Frenchman everywhere. It is true that there are some very great differences among all Frenchmen, not only because of the geography but also because of their occupations.

5. Tell me, Mr. Picard, what are some of these differences?

6. Well, to begin with, in the northwest we have the fishermen and sailors of Brittany, more often at sea than at home; very devout, and very devoted to their brandy, Calvados. Then, the farmers of Normandy, rotund and fond of bantering. And then the workers in the mines and factories of the northeast, resourceful and unionized.

7. All this only to begin with? But, Mr. Picard, we're going to be here all night!

8. I think that we don't need to go on. You realize for example, that the southerner (*Lit.* man of the south), talkative, teller of tall stories, is not much like the taciturn mountaineer of Auvergne.

9. Without knowing the details too well, I do realize that.

10. But in spite of all these differences, they are all Frenchmen; that is to say, that they love to discuss, especially questions of politics; that they are not afraid of ideas; that they are proud of their tradition of democracy, of literature, of philosophy, and of science; and finally that they all love good cooking and good wine.

11. I like them already without knowing them.

12. — Si c'est comme ça à présent, qu'est-ce qui va se passer au mois de juin pendant votre visite?
12. If that's the case now, what will happen in the month of June during your visit?

13. — Ça va être un roman d'amour, M. Picard!
13. It is going to be a love story, Mr. Picard!

NOTE 1. *Lit.* Do the French people resemble each other more or less? 2. **le Midi,** the south of France

Pronunciation and Spelling Aids

Practice aloud

Monsieur Picard, je vais vous poser quelques questions sur les Français. (Muh-syeu pee-**kar**, zhuh veh voo poh-zay kehl-kuh kehst-**yawñ** sur lay frahñ-**seh.**)

Êtes-vous prêt? Voulez-vous encore un cigare? (Eht-voo **preh**? Voo-lay-voo zahñ-kur euñ see-**gar?**)

Voici les allumettes et le cendrier. (Vwa-see lay za-lü-**meht** ay luh sahñ-dree-**ay.**)

Building Vocabulary

A. Points of the compass

le nord (nur) north
le sud (süd) south
l'est (lehst) east
l'ouest (lwehst) west

B. **Quelques locutions de fumer** Some smoking terms

le cigare (see-gar) cigar
la cigarette (see-ga-**reht**)
l'allumette (la-lü-**meht**) match
la pipe (peep) pipe
le tabac (ta-**ba**) tobacco
le cendrier (sahñ-dree-**ay**) ashtray
défense de fumer (day-fahñs duh fü-**may**) no smoking

C. **Des ouvriers** (*m*), **ouvrières** (*f*) Some working men and women

le pêcheur (peh-**sheur**) fisherman
le marin (ma-**rañ**) seaman
le fermier (fehr-**myay**) farmer
la cuisinière (kwee-zu-**nyehr**) cook
le camionneur truck driver
le mécanicien mechanic
les ouvriers des mines (leh-zoo-vree-ay day meen) miners
les ouvriers des usines (leh-zoo-vree-ay day zü-zeen) factory workers
la couturière (koo-tü-rj-**ehr**) dressmaker, seamstress

French Expressions

1. **avoir peur de** (a-vwar **peur** duh) to be afraid of
2. **se passer** (suh pah-**say**) to happen
3. **se passer de** to do without
4. **Qu'est-ce qui se passe?** What is happening?
5. **Qu'est-ce qui arrive?** What is happening?

Exercise No. 128—Completion of Text

1. **Je vais vous poser** (a few) **questions.**
2. **Voici** (the matches and the ashtray).
3. **Je suis** (very comfortable).
4. (They are alike) **plus ou moins.**
5. **Mais un Français est un Français** (everywhere).
6. **Il y a de grandes différences** (as you say).
7. **Quelles sont** (some of these) **différences?**
8. (The fisherman and seaman) **sont très dévots.**
9. (The farmers) **sont ronds et railleurs.**
10. (The mine workers) **sont syndiqués.**
11. (We don't need) **de continuer.**
12. **L'homme du Midi** (does not resemble) **au montagnard.**
13. **Ils aiment beaucoup** (to discuss).

Grammar Notes

1. Reflexive verbs with reciprocal meaning

The reflexive pronouns are sometimes translated *each other* or *one another*. This use is known as the reflexive with reciprocal meaning.

Les Français se ressemblent plus ou moins. French people resemble each other more or less.
Nous nous rencontrons tous les jeudis. We meet each other (one another) every Thursday.

If the meaning is not clear, **l'un (une) l'autre** and **les uns (unes) les autres** are used after the verb. Thus:

Nous nous aimons l'un l'autre. We love one another.
Elles se donnent des cadeaux les unes aux autres. They give gifts to each other.

2. Verbs after prepositions

a. In English the present participle of the verb is used after prepositions. In French the infinitive of the verb is used after any preposition except **en**.

Sans connaître les détails je le comprends. Without knowing the details I realize it.
Avant de sortir il met son pardessus. Before leaving he puts on his overcoat.

b. After the preposition **en** the French use the present participle. In this case **en** is translated by *while, on, by, upon, in,* or is not translated at all.

Ils entrent dans la salle à manger en causant d'un ton animé. They enter the dining room (while) chatting in an animated tone.
En sortant de la gare ils appellent un taxi. (On) leaving the station, they call a taxi.

3. Formation of the present participle

All French verbs, except **être, avoir,** and **savoir,** form the present participle by dropping the ending **-ons** from the **nous** form of the present tense and adding **-ant.** Thus:

donnons we give	**vendons** we sell	**finissons** we finish	**voyons** we see
donnant giving	**vendant** selling	**finissant** finishing	**voyant** seeing

but

avons we have	**sommes** we are	**savons** we know
ayant having	**étant** being	**sachant** knowing

NOTE. Be sure to distinguish the pronunciation of the endings **-ons** (awñ) and **-ant** (ahñ).

Exercise No. 129. Write the **nous** form of the present tense, and the present participle of the following verbs.

Exemple: aller nous allons allant

1. étudier	**4. acheter**	**7. choisir**	**10. connaître**	**13. compter**	**16. faire**
2. venir	**5. vouloir**	**8. finir**	**11. apprendre**	**14. dormir**	**17. avoir**
3. lire	**6. dire**	**9. bâtir**	**12. appeler**	**15. mettre**	**18. être**

4. **quelque, quelqu'un**

a. **quelque** *some* (*plural* **quelques** *some, any, a few*) is an adjective and therefore modifies a noun.

Voulez-vous quelque chose? Do you want something?
Je vais poser quelques questions. I am going to ask a few questions.

b. **quelqu'un, quelqu'une,** *somebody, anybody,* (*plural* **quelques-uns, quelques-unes**) *some, a few, several,* is a pronoun and therefore is not followed by a noun.

Quelqu'un sait la verité. Somebody knows the truth.
Quelques-uns de ces élèves apprennent le français. Several of these pupils are learning French.
Je connais quelques-unes de ces différences. I know several of these differences.

NOTE. **plusieurs** also means several: **Nous avons plusieurs cahiers.**

Exercise No. 130. Complete these sentences with the correct form of **quelque** or **quelqu'un.**

1. **Il y a** (somebody) **dans la cuisine.**
2. **Nous achetons** (a few) **légumes.**
3. (Some) **de ces messieurs sont Français.**
4. (Some) **de ces dames sont Anglaises.**
5. **Quelles sont** (some) **de ces différences?**
6. **Nous apprenons** (some) **locutions françaises.**
7. **J'ai** (some) **livres pour vous.**
8. **Nous avons** (a few) **cadeaux pour maman.**
9. **Voulez-vous** (some) **de ces poires?**
10. **Est-ce que vous attendez** (somebody)?

Exercise No. 131—Questionnaire

1. **Qu'est-ce que M. Potter va faire?**
2. **Qu'est-ce que M. Potter demande pour commencer?**
3. **Est-il vrai qu'il y a de très grandes différences entre tous les Français?**
4. **Pourquoi y a-t-il des différences entre les Français?**
5. **Comment sont les pêcheurs de la Bretagne?**
6. **Comment est l'homme du Midi?**
7. **Est-ce qu'il ressemble au montagnard de l'Auvergne?**
8. **Est-ce que les Français aiment bien discuter?**
9. **De quoi les Français sont-ils fiers?**
10. **Qu'est-ce qu'ils aiment tous?**

CHAPITRE 25 (VINGT-CINQ)

L'ART ET LA MODE
ART AND FASHION

1. — M. Potter vient de recevoir une grande caisse de marchandise que M. Picard est en train d'admirer.

1. Mr. Potter has just received a large case of merchandise that Mr. Picard is admiring.

2. — Ce sont des échantillons de riches étoffes de soie de Lyon, de beaux tissus de lin, de velours, et de laine. Regardez, M. Picard, cette belle étoffe de laine de la maison Dior pour un manteau de dame.

2. These are samples of rich silk materials from Lyons, and of beautiful linen, velvet and woolen fabrics. Look, Mr. Picard, at this fine woolen material from Dior for a lady's coat.

3. — Tiens! Christian Dior? Mais n'est-il pas couturier?

3. Well, well! Christian Dior? But isn't he a couturier? (dress designer)

4. — Certainement. Un des plus connus. Les grandes maisons de couture font le commerce non seulement des robes et des manteaux, mais aussi de la lingerie, des parfums, des gants, des bas, et des tissus; et qui sait si l'année prochaine ils ne vont pas offrir aux élégantes des éviers de cuisine en couleurs assorties, et parfumés.

4. Certainly. One of the best known. The big dressmaking houses do business not only in dresses and coats, but also in lingerie, perfume, gloves, stockings, and fabrics; and who knows if next year they won't offer fashionable women perfumed kitchen sinks in assorted colors.

5. — M. Potter, je crois que vous n'aimez pas la mode.

5. Mr. Potter, I think that you don't like fashion.

6. — J'aime beaucoup les belles choses telles que ces jolies étoffes en couleurs magnifiques; mais la mode, c'est quelque chose d'autre.

6. I'm very fond of beautiful things such as these lovely fabrics in magnificent colors; but fashion, that's another matter.

7. — Pourtant, la couture est un art, n'est-ce pas? Et vous êtes amateur des arts.

7. And yet, dressmaking is an art, isn't it? And you love (*Lit.* are a lover of) the arts.

8. — C'est vrai, mais je préfère les beaux arts: la peinture, la sculpture, l'architecture. Je compte beaucoup sur le plaisir de visiter le Musée du Louvre pour voir l'art des grands maîtres. J'espère aussi visiter les musées de l'art moderne.

8. That's true, but I prefer the fine arts: painting, sculpture and architecture. I am looking forward eagerly to visiting the Louvre Museum to see the art of the great masters. I hope also to visit the museums of modern art.

9. — Vous êtes un homme d'affaires tout à fait exceptionnel. Vous vous intéressez à toutes sortes de choses: l'art, l'histoire, les belles-lettres. Je vous admire.

9. You are a very unusual businessman. You take an interest in all sorts of things, art, history, literature. I admire you.

10. — Et moi, je vous admire aussi. Vous êtes un professeur tout à fait exceptionnel.

10. And I admire you too. You are a very unusual teacher.

11. — Bon. Formons une société d'estime mutuelle.

11. Good. Let us form a mutual admiration society.

12. — Très bien. Prochaine réunion de la société: Mardi à huit heures.

12. Very good. Next meeting of the society: Tuesday at eight o'clock.

13. — Entendu. Au revoir, co-sociétaire.

13. Agreed. Goodby, fellow-member.

14. Ils se serrent la main.

14. They shake hands.

Pronunciation and Spelling Aids

A. Practice aloud

M. Potter vient de recevoir une grande caisse de marchandise que M. Picard est en train de regarder et d'admirer.

(Muh-syeu pu-tehr vyañ duh ruh-suh-**vwar** ün grahñd kehs duh mar-shahñ-**deez** kuh muh-syeu pee-kar eh tahñ **trañ** duh ruh-gar-day ay dad-mee-**ray.**)

B. Remember: **é** is pronounced **ay**, and **è**, **eh**; **e** before a double consonant is pronounced **eh**

je préfère (zhuh pray-**fehr**) **j'achète** (zha-**sheht**) **j'appelle** (zha-**pehl**) **je jette** (zhuh **zheht**)

Building Vocabulary

A. **Les vêtements** (veht-**mahñ**) Clothes

les bas (bah) stockings
la blouse (blooz) blouse
la ceinture (sañ-**tür**) belt
le chapeau (sha-**poh**) hat
le complet (kawñ-**pleh**) suit (man's)
le costume tailleur (tah-**yeur**) suit (woman's)
le fichu (fee-**shü**) small shawl
les gants (gahñ) gloves
la jupe (zhüp) skirt
les chaussettes (*f.*) (shoh-**seht**) socks
la chaussure (shoh-**sür**) shoe, footwear
la chemise (shuh-**meez**) shirt
la cravate (kra-**vat**) necktie
le manteau (mahñ-**toh**) coat, cloak
le pantalon (pahñ-ta-**lawñ**) trousers
le mouchoir (moo-**shwar**) handkerchief
la robe (rub) dress

B. Noun combinations. In English we can put two nouns together using the first one as an adjective, e.g. *a silk dress, a wool coat, a school teacher,* etc. This is not done in French, which uses instead two nouns connected by **de (of)**.

une robe de soie a silk dress
un manteau de laine a wool coat
une ceinture de cuir a leather belt
les tissus de lin linen fabrics
le chapeau de velours velvet hat
l'étoffe de coton cotton cloth
le maître d'école school teacher
la classe de français French class
l'opéra de Paris the Paris opera
les rues de New-York New York streets

French Expressions

1. **venir de** + *infinitive* to have just (done something)
2. **venir de recevoir** to have just received
3. **il vient de recevoir** he has just received
4. **nous venons d'écrire** we have just written
5. **ils viennent de dîner** they have just dined
6. **être en train de** + *infinitive* to be in the act of (doing something)
7. **nous sommes en train de manger** we are eating
8. **il est en train d'admirer** he is admiring
9. **ils font le commerce de** they do business in
10. **c'est quelque chose d'autre** that's something else, another matter
11. **compter sur le plaisir de** + *infinitive* to look forward to (doing something)
12. **je compte sur le plaisir de faire votre connaissance** I look forward to meeting you
13. **se serrer la main** to shake hands
14. **nous nous serrons la main** we shake hands

Exercise No. 132—Completion of Text

1. **Il** (has just received) **des échantillons.**
2. **M. Picard** (is admiring) **les étoffes de soie.**
3. **Les maisons de couture font le commerce** (not only) **des robes** (but also) **de la lingerie, etc.**
4. **Je crois** (that you do not like) **la mode.**
5. **La couture est un art** (isn't it?)
6. **Je préfère** (the fine arts).
7. Painting, sculpture, and architecture.
8. (I look forward) **de visiter le Musée du Louvre.**
9. **Vous êtes un homme d'affaires** (very unusual).
10. I admire you.

Grammar Notes

1. Verbs with spelling changes

acheter, *to buy*	**préférer,** *to prefer*	**appeler,** *to call*
j'achète	**je préfère**	**j'appelle**
tu achètes	**tu préfères**	**tu appelles**
il, elle achète	**il, elle préfère**	**il, elle appelle**
nous achetons	**nous préférons**	**nous appelons**
vous achetez	**vous préférez**	**vous appelez**
ils, elles achètent	**ils, elles préfèrent**	**ils, elles appellent**

These verbs are regular **-er** verbs. There are, however, slight changes in the spelling of the stem before silent endings.

Like **acheter** (**e** of stem becomes **è** before silent endings)

lever, *to raise*	**je lève**	**tu lèves**	**il, elle lève**
	nous levons	**vous levez**	**ils, elles lèvent**

Like **préférer** (**é** of stem becomes **è** before silent endings)

espérer, *to hope*	**j'espère**	**tu espères**	**il, elle espère**
	nous espérons	**vous espérez**	**ils, elles espèrent**
célébrer, *to celebrate*	**je célèbre**	**tu célèbres**	**il, elle célèbre**
	nous célébrons	**vous célébrez**	**ils, elles célèbrent**
répéter, *to repeat*	**je répète**	**tu répètes**	**il, elle répète**
	nous répétons	**vous répétez**	**ils, elles répètent**

Like **appeler** (consonant of stem doubles before silent endings)

jeter, *to throw*	**je jette**	**tu jettes**	**il, elle jette**
	nous jetons	**vous jetez**	**ils, elles, jettent**

Exercise No. 133. Complete each sentence using the correct French verb form:

1. (She is buying) **quelques-uns de ces fichus.**
2. (Do you prefer) **les mouchoirs de soie?**
3. **Non,** (I prefer) **les mouchoirs de lin.**
4. (Let us repeat) **cette phrase.**
5. (I hope) **voir tout cela.**
6. **À quelle heure** (do you get up)?
7. (I get up) **à sept heures du matin.**
8. **En France on** (celebrates) **le 14 juillet.**
9. **Le fils ainé** (is named) **Charles.**
10. **Les enfants** (are throwing) **la balle.**
11. **Le maître** (calls) **les élèves.**
12. (I am raising) **la fenêtre.**

Exercise No. 134—Questionnaire

1. **Qu'est-ce que M. Potter vient de recevoir?**
2. **Que fait M. Picard?**
3. **Qu'y a-t-il dans la grande caisse?**
4. **De quelle maison est la belle étoffe de laine?**
5. **Qu'est-ce que M. Picard croit au sujet de M. Potter et la mode?**
6. **De quoi est-ce que M. Potter est amateur?**
7. **Qu'est-ce que M. Potter va voir au Musée du Louvre?**
8. **Qu'est-ce qu'il espère visiter aussi?**
9. **À quoi M. Potter s'intéresse-t-il?**
10. **Qu'est-ce que les messieurs vont former?**

CHAPITRE 26 (VINGT-SIX)

LES JOURS DE FÊTE DE LA FRANCE
FRENCH HOLIDAYS

1. — Ce soir parlons des jours de fête de la France. Cela va nous égayer un peu, car il fait du vent et il pleut.

1. This evening let's talk about the holidays of France. This will cheer us up a bit, for it's windy and raining.

2. — Volontiers. Je sais bien que le quatorze juillet on célèbre la prise de la Bastille, et que c'est la grande fête nationale. Mais dites-moi, M. Picard, comment est-ce qu'elle est célébrée?

2. Gladly. I know that on the fourteenth of July they celebrate the taking of the Bastille and that it's the big national holiday. But tell me, Mr. Picard, how is it celebrated?

3. — Partout en France, le quatorze juillet est célébré dans les rues. Tout le monde est dans la rue. À Paris chaque quartier a sa troupe de musiciens. On danse toute la journée et presque toute la nuit. On vend des crêpes, des gauffres, des glaces, et toutes sortes de friandises. Il y a les petits chevaux de bois, les Guignols pour les enfants, et naturellement les buvettes pour les grands.

3. Everywhere in France the fourteenth of July is celebrated in the streets. Everybody is in the street. In Paris each district has its band of musicians. They dance all day and nearly all night. They sell crêpes, waffles, ice cream, and all sorts of treats. There are the small carousels, puppet shows for the children, and naturally, bars for the grown-ups.

4. — J'espère voir tout cela et même danser dans les rues au mois de juillet. Et comment le Noël est-il célébré?

4. I hope to see all this and even to dance in the streets in July. And how is Christmas celebrated?

5. — M. Potter, je dois vous corriger. Noël est bien masculin, mais on dit *la* Noël, pas *le* Noël, parce que c'est *la fête de Noël* qu'on veut dire.

5. Mr. Potter, I must correct you. *Noël* is masculine all right, but we say *la Noël,* not *le Noël,* because it is *la fête de Noël* that is meant.

6. — Merci. Je recommence. Comment est-ce qu'on célèbre la Noël?

6. Thank you. I begin again. How is Christmas celebrated?

7. — Eh bien, on la célèbre en dormant.

7. Well, it is celebrated by sleeping.

8. — Comment!

8. What!

9. — Oui, monsieur, c'est ça. On dort parce qu'on a réveillonné toute la nuit. La veille de Noël correspond à la veille du jour de l'An, ici aux États-Unis. Naturellement les bons viveurs ne manquent pas de saisir l'occasion de réveillonner deux fois.

9. Yes, sir, that's right. People sleep because they have been celebrating all night. Christmas Eve corresponds to New Year's Eve here in the United States. Naturally, pleasure-seekers don't miss (*Lit.* fail to seize) the opportunity to celebrate twice.

10. — Et quand est-ce que les enfants reçoivent leurs cadeaux, si tout le monde dort?

10. And when do the children receive their presents, if everyone is sleeping?

11. — Le jour de l'An est le jour des cadeaux, qu'on appelle les étrennes. C'est une fête de réunion de famille. On tient table ouverte. On peut même dire qu'on tient auberge!

11. New Year's Day is the day for gifts which are called *étrennes.* It is a holiday for family gatherings. People keep open house. One can even say that they keep open inn!

12. — Ça doit être très agréable. Y a-t-il d'autres grandes fêtes en France?

12. That must be very agreeable. Are there other big holidays in France?

13. — Pendant la quinzaine de Pâques, on va à la campagne si c'est possible. À l'Assomption (le Quinze-Août) tout le monde quitte Paris si c'est possible ou non. La ville est morte pour la journée.

13. During the Easter fortnight, people go to the country if it's possiple. During the Feast of the Assumption (the 15th of August) everybody leaves Paris, whether it's possible or not. The city is dead for the day.

14. — Tiens! Ça doit être intéressant à voir!

14. Well, well! That must be interesting to see.

15. — Oui. Mais il n'y reste personne pour le voir.[1] Seulement un chien par-ci, par-là, au coin un agent mécontent, et le silence.

15. Yes. But nobody remains there to see it.[1] Only a dog here and there, at the corner a disgruntled policeman, and silence.

NOTE 1. This is almost literally true. Shops are shut and boarded up. One can walk for blocks in the center of the city and see scarcely a soul.

Pronunciation and Spelling Aids

A. Practice aloud

Ce soir parlons des jours de fêtes de la France.

(Suh swar par-lawñ day zhoor duh **feht** duh la **frahñs.**)

Cela va nous égayer un peu, car il fait du vent et il pleut.

(Suh-la va noo zay-geh-yay un **peu,** kar eel feh dü vahñ ay eel **pleu.**)

B. Remember: The letter **c** before **e** or **i** is pronounced like the **s** in *see*. Before **a, o** or **u,** the letter **c** is hard like a *k*. The **c** with a cedilla (**ç**) is always pronounced like the **s** in *see*. For example: **commencer** (ku-mahñ-**say**), **commençons** (ku-mahñ-**sawñ**), but **cacarder** (ka-kar-**day**), *honk like a goose*.

The letter **g**, before **e** or **i,** is pronounced *zh*. Before **a, o,** or **u,** the letter **g** is hard like *g* in *gate*. For example: **manger** (mahñ-**zhay**), **mangeons** (mahñ-**zhawñ**), but **gargouille** (gar-**gweej**), *gargoyle*.

Building Vocabulary

la Noël (nu-ehl) Christmas
le jour de l'An New Year's Day
Pâques *or* **Paque** (pahk) Easter
la veille (vehy) **de Noël** Christmas Eve
le quatorze juillet Bastille Day
Joyeux Noël Merry Christmas
Bonne Année Happy New Year
le Quinze-Août Feast of the Assumption

French Expressions

1. **tout le monde** everybody
2. **les étrennes** New Year's gifts
3. **On tient table ouverte.** People keep open house.
4. **toute la nuit** all night
5. **vouloir dire** to mean
6. **Qu'est-ce que ça veut dire?** What does that mean?

Exercise No. 135—Completion of Text

1. **Le quatorze juillet est** (the big national holiday).
2. (People celebrate) **la prise de la Bastille.**
3. (Everybody) **est dans la rue.**
4. **On danse** (all day) **et presque** (all night).
5. **Il y a** (the puppet shows) **pour les enfants.**
6. **Comment la Noël est-elle** (celebrated)?
7. **On la célèbre** (sleeping).
8. (New Year's Day) **est le jour des cadeaux.**
9. **On appelle ces cadeaux** (the New Year's gifts).
10. **On tient** (open house).
11. **Cela** (must be) **très agréable.**
12. (Everybody leaves Paris) **le Quinze-Août.**
13. **On voit seulement un chien** (here or there).

Grammar Notes

1. Present tense of **tenir,** *to hold, to keep.* The present tense of **tenir** is exactly like that of **venir.**

I hold, you hold, etc.		*I come, you come, etc.*	
je tiens (tyañ)	**nous tenons** (tuh-nawñ)	**je viens**	**nous venons**
tu tiens (tyañ)	**vous tenez** (tuh-nay)	**tu viens**	**vous venez**
il tient (tyañ)	**ils tiennent** (tyehn)	**il vient**	**ils viennent**
elle tient (tyañ)	**elles tiennent** (tyehn)	**elle vient**	**elles viennent**

Other verbs like **tenir** are: **détenir,** *to detain;* **retenir,** *to reserve, to hold back;* **obtenir,** *to obtain;* **appartenir à,** *to belong to;* **contenir,** *to contain;* **soutenir,** *to support.*

2. More verbs with spelling changes. **commencer** to begin; **manger** to eat

I begin, you begin, etc.		*I eat, you eat, etc.*	
je commence	**nous commençons**	**je mange**	**nous mangeons**
tu commences	**vous commencez**	**tu manges**	**vous mangez**
il, elle commence	**ils, elles commencent**	**il, elle mange**	**ils, elles mangent**

Verbs whose infinitives end in **-cer** must add a cedilla under the **c** before the ending **-ons** in order to keep the **c** soft, like *s:* **commençons** (ku-mahñ-sawñ). Verbs whose infinitives end in **-ger** must add an **e** after the **g** before the ending **-ons** to keep the **g** soft (*zh*).

Other verbs like **commencer** are: **placer,** *to place;* **recommencer,** *to begin over or again;* **prononcer,** *to pronounce;* **avancer,** *to advance.* Other verbs like **manger** are: **juger,** *to judge;* **bouger,** *to move;* **changer,** *to change;* **songer,** *to dream, to think;* **plonger,** *to dive;* **voyager,** *to travel;* **agacer,** *to irritate, aggravate.*

Exercise No. 136. Complete each sentence with the correct French verb:

1. (He is holding) **le livre mais il ne le lit pas.**
2. (We are obtaining) **des tissus fins.**
3. (I am not reserving) **les places.**
4. **Les jour de l'An on** (keeps open house).
5. (We begin to work) **à neuf heures.**
6. **Où** (do we change) **de train?**
7. **Comment** (do you pronounce) **ce mot?**
8. (We pronounce it) **"Noël"** (nu-ehl).
9. (We do not eat) **de viande le matin.**
10. **Sur la Côte d'Azur** (we swim) **tous les jours.**
11. (We are correcting) **nos fautes.**
12. Let us begin again.

3. The pronoun **on,** *one, people, we, they, you.* **on** is an indefinite subject pronoun. It takes the third person singular form of the verb (like **il** and **elle**). Note the various ways **on** is translated.

on dit one says, people say, we say, you say, they say, it is said
On danse toute la journée. They (people) dance all day.

In everyday spoken language, **on** is frequently used instead of **nous** for *we*. For example: **Tu viens? On va prendre un café en bas.** Are you coming? We are going to have a coffee downstairs. **Maman, quand est-ce-qu'on va manger?** Mommy, when are we going to eat?

Often **on** is used instead of a passive construction:

Ici on parle français. French is spoken here. (*Lit.* Here one speaks French.)

On célèbre la Noël. Christmas is celebrated. (*Lit.* One celebrates Christmas.)

4. **ne . . . personne,** *nobody, no one, not anybody;* **ne . . . rien,** *nothing, not anything*

a. When used as objects of the verb, **personne** and **rien,** like other negatives (**ne . . . pas, ne . . . jamais, etc.**) require **ne** before the verb.

Je ne vois personne. I do not see anybody. (I see nobody)
Je ne vois rien. I do not see anything. (I see nothing)

b. When used as subjects, **personne** and **rien** are followed by **ne.**

Personne ne sait où il demeure. Nobody knows where he lives.
Rien ne me plaît aujourd'hui. Nothing pleases me today.

c. When **personne** and **rien** are used without a verb, **ne** is omitted.

Qui est chez-vous? Personne. Who is at your house? Nobody.
Que fait-il? Rien. What is he doing? Nothing.

d. The negative **ne . . . personne** must not be confused with the noun **la personne.**

Je ne connais pas cette personne-là. I don't know that person.

Exercise No. 137. Complete each sentence in French:

1. **Ici** (one) **parle français.**
2. **Ici** (nobody) **parle anglais.**
3. (People) **danse dans les rues.**
4. **Nous n'avons** (nothing).
5. **Il ne reste** (nobody) **dans la ville.**
6. **Il n'y a** (nothing) **à voir.**
7. **Que voulez-vous?** (Nothing.)
8. **Qui veut ces billets?** (Nobody)
9. **Il n'aime** (anybody).
10. (Nobody) **l'aime.**

Exercise No. 138—Questionnaire

1. **De quoi est-ce que les messieurs vont parler ce soir?**
2. **Où est-ce qu'on célèbre le quatorze juillet?**
3. **Qu'est-ce qu'on fait dans les rues?**
4. **Qu'est-ce qu'on vend dans les rues?**
5. **Qu'y a-t-il pour les enfants?**
6. **Faut-il dire *la Noël* ou *le Noël* quand on veut dire "la fête de Noël?"**
7. **Pourquoi est-ce qu'on dort la journée de Noël?**
8. **Quand est-ce que les enfants reçoivent leurs cadeaux?**
9. **Comment appelle-t-on les cadeaux du jour de l'An?**
10. **Comment est la ville le jour de l'Assomption (le Quinze-Août)?**

CHAPITRE 27 (VINGT-SEPT)

QUELS ENDROITS VOULEZ-VOUS VISITER, M. POTTER?
WHAT PLACES DO YOU WISH TO VISIT, MR. POTTER?

1. — Vous allez bientôt partir pour la France, M. Potter. Avez-vous décidé quels endroits vous voulez visiter?

1. Soon you are going to leave for France, Mr. Potter. Have you decided what places you want to visit?

2. — Je ne pense à rien d'autre, et je lis beaucoup dans ma collection de guides.

2. I think of nothing else and I am reading a great deal in my collection of guide books.

3. — J'irai à Paris par avion. Je visiterai ce qu'il y a d'intéressant dans la ville, dans les environs de la ville, et ailleurs en France.

4. — C'est un projet ambitieux. Pour voir ce qu'il y a d'intéressant à Paris il vous faudra dix ans.

5. — Je ferai mon possible pour faire l'impossible. À Paris je compte visiter la Cathédrale de Notre-Dame. Au Musée du Louvre, j'irai voir la Vénus de Milo, la Mona Lisa et la salle de la céramique grecque. Vous voyez que je m'intéresse toujours à la céramique.

6. En sortant du Louvre, je passerai à travers le Jardin des Tuileries jusqu'à la Place de la Concorde et puis je continuerai dans l'Avenue des Champs Elysées jusqu'à la Place de l'Étoile. Là je prendrai un taxi pour me promener au Bois de Boulogne. Je reviendrai par Passy pour visiter la Tour Eiffel . . .

7. — Ah bon, je comprends! Vous verrez tout, voilà! Mais vous m'étonnez. Vous connaissez Paris mieux que moi.

8. — Ah non, M. Picard. Pas tout à fait. Je connais le Paris des guides. Mais il me semble qu'à Paris tout me sera familier.

9. — C'est une chose qui arrive à tout le monde. On se sent chez soi à Paris. Et que comptez-vous visiter dans les environs de la ville?

10. — Dans les environs j'irai visiter Versailles, surtout les jardins.

11. — Il faut y aller le quatorze juillet pour voir jouer les fontaines et le feu d'artifice.

12. — Ah, très bien. Je n'y manquerai pas. Je veux voir aussi le château de Chantilly. Et puis Fontainebleau, et puis, Sens, Senlis. . . .

13. — Oh la, la! Laissons les environs, ou nous n'en sortirons jamais. Et après?

14. — Après, je ferai un grand cercle pour visiter la Normandie, surtout le Mont-Saint-Michel, où je mangerai trois omelettes, la spécialité du Mont. Puis je visiterai la Bretagne, et en revenant à Paris, les châteaux de la Loire.

15. — Et quand irez-vous à la Côte d'Azur?

16. — Tout de suite après j'irai à la Côte d'Azur, pour me tremper dans la mer et dans le soleil, et je reviendrai à Paris par la route des Alpes. Qu'en pensez-vous?

17. — Ce que j'en pense? J'ai grande envie de vous accompagner! Mais ce n'est pas possible.

18. — Quel dommage, M. Picard.

3. I'll travel by plane to Paris. I'll visit what there is of interest in the city, in the outskirts of the city and elsewhere in France.

4. It's an ambitious project. To see what there is of interest in Paris you'll need ten years.

5. I'll do everything possible to do the impossible. In Paris I expect to visit Notre Dame Cathedral. At the Louvre Museum I'll go to see the Venus de Milo, the Mona Lisa, and the Greek pottery room. You see that I'm always interested in ceramics.

6. Leaving the Louvre, I shall pass through the Tuileries garden to the Place de la Concorde and then I'll continue on the Champs Elysées up to the Place de l'Etoile. There I'll take a taxi to ride around the Bois de Boulogne. I'll come back by way of Passy to visit the Eiffel Tower and. . . .

7. Ah now I understand. You'll see everything, that's it! But you surprise me. You know Paris better than I.

8. Oh no, Mr. Picard. Not quite. I know the Paris of the guide books. But it seems to me that in Paris everything will be familiar.

9. It's a thing that happens to everybody. One feels at home in Paris. And what do you intend to visit in the outskirts of the city?

10. In the outskirts I'll go to visit Versailles, especially the gardens.

11. You must go there July 14 to see the fountains turned on and the fireworks.

12. Ah, very good. I'll not fail to do so. I also want to see the chateau at Chantilly. Then Fontainebleau, and then Sens, Senlis. . . .

13. Help! Let's leave the outskirts or we'll never get out of them. And afterward?

14. Afterward, I'll make a large circle to visit Normandy, especially Mont St. Michel, where I'll eat three omelettes, the specialty of the Mont. Then I shall visit Brittany, and on the way back to Paris, the chateaus of the Loire valley.

15. And when will you go to the Riviera?

16. Immediately after I'll go to the Riviera, to soak myself in the sea and sun, and I'll come back to Paris by way of the Alps. What do you think of it?

17. What do I think of it? I have a great mind to accompany you. But that isn't possible.

18. What a pity, Mr. Picard.

Pronunciation and Spelling Aids

Practice aloud

Vous allez bientôt partir pour la France, Monsieur Potter.	(Voo za-lay byañ-toh par-teer poor la **frahñs,** muh-syeu pu-**tehr.**)
Avez-vous decidé quels endroits vous voulez visiter?	(A-vay voo day-see-**day** kehl zahñ-drwa voo voo-lay vee-zee-**tay?**)
Je ne pense à rien d'autre.	(Zhuh nuh pahñs a ryañ **dohtr.**)
C'est un projet ambitieux.	(Seh teuñ pru-zheh ahñ-bee-**syeu.**)

Building Vocabulary

Expressions indicating future time

1. **demain** (duh-mañ) tomorrow
2. **après-demain** after tomorrow
3. **le mois prochain** (pru-shañ) next month
4. **lundi (mardi) prochain** next Monday (Tuesday)
5. **la semaine prochaine** (suh-mehn pru-shehn) next week
6. **l'année prochaine** (la-nay pru-shehn) next year

French Expressions

1. **Il vous faudra dix ans.** You will need ten years.
2. **Je ferai mon possible.** I shall do my best, everything I can.
3. **d'abord** first, at first
4. **chez soi** at home
5. **se promener** to go for a walk, drive, sail, etc.
6. **Je me promène en voiture (sur l'eau).** I go for a drive (for a sail).
7. **Je n'y manquerai pas.** I shall not fail to do so. (*Lit.* I shall not miss there.)
8. **J'ai envie de vous accompagner.** I feel like going with you. (*Lit.* I have a desire to accompany you.)

Grammar Notes

1. The future tense. What *shall or will* happen. **parler, vendre, finir**

I shall speak, you will speak, etc.	*I shall finish, etc.*	*I shall sell, etc.*
je parlerai (par-luh-ray)	**je finirai**	**je vendrai**
tu parleras (par-luh-ra)	**tu finiras**	**tu vendras**
il parlera (par-luh-ra)	**il finira**	**il vendra**
elle parlera (par-luh-ra)	**elle finira**	**elle vendra**
nous parlerons (par-luh-rawñ)	**nous finirons**	**nous vendrons**
vous parlerez (par-luh-ray)	**vous finirez**	**vous vendrez**
ils parleront (par-luh-rawñ)	**ils finiront**	**ils vendront**
elles parleront (par-luh-rawñ)	**elles finiront**	**elles vendront**
parlera-t-il? will he speak?	**finira-t-il?** will he finish?	**vendra-t-il?** will he sell?

a. The personal endings of the future tense of all verbs are: **-ai, -as, -a, -ons, -ez, -ont.** They are exactly like the present tense ending of the verb **avoir.**

b. To form the future tense, add the future endings to the infinitive:

parler **je parler-ai, etc.** **finir** **je finir-ai, etc.** **ouvrir** **j'ouvrir-ai, etc.**

c. If the infinitive ends in **-re,** drop the final **e** before adding the future endings:

vendre **je vendr-ai, etc.** **apprendre** **j'apprendr-ai, etc.** **lire** **je lir-ai, etc.**

2. Some verbs with an irregular future. In a number of common verbs there is a change in the infinitive base to which the future endings are added. Among these verbs are:

avoir to have	**j'aurai**	**tu auras**	**il aura**	**nous aurons,** etc.
être to be	**je serai**	**tu seras**	**il sera**	**nous serons,** etc.
aller to go	**j'irai**	**tu iras**	**il ira**	**nous irons,** etc.
voir to see	**je verrai**	**tu verras**	**il verra**	**nous verrons,** etc.
venir to come	**je viendrai**	**tu viendras**	**il viendra**	**nous viendrons,** etc.
faire to do, make	**je ferai**	**tu feras**	**il fera**	**nous ferons,** etc.
pouvoir to be able	**je pourrai**	**tu pourras**	**il pourra**	**nous pourrons,** etc.
falloir to be necessary	**il faut** it is necessary	**il faudra** it will be necessary		

Exercise No. 139—Completion of Text

1. (I shall travel) **en avion.**
2. (I shall visit) **ce qu'il y a d'intéressant.**
3. **Il vous** (will be necessary) **dix ans.**
4. (I shall do) **mon possible.**
5. (I shall go) **voir d'abord la Vénus de Milo.**
6. (I shall pass) **par le jardin des Tuileries.**
7. **Là** (I shall take) **un taxi.**
8. (I shall return) **par Passy.**
9. **Vous connaissez Paris** (better than I).
10. **À Paris tout me** (will be) **familier.**
11. **C'est une chose** (which happens to everybody).
12. **On se sent** (at home) à Paris.

Exercise No. 140. Translate each dialogue. Read each aloud three times.

1. — Où irez-vous l'été prochain?
— J'irai en France.
2. — Combien de temps passerez-vous en France?
— J'y passerai trois mois.
— Est-ce que vous voyagerez en avion ou en bateau?
— Je voyagerai en avion.
3. — Est-ce que vous ferez un voyage au Maroc?
— Oui. Je ferai un voyage au Maroc.
— M. Picard pourra-t-il vous accompagner?
— Hélas! Il ne pourra pas m'accompagner.
— Quand partirez-vous de New-York?
— Je partirai le 31 mai.
4. — Est-ce que vous verrez votre représentant à Paris?
— Mais oui. Il m'attendra à l'aéroport.
— Combien de temps resterez-vous à Paris?
— J'y resterai deux semaines.
5. — Est-ce que vous visiterez la Côte d'Azur?
— Bien entendu, je la visiterai.
— Quand reviendrez-vous aux États Unis?
— Je reviendrai le premier septembre.

Exercise No. 141. Translate:

1. he will visit.
2. I shall travel
3. we shall go
4. they will not write
5. it will be necessary
6. will you see?
7. they will not leave
8. we shall sell
9. will he not finish?
10. she will not learn
11. he will be
12. will you come?
13. I shall have
14. You (**tu**) will not listen
15. we shall study
16. I shall not make
17. will you be able?
18. will you go?

Exercise No. 142—Questionnaire

1. **M. Potter voyagera-t-il en avion ou en bateau?**
2. **Qu'est-ce que M. Potter verra au Louvre?**
3. **En sortant du Louvre par quel jardin passera-t-il?**
4. **Où prendra-t-il un taxi?**
5. **Quelle tour visitera-t-il?**
6. **Où se promènera-t-il?**
7. **Quel est le Paris que M. Potter connaît?**
8. **Qu'est-ce qui arrive à tout le monde?**
9. **Quand est-ce qu'on voit jouer les grandes fontaines à Versailles?**
10. **Que M. Potter fera-t-il à la Côte d'Azur?**
11. **Par quelle route est-ce que M. Potter reviendra à Paris?**

RÉVISION 6
CHAPITRES 24–27 PREMIÈRE PARTIE

NOUNS

1. **l'allumette**	13. **le feu**	25. **l'ouest**	1. match	13. fire	25. west
2. **les bas**	14. **la fête**	26. **l'ouvrier**	2. stockings	14. holiday	26. worker
3. **le bois**	15. **les gants**	27. **le pêcheur**	3. wood	15. gloves	27. fisherman
4. **le cercle**	16. **le jardin**	28. **la peinture**	4. circle	16. garden	28. painting
5. **le cheval**	17. **le lin**	29. **le projet**	5. horse	17. linen	29. project
6. **les chevaux**	18. **la laine**	30. **la robe**	6. horses	18. wool	30. dress
7. **le chien**	19. **le marin**	31. **la soie**	7. dog	19. seaman	31. silk
8. **le costume**	20. **la marchandise**	32. **la sorte**	8. costume	20. merchandise	32. kind, sort
9. **le couturier**	21. **la mode**	33. **le sud**	9. dress designer	21. fashion	33. south
10. **la couturière**	22. **le musicien**	34. **le tissu**	10. dressmaker	22. musician (*m*)	34. fabric, cloth
11. **l'eau de vie**	23. **la musicienne**	35. **le tabac**	11. brandy	23. musician (*f*)	35. tobacco
12. **l'étoffe**	24. **le nord**	36. **le vin**	12. fabric	24. north	36. wine

VERBS

1. **accompagner**	7. **discuter**	13. **se promener**	1. to accompany	7. to discuss	13. to take a walk, ride, etc.
2. **admirer**	8. **étonner**	14. **rester**	2. to admire	8. to astonish	14. to remain
3. **célébrer**	9. **manquer**	15. **recommencer**	3. to celebrate	9. to lack, miss	15. to begin again
4. **corriger**	10. **se passer**	16. **regarder**	4. to correct	10. to happen	16. to look at
5. **danser**	11. **se passer de**	17. **ressembler à**	5. to dance	11. to do without	17. to resemble
6. **décider**	12. **s'intéresser à**	18. **sembler**	6. to decide	12. to interest oneself in	18. to seem

ADJECTIVES

1. ambitieux	**5. bavard**	**9. parfumé**
2. droit	**6. débrouillard**	**10. politique**
3. entendu	**7. mort**	**11. trop**
4. fier (fière *f.*)	**8. mécontent**	**12. tel (telle *f.*)**

1. ambitious	5. talkative	9. perfumed
2. straight, right	6. resourceful	10. political
3. agreed	7. dead	11. too much
4. proud	8. discontented	12. such

ADVERBS

1. alors	**3. bientôt**	**5. partout**
2. autre part	**4. même**	**6. volontiers**

1. then, well	3. soon	5. everywhere
2. elsewhere	4. even	6. gladly

PREPOSITIONS

1. à cause de	**2. malgré**	**3. selon**
1. because of	2. in spite of	3. according to

FRENCH EXPRESSIONS

1. avoir peur (de)	**9. mieux que moi**
2. avoir envie de	**10. par ci par là**
3. être en train de	**11. quelque chose d'autre**
4. faire mon possible	**12. tiens!**
5. faire le commerce	**13. défense de fumer**
6. penser à	**14. Joyeux Noël**
7. venir de + *infinitive*	**15. Bonne Année**
8. plus ou moins	**16. encore un (une)**

1. to be afraid (of)	9. better than I
2. to want to	10. this way and that
3. to be in the act of	11. something else
4. to do my best	12. well!
5. to do business	13. no smoking
6. to think about	14. Merry Christmas
7. to have just (done something)	15. Happy New Year
8. more or less	16. one more

DEUXIÈME PARTIE

Exercise No. 143. In Group II find the words that correspond to the words in Group I.

I

1. the handkerchief
2. the overcoat
3. the suit (man's)
4. the suit (woman's)
5. the coat, cloak
6. the shawl
7. the shoes
8. the necktie
9. the shirt
10. the socks
11. the stockings
12. the belt
13. the dress
14. the trousers
15. the skirt

II

a. le pantalon
b. le manteau
c. le fichu
d. la robe
e. le mouchoir
f. la jupe
g. la pardessus
h. les bas
i. les chaussures
j. les chaussettes
k. la ceinture
l. le complet
m. la chemise
n. le costume tailleur
o. la cravate

Exercise No. 144. Combine each pair of nouns to form compound nouns and give the meaning of each:

Exemple: 1. le chapeau — le velour **le chapeau de velour** the velvet hat

1. **la ceinture — le cuir**
2. **la robe — la soie**
3. **la montre — l'or** (gold)
4. **la salle — le bain**
5. **la chemise — la laine**
6. **le bureau — le poste**
7. **le voyage — les affaires**
8. **le cahier — la musique**
9. **le tissu — le coton**
10. **le bracelet — l'argent**
11. **l'objet — l'art**
12. **le chapeau — la paille** (straw)

Exercise No. 145. Answer these questions in complete sentences (in the future tense) with the help of the words in parentheses:

Exemple: 1. J'achèterai une cravate.

1. **Qu'est-ce que vous achèterez? (une cravate)**
2. **Combien coûtera-t-elle? (cent francs)**
3. **Où irez-vous l'été prochain? (en France)**
4. **Quand reviendrez-vous aux États-Unis? (le 31 décembre)**
5. **À quelle heure vous coucherez-vous? (à minuit)**
6. **À quelle heure vous lèverez-vous? (à six heures du matin)**
7. **Que lui direz-vous? (rien)**
8. **Qui ira avec vous? (personne ne)**
9. **Combien de temps travaillerez-vous? (toute la journée)**
10. **Où nous rencontrerons-nous? (à l'entrée du théâtre)**

Exercise No. 146. Complete these sentences with the help of the French expressions listed below:

Exemple: 1. Ils n'ont pas peur d'exprimer leurs idées.

1. (They are not afraid) **d'exprimer leurs idées.**
2. (We do not need) **de continuer.**
3. (She intends) **de porter son manteau neuf** (new).
4. (Do you want to) **m'accompagner?**
5. (He will do his best) **pour vous aider.**
6. (Will you go shopping) **au Marché aux Puces?**
7. (Mr. Potter is opening) **la caisse.**
8. (Are you afraid) **de dire la vérité?**
9. **Allez-vous** (to take a ride) **au Bois de Boulogne?**
10. **Vous savez que M. Potter** (is not interested in) **la mode.**

a. avoir peur de
b. avoir besoin de
c. avoir envie de
d. avoir l'intention de
e. faire des achats
f. s'intéresser à
g. se promener
h. faire son possible
i. être en train de

Exercise No. 147. Complete these sentences in French. **mettre** here means *to put on.* **aller bien à** means *to be becoming to.*

1. **Je mets** (my hat).
2. **Tu mets** (your coat).
3. **Il met** (his woolen shirt).
4. **Elle met** (her silk dress).
5. **Nous mettons** (our leather belts[1]).
6. **Vous mettez** (your red gloves).
7. **Ils mettent** (their raincoats[1]).
8. **Elles mettent** (their scarves[1]).
9. (This dress) **me va bien.**
10. (This necktie) **lui va bien.**
11. (These gloves) **nous vont bien.**
12. (This skirt) **ne va pas bien à Jeanne.**

NOTE 1. Use the singular. The idea is that each one puts on one item of clothing.

Dialogue 1
Dans l'autobus

1. — Pardon monsieur, où est-ce que je descends pour aller a l'Hôtel des Postes[1] (au boulevard St. Michel) (au Jardin du Luxembourg) (à l'ambassade des États-Unis) (au Marché aux Puces) (à la gare)?

1. Excuse me sir, where do I get off for the Main Post Office (for the boulevard St. Michel) (for the Luxembourg Gardens) (for the United States Embassy) (for the Flea Market) (for the railroad station)?

2. — Vous descendez au coin de la rue du Louvre et la rue Etienne-Marcel (etc).

2. You get off at the corner of the rue du Louvre and the rue Etienne-Marcel (etc.).

3. — Est-ce que c'est loin d'ici?

3. Is it far from here?

4. — Non monsieur, pas trop loin.

4. No sir, not too far.

5. — Quand est-ce que nous y arriverons?

5. When will we get there?

6. — Dans un quart d'heure plus ou moins.

6. In about a quarter of an hour.

7. — Merci beaucoup, monsieur.

7. Thank you very much, sir.

8. — De rien.

8. Don't mention it.

NOTE 1. **Hôtel des Postes** main post office in Paris, **bureau de poste** post office

Dialogue 2
Le courrier

1. — M. Potter, vous avez sans doute une grosse correspondance. Y a-t-il une boîte aux lettres dans votre immeuble?

1. Mr. Potter, no doubt you have much correspondence. Is there a mailbox in your building?

2. — Naturellement. Nous en avons une à chaque étage, où nous jetons nos lettres. Mais nous envoyons les colis postaux au bureau central des postes.

2. Naturally. We have one at each floor where we drop our letters. But we send parcel post packages to the main post office.

3. — Qui est-ce qui les porte?

3. Who takes them?

4. — Le garçon à tout faire. Il nous achète aussi les quantités de timbres dont nous avons besoin, les timbres de service postal aérien, les timbres d'envoi par exprès, etc.

4. The office boy. He also buys us the many stamps that we need, the air mail stamps, the special delivery stamps, etc.

5. — Où est le bureau central des postes?
6. — Il n'est pas loin d'ici.

5. Where is the main post office?
6. It isn't far from here.

Exercise No. 148—Lecture
L'anniversaire[1] de Mme. Potter

C'est le vingt-deux mars, l'anniversaire de Mme. Potter. Elle a trente-cinq ans aujourd'hui. Pour célébrer cette fête la famille Potter va dîner dans un restaurant élégant de la Madison Avenue à New-York.

Quand ils entrent dans le restaurant ils voient sur la table réservée pour les Potter un joli panier rempli de roses blanches. Naturellement Mme. Potter est tout à fait surprise. Elle remercie et embrasse son cher mari avec empressement.

A la fin d'un dîner exquis Anne, la plus jeune, dit tout bas[2] aux autres enfants, — Maintenant! Et chacun des quatre enfants sort d'en bas de[3] la table une jolie petite boîte. Ce sont des cadeaux pour leur mère.

Anne lui donne un mouchoir de soie; Elizabeth, une blouse de lin; Thomas, une paire de gants; et Charles, un fichu de laine.

La semaine prochaine, M. Potter fait le calcul du compte de cette journée, qui suit:

Dîner	**cent soixante**	**$160**
Pourboire	**vingt-quatre**	**24**
Fleurs	**quarante**	**40**
Cadeaux	**cent vingt-six**	**126**
		$350

"Quelle coïncidence!" dit M. Potter. "Trois cent cinquante dollars—dix fois trente-cinq ans!"

NOTE 1. birthday 2. in a low voice 3. from under

CHAPITRE 28 (VINGT-HUIT)

M. POTTER ÉCRIT UNE LETTRE À SON REPRÉSENTANT
MR. POTTER WRITES A LETTER TO HIS AGENT

1. M. Potter et M. Picard sont assis dans le salon chez M. Potter. M. Potter tient deux lettres à la main: une copie de sa lettre à son représentant et la réponse qui vient d'arriver.

2. — M. Picard, je vais vous lire ma lettre à mon représentant à Paris, M. Parmentier.

3. — Cela me fera plaisir.

4. M. Potter lit la lettre qui suit:

New-York, le 4 mai 1987

M. Georges Parmentier
76, rue de Vaugirard
75006 Paris
France

Cher Monsieur Parmentier,

J'ai le plaisir de vous informer que je vais bientôt faire un voyage en France. Je partirai de New-York en avion le 31 mai à sept heures de l'après-midi et j'arriverai à Charles de Gaulle II à sept heures du matin le premier juin.

J'ai l'intention de rester en France deux mois. Je compte faire un voyage d'agrément aussi bien que d'affaires. Je passerai trois semaines à peu près à Paris.

1. Mr. Potter and Mr. Picard are sitting in the living room at Mr. Potter's house. Mr. Potter has two letters in his hand: a copy of his letter to his agent and the answer which has just arrived.

2. Mr. Picard, I am going to read you my letter to my agent in Paris, Mr. Parmentier.

3. That will please me.

4. Mr. Potter reads the letter which follows:

New York, May 4, 1987

Mr. Georges Parmentier
76 Rue de Vaugirard
Paris 75006
France

Dear Mr. Parmentier,

I am pleased to inform you that I am soon going to make a trip to France. I shall leave New York by plane May 31 at 7 P.M. and will arrive at Charles de Gaulle II at 7 A.M. June 1.

I intend to remain in France two months. I expect to make it a pleasure trip as well as a business trip. I shall spend about three weeks in Paris.

Partant de Paris, je ferai quelques excursions pour voir les endroits intéressants en France. J'espère aussi voyager en avion au Maroc et peut-être en Corse.

Pendant mon séjour à Paris j'espère pouvoir saisir l'occasion de faire votre connaissance, car j'ai toujours beaucoup apprécié vos services devoués, qui ont tant contribué à notre réussite.

Je sais que vous êtes très occupé et que vous êtes souvent en voyage. Par conséquent je vous écris d'avance dans l'espoir de pouvoir fixer un rendez-vous. Je vous prie de me faire savoir si j'aurai le plaisir de vous voir à Paris.

Il y a cinq mois que je prends des leçons de français. Cela vous surprendra peut-être. J'espère pouvoir vous parler dans votre belle langue, car depuis quelque temps je cause deux fois par semaine avec mon professeur, M. Auguste Picard, un de vos compatriotes.

Dans l'espoir de vous lire bientôt, agréez, monsieur, l'assurance de ma considération distinguée.

John Potter

Leaving Paris, I shall make a few excursions to see places of interest in France. I hope also to fly to Morocco and perhaps to Corsica.

During my stay in Paris I hope to take advantage of the opportunity to meet you personally, for I have always very much appreciated your dedicated services, which have contributed so much to our success.

I know that you are very busy and that you travel a great deal. For that reason I am writing you beforehand in the hope of being able to arrange an appointment. Please (*Lit.* I pray you) let me know if I shall have the pleasure of seeing you in Paris.

I have been studying French for the last five months. This will surprise you perhaps. I hope to be able to talk with you in your beautiful language, because for some time I have been conversing twice a week with my teacher, Mr. Auguste Picard, a fellow-countryman of yours (*Lit.* one of your fellow-countrymen).

Awaiting your early reply, I remain sincerely yours, (*Lit.* In the hope of reading you soon, accept, sir, the assurance of my marked esteem).

John Potter

5. — Merveilleux, M. Potter, Il n'y pas une seule faute dans toute la lettre.

6. — M. Picard, je dois vous avouer quelque chose. Il y a un livre qui s'appelle "La Correspondance commerciale." Ce livre me rend grand service dans tout ce qui regarde les en-têtes, les conclusions, et les formules de politesse. Naturellement, c'est surtout à vous que je dois les plus vifs remerciements.

7. — Vous êtes très aimable. Et maintenant, voulez-vous bien me lire la réponse que vous venez de recevoir de M. Parmentier?

8. — Avec plaisir, Monsieur.

(La suite au Chapitre 29.)

5. Marvellous, Mr. Potter. There is not a single error in the whole letter.

6. Mr. Picard, I must confess something to you. There is a book entitled "Commercial Correspondence." This book helps me a great deal in everything that concerns headings, conclusions, and expressions of courtesy. Of course, to you especially I owe the most sincere thanks.

7. You are very kind. And now will you kindly read me the answer which you have received from Mr. Parmentier?

8. With pleasure, sir.

(Continued in Chapter 29.)

Pronunciation and Spelling Aids

Practice aloud

J'ai le plaisir de vous informer que je vais bientôt faire un voyage en France.

(Zhay luh pleh-zeer duh voo zañ- fur-**may** kuh zhuh veh byañ-toh fehr euñ vwa-**yazh** ahñ **frahñs**.)

Je partirai de New-York en avion le 31 (trente et un) mai à sept heures.

(Zhuh par-tee-ray duh New-York ahñ na-**vyawñ** luh trahñ-tay-euñ **meh** a seh **teur**.)

Building Vocabulary

Related expressions

1. **la main** hand
2. **la main droite** the right hand
3. **la main gauche** the left hand
4. **à droite** on, to the right
5. **à gauche** on, to the left
6. **tourner** *or* **prendre la droite (gauche)** to turn to the right (left)
7. **tout droit** straight ahead
8. **à la main** in his or her hand
9. **Ils se serrent la main** they shake hands

NOTE: Often when referring to parts of the body, French uses the definite article instead of **mon, ton, son, etc.** Thus:

Il tient deux lettres à la main. He has two letters in his hand.

Elle a un panier sur la tête. She has a basket on her head.

French Expressions

1. **avoir l'intention de** to intend to
2. **saisir l'occasion** to seize (take advantage of) the opportunity
3. **par conséquent** consequently
4. **d'avance** in advance, beforehand
5. **faire le connaissance de** to make the acquaintance of, to meet
6. **faire savoir** to let know, to inform
7. **deux fois par semaine** twice a week
8. **voulez-vous bien** will you kindly
9. **cela me fera plaisir** that will please me
10. **être occupé** to be busy

Exercise No. 149—Completion of Text

1. **M. Potter a deux lettres** (in his hand).
2. **Voici la réponse qui** (has just arrived).
3. **M. Potter lit la lettre** (which follows).
4. (I shall leave) **le 31 mai.**
5. (I intend) **de rester en France deux mois.**
6. **Je sais que vous êtes** (very busy).
7. (Consequently) **je vous écris d'avance.**
8. (For some time) **je cause** (twice a week) **avec mon professeur.**
9. **Il n'y a pas** (a single mistake) **dans toute la lettre.**
10. (Will you kindly) **me lire la réponse de M. Parmentier.**

Grammar Notes

1. Present tense of **suivre,** *to follow,* **traduire,** *to translate*

I follow, you follow, etc.

je suis	**nous suivons**
tu suis	**vous suivez**
il, elle suit	**ils, elles suivent**

Imperative

suis **suivons** **suivez**

I translate, you translate, etc.

je traduis	**nous traduisons**
tu traduis	**vous traduisez**
il, elle traduit	**ils, elles traduisent**

Imperative

traduis **traduisons** **traduisez**

Like **suivre** is: **poursuivre,** *to pursue.* Like **traduire: conduire,** *to lead, conduct;* **produire,** *to produce;* **construire,** *to construct.*

2. More verbs with an irregular future

tenir to hold	**je tiendrai,** etc.
devoir to owe	**je devrai,** etc.
recevoir to receive	**je recevrai,** etc.
vouloir to want	**je voudrai,** etc.
valoir to be worth	**il vaudra,** etc.
envoyer to send	**j'enverrai,** etc.
courir to run	**je courrai,** etc.
savoir to know	**je saurai,** etc.

Exercise No. 150. Complete the following sentences in French:

Exemple: 1. Je leur enverrai les journaux français.

1. (I shall send them) **les journaux français.**
2. **Mme. Potter** (will receive) **beaucoup de cadeaux.**
3. (They will know) **où me trouver.**
4. (He will not want) **nous accompagner.**
5. **Les enfants** (will run) **pour voir le Guignol.**
6. **Les billets** (will not be worth) **plus de cinq dollars.**
7. (They will owe us) **moins de dix dollars.**
8. (They will hold) **table ouverte.**
9. (Will you translate) **cet exercice?**
10. (We shall not follow) **la mode.**
11. (I shall make) **la connaissance de M. Parmentier.**
12. (We shall be able) **fixer un rendez-vous.**

3. **depuis, depuis quand, combien de temps, pendant**

a. When an action that began in the past continues in the present, French uses **depuis** (*since, for*) or **depuis quand?** (*since when?*) or **combien de temps?** (*how long?*), with the present tense of the verb. English uses the present perfect tense to express the same notion.

Depuis quand est-ce que M. Potter *étudie* le français? — Since when *has* Mr. Potter *been studying* French?

Il *étudie* le français depuis cinq mois. — He *has been studying* (*has studied*) French for (since) five months.

Combien de temps y a-t-il que M. Potter *étudie* le français? — How long (is it that) has Mr. Potter *been studying* (*has studied*) French?

Il y a cinq mois qu'il *étudie* le français. — He *has been studying* (*has studied*) French for five months.

b. For future action, French uses **combien de temps?** (*how long?*) and **pendant** (*for, during*) plus the future tense of the verb, as in English.

The word *for* in English, **pendant,** is often omitted in French.

Combien de temps restera-t-il à Paris? — How long will he remain in Paris?

Il y restera (pendant) trois semaines. — He will remain there (for) three weeks.

Exercise No. 151. Complete the following sentences in French:

Exemple: 1. Combien de temps resterez-vous à Paris?

1. (How long) **resterez-vous à Paris?**
2. **Nous resterons à Paris** (during the months) **de juin et juillet.**
3. (Since when) **le connaissez-vous?**
4. **Nous le connaissons** (for ten years).
5. **J'étudie le français** (for two years).
6. **Il écrit des lettres** (for three hours).
7. (How long) **m'attendrez-vous?**
8. (It is three days) **qu'elle est malade.**
9. (Since when have you been living) **dans cette maison?**
10. (We have been living there) **depuis trois ans.**

Exercise No. 152—Questionnaire

1. **Où est-ce que les messieurs sont assis?**
2. **Qu'est-ce que M. Potter tient à la main?**
3. **Qu'est-ce qu'il va lire à M. Picard?**
4. **Quand est-ce que M. Potter partira de New-York?**
5. **Combien de temps passera-t-il en France?**
6. **Combien de temps restera-t-il à Paris?**
7. **Où espère-t-il voyager en avion?**
8. **Qui est très occupé?**
9. **De qui est-ce que M. Potter veut faire la connaissance?**
10. **Pourquoi écrit-il d'avance?**
11. **Combien de temps y a-t-il que M. Potter prend des leçons de français?**

CHAPITRE 29 (VINGT-NEUF)

M. POTTER REÇOIT UNE LETTRE
MR. POTTER RECEIVES A LETTER

M. Potter a écrit une lettre à son représentant à Paris. Dans le dernier chapitre il a lu une copie de cette lettre à son professeur, M. Picard. Celui-ci n'a pas trouvé une seule faute dans la lettre. M. Potter a reçu une réponse de son représentant. Maintenant il la tient à la main et il est en train de la lire.

Mr. Potter has written a letter to his representative in Paris. In the last chapter he read a copy of that letter to his teacher, Mr. Picard. He did not find a single error in the letter. Mr. Potter has received an answer from his agent. Now he has it in his hand and is reading it.

1. Cher M. Potter, — 1. Dear Mr. Potter,

2. J'ai reçu avec beaucoup de plaisir votre lettre du 4 mai dans laquelle[1] vous m'informez que vous allez bientôt faire un voyage en France. — 2. I have received with great pleasure your letter of May 4 in which[1] you inform me that you will soon make a trip to France.

3. Heureusement je serai à Paris pendant les mois de juin et juillet, et je serai tout à fait à votre disposition. — 3. Fortunately I shall be in Paris during the months of June and July, and I shall be entirely at your service.

4. Je compte sur le plaisir de vous rencontrer à Charles de Gaulle II aéroport à sept heures du matin le premier juin. J'espère pouvoir rendre votre séjour agréable quant aux distractions aussi bien que profitable quant aux affaires.

5. C'est avec plaisir que je causerai en français avec vous et je suis sûr que vous le parlez à la perfection. En vérité vous écrivez le français à merveille. Je veux vous féliciter aussi bien que votre professeur. Comme M. Picard est Français, je comprends bien votre connaissance de beaucoup de gallicismes.

6. Dans l'attente de faire votre connaissance, je vous prie de croire, monsieur, à ma parfaite considération.

Georges Parmentier

7. — C'est une gentille lettre, dit M. Picard. Jusqu'à présent vous avez connu M. Parmentier comme représentant sérieux. Sans doute vous allez voir qu'il est aussi très sympathique comme un bon nombre de ses compatriotes. Pardonnez-moi si je suis fier des Français, mais vous verrez vous-même.

8. — Je suis certain que je serai très content parmi les Français; et le plus beau de l'affaire c'est que je pourrai parler avec eux dans leur propre langue.

9. — C'est certain. Alors, M. Potter, mardi prochain c'est le dernier rendez-vous avant votre départ. Nous nous rencontrerons à votre bureau, n'est-ce pas?

10. — Oui, monsieur. Et vous me donnerez quelques derniers conseils?

11. — Avec plaisir, M. Potter.

4. I am looking forward to meeting you at Charles de Gaulle II airport at 7 A.M. June 1. I hope to be able to make your stay pleasant in terms of entertainment as well as profitable in terms of business.

5. I shall be happy to talk with you in French and I am sure that you speak it perfectly. Indeed, you write French extremely well. I want to congratulate you as well as your teacher. Since Mr. Picard is French, I understand very well your familiarity with many French idioms.

6. Looking forward to making your acquaintance, I remain, Sincerely yours, (*Lit.* I beg you to believe, sir, in my complete esteem)

Georges Parmentier

7. "It's a nice letter," says Mr. Picard. "Until now you have known Mr. Parmentier as a reliable agent. No doubt, you will see that he is also very likeable like a good number of his fellow-countrymen. Pardon me if I am proud of the French people, but you will see for yourself."

8. I am certain that I shall be very happy among the French; and the best part of it is that I'll be able to converse with them in their own language.

9. That's right. Well, Mr. Potter, next Tuesday is the last meeting before your departure. We'll meet in your office, no?

10. Yes, sir. And you will give me some final advice?

11. With pleasure, Mr. Potter.

NOTE 1. **lequel (laquelle, lesquels, lesquelles)**, *which*, is a relative pronoun used after prepositions. It agrees with its antecedent in number and gender.

Pronunciation and Spelling Aids

Practice aloud

J'ai reçu avec beaucoup de plaisir votre lettre du 4 (quatre) mai dans laquelle vous m'informez que vous allez bientôt faire un voyage en France.

(Zhay ruh-sü a-vehk boh-koo duh pleh-zeer vutr lehtr dü katr **meh** dahñ la-kehl voo mañ-fur-**may** kuh voo za-lay byañ-toh fehr euñ vwa-yazh ahñ **frahñs.**)

Building Vocabulary

Expressions referring to past time

1. **hier** (yehr) yesterday
2. **hier soir** yesterday evening
3. **hier matin** yesterday morning
4. **avant-hier** day before yesterday
5. **la semaine dernière** last week
6. **l'année dernière** last year
7. **il y a deux jours (mois, ans)** two days (months, years) ago
8. **il y a huit jours** a week ago
9. **il y a quinze jours** two weeks ago

French Expressions

1. **je compte sur le plaisir de** I look forward to
2. **quant à** in the matter of, in terms of
3. **en vérité** indeed
4. **jusqu'à présent** until now
5. **ma (sa, leur) propre langue** my (his, their) own language

Salutations: business letters

1. **Monsieur:** Dear Sir:
2. **Messieurs:** Gentlemen:
3. **Cher Monsieur A.:** Dear Mr. A.:
4. **Chère Madame B.:** Dear Mrs. B.:

Closings: business letters. Literally translated, the formulas for closing French business letters may sound very flowery to English-speakers' ears, but they are merely the equivalent of Sincerely yours, Yours truly, etc.

1. **Agréez, monsieur, mes salutations distinguées.** Accept, sir, my distinguished greetings. Yours truly.
2. **Agréez, monsieur, mes salutations empressés.** Accept, sir, my earnest greetings. Yours truly.
3. **Agréez, je vous prie, l'expression de mes salutations les plus distinguées.** Please accept the expression of my most distinguished greetings. Yours truly.
4. **Veuillez agréer, monsieur, mes sincères salutations.** Please accept, sir, my sincere greetings. Yours truly.

Exercise No. 153—Completion of Text

1. (He is in the act of reading) **la lettre.**
2. (I have received) **votre lettre du 4 mai.**
3. **Je serai à Paris** (during the months) **de juin et juillet.**
4. (I am looking forward) **de vous rencontrer à l'aéroport.**
5. **C'est avec plaisir** (that I shall talk in French) **avec vous.**
6. **Je veux** (to congratulate you).
7. (You have known) **M. Parmentier comme représentant sérieux.**
8. **Pardonnez-moi** (if I am proud) **des Français.**
9. (You will see) **vous-même.**
10. (I shall be able) **parler avec eux en français.**

Grammar Notes

1. Conversational past tense (present perfect). What happened, has happened, did happen. Model verbs **parler, finir, vendre, être**

I have spoken, spoke, did speak, etc.

j'ai parlé	**nous avons parlé**
tu as parlé	**vous avez parlé**
il, elle a parlé	**ils, elles ont parlé**

I have not finished, did not finish, etc.

je n'ai pas fini	**nous n'avons pas fini**
tu n'as pas fini	**vous n'avez pas fini**
il, elle n'a pas fini	**ils, elles n'ont pas fini**

I have sold, did sell, etc.

j'ai vendu	**nous avons vendu**
tu as vendu	**vous avez vendu**
il a vendu	**ils, elles ont vendu**

I have been, was, etc.

j'ai été	**nous avons été**
tu as été	**vous avez été**
il a été	**ils, elles ont été**

Interrogative: **a-t-il parlé?**[2], **avons-nous fini?, avez-vous vendu?, ont-ils été?**
Negative interrogative: **n'a-t-il pas parlé?, n'avons-nous pas fini? etc.**

Like the present perfect tense in English, the conversational past tense in French is formed by means of an auxiliary verb plus the past participle. The auxiliary verb is usually **avoir,** *to have,* but it is sometimes **être,** *to be.* The use of **être** as an auxiliary verb will be discussed later, in Chapter 32.

2. How to form the regular past participle

-er verbs drop **-er** and add **é**

Infinitive	*Past Participle*	*Infinitive*	*Past Participle*
parler to speak	**parlé** spoken	**apporter** to bring	**apporté** brought

trouver to find	**trouvé** found	**écouter** to listen to	**écouté** listened to
demander to ask	**demandé** asked	**envoyer** to send	**envoyé** sent
casser to break	**cassé** broken	**manger** to eat	**mangé** eaten
fermer to close	**fermé** closed	**porter** to carry	**porté** carried

-ir verbs drop **-ir** and add **-i**

Infinitive	*Past Participle*	*Infinitive*	*Past Participle*
finir to finish	**fini** finished	**dormir** to sleep	**dormi** slept
choisir to choose	**choisi** chosen	**sentir** to feel	**senti** felt
bâtir to build	**bâti** built	**servir** to serve	**servi** served
obéir to obey	**obéi** obeyed	**punir** to punish	**puni** punished
saisir to seize	**saisi** seized	**remplir** to fill	**rempli** filled

-re verbs drop **-re** and add **-u**

Infinitive	*Past Participle*	*Infinitive*	*Past Participle*
vendre to sell	**vendu** sold	**entendre** to hear	**entendu** heard
répondre to answer	**répondu** answered	**rendre** to give back	**rendu** gave, given back
perdre to lose	**perdu** lost	**attendre** to wait for	**attendu** waited for

3. Some irregular past participles

Infinitive	*Past Participle*	*Infinitive*	*Past Participle*
connaître to know	**connu** known	**écrire** to write	**écrit** written
lire to read	**lu** read	**faire** to make	**fait** made
dire to say	**dit** said	**recevoir** to receive	**reçu** received

Exercise No. 154. Translate each dialogue. Read each dialogue aloud three times.

1. — M. Picard a-t-il posé des questions difficiles à M. Potter?
— Oui. Il lui a posé des questions difficiles.
— Est-ce que M. Potter a bien[1] répondu?
— Oui, il a bien répondu à toutes les questions.

2. — Quand est-ce que M. Potter a écrit la lettre à son représentant?
— Il y a aujourd'hui quinze jours qu'il a écrit la lettre.
— À qui a-t-il lu une copie de cette lettre?
— Il a lu la copie à M. Picard.

3. — Est-ce que M. Picard a trouvé beaucoup de fautes dans la lettre?
— Non. Il n'a pas trouvé une seule faute.
— Quel livre a rendu grand service à M. Potter?
— Le livre, "La Correspondance commerciale," lui a rendu grand service.

4. — M. Potter a-t-il apprecié les services de M. Parmentier?
— Oui. Il a toujours[1] apprecié ses services dévoués.
— Qu'est-ce que M. Picard a dit quand M. Potter a fini de lire la lettre?
— Il a dit: C'est une gentille lettre.

NOTE 1. Most adverbs (**bien, déjà, encore, toujours, souvent, etc.**) precede the past participle. The adverbs **hier, aujourd'hui, demain, ici, là, tôt, tard,** however, follow the past participle.

Il a déjà écrit la lettre.	He has already written the letter.
Il a écrit la lettre hier.	He wrote the letter yesterday.

Exercise No. 155. Complete the following sentences with the past participle of the verb indicated. Read each completed sentence aloud.

Exemple: 1. J'ai reçu votre lettre du 4 mai.

1. **J'ai (recevoir) votre lettre du 4 mai.**
2. **Nous avons (décider) de visiter le Musée du Louvre.**
3. **Il a toujours (apprécier) vos services devoués.**
4. **Ces services ont (contribuer) à notre réussite.**
5. **M. Potter a (vendre) beaucoup d'objets d'art.**
6. **Nous n'avons pas (écrire) beaucoup de lettres.**
7. **N'avez-vous pas (lire) tous les guides?**
8. **Ont-ils (rendre) les livres à la bibliothèque?**
9. **Avez-vous (faire) la connaissance de votre représentant?**
10. **Je n'ai pas (entendre) ce qu'il a (dire).**
11. **Elles n'ont pas encore (finir) l'examen.**
12. **La bonne a déjà (servir) le thé au rhum.**

Exercise No. 156—Questionnaire

1. **Qui a écrit une lettre à son représentant?**
2. **À qui a-t-il lu une copie de cette lettre?**
3. **M. Picard a-t-il trouvé beaucoup de fautes dans la lettre de M. Potter?**
4. **Quand est-ce que M. Parmentier sera à Paris?**
5. **Où est-ce qu'il va rencontrer M. Potter?**
6. **Dans quelle langue va-t-il causer avec lui?**
7. **Comment est-ce que M. Potter a connu M. Parmentier jusqu'à présent?**
8. **De quoi M. Potter est-il certain?**
9. **Quand est-ce que les deux messieurs auront leur dernier rendez-vous?**
10. **Où est-ce qu'ils se rencontreront?**
11. **Qu'est-ce que M. Picard donnera à M. Potter?**

CHAPITRE 30 (TRENTE)

LES DERNIERS CONSEILS DE M. PICARD
MR. PICARD'S FINAL WORDS OF ADVICE

1. Il fait chaud dans là maison de M. Potter. Il n'y a pas un souffle d'air. Par la fenêtre ouverte on entend les bruits de la rue.

1. It is hot in Mr. Potter's house. There is not a breath of air. Through the open window one hears the noises of the street.

2. — Je suis content de quitter la ville, dit M. Potter à M. Picard.

2. "I am happy to leave the city," says Mr. Potter to Mr. Picard.

3. — J'ai envie de vous accompagner, répond M. Picard.

3. "I have a mind to go with you," answers Mr. Picard.

4. — Pourrez-vous venir avec moi?

4. Will you be able to go with me?

5. — Malheureusement, ce n'est pas possible.

5. Unfortunately, it isn't possible.

6. — Quel dommage! Eh bien, voulez-vous bien me donner quelques derniers conseils? Est-ce que la vie en France est différente de la vie aux États-Unis?

6. What a pity! Well then, will you kindly give me some final advice? Is life in France different from life in the United States?

7. — Oui, Mr. Potter, les coutumes du pays sont assez différentes. En général on fait les choses avec plus de formalité qu'ici. La question de politesse, il me semble, est d'une valeur profonde; c'est à dire que chaque homme est digne d'être respecté.

7. Yes Mr. Potter, the customs of the country are quite different. In general things are done with more formality than they are here. The question of courtesy it seems to me has a profound meaning; that is, every man is worthy of respect.

8. — C'est vrai, répond M. Potter.

8. "That's true," answers Mr. Potter.

9. — J'ai remarqué que les affaires se traitent en France avec plus de formalité qu'aux États-Unis. Les hommes d'affaires aiment bien causer un peu avant d'entamer une affaire. Ils désirent se connaître les uns les autres.

9. I have noticed that in France business is done with more formality than it is in the United States. Businessmen like to chat a little with each other before taking up a business matter. They want to get to know one another.

10. — Je serai très content en France.

10. I'll be very happy in France.

11. — Il faudra vous habituer à un train de vie moins agité. En général la vie en France est plus tranquille.

11. You'll have to (*Lit.* It will be necessary to) get used to a less turbulent way of life. In general, life in France is quieter.

12. — Je l'espère. Je suis las d'être toujours bousculé.

12. I hope so. (*Lit.* I hope it.) I am tired of being forever jostled.

13. — Parlant d'autre chose, avez-vous lu les livres sur la France que je vous ai recommandés?

13. To speak of something else; did you read the books on France which I recommended to you?

14. — Oui, je les ai tous lus avec beaucoup d'intérêt.

14. Yes. I read them all with much interest.

15. — J'ai parcouru aussi les deux guides que vous m'avez prêtés. Le Guide Michelin et le Guide Bleu. Il me semble que ces deux guides me rendront grand service.

15. I have also glanced through the two guides which you lent me: the Michelin Guide and the Blue Guide. It seems to me that these two guides will be helpful to me.

16. — Sans aucune[1] doute. Quant à moi, je passerai l'été à New-York. Nos conversations m'ont donné beaucoup de plaisir. Vous allez me manquer.

16. Without any doubt. As for me, I'll spend the summer in New York. I have enjoyed our conversations very much. I shall miss you.

17. — Je penserai à vous très souvent et de temps en temps je vous écrirai.
17. I'll think of you often and from time to time I'll write you.

18. — Je serai content de recevoir vos lettres. Alors, voilà, il faut nous dire au revoir. Vous serez bien gentil de faire mes amitiés à Mme. Potter et d'embrasser les enfants de ma part.
18. I'll be happy to receive your letters. Well, then we must say goodbye. Kindly give my regards to Mrs. Potter and kiss the children for me.

19. — Merci, et bonne chance!
19. Thank you, and good luck!

20. — Bon voyage, M. Potter.
Ils se serrent la main.
20. Happy voyage, Mr. Potter.
They shake hands.

NOTE 1. **aucun (aucune** *f*) not any, none, no one. Except after **sans,** it is used with **ne. Je n'ai pas aucune doute.** I haven't any doubt. **Aucun de ces élèves n'est Français.** None of these pupils is French.

Pronunciation and Spelling Aids

Practice aloud

— Je suis content de quitter la ville, dit Monsieur Potter à Monsieur Picard.
(Zhuh süee kawñ-tahñ duh kee-tay la **veel,** dee muh-syeu pu-**tehr** a muh-syeu pee-**kar.**)

— J'ai envie de vous accompagner, répond M. Picard.
(Zhay ahñ-vee duh voo za-kawñ-pa-**nyay,** ray-pawñ muh-syeu pee-**kar.**)

— Ne pouvez-vous pas venir avec moi?
(Nuh poo-vay-voo pah vuh-neer a-vehk **mwa**?)

— Malheureusement, ce n'est pas possible.
(Ma-leu-reuz-**mahñ,** suh neh pah pu-**seebl.**)

Building Vocabulary

Words whose appearance deceives

demander means to ask or ask for *not* to demand; **exiger** means to demand
rester means to stay or remain *not* to rest; **se reposer** means to rest
le crayon means the pencil *not* the crayon; **le pastel** means the crayon
la fabrique means the factory *not* the fabric; **le tissu** means the fabric
la lecture means the reading selection *not* lecture; **la conférence** means the lecture
la librairie means the bookstore *not* the library; **la bibliothèque** means the library
le magasin means the store *not* the magazine; **la revue** means the magazine
actuellement means now, at present *not* actually; **réellement** means actually
large means wide *not* large; **grand** means large
les nouvelles means the news *not novels;* **le roman** means the novel

French Expressions

1. **les affaires se traitent** business is done
2. **entamer** to start, to begin; **entamer une affaire** to take up a business matter
3. **sans aucune doute** without any doubt
4. **manquer** to miss, to be lacking, to fail, to be in need of
5. **Vous allez me manquer.** I shall miss you. (*Lit.* You will be missing to me.)
6. **L'argent lui manque.** He lacks money. (*Lit.* Money is lacking to him.)
7. **Je n'y manquerai pas.** I shall not fail to do so.
8. **faire ses amitiés** to give one's regards
9. **faites-lui mes amitiés** give him my regards
10. **mes amitiés à tout le monde** regards to all
11. **Point de nouvelles, bonnes nouvelles.** No news is good news.

Exercise No. 157—Completion of Text

1. (Through the open window) **on entend les bruits de la rue.**
2. (I have a mind) **de vous accompagner.**
3. (Will you give me) **quelques derniers conseils?**
4. **On fait les choses** (with more formality) **qu'ici.**
5. (Each man is worthy) **d'être respecté.**
6. **Ils désirent** (want to get to know one another).
7. **En général la vie en France** (is more tranquil).
8. (Have you read) **les livres sur la France?**
9. (I have glanced through) **les deux guides.**
10. (I shall spend) **l'été à New-York.**
11. I shall miss you.
12. (I shall be happy) **de recevoir vos lettres.**

Grammar Notes

1. More irregular past participles

courir to run	**couru** run	**parcourir** to scan	**parcouru** scanned
mettre to put	**mis** put	**promettre** to promise	**promis** promised
prendre to take	**pris** taken	**apprendre** to learn	**appris** learned
voir to see	**vu** seen	**comprendre** to understand	**compris** understood

Exercise No. 158. Complete each of the following sentences with the correct past participle. Read each completed sentence aloud.

1. **J'ai déjà** (scanned *or* glanced through) **tous les guides.**
2. **Avez-vous** (understood) **tout ce que le maître a** (said)?
3. **A-t-il** (put on) **son pardessus?**
4. **Elle a** (promised) **de nous rencontrer a l'aéroport.**
5. **J'ai tout** (heard) **mais je n'ai pas tout** (understood).
6. **Avez-vous** (seen) **Mme. Picard?**
7. **Les enfants ont** (run) **à l'école.**
8. **Les élèves ont** (learned) **beaucoup de locutions françaises.**
9. **Ils n'ont pas** (taken) **leurs caoutchoucs.**
10. **Nous n'avons pas** (taken) **la bouteille.**

2. Agreement of the past participle

When a direct object precedes the verb the past participle must agree with that direct object in number and gender.

Direct object after verb (*No agreement*)	Direct object before verb (*Agreement*)
Avez-vous trouvé ***le livre?***	**Je** ***l'*****ai trouvé.** (*masc. sing.*)
Avez-vous trouvé ***la lettre?***	**Je** ***l'*****ai trouvée.** (*fem. sing.*)
Avez-vous trouvé ***les livres?***	**Je** ***les*** **ai trouvés.** (*masc. plur.*)
Avez-vous trouvé ***les lettres?***	**Je** ***les*** **ai trouvées.** (*fem. plur.*)

The past participle does not agree with an *indirect* object preceding the verb.
Nous ne ***leur*** **avons pas donné de cadeaux.** We did not give *them* any gifts.

Exercise No. 159. Translate each question and answer. Read each question and answer aloud in French three times. Note the agreement of the past participle.

1. **— Avez-vous recommandé ces guides** (*m*)*?*
2. **— Est-ce qu'il a écrit la réponse?**
3. **— Où a-t-il trouvé l'argent** (*m*)*?*
4. **— Avez-vous compris la question?**
5. **— A-t-elle appris le proverbe?**
6. **— Qui a reservé les deux places** (*f*)*?*
7. **— Quand avez-vous vu votre amie?**
8. **— Quand ont-ils fini l'examen** (*m*)*?*
9. **— Quand est-ce que le facteur** (postman) **a apporté les lettres?**
10. **— Avez-vous entendu la sonnette** (door bell)?
11. **— M. Potter a-t-il parcouru tous les guides?**
12. **— Quelle lettre a-t-il lue**[1] **à M. Picard?**

1. **— Oui, monsieur, je les ai** ***recommandés.***
2. **— Oui monsieur, il l'a** ***écrite.***
3. **— Il l'a** ***trouvé*** **au bureau.**
4. **— Non monsieur, je ne l'ai pas** ***comprise.***
5. **— Non madame, elle ne l'a pas** ***appris.***
6. **— Mon père les a** ***réservées*** **hier.**
7. **— Je l'ai** ***vue*** **hier soir.**
8. **— Ils l'ont** ***fini*** **à deux heures.**
9. **— Il les a** ***apportées*** **ce matin.**
10. **— Non, monsieur, je ne l'ai pas** ***entendue.***
11. **— Il les a** ***parcourus*** **tous.**
12. **— Il a** ***lu*** **la lettre qu'il a** ***reçue***[2] **de M. Parmentier.**

NOTE 1. The direct object preceding the verb, with which **lue** agrees, is **quelle lettre.**

NOTE 2. The direct object preceding the verb, with which **reçue** agrees, is the relative pronoun **qu'**, which is feminine because it refers to **lettre** (*f*).

Exercise No. 160—Questionnaire

1. **Où se trouvent M. Potter et M. Picard?**
2. **Quel temps fait-il?**
3. **Qu'est-ce qu'on entend par la fenêtre?**
4. **Qui est content de quitter la ville?**

5. Qui a envie d'accompagner M. Potter?
6. Qu'est-ce que M. Picard répond à la question, "Ne pourrez-vous pas venir avec moi"?
7. Comment fait-on les choses en France?
8. Qu'est-ce que M. Picard a remarqué en France?
9. Qui est las d'être bousculé?
10. Qui a lu des livres sur la France?
11. Qui les a recommandés?
12. Quant à M. Picard, où passera-t-il l'été?
13. A qui M. Potter pensera-t-il souvent?

CHAPITRE 31 (TRENTE ET UN)

M. POTTER PART POUR LA FRANCE
MR. POTTER LEAVES FOR FRANCE

1. Il y a cinq mois que M. Potter étudie le français. Il a passé beaucoup de temps en conversation avec son professeur, M. Picard. Il a appris les règles essentielles de la grammaire et il a lu beaucoup de livres sur la France. Il a vraiment travaillé dur. Maintenant il parle bien le français et il compte se tirer d'affaires en France sans difficulté.

2. M. Potter a obtenu son billet pour le voyage, son passeport, et ses chèques de voyage. Il a tout ce qui lui faut.

3. Naturellement M. Potter a écrit une lettre à son représentant en France pour lui faire savoir l'heure de son arrivée. M. Parmentier, le représentant, a promis de le rencontrer à l'aéroport.

4. C'est enfin le 31 mai, ce jour entre tous. L'avion de M. Potter part de l'aéroport Kennedy International à sept heures précises du soir. Il doit être à l'aéroport une heure d'avance pour faire contrôler son billet et son passeport et pour faire peser ses bagages.

5. La famille ne l'accompagne pas en France parce que les enfants doivent finir l'année scolaire, et sa femme doit rester à la maison pour s'occuper des enfants. D'ailleurs, voyager avec quatre enfants entre cinq et douze ans est non seulement difficile, mais aussi assez coûteux.

6. Naturellement la famille est dans tous ses états. Les enfants ont très peu dormi et à sept heures du matin ils sont tous levés, lavés, et habillés.

7. À cinq heures de l'après-midi la famille est prête à partir pour l'aéroport. M. Potter a fait ses deux valises et il les a déjà mises dans l'auto. Ils montent tous en voiture. M. Potter se met en route et ils arrivent à l'aéroport vers six heures.

8. M. Potter fait contrôler son billet et son passeport, et il fait peser ses bagages. Il doit payer vingt dollars en supplément parce que le poids total dépasse les soixante-six livres permis gratis.

9. Alors M. Potter fait ses adieux à sa femme et aux enfants qui lui souhaitent "bon voyage." Il monte dans l'avion, saluant de la main son petit monde qui le regarde d'un air ému. À sept heures précises l'avion prend son vol.

10. M. Potter est en route.

1. Mr. Potter has been studying French for five months. He has spent a lot of time in conversation with his teacher, Mr. Picard. He has learned the essential rules of grammar and he has read many books on France. He really has worked very hard. Now he speaks French quite well and he expects to get along in France without difficulty.

2. Mr. Potter has obtained his ticket for the trip, his passport, and his travelers' checks. He has everything he needs.

3. Of course Mr. Potter has written a letter to his agent in France letting him know the time of his arrival. Mr. Parmentier, the agent, has promised to meet him at the airport.

4. It is May 31 at last, the day of days. Mr. Potter's plane leaves Kennedy International Airport at 7 p.m. sharp. He must be at the airport one hour before to have his ticket and passport checked and his baggage weighed.

5. The family is not going with him to France because his children have to finish the school year and his wife has to remain at home to take care of the children. Besides, traveling with four children from five to twelve years of age is not only difficult but also quite expensive.

6. Of course the family is extremely excited. The children have hardly slept and at seven in the morning they are all awake, washed and dressed.

7. At five in the afternoon the whole family is ready to leave for the airport. Mr. Potter has packed two valises and he has already put them in the car. They all get into the car. Mr. Potter starts off and they arrive at the airport at about six.

8. Mr. Potter has his ticket and his passport checked and he has his baggage weighed. He has to pay twenty dollars extra, because the total weight exceeds the 66 pounds allowed free.

9. Then Mr. Potter says goodbye to his wife and children, who wish him a good trip. He goes up into the plane waving to his little world, who are watching him with emotion. At 7 o'clock sharp the plane takes off.

10. Mr. Potter is on his way.

Building Vocabulary

A. Antonyms

1. **il a ouvert** he opened
   il a fermé he closed
2. **j'ai commencé** I began
   j'ai fini I finished
3. **nous avons trouvé** we found
   nous avons perdu we lost
4. **vous avez envoyé** you sent
   vous avez apporté you brought
5. **ils ont acheté** they bought
   ils ont vendu they sold
6. **elles ont donné** they gave
   elles ont reçu they received

French Expressions

1. **se tirer d'affaire, s'en tirer** to get along, to cope
2. **pour lui faire savoir** to let him know
3. **ce jour entre tous** this day of days
4. **pour faire contrôler son billet** to have his ticket checked
5. **pour faire peser ses bagages** to have his baggage weighed
6. **s'occuper de** to busy oneself with, to take care of
7. **être dans tous ses états** to be extremely excited
8. **faire les valises** to pack the suitcases
9. **monter en voiture** to get in the car
10. **se mettre en route** to set out
11. **faire ses adieux à** to say goodbye to
12. **Il est en route.** He is on his way.

Exercise No. 161—Completion of Text

1. (It is five months) **que M. Potter étudie le français.**
2. (He has learned) **les règles essentielles.**
3. (He has really worked) **beaucoup.**
4. (He has obtained) **son billet pour le voyage.**
5. (He has written) **une lettre à son représentant.**
6. **M. Parmentier** (has promised) **de le rencontrer.**
7. **À six heures** (he must be) **à l'aéroport.**
8. **La famille** (is not going with him).
9. **Les enfants** (must finish) **l'année scolaire.**
10. **M. Potter** (has packed) **les deux valises.**
11. (They all get) **en voiture.**
12. **M. Potter** (has his baggage weighed).
13. (He must pay) **vingt dollars en supplément.**
14. **M. Potter** (says goodbye to) **sa femme et ses enfants.**
15. **Il est** (on his way).

Grammar Notes

1. More irregular past participles

ouvrir to open	**ouvert** opened	**vivre** to live	**vécu** lived
couvrir to cover	**couvert** covered	**plaire** to please	**plu** pleased
offrir to offer	**offert** offered	**devoir** to owe	**dû** owed
savoir to know	**su** learned[1]	**falloir** must[2]	**fallu** had to[2]
vouloir to want	**voulu** wanted	**paraître** to appear	**paru** appeared
avoir to have	**eu** had	**boire** to drink	**bu** drunk
être to be	**été** been	**croire** to believe	**cru** believed

NOTE 1. The conversational past of **savoir — j'ai su,** etc.—means I have learned (found out), etc., *not* I have known, etc. NOTE 2. The verb **falloir** is used only in the third person singular, thus **il a fallu** is the only form used in the conversational past tense.

Exercise No. 162. Translate. Use the conversational past for these verbs.

Exemple: I have had (I had, I did have), **j'ai eu**

1. he has wanted
2. you opened
3. I have found out
4. did he open?
5. we have had
6. they have been
7. I have not covered
8. have they found out?
9. we did not open
10. she was
11. did he want?
12. I offered

2. Past participles used as adjectives

Past participles are often used as adjectives. Like other adjectives they usually follow the noun they modify and always agree with it in number and gender.

le vase cassé	the broken vase	**le livre ouvert**	the open book
les vases cassés	the broken vases	**les livres ouverts**	the open books
la tasse cassée	the broken cup	**la porte ouverte**	the open door
les tasses cassées	the broken cups	**les portes ouvertes**	the open doors

Exercise No. 163. Complete each sentence with the correct form of the past participle in parentheses:

Exemple: 1. Il est assis près de la fenêtre ouverte.

1. **Il est assis près de la fenêtre (ouvert)**
2. **Au mur il y a des affiches (*f*) (illustré)**
3. **Toutes les portes sont (fermé)**
4. **Le couturier Dior est bien (connu)**
5. **Beaucoup de ces tasses (*f*) sont (cassé)**
6. **Tous les enfants sont (levé)**
7. **Jean n'est pas encore (habillé)**
8. **Voici des revues (*f*) (envoyé) par M. Picard**
9. **Où est la chambre (réservé) pour M. Adams**
10. **Nous avons trouvé les billets (perdu)**

Exercise No. 164—Questionnaire

1. **Combien de temps y a-t-il que M. Potter étudie le français?**
2. **Avec qui a-t-il passé beaucoup de temps en conversation?**
3. **Qu'est-ce qu'il a appris?**
4. **Comment est-ce qu'il a travaillé?**
5. **Comment est-ce qu'il parle français maintenant?**
6. **Qu'est-ce que M. Potter a obtenu?**
7. **A qui M. Potter a-t-il écrit?**
8. **Qu'est-ce que son représentant lui a promis?**
9. **À quelle heure les enfants sont-ils levés?**
10. **À quelle heure est-ce que l'avion part de l'aéroport?**
11. **Qu'est-ce que chaque voyageur doit faire contrôler?**
12. **Est-ce que sa famille accompagne M. Potter en France?**
13. **Pourquoi est-ce que les enfants doivent rester à New-York?**
14. **Pourquoi est-ce que Mme. Potter doit rester à New-York?**

RÉVISION 7
CHAPITRES 28–31 PRÈMIERE PARTIE

NOUNS

1. l'aéroport	**7. la familiarité**	**13. la politesse**	1. airport	7. familiarity	13. courtesy
2. le bruit	**8. la faute**	**14. la règle**	2. noise	8. mistake, fault	14. rule
3. l'arrivée	**9. la formalité**	**15. le séjour**	3. arrival	9. formality	15. stay, sojourn
4. la copie	**10. l'intérêt**	**16. la sortie**	4. copy	10. interest	16. exit, departure
5. la difficulté	**11. la main**	**17. le valeur**	5. difficulty	11. hand	17. value
6. l'espoir	**12. le passeport**	**18. l'homme d'affaires**	6. hope	12. passport	18. businessman

VERBS

1. apprécier	**7. s'occuper de**	**13. traiter**	1. to appreciate	7. to be busy with	13. to treat
2. j'apprécie	**8. elle s'occupe de**	**14. courir**	2. I appreciate	8. she takes care of	14. to run
3. avouer	**9. pardonner**	**15. parcourir**	3. to avow	9. to pardon	15. to scan, glance
4. contrôler	**10. pardonnez-moi**	**16. permettre**	4. to control, check	10. pardon me	16. to permit
5. dépasser	**11. prier**	**17. souhaiter**	5. to exceed	11. to pray, to beg	17. to wish
6. s'habituer à	**12. remarquer**	**18. surprendre**	6. to get used to	12. to notice	18. to surprise

ADJECTIVES

1. différent	**4. distingué**	**7. sérieux (euse *f.*)**	1. different	4. distinguished	7. serious
2. dernier	**5. nerveux (euse *f.*)**	**8. seul**	2. last	5. nervous	8. alone
3. digne	**6. propre**	**9. las (lasse *f.*)**	3. worthy	6. own	9. tired

ADVERBS

1. d'avance	**2. malheureusement**	**3. heureusement**	1. in advance	2. unfortunately	3. fortunately

FRENCH EXPRESSIONS

1. faire ses adieux à	**10. se tirer d'affaire, s'en tirer**	1. to say goodbye to	10. to get along, to cope
2. faire ses amitiés à	**11. voulez-vous bien**	2. to give his regards to	11. will you kindly
3. faire votre connaissance	**12. à la perfection**	3. to make your acquaintance	12. perfectly
	13. quant à moi		13. as for me
4. faire peser les valises	**14. par conséquent**	4. to have bags weighed	14. consequently
5. faire venir	**15. deux fois par semaine**	5. to send for	15. two times a week
6. faire savoir	**16. votre propre langue**	6. to let know	16. your own language
7. descendre de la voiture	**17. je vous prie**	7. to get out of the car	17. I beg you, please
8. monter en voiture	**18. vers six heures**	8. to get into the car	18. about six o'clock
9. se mettre en route		9. to set out	

DEUXIÈME PARTIE

Exercise No. 165. Translate each past participle and give the infinitive of the verb from which it is derived.

Exemple: vendu sold **vendre** to sell

1. obtenu	**6. voulu**	**11. su**	**16. mangé**	**21. compris**
2. laissé	**7. reçu**	**12. rendu**	**17. fait**	**22. ouvert**
3. été	**8. écrit**	**13. mis**	**18. pris**	**23. eu**
4. dit	**9. lu**	**14. obéi**	**19. écouté**	**24. permis**
5. fini	**10. appris**	**15. vu**	**20. couvert**	**25. pu**

Exercise No. 166. Select the group of words in Column II which best completes each sentence begun in Column I:

I	II
1. M. Potter a appris rapidement	**a. qui l'attendra à l'aéroport.**
2. Il parle bien le français; par conséquent	**b. me rendront grand service.**
3. Il a un représentant à Paris	**c. deux fois par semaine chez M. Potter.**
4. M. Picard n'a pas trouvé une seule faute	**d. est digne d'être respecté.**
5. Il y a cinq mois qu'ils se rencontrent	**e. il pourra se tirer d'affaires en France.**
6. Mme. Potter s'occupera des enfants	**f. l'heure de votre arrivée?**
7. Les Français croient que chaque homme	**g. parce qu'il a travaillé dur.**
8. Avant le départ de M. Potter	**h. dans la lettre que M. Potter a écrite.**
9. Les deux guides que vous m'avez prêtés	**i. pendant l'absence de son mari.**
10. Voulez-vous bien me faire savoir	**j. son professeur lui a donné de bons conseils.**

Exercise No. 167. Complete each sentence in Column I by choosing the correct expression from Column II. Be sure to use the correct verb form.

I	II
1. (Have you packed) **les valises?**	**a. monter en voiture**
2. (Give my regards) **à Mme. Potter.**	**b. descendre de la voiture**
3. **Embrassez les enfants** (for me).	**c. faire ses adieux**
4. **Je parlerai avec vous** (in your own language).	**d. me tirer d'affaire**
5. (Pardon me) **si je suis fier de mes compatriotes.**	**e. faire les valises**
6. **Je pourrai** (to get along) **en France.**	**f. pardonnez-moi**
7. **J'aurai le plaisir** (of meeting you).	**g. votre propre langue**
8. (They get into the car) **et se mettent en route.**	**h. faire votre connaissance**
9. (They get out of the car) **à l'aéroport.**	**i. faire mes amitiés**
10. **Là M. Potter** (said goodbye) **à sa famille.**	**j. de ma part**

Exercise No. 168. Read each question. Translate the English answers into French. In seven of the answers there is a direct object pronoun before the verb. Be sure that the past participle agrees with the direct object pronoun in number and gender.

Exemple: 1. Oui, monsieur, je l'ai reçue.

1. Avez-vous reçu ma lettre?	1. Yes sir, I have received it (*f*).
2. À qui est-ce que M. Potter à écrit la lettre?	2. He wrote it (*f*) to Mr. Parmentier.
3. M. Potter a-t-il apprécié ses services?	3. Yes sir, he has appreciated them (*m*).
4. Qui a fait la valise?	4. Mr. Potter has packed it (*f*).
5. Est-ce que les guides vous ont rendu grand service?	5. Yes, sir, they have rendered me great service.
6. Qu'est-ce que la bonne a servi?	6. She served tea with rum.
7. Avez-vous compris la question?	7. No sir, I did not understand it (*f*).
8. Qui n'a pas fait les leçons?	8. Philippe has not done them (*f*).
9. Avez-vous vu le nouveau film?	9. No madame, we have not seen it (*m*).
10. Qu'est-ce que le facteur a apporté?	10. He has brought a parcel-post package (**colis postal** *m*).

Dialogue 1 — À l'aéroport

1. — Bonjour, M. Parmentier. Est-ce que vous attendez quelqu'un?	1. Good day, Mr. Parmentier. Are you expecting someone?
2. — Oui, monsieur, J'attends M. Potter de New-York, le chef de la maison que je représente à Paris.	2. Yes, sir, I am waiting for Mr. Potter of New York, the head of the firm I represent in Paris.
3. — Est-ce que vous le connaissez?	3. Do you know him?
4. — Je le connais seulement par correspondance. Mais j'ai sa photo et je crois que je le reconnaîtrai. C'est un homme d'à peu près quarante ans.	4. I know him only by correspondence. But I have his photo and I think I'll recognize him. He is a man about forty years old.
5. — À quelle heure doit-il arriver?	5. At what time should he arrive?
6. — L'avion est annoncé pour sept heures.	6. The plane is scheduled to arrive at noon.
7. — Est-il en retard?	7. Is it late?
8. — Non, il est à temps. Ah! Le voilà. Il arrive. Il s'approche. Il s'atterre.	8. No, it's on time. Ah! There it is. It's coming. It's approaching. It is landing.
9. — Excusez-moi, monsieur, je vais à la rencontre de M. Potter.	9. Excuse me, sir, I am going to meet Mr. Potter.

Dialogue 2 — Bienvenu en France

1. — (Soyez le) Bienvenu en France, M. Potter. Comment le voyage s'est-il passé?	1. Welcome to France, Mr. Potter. How did the trip go?
2. — Merveilleusement bien! Je suis heureux d'être en France. J'ai tellement songé à ce moment.	2. Marvelously well. I am happy to be in France. I have thought about this moment so much.
3. — Et vous voilà! Je suis sûr que vous serez très content ici.	3. And here you are! I am sure that you will be very happy here.

Exercise No. 169—Lecture
Un Programme Exceptionnel Au Cinéma

Ce soir M. et Mme. Potter vont au cinéma. Ils n'aiment pas la plupart des films de Hollywood, surtout les "Westerns" dans lesquels les "cowboys" tirent des coups de feu sur tout le monde et galopent sans cesse. Les films policiers ne les intéressent pas non plus.

Mais ce soir il y a un programme exceptionnel dans un théâtre qui est tout près de chez eux. Le film s'appelle "Un Voyage en France." C'est un film de reportage sur le pays que M. Potter va visiter dans quelques mois. Il y a des scènes qui représentent l'histoire de la France, d'autres qui montrent ses paysages, ses rivières, ses montagnes, ses grandes villes, etc. C'est à dire que c'est un film très intéressant pour les touristes.

Les Potter arrivent au théâtre à huit heures et demie. Presque toutes les places sont prises, donc ils doivent s'asseoir au troisième rang. Ceci ne plaît pas à M. Potter parce que les mouvements sur l'écran lui font mal aux yeux. Heureusement ils peuvent changer de place après un quart d'heure et ils se mettent au treizième rang.

Les Potter aiment beaucoup ce film. Ils le trouvent passionnant.

En sortant du théâtre M. Potter dit à sa femme, — Sais-tu, Alice, je crois que je me tirerai bien d'affaire en France. J'ai compris presque tout ce qu'on dit.

CHAPITRE 32 (TRENTE-DEUX)

USAGE REND MAÎTRE
PRACTICE MAKES PERFECT

Foreword

Mr. Potter is now in France and he writes nine letters to Mr. Picard about some of the places he visits and about some of his experiences and impressions.

There are many references in his letters to things he has discussed with his teacher. Much of the vocabulary of Chapters 3 to 31 is repeated in the letters.

Reread the texts and dialogues of the previous chapters *before* proceeding with Chapter 32 to review the vocabulary and important expressions. You will be able to do this easily and rapidly, with little or no reference to the English translation.

You should continue your pronunciation practice by reading aloud dialogues and parts of conversational texts from previous chapters as often as possible.

L'Arrivée À Paris
Arrival in Paris

La Première Lettre De Paris

Paris, le 4 juin 1987

Cher ami,

1. Quand l'avion est arrivé[1] à Roissy,[2] j'ai passé par la douane et je suis allé à la salle d'attente.

2. Tout de suite un bel homme s'est approché[3] et il m'a demandé, — Pardon monsieur, êtes-vous M. Potter?

3. J'ai répondu, — À votre service. Et vous êtes M. Parmentier, n'est-ce pas? Je suis très content de faire votre connaissance.

Nous nous sommes serré la main.

4. — Le plaisir est à moi, M. Parmentier a répondu.

5. Vous vous rappelez, M. Picard, que M. Parmentier est le représentant de notre maison à Paris.

6. Nous sommes sortis ensemble et nous avons pris un taxi pour l'Hôtel du Quai Voltaire.

7. Le taxi a pris le chemin de la ville en allant à toute vitesse. J'ai pensé à moi-même, — M. Picard se trompe au sujet de la vie tranquille en France.

8. En regardant autour de nous j'ai vu que tout, autos, camions, autobus, taxis, tout courait à vitesse vertigineuse.

9. A la fin j'ai crié au chauffeur, — Pas si vite, s'il vous plaît! Je ne suis pas pressé!

10. — Ni moi non plus, monsieur, m'a-t-il répondu, tournant le coin à toute vitesse.

Paris, June 4, 1987

Dear Friend,

1. When the plane arrived at Roissy, I got through the customs and went to the waiting room.

2. A fine-looking man immediately approached me and asked, "Pardon me, sir, are you Mr. Potter?"

3. "At your service," I answered. "And you are Mr. Parmentier, are you not? I am delighted to know you."

We shook hands.

4. "The pleasure is mine," answered Mr. Parmentier.

5. You remember, Mr. Picard, that Mr. Parmentier is the agent of our firm in Paris.

6. We went out together and took a taxi to the Hotel du Quai Voltaire.

7. The taxi drove (*Lit.*, took the road) to the city (going) at full speed. I thought to myself, "Mr. Picard is mistaken about the quiet life of France."

8. Looking around us I saw that everything—cars, trucks, buses, taxis—everything was rushing at a dizzying speed.

9. At last I shouted to the driver, "Not so fast, please! I am not in a hurry!"

10. "Neither am I, sir," he answered me, turning the corner at full speed.

11. Enfin nous sommes arrivés à l'hôtel sain et saufs. Le taxi s'est arrêté et nous sommes descendus. M. Parmentier est entré avec moi.

11. At last we arrived safe and sound (*Lit.* healthy and safe) at the hotel. The taxi stopped and we got out. Mr. Parmentier went in with me.

12. Je suis allé au bureau de réception, et j'ai dit à l'employé, — Bonjour, monsieur. Avez-vous une chambre réservée pour Potter?

12. I went to the reception desk and said to the clerk, "Good day, sir. Do you have a room reserved for Potter?"

13. — Bienvenu à Paris, M. Potter. Certainement. Nous vous avons réservé une belle chambre au troisième étage qui donne sur le quai. C'est le numéro 35.

13. Welcome to Paris, Mr. Potter. Certainly. We have reserved for you a fine room on the third floor, which faces the quay. It is number 35.

14. — Très bien, merci. Et quel est le prix, s'il vous plaît?

14. Very good, thank you. And what is the rate, please?

15. — Quatre cent francs par jour, service compris.

15. Four hundred francs a day, including service.

16. — Bon. Voulez-vous bien faire monter mes bagages?

16. Good. Would you please have my bags taken up?

17. — Tout de suite, monsieur. Porteur! Mais vous parlez très bien le français. Y a-t-il longtemps que vous êtes en France?

17. Right away, sir. Porter! But you speak French very well. Have you been in France long?

18. — Je viens d'arriver, ai-je dit, assez fier de moi-même.

18. "I have just arrived," I said, quite proud of myself.

19. — Est-ce que vous faites un voyage d'agrément?

19. Are you on a pleasure trip?

20. — C'est à la fois un voyage d'agrément et un voyage d'affaires.

20. This is both a pleasure trip and a business trip.

21. J'ai causé un peu plus avec M. Parmentier et ensuite nous nous sommes dit au revoir. M. Parmentier m'a promis en partant de me téléphoner pour prendre rendez-vous.

21. I chatted a little more with Mr. Parmentier and then we said goodbye. On leaving Mr. Parmentier promised to telephone me to make an appointment.

22. Je suis monté par l'ascenseur à ma chambre, numéro 35. Elle est très commode. Je ne manque de rien. Je vous répète encore une fois, M. Picard, que je serai très content en France.

Cordialement, votre ami,
John Potter

22. I went up in the elevator to my room, number 35. It is very comfortable. I lack nothing. I repeat once more, Mr. Picard, that I shall be very happy in France.

Cordially, your friend,
John Potter

NOTE 1. Sixteen French verbs form their conversational past by using **être** as an auxiliary (**je suis, tu es, il est**, etc.) instead of **avoir** (**j'ai, tu as, il a**, etc.). These so-called **être**-verbs are fully explained in the Grammar Notes of this chapter. 2. Roissy, a town outside Paris where Charles de Gaulle International Airport is located. 3. All reflexive verbs use **être** (**je suis, tu es, il est**, etc.) to form their conversational past. This use is fully explained in the Grammar Notes of the next chapter.

Building Vocabulary

A. Antonyms

1. **il est allé** he went
   il est venu he came
2. **il est arrivé** he arrived
   il est parti he left
3. **il est entré** he entered
   il est sorti he went out
4. **il est monté** he went up
   il est descendu he went down
5. **il s'est rappelé** he remembered
   il a oublié he forgot
6. **il a demandé** he asked
   il a répondu he answered

B. Related words

1. **appeler** to call; **s'appeler** to be called, to be named; **se rappeler** to recall, remember
2. **entrer** to enter; **rentrer** to re-enter, return home
3. **tourner** to turn; **retourner** to return, go back; **détourner** to reroute
4. **venir** to come; **revenir** to come back; **devenir** to become; **prevenir** to warn
5. **voir** to see; **revoir** to see again

French Expressions

Présentations (pray-zahñ-tah-syawñ)	Introductions
1. **Permettez-moi de vous présenter M. Parmentier, un de mes amis.**	1. Allow me to introduce you to Mr. Parmentier, a friend of mine.
2. **Enchanté de faire votre connaissance.**	2. Delighted to make your acquaintance; to know you.
3. **Le plaisir est à moi.**	3. The pleasure is mine.
4. **Veuillez** (veu-yay) **me présenter à monsieur (madame)?**	4. Would you kindly introduce me to the gentleman (lady)?

Salutations: letters to friends

1. **Mon cher Louis,** Dear Louis,
2. **Ma chère Colette,** Dear Colette,
3. **Cher ami,** Dear Friend (*m*),
4. **Chère amie,** Dear Friend (*f*),

Closings: letters to friends

1. **Cordialement, votre ami,**
   Cordially yours,
2. **Salutations amicales de votre ami,**
   Warm greetings from your friend,
3. **Très affectueusement,**
   Very affectionately yours,
4. **Embrasse tout le monde pour moi,**
   Kiss everybody for me,
5. **Rappelle-moi au bon souvenir de ta famille,**
   Remember me to your family,

Exercise No. 170—Completion of Text

1. **Je suis allé** (to the waiting-room).
2. (Immediately) **un bel homme s'est approché.**
3. (He asked me), **— Êtes-vous M. Potter?**
4. (I answered), **— À votre service.**
5. **Je suis content** (to make your acquaintance).
6. (The pleasure is mine), **a-t-il répondu.**
7. (I thought to myself), **— M. Parmentier se trompe.**
8. (We took) **un taxi.**
9. **Tout courait** (at a dizzying speed).
10. Not so fast!
11. **J'ai crié, —** (I am not in a hurry).
12. — (Neither am I), **m'a-t-il répondu.**
13. **Avez-vous une chambre** (reserved for Potter)?
14. (What is the rate), **s'il vous plaît?**
15. (Four hundred francs per day) **service compris.**

Grammar Notes

1. Verbs with the auxiliary **être** instead of **avoir**

You have learned that the conversational past tense (present perfect) in French usually consists of the auxiliary **avoir** (*have*) plus the past participle of the verb.

In French there are sixteen verbs which take some form of the auxiliary **être** (*be*) instead of **avoir** (*have*). They are called **être**-verbs. They are translated into English the same way as **avoir**-verbs. The two most common **être**-verbs are **aller** *to go* and **venir** *to come*. Observe carefully the conversational past tense of **aller**, noting the auxiliary verb and the changes in the past participle.

I have gone, I went, I did go; you have gone, you went, you did go, etc.

je suis	**allé** (*m*) **allée** (*f*)	(zhuh süee za-**lay**)	**nous sommes**	**allés** (*m. plur.*) **allées** (*f. plur.*)	(noo sum za-**lay**)
tu es	**allé** (*m*) **allée** (*f*)	(tu eh za-**lay**)	**vous êtes**	**allé allés** **allée allées**	(voo zeht za-**lay**)
il est	**allé**	(eel eh ta-**lay**)	**ils sont**	**allés**	(eel sawñ ta-**lay**)
elle est	**allée**	(ehl eh ta-**lay**)	**elles sont**	**allées**	(ehl sawñ ta-**lay**)

a. The past participle of an **être**-verb agrees with the subject in number and gender.

b. **je, tu,** and **nous** may be masculine or feminine. If **je** or **tu** are feminine the agreeing past participle adds the feminine singular ending **-e.** If **nous** is masculine, the agreeing past participle adds **-s.** If **nous** is feminine, the past participle adds **-es.**

Vous, like *you* in English, may be masculine or feminine singular, or masculine or feminine plural. The agreeing past participle therefore has four possible forms.

(*masc. sing.*) **allé** (*fem. sing.*) **allée** (*masc. plur.*) **allés** (*fem. plur.*) **allées**

2. List of **être**-verbs

Infinitive		*Conversational Past*	
aller	to go	**il (elle) est allé(e)**	**nous sommes allés (allées)**
arriver	to arrive	**il (elle) est arrivé(e)**	**nous sommes arrivés (arrivées)**
entrer	to enter, come (go) in	**il (elle) est entré(e)**	**nous sommes entrés (entrées)**
rentrer	to return, go home	**il (elle) est rentré(e)**	**nous sommes rentrés (rentrées)**
monter	to climb, mount	**il (elle) est monté(e)**	**nous sommes montés (montées)**
retourner	to return, go back	**il (elle) est retourné(e)**	**nous sommes retournés (retournées)**
tomber	to fall	**il (elle) est tombé(e)**	**nous sommes tombés (tombées)**
rester	to remain, stay	**il (elle) est resté(e)**	**nous sommes restés (restées)**
partir	to leave, depart	**il (elle) est parti(e)**	**nous sommes partis (parties)**
sortir (de)	to go out (of)	**il (elle) est sorti(e) de**	**nous sommes sortis (sorties) de**
venir	to come	**il (elle) est venu(e)**	**nous sommes venus (venues)**
revenir	to return, come back	**il (elle) est revenu(e)**	**nous sommes revenus (revenues)**
devenir	to become	**il (elle) est devenu(e)**	**nous sommes devenus (devenues)**
descendre	to go (come) down	**il (elle) est descendu(e)**	**nous sommes descendus (descendues)**
naître	to be born	**il (elle) est né(e)**	**nous sommes nés (nées)**
mourir	to die	**il (elle) est mort(e)**	**nous sommes morts (mortes)**

Note that all the **être**-verbs except **devenir** *to become,* **mourir** *to die* and **naître** *to be born,* are verbs of motion. They are all intransitive, that is, they do not take objects.

Exercise No. 171. Translate each short dialogue. Note the agreement of the past participle. Read each dialogue aloud three times.

1. **— Philippe est-il allé à la gare pour rencontrer son père?**
   — Oui. Il est sorti de la maison il y a vingt minutes.
   — Est-ce que sa soeur Marie est allée avec lui?
   — Oui. Sa soeur, Marie, et aussi son frère, Henri, sont allés avec lui.
2. **— Madame Potter est-elle revenue de la ville?**
   — Elle n'est pas encore revenue, mais elle reviendra bientôt.
   — Pourquoi est-elle allée en ville?
   — Elle y est allée pour faire ses achats.
3. **— Pourquoi est-ce que M. Potter est revenu tard ce soir?**
   — Beaucoup de clients sont venus le voir l'après-midi.
   — A quelle heure part-il de son bureau d'habitude?
   — D'habitude il part à cinq heures précises mais aujourd'hui il n'est pas parti jusqu'à six heures moins le quart.
4. **— À quelle heure est-ce que M. Potter est parti pour l'aéroport?**
   — Il est parti à six heures du matin.
   — À quelle heure est-il monté dans l'avion?
   — Il est monté dans l'avion à huit heures moins le quart.

Exercise No. 172. Supply the correct form of the participle of the verb in parentheses. Watch your endings. Read each completed sentence aloud three times.

Exemple: 1. Elle est arrivée chez elle à six heures et demie.

1. **Elle est (arriver) chez elle à six heures et demie.**
2. **Nous (*f*) sommes (aller) à la gare en voiture.**
3. **Abraham Lincoln est (naître) le 12 février 1809.**
4. **Il est (mourir) le 15 avril 1865.**
5. **Les enfants sont (devenir) très agités quand leur père est (monter) dans l'avion.**
6. **Mme. Potter est (retourner) de la ville à trois heures et quart.**

7. À quelle heure est-ce que la famille Potter est (partir) pour l'aéroport?
8. A cinq heures précises ils sont (entrer) dans la salle d'attente.
9. Je (*m*) suis (rester) trois semaines à Paris.
10. Quand vous (*m plur.*) êtes (partir) nous (*m*) sommes (arriver).

Exercise No. 173—Questionnaire

1. Qu'est-ce que M. Potter a fait quand l'avion est arrivé?
2. Qui s'est approché dans la salle d'attente?
3. Qu'est-ce que le monsieur a dit?
4. Qu'est-ce que M. Potter a répondu?
5. Comment le taxi est-il allé en ville?
6. Qu'est-ce qu'il a crié à la fin?
7. Qu'est-ce que le chauffeur a répondu?
8. Qu'est-ce que M. Potter a dit à l'employé?
9. Qu'est-ce qu'il a répondu?

CHAPITRE 33 (TRENTE-TROIS)

M. POTTER REND VISITE À LA FAMILLE PARMENTIER
MR. POTTER VISITS THE PARMENTIER FAMILY

Deuxième Letter De Paris

Cher ami,

1. Lundi passé, M. Parmentier m'a appelé par téléphone pour m'inviter à prendre le thé chez lui le lendemain.[1] Naturellement, j'ai sauté sur l'offre de visiter une famille française.

2. J'ai pris un taxi et à cinq heures de l'après-midi nous nous sommes arrêtés devant une maison charmante dans la rue Vaugirard. Je suis monté au troisième étage par un escalier gracieux.

3. J'ai sonné et aussitôt j'ai entendu des pas rapides. Une petite bonne fraîche m'a ouvert la porte et elle m'a invité à entrer.

4. M. Parmentier s'est approché pour me saluer. — Bonjour M. Potter, a-t-il dit, je suis content de vous voir.

5. Je lui ai dit, — Cette maison a l'air du dix-huitième siècle. Elle est charmante.

6. — Il y a beaucoup de maisons de cette époque à Paris, et plusieurs qui datent d'encore beaucoup plus loin, comme vous le savez sans doute.

7. Nous sommes entrés dans un grand salon, meublé avec beaucoup de goût dans le style Louis XV (quinze). M. Parmentier m'a présenté à sa femme, et à ses deux fils, des jeunes gens très sérieux et intelligents.

8. Les garçons font leurs études au Lycée Henri IV. L'aîné veut être docteur; le cadet, avocat.

9. Après un peu de conversation ils se sont retirés pour aller faire leurs devoirs.

10. Nous nous sommes mis à table et Mme. Parmentier m'a servi une tasse de thé et quelques petits gâteaux délicieux. En prenant le thé, nous avons parlé de la vie en France, des coutumes du pays, et de l'art.

Dear Friend,

1. Last Monday Mr. Parmentier called me on the telephone to invite me to have tea at his house the next day. Naturally I jumped at the chance to visit a French family.

2. I took a taxi and at five o'clock in the afternoon we stopped in front of an attractive house in Vaugirard Street. I went up to the third floor by a graceful staircase.

3. I rang and immediately heard rapid footsteps. A bright-faced little maid opened the door (for me) and invited me to come in.

4. Mr. Parmentier approached to greet me. "Good day, Mr. Potter," he said. "I'm glad to see you."

5. I said to him, "This house has an eighteenth century air. It is charming."

6. "There are many houses of that period in Paris and several which date from even longer ago, as you no doubt know."

7. We went into a large living room furnished with good taste in the style of Louis XV. Mr. Parmentier introduced me to his wife and to his two sons, very serious and intelligent young men.

8. The boys are studying at the Henri IV lycée. The older one wants to be a doctor; the younger one, a lawyer.

9. After a bit of conversation, they withdrew to do their homework.

10. We sat down at the table and Madame Parmentier served me a cup of tea and some delicious little cakes. While drinking tea we talked of life in France, of the customs of the country and of art.

11. M. Parmentier m'a recommandé comme curiosité de Paris le Marché aux Puces dont nous avons parlé il y a longtemps. Et Mme. Parmentier m'a invité à l'accompagner au Marché aux Fleurs le dimanche matin.

12. J'ai répondu que toutes les deux excursions m'intéressaient beaucoup et j'ai accepté l'aimable invitation de Madame.

13. Après avoir passé une heure agréable en parlant d'une chose et d'une autre, je suis parti, charmé de mes nouveaux amis.

14. Je suis revenu à l'hôtel à pied, passant par les vieux quartiers de la Rive Gauche qui évoquent d'une manière frappante l'histoire de la France.

Votre ami,
John Potter

11. Mr. Parmentier recommended (to me) as a curiosity of Paris the Flea Market, which we talked about a long time ago. And Madame Parmentier invited me to accompany her to the Flower Market on Sunday morning.

12. I answered that both excursions interested me very much and I accepted Madame's kind invitation.

13. After having spent a delightful hour in talking of one thing and another, I left, charmed by my new friends.

14. I returned to the hotel on foot, passing through the old sections of the Left Bank which evoke in a striking manner the history of France.

Your friend,
John Potter

NOTE 1. **lendemain** means tomorrow; **le lendemain** means the next day.

Building Vocabulary

Quelques professions Some professions

1. **un docteur** doctor
2. **un médecin** medical doctor
3. **un avocat** lawyer
4. **un professeur** professor, teacher in a secondary school (**lycée**)
5. **un maître d'école** teacher in elementary school
6. **un ingénieur** (añ-zhay-**nyeur**) engineer
7. **un écrivain** writer
8. **une femme docteur** woman doctor
9. **une femme avocat** woman lawyer
10. **une maîtresse** elementary school teacher
11. **un acteur, un comédien** actor
12. **une actrice, une comédienne** actress

French Expressions

1. **rendre visite à** *or* **faire visite à**
   to visit (a person), to pay a visit to
2. **visiter**
   to visit (a place)
3. **ils font leurs études**
   they are studying (*Lit.* making their studies)
4. **ils font leurs devoirs**
   they are doing their homework
5. **Il veut être docteur (avocat).**
   He wants to be a doctor (a lawyer).
6. **beaucoup plus loin**
   much longer ago, much farther away
7. **en parlant d'une chose et d'une autre**
   speaking of one thing and another
8. **il y a longtemps**
   a long time ago

Exercise No. 174—Completion of Text

1. **M. Parmentier** (called me) **par téléphone.**
2. **Il m'a invité** (to have tea) **chez lui.**
3. (We stopped) **devant une maison charmante.**
4. (I went up) **au troisième étage.**
5. (I rang). **La bonne** (invited me) **à entrer.**
6. **M. Parmentier** (approached to greet me).
7. **Il a dit, —** (I'm glad to see you).
8. (There are many houses) **de cette époque à Paris.**
9. (We entered) **dans un grand salon.**
10. **M. Parmentier** (introduced me) **à ses deux fils.**
11. **L'aîné** (wants to be a) **docteur.**
12. **Ils** (retired) **pour aller faire** (their homework).
13. (We sat down) **à table.**
14. (We spoke) **de la vie en France.**
15. (I returned) **à l'hôtel à pied.**
16. **J'ai passé** (through the old sections).

Grammar Notes

1. Conversational past (present perfect) of reflexive verbs
Observe carefully the conversational past (present perfect) of the reflexive verb **se laver** *to wash oneself*. Note the auxiliary verb and the changes in the past participle.

I have washed (I washed, did wash) myself

je me suis lavé (lavée)	**nous nous sommes lavés (lavées)**
tu t'es lavé (lavée)	**vous vous êtes lavé(e), (lavés lavées)**
il s'est lavé	**ils se sont lavés**
elle s'est lavée	**elles se sont lavées**

s'est-il lavé?
est-ce qu'il s'est lavé did he wash himself?
il ne s'est pas lavé he did not wash himself
est-ce qu'il ne s'est pas lavé? did he not wash himself?

a. The auxiliary verb **être** is used to form the conversational past of reflexive verbs.

b. The past participle agrees with the reflexive pronoun in number and gender when the reflexive pronoun is the *direct object* of the verb. The reflexive pronoun has the same gender and number as the subject.

c. The reflexive pronoun is sometimes the *indirect object* of the verb. In that case the past participle does *not* agree with it.

Ils se sont donné des cadeaux.	They gave gifts *to* each other.
Ils se sont serré la main.	They shook hands. (*Lit.* They shook *to* themselves the hand.)
Elles s'est lavé la figure.	She washed her face. (*Lit.* She washed *to* herself the face.)

2. Present and conversational past of **s'asseoir,** *to sit down*

I sit down (I seat myself), you sit down (you seat yourself), etc.

je m'assois (ma-swa)	**nous nous asseyons** (za-say-yawñ)
tu t'assois (ta-swa)	**vous vous asseyez** (za-say-yay)
il, elle s'assoit (sa-swa)	**ils, elles s'assoient** (sa-swa)

assieds-toi sit down **asseyons-nous** let us sit down **asseyez-vous** sit down

I have sat down (I sat down, I did sit down), etc.

je me suis assis (assise)	**nous nous sommes assis (assises)**
tu t'es assis (assise)	**vous vous êtes assis(e), assis(es)**
il s'est assis	**ils se sont assis**
elle s'est assise	**elles se sont assises**

3. Some reflexive verbs you have met

Infinitive	*Conversational Past*
se lever to get up	**je me suis levé(e)**
se coucher to go to bed	**tu t'es couché(e)**
s'habiller to dress	**il s'est habillé**
s'amuser to enjoy oneself, have a good time	**elle s'est amusée**
s'arrêter to stop	**nous nous sommes arrêtés**
s'approcher to approach	**vous vous êtes approchés**
se rencontrer to meet each other	**ils se sont rencontrés**
se connaître to know each other	**elles se sont connues**
se promener to go for a walk	**je ne me suis pas promené(e)**
se tromper to be mistaken	**il ne s'est pas trompé**
se retirer to withdraw	**ne se sont-ils pas retirés?**
s'asseoir to sit down	**est-ce qu'ils ne se sont pas assis?**

Exercise No. 175. Translate the conversational past tense of the verbs listed above:

Exemple: 1. je me suis levé(e) = I got up

Exercise No. 176. Translate each question and answer. Read each question and answer aloud three times.

1. **Est-ce que les enfants se sont couchés de bonne heure?**
   Oui. Ils se sont couchés de bonne heure.
2. **Est-ce que Jean s'est levé tard?**
   Non. Il ne s'est pas levé tard.

3. **Est-ce que Marie s'est habillée vite?**
   Oui. Elle s'est habillée vite.
4. **Est-ce que vous vous êtes trompé, Charles?**
   Non. Je ne me suis pas trompé.
5. **Est-ce que vous vous êtes amusée, Anne?**
   Non. Je ne me suis pas amusée.
6. **Où est-ce que vous vous êtes rencontrés, messieurs?**
   Nous nous sommes rencontrés au bureau.
7. **Où est-ce que l'autobus s'est arrêté?**
   Il s'est arrêté au coin là-bas.
8. **Est-ce que Mme. Potter s'est occupée des enfants?**
   Oui. Elle s'est occupée des enfants.
9. **Est-ce que le touriste s'est senti chez lui à Paris?**
   Comme tous les touristes il s'est senti chez lui.

Exercise No. 177—Questionnaire

1. **Qui a appelé M. Potter par téléphone?**
2. **À quelle heure est-ce que le taxi s'est arrêté chez M. Parmentier?**
3. **Qui a ouvert la porte?**
4. **Qui s'est approché pour saluer M. Potter?**
5. **Quel air cette maison a-t-elle?**
6. **Où les messieurs sont-ils entrés?**
7. **Qui sont les jeunes gens sérieux et intelligents?**
8. **Où font-ils leurs études?**
9. **Qu'est-ce que l'aîné veut faire?**
10. **Pourquoi se sont-ils retirés?**
11. **De quoi est-ce qu'on a parlé en prenant le thé?**
12. **Qu'est-ce que M. Parmentier a recommandé comme curiosité?**
13. **Où est-ce que Mme. Parmentier l'a invité à l'accompagner?**
14. **Comment est-ce que M. Potter a passé une heure agréable?**
15. **Est-il revenu à son hôtel à pied ou en voiture?**

CHAPITRE 34 (TRENTE-QUATRE)

UNE BELLE PROMENADE
A PLEASANT STROLL

Troisième Lettre

Cher ami,

1. Je vous écris attablé dans le café que vous m'avez fort recommandé: le Royale-Concorde. Il me reste peut-être des pieds,[1] mais certainement pas de jambes.

2. Ce matin M. Parmentier est venu me chercher à l'hôtel et nous avons commencé notre promenade en suivant les quays jusqu'au Pont Neuf.

3. Nous sommes restés très longtemps sur le pont, en regardant les pêcheurs qui restent des heures sans rien attraper; en regardant aussi les bateaux-mouches, et les enfants qui s'amusent à jeter des pierres dans l'eau.

4. Nous avons traversé le pont et continué sur la Rive Droite jusqu'à la Place de la Concorde. Je pense que cela doit être la plus belle place du monde. Les fontaines, l'obélisque, les jardins d'un côté, l'avenue des Champs-Elysées[2] de l'autre, tout est disposé en parfaite harmonie.

5. Nous avons pris l'avenue des Champs-Elysées. Quelle belle avenue avec ses grands arbres, son étendue royale!

6. Nous nous sommes attablés dans un de ces cafés immenses pour prendre un café, mais surtout pour nous reposer. Ce qui m'a frappé tout de suite en France, c'est l'importance du café dans la vie quotidienne.

Dear Friend,

1. I am writing you seated at a table in the café which you have strongly recommended to me: the Royale-Concorde. I may have feet left, but certainly no legs.

2. This morning Mr. Parmentier came to call for me at the hotel and we started our walk along the quays to the Pont Neuf.

3. We stayed on the bridge for a long time watching the fishermen, who stand for hours without catching anything, also watching the tour boats and the children amusing themselves by throwing stones in the water.

4. We crossed the bridge and continued on the Right Bank to the Place de la Concorde. I believe that this must be the most beautiful square in the world. The fountains, the obelisk, the gardens on one side, the Champs Elysées on the other, everything is arranged in perfect harmony.

5. We walked up the Champs Elysées. What a lovely avenue with its large trees, its splendid spaciousness!

6. We sat down at a table in one of those huge cafés to have coffee but especially to rest. What struck me at once in France is the importance of the café in daily life.

7. Le café est un club. On y rencontre ses amis, on y joue aux échecs; on y écrit des lettres comme voici moi-même.

7. The café is a club. There people meet their friends; they play chess; they write letters as I am doing right now.

8. Le café est aussi un centre de commerce. Pour les hommes d'affaires c'est un deuxième bureau, même peut-être le premier.

8. The café is also a business center. For businessmen it is a second office, perhaps even the first.

9. Le café est un théâtre: les passants sont les acteurs et les actrices parfois tragiques, plus souvent comiques, mais toujours intéressants.

9. The café is a theater: the passers-by are the actors and actresses, sometimes tragic, more often comic, but always interesting.

10. Ensuite nous avons continué notre route sur l'avenue des Champs-Elysées jusqu'à la Place de l'Étoile.[3] Nous avons contemplé l'immense Arc de Triomphe qui se trouve au centre de la Place de l'Étoile.

10. Then we continued on our way along the Champs Elysées up to the Place de l'Étoile. We looked at the immense Arch of Triumph which is in the center of the Place de l'Étoile.

11. Pour revenir au Café Royale-Concorde nous avons pris la belle Avenue Marceau. À la Place de l'Alma M. Parmentier m'a quitté. J'ai suivi les quais en admirant la Seine tout le long du chemin jusqu'à la Place de la Concorde.

11. To return to the Café Royale-Concorde we took the beautiful Avenue Marceau. At the Place de l'Alma Mr. Parmentier left me. I followed the quays admiring the Seine all along the way to the Place de la Concorde.

12. Ensuite j'ai pris la Rue Royale et enfin je suis tombé dans la chaise la plus proche du Café Royale-Concorde, fatigué, épuisé, et enchanté.

Votre ami, grand amoureux de Paris,
John Potter

12. Then I took the rue Royale, and finally I fell into the nearest chair of the Royale-Concorde Café, tired, worn out, and delighted.

Your friend, in love with Paris,
John Potter

NOTE 1. *Lit.* Feet perhaps remain to me. 2. Shahñ zay-lee-zay. 3. *Lit.* Place of the star, because at this place a dozen avenues spread out from the Arch of Triumph like the points of a star. It has been renamed Place Charles de Gaulle but most people still call it Place de l'Etoile or simply l'Etoile.

Building Vocabulary

Related words

1. **arrêter** to stop (someone, something);
   s'arrêter to stop (stand still);
   l'arrêt (*m*) stop, halt
2. **approcher** to bring nearer;
   s'approcher to come nearer;
   l'approche (*f*) approach; **proche** near
3. **écrire** to write; **décrire** to describe;
   l'écrivain the writer;
   l'écriture writing, handwriting
4. **la table** table;
   s'attabler to sit down at a table;
   attablé seated at a table
5. **se reposer** to rest; **le repos** rest
6. **l'amour** love;
   amoureux enamored, in love;
   l'amoureux the lover
7. **le pays** country; **le paysan** farmer, peasant;
   le paysage landscape
8. **tirer** to pull, to shoot; **s'en tirer** to cope, to manage; **retirer** to pull back;
   se retirer to retire
9. **vite** quick, quickly; **la vitesse** speed
10. **curieux** curious, strange; **la curiosité** curiosity

French Expressions

1. **Il vient me chercher.**
   He comes to call for (*Lit.* look for) me.
2. **d'un côté** on one side
   de l'autre côté on the other side
3. **jouer aux cartes (aux échecs, au billard)**
   to play cards (chess, billiards)
4. **tout le long du chemin** all along the way
5. **combien de fois?** how many times?
   une fois once; **deux fois** two times, twice;
   quelquefois sometimes; **des fois** at times;
   à la fois at once, together; **encore une fois** one more time; **plusieurs fois** several times

Exercise No. 178—Completion of Text

1. **M. Parmentier est venu** (to look for me).
2. (We stayed) **très longtemps sur le pont.**
3. **Les pêcheurs restent des heures** (without catching anything).

4. **Les enfants s'amusent** (throwing stones).
5. (We continued) **sur le quai.**
6. **Cela doit être** (the most beautiful square) **du monde.**
7. What a beautiful avenue!
8. **Ce qui** (struck me) **c'est l'importance du café.**
9. (There people play) **aux cartes.**
10. (There one writes) **des lettres.**
11. (The passers-by) **sont les acteurs et les actrices.**
12. (Then) **nous avons continué** (our way).
13. **À la Place de l'Alma M. Parmentier** (left me).
14. (I followed) **les quais.**
15. **Je suis tombé** (into the nearest chair).

Grammar Notes

1. Relative pronouns

a. **qui**—*who, which, that*—is used as a subject relative pronoun.

Connaissez-vous les acteurs *qui* sont assis à cette table? Do you know the actors *who* are seated at that table?

Où est le quai *qui* mène au Pont Neuf? Where is the quay *that* leads to the Pont Neuf?

J'aime bien me promener dans le parc Monceau, qui se trouve pas loin de l'Etoile. I like to walk in Monceau Park, which is not far from the Etoile.

b. **que** *or* **qu'**—*whom, which, that,*—is used as a direct object relative pronoun.

Je suis attablé dans le café *que* vous m'avez recommendé. I am seated at a table in the café *that* you recommended to me.

C'est un professeur *que* les étudiants admirent. He is a teacher *whom* the students admire.

c. **ce qui** (*subject*) and **ce que** *or* **ce qu'** (*object*) mean *what* (*that which*).

Savez-vous *ce qui* est dans cette grande caisse? Do you know *what* (*that which*) is in that large case?

Nous avons lu tout *ce que* vous avez écrit. We have read all *that* (*which*) you wrote.

Je n'ai pas entendu *ce qu'il* a dit. I did not hear *what* (*that which*) he said.

d. **qui**—*whom*—is used as the object of a preposition.

Je ne connais pas la dame *à* (*avec*) *qui* vous avez parlé. I do not know the lady *to* (*with*) *whom* you spoke.

e. **lequel (laquelle, lesquels, lesquelles)**—*which, whom*—is most often used after a preposition. It agrees with its antecedent in number and gender.

J'ai reçu votre lettre *dans laquelle* vous décrivez "Une Belle Promenade." I have received your letter *in which* you describe "A Pleasant Stroll."

f. **dont**—*whose, of whom, of which*—is used as a relative pronoun instead of **de + qui** or **de +** any form of **lequel.**

Nous allons rendre visite au professeur *dont* nous avons parlé hier. We are going to visit the teacher *of whom* we spoke yesterday.

Le Mont Saint Michel est un endroit *dont* les omelettes sont célèbres. Mont Saint Michel is a place *whose* omelettes are famous.

g. A relative pronoun may sometimes be omitted in English. It is never omitted in French.

Les pêcheurs *que* vous voyez sur le quai sont Bretons. The fishermen (*whom*) you see on the quay are Bretons.

Exercise No. 179. Translate each question and answer. Then read each one aloud three times.

1. **Avez-vous compris tout ce que le maître a dit?**
   Je n'en ai pas compris tout.
2. **Avez-vous lu les deux guides que je vous ai prêtés?**
   Je les ai lus avec beaucoup d'intérêt.
3. **Quel est le premier secret de la bonne cuisine?**
   Tout ce qui entre dans un plat doit être de bonne qualitè.
4. **Est-ce qu'on peut faire du ski en montagne?**
   Ceux qui sont jeunes et forts le font tout le temps.

5. **Quel café avez-vous visité aujourd'hui?**
J'ai visité le Royale-Concorde dont nous avons souvent parlé.
6. **Où sont les valises dans lesquelles j'ai mis mes vêtements?**
Elles sont dans votre chambre.

Exercise No. 180. Complete each sentence with the correct French relative pronoun:

1. **Montrez-moi le chapeau** (that) **vous venez d'acheter.**
2. **Vous rappelez-vous** (what) **il vous a dit?**
3. **Les touristes** (who) **visitent Paris se sentent chez eux.**
4. **Voyons** (what) **se trouve dans cette caisse.**
5. **Voilà le guide avec** (whom) **nous allons visiter la cathédrale.**
6. **Je cherche la boîte dans** (which) **j'ai mis ma montre.**
7. **Il y a trois élèves dans ma classe** (whose) **les parents sont Français.**
8. **Tous les endroits** (which) **j'ai visités sont très intéressants.**
9. **Tout** (that) **se passe aux cafés est intéressant.**
10. **Nous ne pouvons pas trouver les élèves** (whom) **nous cherchons.**

Exercise No. 181—Questionnaire

1. **Où est-ce que M. Potter écrit sa lettre?**
2. **Où est-ce que M. Parmentier est venu le chercher?**
3. **Où sont-ils restés très longtemps?**
4. **Qu'est-ce qu'ils ont vu?**
5. **Qu'est-ce que M. Potter pense au sujet de la Place de la Concorde?**
6. **Pourquoi les messieurs se sont-ils attablés?**
7. **Qu'est-ce qui a frappé M. Potter?**
8. **Qu'est-ce qu'on joue dans un café?**
9. **Qu'est-ce que c'est qu'un café pour les hommes d'affaires?**
10. **Qu'est-ce qu'ils ont contemplé?**
11. **Où est-ce que M. Parmentier a quitté M. Potter?**
12. **Qu'est-ce que M. Potter a admiré tout le long du chemin?**
13. **Comment M. Potter est-il tombé dans la chaise du café?**

CHAPITRE 35 (TRENTE-CINQ)

LE MONT ST. MICHEL
MONT ST. MICHEL

Quatrième Lettre

Cher ami,

1. Devinez un peu d'où je vous écris. C'est ça! Vous avez raison. Je vous écris attablé dans un café. Vous allez croire que je ne fais que ça. C'est que le métier de touriste demande beaucoup de repos. Et où est-ce qu'on se repose mieux que dans un café?

2. Vous rappelez-vous notre conversation au sujet de mes voyages? Eh bien, j'ai commencé mon grand cercle en partant de Paris pour la Normandie. J'ai visité le Mont Saint Michel et me voilà à Perros-Guirec en Bretagne. En l'honneur de ma première visite en Bretagne, je prends un Calvados.

3. Je veux vous décrire ma visite au Mont Saint Michel, pendant que j'en ai la mémoire fraîche.[1]

4. Pendant que le train traversait les champs et les forêts, je regardais par la fenêtre. En filant à toute vitesse je voyais les paysans qui travaillaient dans les champs. Très souvent nous avons passé par les villages.

Dear Friend,

1. Just guess from where I'm writing you. That's it! You're right. I am writing you seated at a table in a café. You're going to think that it's all I do. The thing is that the profession of tourist demands a great deal of rest. And where can you rest better than in a café?

2. Do you recall our conversation on the subject of my travels? Well, I started my great circle leaving Paris for Normandy. I visited Mont Saint Michel and here I am in Perros-Guirec in Brittany. In honor of my first visit to Brittany, I am drinking a Calvados (apple brandy).

3. I want to describe to you my visit to the Mont Saint Michel while it is still fresh in my memory.[1]

4. While the train was crossing the fields and forests, I was looking out the window. Going along at top speed, I saw the country people working in the fields. Very often we passed through villages.

5. A Pontorson, j'ai pris un taxi pour le Mont. Presque tout de suite j'ai vu ce rocher monumental isolé au milieu des sables.

6. Mais quand je suis arrivé au pittoresque village situé aux flancs du rocher, j'ai entendu un bruit terrifiant.

7. On criait, on hurlait. — Monsieur! Par ici! Les souvenirs du Mont! Les cartes postales! Monsieur! La véritable omelette de la Mère Poularde! Monsieur! Ici la vraie! Monsieur! Ici l'omelette Poularde! Les cartes! Les souvenirs! L'omelette! Ici! Ici! Monsieur! Monsieur! Monsieur!

8. La tête me tournait comme une toupie. J'avais envie de partir. Mais enfin je me suit dit, — En avant l'art et l'histoire. Courage!

J'ai fermé les oreilles mentalement et j'ai vite grimpé la pente rapide jusqu'à l'escalier de l'Abbaye.

9. La visite à l'Abbaye a duré une heure environ. Ce bâtiment gothique avec ses grandes salles, ses escaliers, ses galeries, ses cloîtres, ses jardins en terrasses est un spectacle grandiose. Je voulais rester pour contempler la sculpture mais ce n'était pas possible.

10. Vous savez que le visiteur d'un monument historique n'a pas de droits. On est poussé par ici, on est tiré par là et on doit suivre comme un mouton. Malgré tout j'ai reçu une impréssion imposante de cet îlot rocheux.

11. Maintenant je me tourne vers la Bretagne: la mer, les marins, les poissons, les chapelles et le Calvados auquel les marins de la Bretagne sont dévoués. Perros-Guirec me plaît beaucoup. Je finirai peut-être par aimer le Calvados.

Très cordialement,
Votre ami,
John Potter

5. At Pontorson, I took a taxi to the Mont. Almost at once I saw this monumental rock isolated in the middle of the sands.

6. But when I reached the picturesque village situated on the sides of the rocky hill, I heard a terrifying din.

7. People were calling, yelling. "Mister! Right here! Souvenirs of the Mont! Post cards! Sir! The authentic Mother Poularde omelet! Sir! Here you get the real one! Sir! The Poularde omelet! Cards! Souvenirs! The omelet! Here! Here! Sir! Sir! Sir!"

8. My head was spinning like a top. I wanted to go away. But in the end I said to myself, "Onward with art and history. Courage!"

I mentally closed my ears and I quickly climbed the steep slope up to the stairs of the Abbey.

9. The visit to the Abbey lasted about an hour. This Gothic structure with its vast halls, its stairways, its galleries, its cloisters, its terraced gardens is a grandiose spectacle. I wanted to stop to contemplate the sculpture but it wasn't possible.

10. You know that the visitor at a historic site has no rights. You are pushed this way, pulled that way, and you have to follow like sheep. In spite of everything I received an imposing impression of this rocky islet.

11. Now I turn toward Brittany: the sea, the sailors, the fish, the chapels and the Calvados to which the sailors of Brittany are devoted. I like Perros-Guirec very much. Perhaps I shall end up by liking Calvados.

Cordially,
Your friend,
John Potter

NOTE 1. *Lit.* While I still have the fresh memory of it.

Building Vocabulary

le corps (kur) body
la tête (teht) head
les cheveux (shuh-veu) hair
la figure (fee-gür) face
l'oeil (leuy) eye
les yeux (lay-**zyeu**) eyes
le nez (nay) nose
la bouche (boosh) mouth
la langue (lahñg) tongue
la main (mañ) hand
le doigt (dwa) finger
le pied (pyay) foot
le bras (brah) arm
la jambe (zhahñb) leg
le coeur (keur) heart

French Expressions

me voici here I am
te voici here you are
le (la) voici here he (she) is
le (la) voilà there he (she) is
nous voici here we are
vous voici here you are
les voici here they are
les voilà there they are

Exercise No. 182—Completion of Text

1. (You are right).
2. (Here I am) **dans un café.**
3. (I am drinking) **un Calvados.**
4. **Le train traversait** (the fields and the forests).

5. **Je regardais** (out of the window).
6. (The farmers) **travaillaient dans** (the fields).
7. (I took a taxi) **pour le Mont.**
8. (Almost at once) **j'ai vu ce rocher monumental.**
9. **On criait, — Monsieur,** (right here)!
10. **J'ai fermé** (my ears).
11. **La visite à l'abbaye** (lasted) **une heure.**
12. **Je voulais** (to stop to contemplate) **la sculpture.**
13. **On** (is pushed) **par ici, on** (is pulled) **par là.**
14. (You must follow) **comme un mouton.**

Grammar Notes

The imperfect tense. What *was happening, used to happen.*

The conversational past, as you have seen, tells what *has happened, happened,* or *did happen.*

The imperfect tense tells what *was happening* or *used to happen.* For convenience we can call the imperfect the *was, were, used to* tense.

Note carefully the endings of the imperfect tense of **parler, finir, vendre, prendre, avoir,** and **être.**

I was speaking, you were speaking, etc.

je	**parlais**	**nous**	**parlions**
tu	**parlais**	**vous**	**parliez**
il	**parlait**	**ils**	**parlaient**
elle	**parlait**	**elles**	**parlaient**

I was finishing, you were finishing, etc.

je	**finissais**	**nous**	**finissions**
tu	**finissais**	**vous**	**finissiez**
il	**finissait**	**ils**	**finissaient**
elle	**finissait**	**elles**	**finissaient**

I was selling, you were selling, etc.

je	**vendais**	**nous**	**vendions**
tu	**vendais**	**vous**	**vendiez**
il	**vendait**	**ils**	**vendaient**
elle	**vendait**	**elles**	**vendaient**

I was taking, you were taking, etc.

je	**prenais**	**nous**	**prenions**
tu	**prenais**	**vous**	**preniez**
il	**prenait**	**ils**	**prenaient**
elle	**prenait**	**elles**	**prenaient**

I had, you had, etc.

j'	**avais**	**nous**	**avions**
tu	**avais**	**vous**	**aviez**
il	**avait**	**ils**	**avaient**
elle	**avait**	**elles**	**avaient**

I was, you were, etc.

j'	**étais**	**nous**	**étions**
tu	**étais**	**vous**	**étiez**
il	**était**	**ils**	**étaient**
elle	**était**	**elles**	**étaient**

a. The imperfect tense endings of all French verbs are: Singular: **-ais** (*eh*) **-ais** (*eh*) **-ait** (*eh*); Plural: **-ions** (*yawñ*) **-iez** (*yay*) **-aient** (*eh*).

b. To form the imperfect tense drop the ending **-ons** from the **nous** form of the present tense and add the imperfect tense endings. This way of forming the imperfect tense applies to all verbs except **être.** Thus:

Infinitive	*Nous form of Present*	*Imperfect (was, were, used to)*
parler	**nous parlons**	**je parlais, tu parlais, etc.**
vendre	**nous vendons**	**je vendais, tu vendais, etc.**
finir	**nous finissons**	**je finissais, tu finissais, etc.**
dormir	**nous dormons**	**je dormais, tu dormais, etc.**
prendre	**nous prenons**	**je prenais, tu prenais, etc.**
dire	**nous disons**	**je disais, tu disais, etc.**
faire	**nous faisons**	**je faisais, tu faisais, etc.**
lire	**nous lisons**	**je lisais, tu lisais, etc.**
écrire	**nous écrivons**	**j'écrivais, tu écrivais, etc.**
vouloir	**nous voulons**	**je voulais, tu voulais, etc.**
avoir	**nous avons**	**j'avais, tu avais, etc.**
être	**nous sommes**	**j'étais, tu étais, etc.**

c. Present and imperfect of **il y a, venir de,** and **aller**

Present		*Imperfect*	
il y a	there is (are)	**il y avait**	there was (were)
y a-t-il?	is (are) there?	**y avait-il?**	was (were) there?
qu'y a-t-il?	what is (are) there?	**qu'y avait-il?**	what was (were) there?
il n'y a pas	there is (are) not	**il n'y avait pas**	there was (were) not
Il vient de voir.	He has just seen.	**Il venait de voir.**	He had just seen.
Je vais arriver.	I am going to arrive.	**J'allais arriver.**	I was going to arrive.

Exercise No. 183. Translate the following brief dialogues. Practice them aloud.

1. **— Qu'est-ce M. Potter faisait quand vous êtes entré dans le salon?**
   — Il lisait à haute voix (aloud) **une lettre qu'il venait de recevoir de son représentant à Paris.**
   — M. Picard que faisait-il?
   — Il l'écoutait.
2. **— Que faissiez-vous pendant que le train traversait les champs et les forêts?**
   — Je regardais par la fenêtre.
   — Qu'est-ce que vous voyiez?
   — Je voyais les paysans qui travaillaient dans les champs.
3. **— Y avait-il beaucoup de vendeurs au Mont Saint Michel?**
   — Il y en avait une armée.
   — Qu'est-ce qu'ils vendaient?
   — Ils vendaient les souvenirs du Mont.
4. **— Jouez-vous souvent au tennis?**
   — Autrefois (formerly) **je jouais presque tous les jours mais cette année j'ai joué une fois seulement.**

Exercise No. 184. Each of these sentences indicates an action that was happening (*imperfect tense*) and another action that interrupted it at a definite time (*conversational past tense*). Complete with the correct French verbs. Translate the completed sentences.

1. **Le vendeurs** (were calling and yelling) **quand je suis arrivé au marché.**
2. **Pendant que** (I was listening to) **la radio, on m'a telephoné.**
3. **Quand** (we were doing) **nos devoirs, ils sont entrés dans notre chambre.**
4. **Elle est tombée quand elle** (was getting out) **de l'auto.**
5. **Quand le taxi** (was going) **à toute vitesse, j'ai crié: — Pas si vite!**
6. **Nous lui avons rendu visite quand** (he was) **malade.**
7. (There were) **beaucoup de personnes à l'aéroport quand notre avion est arrivé.**
8. **Pendant que** (we were waiting for) **l'autobus, il a commencé à pleuvoir.**
9. **Nous les avons rencontrés quand** (we were coming) **du cinéma.**
10. **M. Potter est revenu pendant que les enfants** (were sleeping).

Exercise No. 185—Questionnaire

1. **D'où est-ce que M. Potter écrit?**
2. **Qu'est-ce que le métier de touriste demande?**
3. **Où est le café?**
4. **Qu'est-ce que M. Potter prend en l'honneur de sa première visite en Bretagne?**
5. **Qu'est-ce que M. Potter faisait pendant que le train traversait les champs et les forêts?**
6. **Qu'est-ce qu'il voyait?**
7. **Qu'est-ce qu'il pouvait voir dans les villages?**
8. **Qu'a-t-il entendu quand il est arrivé?**
9. **Pourquoi avait-il d'abord envie de partir?**
10. **Pourquoi est-ce que M. Potter voulait rester?**
11. **Quelle impression M. Potter a-t-il reçue?**
12. **Où se tourne-t-il maintenant?**

CHAPITRE 36 (TRENTE-SIX)

GUIGNOL
PUPPET SHOW

Cinquième Lettre

Cher ami,

1. Je suis revenu à Paris de mon voyage en Bretagne de plus en plus amoureux de la France.

2. Ce matin je suis allé au Louvre pour le visiter à fond. Je l'ai visité tellement à fond que je ne peux rien vous dire.

3. Si la tête me tournait comme une toupie au Mont Saint Michel à cause du bruit, elle me tournait dix fois plus vite en sortant du silence du Louvre. Je me suis dit, — Imbécile! Pourquoi n'es-tu pas sorti il y à deux heures? Crois-tu que le Louvre va s'envoler?

Dear Friend,

1. I returned from my trip to Brittany more and more in love with France.

2. This morning I went to the Louvre to visit it thoroughly. I visited it so thoroughly that I am not able to tell you anything.

3. If my head was spinning like a top at Mont Saint Michel because of the noise, it was spinning ten times faster when I left the silence of the Louvre. I said to myself, "Fool! Why didn't you leave two hours ago? Do you think the Louvre is going to fly away?"

4. Enfin, après un bon déjeuner arrosé d'un bon vin, j'étais délassé et avide de nouvelles aventures.

4. Well, after a good lunch washed down with a good wine, I was refreshed and eager for new adventures.

5. Je me suis tourné vers le Jardin des Tuileries attiré par le soleil et les fleurs. Je marchais tranquillement quand tout à coup j'ai entendu des rires immodérés. Je me suis approché, tout curieux.

5. I turned toward the Tuileries Gardens attracted by the sun and the flowers. I was strolling quietly along when all of a sudden I heard unrestrained laughter. I drew near, very curious.

6. J'ai vu un joli petit théâtre, la scène encadrée d'un rideau de velours bleu ciel. Les bancs qui formaient la petite salle étaient comblés d'enfants. Ils riaient à la folie.

6. I saw a pretty little theatre, the stage framed by a sky blue velvet curtain. The benches which formed the tiny auditorium were crowded with children. They were laughing wildly.

7. Sur la scène il n'y avait que Guignol.[1] Il ne bougeait pas. Il ne disait rien. Mais ce n'était pas nécessaire. Il n'avait qu'à apparaître, et les enfants éclataient de rire.

7. On the stage there was only Guignol.[1] He was not moving. He was not saying anything. But it wasn't necessary. He had only to appear and the children would burst out laughing.

8. J'ai pris une place à coté d'une toute petite fille qui m'a saisi par la main en criant, — Papa! Très flatté, j'ai répondu, — Bonjour, ma chérie.

8. I took a seat next to a very little girl who seized my hand and called out "Daddy!" Very flattered, I answered, "Hello, my dear."

9. Sa maman, toute rose, lui a dit, — Regarde, Cri-Cri, voilà Gringalet, le fils de Guignol. Et à moi, — Christine pense que tous les messieurs s'appellent papa.

9. Her mother said to her, blushing, "Look Cri-Cri, here is Gringalet, Guignol's son." And to me, "Christine thinks that all men are called daddy."

— Mais j'en suis ravi, madame, ai-je dit, en souriant.

"But I'm delighted, Madame," I said, smiling.

10. Un fou rire nous a fait regarder la scène. Le petit Gringalet était en train de donner de grands coups de tête dans le ventre de Guignol. Les enfants n'étaient pas du tout fâchés. Au contraire, ils en étaient ravis.

10. A wild shout of laughter made us look at the stage. Little Gringalet was butting Guignol in the stomach with his head. The children were not at all annoyed. On the contrary, they were delighted.

11. J'ai dit au revoir à Cri-Cri et à sa mère, et l'enfant m'a répondu gentiment, — Au revoir, papa.

11. I said goodbye to Cri-Cri and her mother and the child answered nicely, "Goodbye, daddy."

12. Je dois vous dire qu'à ce moment là ma femme et mes enfants me manquaient beaucoup.[2]

12. I must tell you that at that moment I missed my wife and my children[2] very much.

Salutations amicales de votre ami,
John Potter

Greetings from your friend,
John Potter

NOTE 1. **Guignol** (geen-yul) Chief character in French puppet shows. His son is called **Gringalet** (grañ-ga-lay). 2. *Lit.* My wife and children were missing very much to me.

Building Vocabulary

Antonyms

1. **le bruit** noise, **le silence** silence
2. **fatigué** tired, **délassé** refreshed
3. **apparaître** to appear; **désapparaître** to disappear
4. **rire** to laugh, **pleurer** to weep
5. **fâché** annoyed; **ravi** delighted
6. **nouveau (nouvel) nouvelle** (*f*) new, **vieux (vieil) vieille** (*f*) old
7. **mener** to lead **suivre** to follow
8. **monter en voiture** to get into the car; **descendre de la voiture** to get out of the car

NOTE: **nouvel** and **vieil** are forms used before masculine nouns beginning with a vowel or **h** (usually). Thus: **un nouvel article; un vieil homme**

French Expressions

1. **de plus en plus** more and more
2. **à fond** thoroughly
3. **tout à coup** suddenly
4. **à la folie** wildly, uproariously
5. **il n'y avait que Guignol** there was only Guignol
6. **éclater de rire** to burst out laughing

Exercise No. 186—Completion of Text

1. (I returned) **de mon voyage.**
2. **J'étais** (more and more) **amoureux de la France.**
3. **Ce matin** (I went) **au Louvre.**
4. (I am not able) **rien vous dire.**

5. (My head) **me tournait comme une toupie.**
6. (I said to myself) **— Imbécile.**
7. **Pourquoi n'es-tu pas sorti** (two hours ago)?
8. (I was) **délassé.**
9. (I was walking) **tranquillement.**
10. (I approached) **tout curieux.**
11. **Les bancs** (were) **combles d'enfants.**
12. (They were laughing) **à la folie.**
13. **Guignol** (was not moving).
14. He was saying nothing.
15. **Les enfants** (were not at all) **fâchés.**
16. (I said) **au revoir à Cri-Cri et à sa mère.**

Grammar Notes

1. Present, imperfect, conversational past of **rire,** *to laugh;* **vivre,** *to live*

Present

I laugh, you laugh, etc.		*I live, you live, etc.*	
je ris (ree)	**nous rions**	**je vis**	**nous vivons**
tu ris (ree)	**vous riez**	**tu vis**	**vous vivez**
il rit (ree)	**ils rient** (ree)	**il vit**	**ils vivent**
elle rit (ree)	**elles rient** (ree)	**elle vit**	**elles vivent**

Imperative: **ris rions riez** — **vis vivons vivez**

Imperfect

I was laughing, you were laughing, etc.		*I was living, you were living, etc.*	
je riais	**nous riions**	**je vivais**	**nous vivions**
tu riais	**vous riiez**	**tu vivais**	**vous viviez**
il riait	**ils riaient**	**il vivait**	**ils vivaient**
elle riait	**elles riaient**	**elle vivait**	**elles vivaient**

Conversational Past

I laughed, you laughed, etc.		*I lived, you lived, etc.*	
j'ai ri	**nous avons ri**	**j'ai vécu**	**nous avons vécu**
etc.	**etc.**	**etc.**	**etc.**

Like **rire: sourire,** *to smile;* like **vivre: survivre,** *to survive;* **revivre,** *to revive*

2. **vouloir, pouvoir, savoir, devoir** and **avoir** generally use the imperfect; they seldom use the conversational past.

Il nous devait cinq dollars. He owed us five dollars.
Je ne pouvais pas lui écrire. I was not able to write him.

3. The past infinitive

a. The *past infinitive* is formed by the auxiliary **avoir** or **être** plus the *past participle* of the verb.

Present Infinitive	*Past Infinitive*
parler to speak	**avoir parlé** to have spoken
finir to finish	**avoir fini** to have finished
aller to go	**être allé** to have gone
sortir to go out	**être sorti** to have gone out

b. You have learned that prepositions (except **en**) take the present infinitive in French instead of the present participle as in English.

sans apprendre without learning — **en admirant** (while) admiring
avant de partir before leaving — **en sortant** (on) leaving

Prepositions may also take past infinitives

avant avoir appris before learning (*Lit.* before to have learned)
après être allé after going (*Lit.* after to have gone)

NOTE: **après** *always* takes a past infinitive.

Exercise No. 187. Complete the following sentences in French with the imperfect tense of the verbs in parentheses:

Exemple: 1. Les enfants riaent à la folie.

1. **Les enfants** (were laughing) **à la folie.**
2. **M. Parmentier** (was living) **à Paris.**
3. **Les femmes** (were washing) **le linge.**
4. (Were they) **fâchés?**
5. **Jean** (was coming) **du cinéma.**
6. **Nous** (were paying a visit to) **M. Duval.**
7. **M. Potter** (was he thinking) **à sa famille?**
8. **Marie** (was getting out) **de la voiture.**
9. **Je** (was coming back) **de l'hôtel à pied.**
10. **Nous** (were going up) **au troisième étage.**
11. **Toute la ville** (was smiling).
12. (I was) **content de vous voir.**
13. **Un bel homme** (was approaching).
14. **Ils** (were beginning)[1] **à parler français.**
15. **Elle** (was eating)[1] **des gâteaux délicieux.**
16. **Ils** (used to meet) **tous les jeudis.**
17. **Nous** (did not have) **d'argent.**
18. **Elles** (did not want) **aller.**
19. (Were you able) **lui rendre visite.**
20. **Personne ne** (knew) **combien il** (owed).

NOTE 1: Verbs ending in **-cer** have a soft **c** (like *s*) and verbs ending in **-ger** have a soft **g** (*zh*) before **e** or **i**. To keep the **c** and **g** soft before endings beginning with **a** or **o**, the **c** must add a cedilla; and the **g** must be followed by a silent **e**. Thus:

commencer	**manger**
Present: **nous commençons**	Present: **nous mangeons**
Imperfect: **je commençais, il commençait**	Imperfect: **je mangeais, ils mangeaient**

but

Imperfect: **nous commencions**	Imperfect: **nous mangions**
Future: **nous commencerons**	Future: **nous mangerons**

Exercise No. 188—Questionnaire

1. **Pourquoi M. Potter est-il allé au Louvre?**
2. **Qu'est-ce que M. Potter s'est dit?**
3. **Où s'est-il tourné?**
4. **Qu'est-ce qu'il a entendu tout à coup?**
5. **Qu'est-ce qu'il a vu quand il s'est approché?**
6. **Qui ne bougeait pas?**
7. **Qu'est-ce que les enfants faisaient chaque fois que Guignol apparaissait?**
8. **Où est-ce que M. Potter a pris une place?**
9. **Qu'est-ce que la petite fille a crié?**
10. **Qu'est-ce que le petit Gringalet était en train de faire?**
11. **Est-ce que les enfants étaient fâchés?**
12. **Qu'est-ce que l'enfant a répondu quand M. Potter lui a dit au revoir?**

RÉVISION 8
CHAPITRES 32–36 PREMIÈRE PARTIE

NOUNS

1. **l'arbre**	10. **l'écrivain**	19. **la manière**	1. tree	10. writer	19. manner
2. **l'avocat**	11. **l'escalier**	20. **le paysan**	2. lawyer	11. staircase	20. peasant
3. **l'ascenseur**	12. **la figure**	21. **le pas**	3. elevator	12. face	21. step
4. **le banc**	13. **la fontaine**	22. **la pierre**	4. bench	13. fountain	22. stone
5. **le camion**	14. **la forêt**	23. **le repos**	5. truck	14. forest	23. rest
6. **le champ**	15. **les gens**	24. **la rivière**	6. field	15. people, folk	24. stream, river
7. **le chemin**	16. **la jambe**	25. **le village**	7. road	16. leg	25. village
8. **le docteur**	17. **le lycée**	26. **la vitesse**	8. doctor	17. high school	26. speed
9. **la douane**	18. **la mémoire**	27. **le ventre**	9. customs	18. memory	27. stomach

VERBS

1. **s'approcher (de)**	8. **durer**	15. **se rappeler**	1. to approach	8. to last	15. to recall
2. **s'arrêter**	9. **essayer**	16. **se retirer**	2. to stop	9. to try	16. to retire
3. **boire**	10. **jeter**	17. **retourner**	3. to drink	10. to throw	17. to go back
4. **crier**	11. **marcher**	18. **rentrer dans**	4. to cry, to shout	11. to walk	18. to reenter
5. **décrire**	12. **monter**	19. **rire**	5. to describe	12. to go up, mount	19. to laugh
6. **désapparaître**	13. **oublier**	20. **sauter**	6. to disappear	13. to forget	20. to leap, to jump
7. **descendre**	14. **pousser**	21. **se tromper**	7. to descend	14. to push	21. to be mistaken

ADJECTIVES

1. amoureux (amoureuse *f*)	**7. fier (fière *f*)**	**13. nouveau (nouvelle *f*)**	1. amorous, in love	7. proud	13. new, another
2. chéri	**8. frais (fraîche *f*)**	**14. plusieurs**	2. dear, beloved	8. fresh	14. several
3. délassé	**9. frappant**	**15. proche**	3. rested	9. striking	15. near
4. fâché	**10. gracieux (gracieuse *f*)**	**16. sain**	4. angry, vexed	10. graceful	16. healthy
5. fatigué	**11. meublé**	**17. sauf**	5. tired	11. furnished	17. safe
6. flatté	**12. neuf (neuve *f*)**		6. flattered	12. new	

ADVERBS

1. aussitôt que	**3. ensuite**	**5. cordialement**	1. as soon as	3. then, afterward	5. cordially
2. enfin	**4. longtemps**	**6. tellement**	2. finally	4. long, a long while	6. so, in such manner

PREPOSITIONS

1. parmi	**2. au bord de**	**3. au milieu de**	1. among	2. on the edge of	3. in the middle of

FRENCH EXPRESSIONS

1. d'accord	**7. faire leurs devoirs**	1. agreed, in agreement	7. to do their homework
2. en avant	**8. rendre visite à**	2. forward, onward	8. to pay a visit to
3. à la fois	**9. jouer aux cartes**	3. together, at the same time	9. to play cards
4. de plus en plus	**10. le plaisir est à moi**	4. more and more	10. the pleasure is mine
5. tout à coup	**11. le café me plaît**	5. suddenly	11. I like the café
6. faire leurs études	**12. je ne manque de rien**	6. to continue their studies	12. I lack nothing

DEUXIÈME PARTIE

Exercise No. 189. Translate each sentence. Then read it aloud three times.

1. **M. Potter est parti pour Paris.**
2. **Sa femme est restée à la maison.**
3. **Mme. Picard est sortie il y a une heure.**
4. **Elle n'est pas encore rentrée.**
5. **Nous sommes montés en ascenseur.**
6. **Ils sont descendus à pied.**
7. **Pourquoi êtes-vous revenue si tard, Marie?**
8. **Je suis allée au marché pour faire mes achats.**
9. **Son grand-père est mort ce matin.**
10. **Ma grand'mère est née le cinq juin 1927.**

Exercise No. 190. Fill in the correct form of the past participle of each verb in parentheses:

Exemple: 1. Un bel homme s'est approché.

1. **Un bel homme s'est (approcher).**
2. **Ils se sont (rencontrer) à la gare.**
3. **J'ai (prendre) un taxi pour l'hôtel.**
4. **Nous sommes (sortir) ensemble.**
5. **Le taxi s'est (arrêter) devant le théâtre.**
6. **Elle est (arriver) saine et sauve.**
7. **M. Potter est (descendre) de la voiture.**
8. **On lui a (réserver) un belle chambre.**
9. **Ma soeur est (naître) le 5 janvier.**
10. **Il a (mettre) son pardessus.**
11. **Qu'est-ce que vous avez (dire)?**
12. **Je n'ai pas (faire) les valises.**
13. **Ont-ils (demander) des renseignements?**
14. **Les fenêtres sont (ouvrir). Qui les a (ouvrir)?**

Exercise No. 191. Complete each sentence by selecting from the parentheses the tense of the verb that fits best. Translate each sentence.

1. **Demain nous _____ visite à la famille Potter. (rendrons, rendions, avons rendu)**
2. **Hier soir les enfants _____ au ciné. (iront, allaient, sont allés)**
3. **Les élèves n'écoutaient pas pendant que le professeur _____. (parlera, parlait, a parlé)**
4. **Où _____ l'hiver dernier? (passerez-vous, passiez-vous, avez-vous passé)**
5. **Je ne les _____ jusqu'à demain. (verrai pas, voyais pas, ai pas vu)**
6. **Nous faisions nos devoirs pendant qu'ils _____ aux cartes. (joueront, jouaient, ont joué)**
7. **Elles sont restées à la maison parce qu'il _____ à verse. (pleuvra, pleuvait, a plu)**
8. **_____ un voyage en Europe l'été prochain? (ferez-vous, faisiez-vous, avez-vous fait)**
9. **Il nous _____ cinq dollars hier. (prêtera, prêtait, a prêté)**
10. **À quelle heure est-ce que _____ hier matin? (vous vous lèverez, vous vous leviez, vous vous êtes levé)**

Exercise No. 192. Complete each sentence in French. Then read it aloud three times.

1. (It was raining buckets) **quand M. Picard a frappé à la porte.**
2. (I was very happy) **lorsque** (*when*) **j'ai reçu sa lettre.**
3. **Ils prenaient du thé au rhum** (when Mr. Potter received) **un télégramme.**
4. **Nous dînions** (when my agent telephoned me).
5. **Autrefois** (we used to go) **souvent au théâtre.**
6. (I did not know)[1] **ce qu'ils disaient.**
7. (We were not able)[1] **trouver le stylo.**
8. (Did they want)[1] **voyager partout?**
9. (She did not have[1] time) **d'aller au ciné.**
10. (She was to)[2] **nous rendre visite hier.**

NOTE 1. Use the imperfect. 2. Use the imperfect of **devoir.**

Dialogue
Au poste d'essence

M. Potter entre au poste d'essence pour faire le plein d'essence.

Mr. Potter goes to the gas station to fill up the tank.

Tout de suite un jeune homme s'approche pour le servir.

Immediately a young man approaches to serve him.

— Bonjour, monsieur, lui dit le jeune homme.

"Good day, sir," the young man greets him.

— Bonjour, jeune homme, répond M. Potter. Voulez-vous bien faire le plein?

"Good day, young man," answers Mr. Potter. "Will you fill it up, please?"

— Tourisme ou super?

"Regular or Super?"

— Tourisme, s'il vous plaît. Voulez-vous bien vérifier l'huile, l'eau, et les pneus?

"Regular, please. Will you please check the oil, water, and the tires?"

— Avec plaisir, monsieur, répond l'employé.

"With pleasure, sir," the employee replies.

Le jeune homme fait le plein, vérifie l'huile, l'eau et les pneus.

The young man fills the tank, checks the oil, the water and the tires.

— Tout est bien, dit-il à notre touriste.

"Everything is all right," he says to our tourist.

— Merci beaucoup. Combien est-ce que je vous dois?

"Many thanks. How much do I owe you?"

— Ça fait cent soixante-huit francs.

"It comes to one hundred sixty-eight francs."

M. Potter lui donne deux billets de cent francs, et le jeune homme lui rend la monnaie, trente-deux francs.

Mr. Potter gives him two hundred-franc notes and the young man gives him the change, thirty-two francs.

M. Potter fait le compte et il voit que tout est en ordre.

Mr. Potter figures out the amount and sees that all is in order.

— Très bien, dit-il à l'employé. Merci beaucoup et au revoir.

"Very good," he says to the employee. "Thank you very much and goodbye."

Le jeune homme répond, —Au revoir et bon voyage.

The young man answers, "Goodbye and a happy trip."

Exercise No. 193—Lecture 1
Une Excursion À Versailles

Un jour M. Potter a invité les fils de M. Parmentier à l'accompagner en excursion à Versailles. Ce n'est pas très loin de Paris et ils sont arrivés sans aucune difficulté. En route pour le palais M. Potter a eu une idée originale.

— Mangeons sur l'herbe[1] dans le grand parc au bord du lac. On m'a dit que c'est permis.

— Merveilleux! Allons-y.

Ils sont entrés dans une épicerie pour acheter du jambon, un fromage de camembert et une bouteille de vin rouge. Dans une boulangerie à côté ils ont acheté deux baguettes[2] et trois éclairs.

— Moi, j'ai un appétit de loup, a dit l'aîné en sortant de la boulangerie.

— Allons manger tout de suite, a dit M. Potter. Mais que faire pour les ustensiles?

— Voyons ce qu'il y a dans nos poches, a dit le cadet. Les deux garçons ont trouvé des canifs.[3]

— Voilà! Et nous allons boire dans la bouteille.[4]

Ils sont entrés au palais par la grande grille, mais au lieu de faire la visite ils sont sortis pour traverser le jardin immense.

Le jardin avec ses statues, fontaines et bosquets[5] a fait une forte impression sur M. Potter. Les deux garçons étaient d'accord. — Je vous assure que le jardin est le bijou de Versailles, a dit le cadet. Mais le palais nous ennuie à mourir.

M. Potter a répondu en riant, — Nous ne sommes pas forcés d'y aller.

Arrivés au lac ils se sont assis sur l'herbe pour manger. Ils ont causé d'une chose et d'une autre en mangeant, et M. Potter était frappé encore une fois par leur intelligence. Les garçons ont mangé comme deux loups et ils se sont amusés énormément.

Tous les trois ils se souviendront[6] longtemps de cette excursion à Versailles.

NOTE 1. on the grass 2. long loaves of bread 3. penknives 4. from the bottle 5. groves of trees 6. will remember; **se souvenir de,** *to remember*.

Exercise No. 194—Lecture 2
L'Avenue de L'Opéra

Nous nous promenons sur l'Avenue de l'Opéra. C'est une belle avenue large qui mène du Palais Royal à l'Opéra.

Il y a beaucoup de monde sur l'avenue. Tous les touristes s'y rencontrent. Les trottoirs sont bordés de boutiques de luxe où on peut acheter toutes sortes de belles choses, si on a de l'argent: des bijoux, de la lingerie fine, des gants, de la céramique, des blouses, des articles de cuir, et aussi des livres, car nous sommes en France où on aime lire. Il y a même une petite boutique et une librairie dans l'Opéra.

Il y a aussi un café-restaurant bien connu sur la Place de l'Opéra: le Café de la Paix. Allons-y prendre un demi,[1] voulez-vous? Avec plaisir.

NOTE 1. a beer

CHAPITRE 37 (TRENTE-SEPT)

Foreword

In Chapters 37–40 there is no parallel translation of the texts. However, the new words and expressions that appear are given in the vocabularies which follow each text. There is also the French-English dictionary in the Appendix to which you can refer for words you may have forgotten.

You should therefore have no difficulty in reading and understanding the texts. As a means of testing your understanding, a series of English questions to be answered in English are given under the heading Test of Reading Comprehension, instead of the usual French Questionnaire. You can check your answers in the Answers Section at the back of the book.

LE GRANDE RUE DU VILLAGE
MAIN STREET

Cher ami,

J'ai remarqué que malgré la difference qui existe entre les villages français, ils ont tous une grande rue qui mène à une place entourée d'arbres.

Derrière les arbres, les boutiques du village sont bien rangées, en ordre. La teinturerie est souvent peinte en violet. La vitrine de la boulangerie-pâtisserie à côté est remplie de gâteaux délicieux. Le boucher au coin a pendu ses gigots élégants à l'air libre. Quelques mouches s'y promènent tranquillement, mais personne n'y prête attention.

Dans la vitrine de l'épicerie on voit un tas de boîtes de sardines, et quand on y passe on sent le parfum fort de café. La blanchisseuse est une artiste. Elle arrange sa vitrine avec des papiers bleus, roses et violets pour faire un tableau d'une blouse blanche. La laiterie est toujours comblée.

Sur la place, à peu près au milieu du village, il y a la mairie d'un côté et l'église de l'autre. Au fond de la place se trouve l'école. Quelquefois on entend des rires, des chansons, mais en général le silence domine. Les enfants sont sages en France.

L'aspect de la rue change à toute heure. Pour ne rien manquer du spectacle je me lève de bonne heure. La matinée est grise. Toutes les fenêtres et tous les volets sont fermés. On dort. J'entends un coq. Puis un autre. Les chiens réveillés commencent à se saluer. Tout le monde se réveille. On ouvre les volets, on ouvre les fenêtres.

Voilà un garçon, le premier, qu'on envoie chercher le pain. Il se précipite dans la rue, court à vitesse vertigineuse, et s'arrête soudain au coin pour examiner quelque chose qui attire son attention. Ensuite il reprend sa route au pas militaire. En voilà un autre. Et encore un. Ce que les Français mangent comme pain! Notre héros, le premier, revient avec un pain presque aussi long que lui, qu'il fait tourner comme une canne.

Il n'est que sept heures et demie. Je dois tout de même vous quitter, car j'ai rendez-vous avec les jeunes Parmentier pour faire une excursion à Chartres.

Je vous laisse en vous serrant la main, jusqu'à ma prochaine lettre dans laquelle je vous décrirai nos aventures de cet après-midi.

Votre ami,
John Potter

Vocabulaire

la canne cane
la chanson song
le coq (kuk) rooster
l'église church
le gigot (zhee-**goh**) leg of lamb
la mairie townhall
la mouche fly
le tableau picture, painting
le volet shutter
la vitrine shop window
dominer to reign
pendre to hang
se précipiter to hurl oneself, rush
reprendre to take again
se réveiller to wake up
comblé crowded
entouré surrounded
peint painted
rangé arranged
réveillé awakened
sage well-behaved
soudain suddenly
à l'air libre in the open air
au milieu de in the middle of
pour ne rien manquer in order to miss nothing

Boutiques et marchands Shops and shopkeepers

la blanchisseuse laundress
la blanchisserie laundry
le boucher butcher
la boucherie butcher shop
le boulanger baker
la boulangerie bakery
le bureau de tabac tobacco shop
le coiffeur hairdresser
la confiserie candy shop
le cordonnier shoemaker
la couturière dressmaker
la droguerie hardware store
l'épicier grocer
l'épicerie grocery
la laiterie dairy
la papeterie stationery shop
la pâtisserie pastry shop, pastry
la pharmacie pharmacy, drug store
le tailleur tailor
la teinturerie dry-cleaners

Exercise No. 195—Test of Reading Comprehension

Answer these questions fully in English:

1. What has Mr. Potter noticed?
2. Where does the street often lead to?
3. What is behind the trees?
4. What shop is often painted violet?
5. Where can one see delicious cakes? A heap of cans of sardines? A white blouse that looks like a painting?
6. Where are the flies walking tranquilly about?
7. What three buildings are on the square?
8. How do the children behave in France?
9. Why does Mr. Potter get up early?
10. What does he hear first?
11. Who rushes into the street?
12. Why does he suddenly stop?
13. With what does our hero return?
14. Why must Mr. Potter stop writing?
15. What will he describe in his next letter?

Exercise No. 196—Completion of Text

1. **La rue mène** (to a square surrounded by trees).
2. **Les boutiques du village sont** (well arranged).
3. **La teinturerie** (is painted) **en violet.**
4. **La vitrine de la pâtisserie** (is filled with delicious cakes).
5. **Le boucher** (has hung his legs of lamb) **à l'air libre.**
6. **Quelques mouches** (are walking on them) **tranquillement.**
7. (In the middle of the village) **il y a la mairie.**

8. **Des fois on entend** (laughter and songs).
9. (In order not to miss anything of the spectacle) **je me lève de bonne heure.**
10. People are sleeping.
11. **Les chiens réveillés commencent** (to greet each other).
12. **Tout le monde** (wakes up).
13. (What the French eat) **comme pain!**
14. **Notre héros** (returns with a loaf of bread).
15. (I must nevertheless) **vous quitter.**

Grammar Notes

1. Position of single object pronouns

You have learned:

a. The direct object and indirect object pronouns.

Direct Object

me	me	**nous**	us
te	you (*fam.*)	**vous**	you
le	him, it (*m*)	**les**	them
la	her, it (*f*)		

Indirect Object

me	(to) me	**nous**	(to) us
te	(to) you	**vous**	(to) you
lui	(to) him, (to) her	**leur**	(to) them

Reflexives (*Direct and Indirect Objects*)

me	myself	**nous**	ourselves
te	yourself	**vous**	yourself, yourselves
se	himself, herself, itself, oneself	**se**	themselves

b. The partitive pronoun (**en**—*some, any, none, not any, of it, of them*) is often omitted in English, but **en** is never omitted in French.

Avez-vous du beurre?	Have you any butter?
J'en ai une livre.	I have a pound (of it).
A-t-elle acheté des oeufs?	Has she bought some eggs?
Elle en a acheté une douzaine.	She has bought a dozen (of them).

c. The use of **y** to refer to a place already mentioned.

Combien de temps restera-t-il à Paris?	How long will he stay in Paris?
Il y restera trois semaines.	He will stay there three weeks.

d. Object pronouns precede the verb except in the affirmative imperative.

Avez-vous acheté les peintures?	Have you bought the paintings?
Je ne les ai pas achetées.	I have not bought them.
Ne les achetez pas.	Do not buy them.
Achetez-les.	Buy them.

2. Two object pronouns

When a verb has two object pronouns their placement is as follows:

a. If there are two pronoun objects of different persons, both precede the verb with **me, te, nous, vous** (first and second persons) coming before **le, la, l', les** (third person). The order is different in English.

M'enverrez-vous les billets?	Will you send me the tickets?
Nous *vous les* enverrons demain.	We shall send *them to you* tomorrow.

b. If there are two pronoun objects of the third person, the direct object (**le, la, l', or les**) precedes the indirect object (**lui** or **leur**).

Avez-vous prêté votre crayon à Jean?	Did you lend your pencil to John?
Oui. Je *le lui* ai prêté.	Yes. I lent *it to him*.

c. When **y** or **en** is used with another object pronoun, it follows that object pronoun.

A-t-elle mis les tasses sur le buffet?	Has she put the cups on the buffet?
Elle *les y* a mises.	She has put *them there*.
Il n'a pas eu l'occasion de *m'en* informer.	He did not have a chance to let *me* know *about it*.

d. If y and **en** both appear, y precedes **en.**
This combination is rarely seen except with **il y a** (*there is, are*).

Combien de chaises y a-t-il dans le salon?	How many chairs are there in the parlor?
Il *y en* a six.	There are six (*of them*).

e. In the affirmative imperative the order of two object pronouns is exactly as in English.

Donnez-*les-moi*. Envoyez-*m'en*.	Give *them to me*. Send *me some* (*of it*).

NOTE: **moi** is used for **me** in the affirmative imperative, except before **en** when the contraction **m'en** is used.

Exercise No. 197. Translate the following sentences. Practice them aloud. They will help give you a feel for the double object pronoun. Remember, however, that in ordinary conversation a simple *yes* or *no* answer would serve, or an answer with only one pronoun object. Thus in Question No. 1 the answer might also be:

Oui. *or* **Oui, nous l'avons envoyée. Non.** *or* **Non, nous ne l'avons pas envoyée.**

1. **Est-ce que vous avez envoyé la poterie à M. Potter?
Oui, nous la lui avons envoyée.**
2. **Est-ce que beaucoup de monde se rencontre sur l'Avenue de l'Opéra?
Tous les touristes s'y rencontrent.**
3. **Envoyez-moi les journaux français, s'il vous plaît.
Nous vous les enverrons demain.**
4. **Est-ce que le garçon vous a donné l'addition?
Il ne me l'a pas encore donnée.**
5. **Avez-vous demandé les billets à l'employé?
Je ne les lui ai pas encore demandés parce qu'il est très occupé.**
6. **Combien de plats y a-t-il dans cette caisse?
Il y en a vingt-cinq douzaines.**
7. **Lui avez-vous rendu l'argent que vous lui avez emprunté?** (borrowed)
Je le lui rendrai ce soir.
8. **La bonne a-t-elle mis sur le bureau la porcelaine que M. Potter vient de recevoir?
Elle l'y a mise.**
9. **Me prêterez-vous votre parapluie?
Je vous le prêterai; mais rendez-le-moi demain, s'il vous plaît.
Merci beaucoup. Je vous le rendrai demain.**
10. **Montrez-moi, s'il vous plaît, la nouvelle robe que vous avez achetée.
Je ne peux pas vous la montrer parce qu'elle n'est pas encore arrivée du magasin.**

CHAPITRE 38 (TRENTE-HUIT)

UNE EXCURSION À CHARTRES
A TRIP TO CHARTRES

Cher ami,

Mes jeunes amis sont venus me chercher de bonne heure car j'ai voulu revenir à temps pour aller à l'opéra le soir. Cette fois-ci ils avaient préparé (*they had prepared*) un bon déjeuner qu'on avait l'intention de prendre en route sur l'herbe, comme à Versailles. Mais cette fois-ci ils avaient apporté (*they had brought*) un beau panier rempli d'une nappe, de serviettes, de couteaux, de fourchettes, et aussi d'un poulet.

La voiture que j'avais louée (*I had rented*) nous attendait en bas. Nous y sommes montés tout en parlant et riant, et nous voilà en route.

Je conduisais à mon aise, quand tout à coup j'ai entendu un son que j'ai reconnu tout de suite.

— Qu'est-ce que c'est? ont demandé les garçons.

J'ai stoppé et nous sommes descendus. — Nous avons crevé un pneu, ai-je répondu.

J'ai voulu changer le pneu et les jeunes gens voulaient m'aider. Très heureux ils ont commencé à chercher le cric. Mais, malheur! il n'y avait pas de cric dans l'outillage. Que faire?

De temps en temps une auto passait à toute vitesse. Malgré nos signaux désespérés personne ne s'est arrêté. Il était presque midi et le soleil donnait à plomb sur nos têtes. Nous nous sommes assis sous un arbre près de la route pour attendre notre destin.

Bientôt un grand camion s'est approché rapidement et il s'est arrêté court avec un grand bruit de freins devant nous. Le camionneur est descendu.

— Vous êtes à plat? Voulez-vous un coup de main? Ce grand gaillard avait une voix très douce. Il souriait.

— Nous n'avons pas de cric, lui ai-je dit.
— Mais c'est un désastre, m'a-t-il répondu, en cherchant le sien (*his*).
— En tout cas nous avons un pneu de rechange.
— C'est toujours ça! Tout le monde s'est mis à la besogne. En cinq secondes tout était prêt.

Je n'osais pas lui offrir un pourboire. Il avait tant de dignité naturelle. Mais les deux garçons ont eu une idée astucieuse. — Voulez-vous bien déjeuner avec nous? Nous avons un poulet énorme.

— Très volontiers, a répondu le camionneur. À condition que j'ajoute mon jambon et ma bouteille de vin.

Nous nous sommes assis au-dessous de notre arbre et nous avons déjeuné gaiement de bon appétit.

— Le jambon est délicieux, avons-nous dit avec enthousiasme.

Il a souri. — Ma femme ne me néglige pas.

Le déjeuner fini, nous avons tous fait la sieste. Ensuite nous avons fait nos adieux. Le gros camion est parti vers Paris et nous avons repris la route pour Chartres.

Et violà qu'encore une fois je n'ai pas le temps de vous décrire mes impressions, car ce soir je vais à l'opéra et je dois m'habiller.

Bien cordialement à vous,
John Potter

Vocabulaire

A.
le camion truck, bus
le camionneur truckdriver
le désastre disaster
le coup de main a helping hand
le destin fate
le gaillard jovial fellow
le malheur misfortune
le panier basket
la nappe tablecloth
la serviette napkin
le son sound
ajouter to add, join
couper to cut
louer to rent
négliger to neglect
oser to dare
court short
désespéré desperate
gros (grosse *f*) big, fat
au-dessous de under
en bas below, downstairs

B.
l'automobile (la voiture) the car
le cric (kree) jack
le poste d'essence gas station
les freins brakes
le pneu tire
le pneu de rechange spare tire
l'outillage tool kit
le volant steering wheel
changer l'huile to change the oil
conduire to drive, to conduct
être à plat to have a flat
crever un pneu to burst (puncture) a tire
faire le plein d'essence to fill up the tank
stationner to park
stopper to stop
vérifier to check

French Expressions

1. **Qu'est-ce qui est arrivé?** What happened?
2. **crever un pneu** to get a flat
3. **le soleil donnait à plomb** the sun was shining directly
4. **être à plat** to have a flat
5. **un coup de main** a helping hand
6. **c'est toujours ça** that's all to the good
7. **se mettre à la besogne** to set to work
8. **et voilà qu'encore une fois** and so it is that once more

Exercise No. 198—Test of Reading Comprehension

1. Why did Mr. Potter's young friends call for him early?
2. What had they prepared?
3. Where was the car that Mr. Potter had rented?
4. What did he hear all of a sudden?
5. What had happened?
6. What did the young men want to do?
7. Why could they not change the tire?
8. What did the truckdriver who came along soon offer to do?
9. Why didn't Mr. Potter dare to offer him a tip?
10. What clever idea did the boys have?
11. What did they eat and drink for lunch?
12. What did the boys say about the truckdriver's ham?
13. What did the truckdriver say about his wife?
14. What did they do after lunch?
15. Why, once again, doesn't Mr. Potter have time to describe his impressions of Chartres?

Exercise No. 199—Completion of Text

1. **Mes amis sont venus** (to get me).
2. (They had prepared) **un bon déjeuner.**
3. a tablecloth, some napkins, some knives, some forks
4. (And there we were) **en route.**
5. (All of a sudden) **j'ai entendu un son.**
6. We have blown a tire.
7. (There was no jack) **dans l'outillage.**
8. (Nobody) **s'est arrêté.**
9. (We sat down) **au-dessous d'un arbre.**
10. (Soon a large truck) **s'est approché rapidement.**
11. **Voulez-vous** (a helping hand)?
12. (At any rate) **nous avons un pneu de rechange.**
13. **Tout le monde** (set to work).
14. **Je n'osais pas** (to offer him a tip).
15. **Voulez-vous bien** (to have lunch with us)?

Grammar Notes

1. The past perfect (pluperfect) tense. What *had happened.* Model verbs, **parler, finir, vendre.**

j'avais parlé (fini, vendu)	I had spoken (finished, sold)
tu avais parlé (fini, vendu)	you had spoken (finished, sold)
il avait parlé (fini, vendu)	he had spoken (finished, sold)
elle avait parlé (fini, vendu)	she had spoken (finished, sold)
nous avions parlé (fini, vendu)	we had spoken (finished, sold)
vous aviez parlé (fini, vendu)	you had spoken (finished, sold)
ils avaient parlé (fini, vendu)	they had spoken (finished, sold)
elles avaient parlé (fini, vendu)	they had spoken (finished, sold)
avait-il parlé (fini, vendu)?	had he spoken (finished, sold)?
il n'avait pas parlé (fini, vendu)	he had not spoken (finished, sold)
n'avait-il pas parlé (fini, vendu)?	had he not spoken (finished, sold)?

The past perfect tense is usually formed by the auxiliary verb **j'avais, etc.** (*I had, etc.*) plus the past participle of the verb. See below for **être**-verbs.

Exercise No. 200. Change these sentences from the conversational past to the past perfect. Translate each sentence in the past perfect.

Exemple: 1. Il avait appris les règles essentielles. He had learned the essential rules.

1. **Il a appris les règles essentielles.**
2. **Nous avons vraiment travaillé dur.**
3. **Ils n'ont pas encore obtenu leurs billets.**
4. **A-t-il écrit une lettre à son ami?**
5. **Qui a promis de le rencontrer à l'aéroport?**
6. **J'ai oublié mon parapluie.**
7. **Ont-ils réservé une chambre pour M. Potter?**
8. **Avez-vous lu beaucoup de guides?**
9. **Ses jeunes amis ont préparé un bon déjeuner.**
10. **N'a-t-il pas loué une voiture?**

2. The past perfect of **être**-verbs. Model verb **aller.**

I had gone, you had gone, etc.

j'étais allé (allée)	**nous étions allés (allées)**
tu étais allé (allée)	**vous étiez allé(s), allée(s)**
il était allé	**ils sont allés**
elle était allée	**elles sont allées**

être-verbs in the past perfect take the auxiliary **j'étais, etc.,** instead of **j'avais, etc. J'étais, etc.,** is the imperfect of **être,** *to be.* As an auxiliary verb it is translated *I had,* etc., not *I was,* etc.

Reflexive verbs also take the auxiliary **j'étais, etc.,** in the past perfect.

Conversational Past **Un bel homme s'est approché.** A handsome man approached.
Past Perfect **Un bel homme s'était approché.** A handsome man had approached.

Exercise No. 201. Change these sentences from the conversational past to the past perfect. Translate each sentence in the past perfect.

Exemple: 1. Mes jeunes amis étaient venus me chercher. My young friends had come to get me.

1. **Mes jeunes amis sont venus me chercher.**
2. **Un grand camion s'est approché rapidement.**
3. **Nous nous sommes assis sous un grand arbre.**
4. **Je suis allé à la salle d'attente.**

5. **Nous ne sommes pas sortis ensemble.**
6. **Ils sont arrivés sains et saufs.**
7. **Le taxi s'est arrêté devant l'hôtel.**
8. **Êtes-vous allé au bureau de douane?**
9. **Nous nous sommes dit au revoir.**
10. **Elles ne sont pas restées à Paris deux semaines.**

3. The possessive pronouns **le mien,** *mine,* **le tien,** *yours,* etc.

a. In French as in English there are possessive adjectives and possessive pronouns. The possessive adjectives (**mon, ton, son, etc.**) are very important and useful words. You have learned and used them a great deal. The possessive pronouns are used rather infrequently. Study the following examples:

Possessive Adjectives	*Possessive Pronouns*
Son père (his or her father) **est docteur.**	**Le mien** (mine) **est avocat.**
Sa soeur (his or her sister) **est petite.**	**La mienne** (mine) **est grande.**
Ses livres (his or her books) **sont neufs.**	**Les miens** (mine) **sont vieux.**
Ses plumes (his or her pens) **sont bonnes.**	**Les miennes** (mine) **sont mauvaises.**

The possessive pronoun agrees in number and gender with the noun for which it stands. The complete table of possessive pronouns follows:

Singular			*Plural*	
Masc.	*Fem.*		*Masc.*	*Fem.*
le mien	**la mienne**	(mine)	**les miens**	**les miennes**
le tien	**la tienne**	(yours)	**les tiens**	**les tiennes**
le sien	**la sienne**	(his, hers)	**les siens**	**les siennes**
le nôtre (nohtr)	**la nôtre**	(ours)	**les nôtres**	**les nôtres**
le vôtre (vohtr)	**la vôtre**	(yours)	**les vôtres**	**les vôtres**
le leur	**la leur**	(theirs)	**les leurs**	**les leurs**

b. After the verb **être, à** + an independent pronoun is generally used rather than the possessive pronoun:

Cette montre est à moi,	This watch is mine,
à toi, à lui, à elle.	yours, his, hers.
Ces places sont à nous,	These seats are ours,
à vous, à eux, à elles.	yours, theirs (*m*) theirs (*f*).

Exercise No. 202. Translate these sentences. Practice them aloud.

1. **Nous avons de bons professeurs. Comment trouvez-vous les vôtres?**
2. **Allons au bureau de poste dans votre voiture. La nôtre a crevé un pneu.**
3. **Prêtez-moi votre plume, s'il vous plaît. La mienne n'écrit pas.**
4. **J'ai oublié mon parapluie. Voulez-vous bien me prêter le vôtre?**
5. **Vous n'avez pas de cric. Voulez-vous emprunter** (borrow) **le mien?**
6. **La bicyclette de Paul coûte plus cher que la mienne, mais la mienne est meilleure que la sienne.**
7. **Louise et moi nous avons acheté des billets de théâtre hier. J'ai les miens, mais elle a malheureusement perdu les siens.**
8. **Voici nos chapeaux. Celui-ci est à moi. Celui-là est à vous.**

CHAPITRE 39 (TRENTE-NEUF)

M. POTTER ACHÈTE UN BILLET DE LOTERIE
MR. POTTER BUYS A LOTTERY TICKET

Cher ami,

Je ne suis pas joueur, M. Picard. C'est à dire que jusqu'à la semaine dernière je n'avais jamais été joueur.

Ce que est arrivé? Je vais vous raconter tout.

Comme vous le savez bien il y a des postes de vente de billets de loterie partout à Paris.

Quand je suis arrivé à Paris j'ai remarqué tout de suite qu'on s'occupait beaucoup de la Loterie Nationale. Je voyais des affiches illustrées dans le métro, dans les autobus, dans les rues, enfin un peu partout. Quand (*Whenever*) je voyais une de ces affiches je commençais à rêver: — Si je gagnais le premier prix, le gros lot, j'aurais (*would have*) assez d'argent pour voyager partout en Europe l'année prochaine. Ma femme m'accompagnerait (*would accompany me*) et les enfants iraient (*would go*) à l'école quelque part en France pour apprendre le français. Ma femme pourrait (*would be able*) faire la connaissance des Parmentiers et nous pourrions (*could*) peut-être faire un voyage ensemble tous les quatre.

Je pourrais (*would be able*) acheter beaucoup de belles choses. J'achèterais (*would buy*) des objets d'art, non pas pour les vendre, mais pour les garder chez moi. Je serais (*would be*) l'homme le plus heureux du monde.

C'est ainsi que je rêvais.

Mercredi passé je descendais la Rue de Rivoli. Au coin de la Rue Cambon j'ai vu un de ces petits postes de vente de billets de loterie. La jeune fille qui était de service m'a vu regarder l'annonce "Loterie Nationale." Elle m'a dit:

— Monsieur, achetez ce billet. C'est le bon. Il vous portera bonheur.

— Comment savez-vous que celui-là est le bon?

— Parce qu'il a trois zéros. Regardez.

J'ai regardé et en effet le numéro finissait en trois zéros. Je me suis dit, — Celui-là, il sort de l'ordinaire. Allons-y!

Et voilà comment je suis devenu joueur!

Le lendemain, je me suis levé de bonne heure, j'ai sonné tout de suite pour demander mon café, mes croissants et mon journal. Ils sont arrivés tous à la fois, mais à ce moment je ne m'intéressais qu'au journal. Je l'ai ouvert vite, le coeur battant. Mais où est-ce qu'on les a caché, ces numéros? Ah, les voilà! Qu'est-ce que je vois? Le numéro qui a gagné le gros lot finit en trois zéros: 26,000. Je ne respire plus. Je cherche mon billet, en faisant des voyages dans la lune. Enfin je le trouve. Je peux à peine le tenir. Voilà les trois zéros. Voilà le deux. Mais, malheur! C'est un cinq, pas un six. Tant pis! Et j'ai pris mon petit déjeuner, en riant de moi-même. J'ai décidé que les émotions d'un joueur ne sont pas pour moi. J'aime la vie tranquille comme je vous l'ai dit à New-York.

Très cordialement, votre ami,
John Potter

Vocabulaire

l'affiche (*f*) poster
l'annonce (*f*) advertisement
le bonheur happiness
le coeur heart
le gros lot first prize
la lune moon
le joueur gambler
le poste de vente booth
battre to beat
cacher to hide, conceal
gagner to win, gain, earn
s'occuper de to be busy with
respirer to breathe
rêver to dream
rire de to laugh at

French Expressions

1. **être de service** to be on duty
2. **il sort de l'ordinaire** it is something out of the ordinary
3. **allons-y** let's go, let's take it
4. **tant pis** so much the worse
5. **à peine** scarcely
6. **quelque part** somewhere

Exercise No. 203—Test of Reading Comprehension

1. What kind of man had Mr. Potter never been?
2. What had he noticed right away when he came to France?
3. When he saw one of the illustrated posters what did he dream of doing?
4. If he won the first prize, for what would he have sufficient money?
5. What would his wife do?
6. What would the children do?
7. From whom did Mr. Potter buy a lottery ticket, whose number ended in three zeros?
8. What did he ring for the next morning?
9. What was the only thing that interested him at the moment?
10. What happened when he saw that the winning number had three zeros?
11. What was he doing mentally while he looked for his ticket?
12. What number did Mr. Potter have?
13. What number won the prize?
14. What did Mr. Potter decide?
15. What sort of life does he like?

Exercise No. 204—Completion of Text

1. (I had never been) **joueur.**
2. **Il y a** (lottery ticket stalls) **partout à Paris.**
3. **J'ai remarqué tout de suite** (that people were very much taken up with) **la Loterie Nationale.**
4. (I saw illustrated posters) **dans le métro.**
5. (If I won the first prize) **j'aurais assez d'argent pour voyager partout en Europe.**
6. (I would be able to buy) **beaucoup de belles choses.**
7. **Je serais** (the happiest man in the world).
8. (And that is how) **je suis devenu joueur.**
9. **Je me suis levé** (early).
10. **À ce moment** (I was interested only in the newspaper).
11. (I look for) **mon billet.**
12. **Je peux** (scarcely hold it).
13. **Mais malheur!** (It's a five, not a six).
14. **J'ai pris mon petit déjeuner** (laughing at myself).

Grammar Notes

1. The present conditional. What *would happen*. Model verbs **parler, finir, vendre.**

The present conditional may be called the *would* tense. Its use in French is much the same as in English.

je parlerais (finirais, vendrais)	I would speak (finish, sell)
tu parlerais (finirais, vendrais)	you would speak (finish, sell)
il parlerait (finirait, vendrait)	he would speak (finish, sell)
elle parlerait (finirait, vendrait)	she would speak (finish, sell)
nous parlerions (finirions, vendrions)	we would speak (finish, sell)
vous parleriez (finiriez, vendriez)	you would speak (finish, sell)
ils parleraient (finiraient, vendraient)	they (*m*) would speak (finish, sell)
elles parleraient (finiraient, vendraient)	they (*f*) would speak (finish, sell)

a. The personal endings of the present conditional of all verbs are **-ais, -ais, -ait; -ions, -iez, -aient.** They are exactly like the endings of the imperfect tense.

b. To form the present conditional, add the conditional endings to the *infinitive* as a base. If the *infinitive* ends in **-re,** as in **vendre,** drop the final **e** before adding the conditional endings.

Thus the base for the present conditional is the same as the base for the future.

Infinitive	*Future*	*Present Conditional*
to	*I shall, you will, etc.*	*I would, you would, etc.*
parler	**je parlerai, tu parleras, etc.**	**je parlerais, tu parlerais, etc.**
finir	**je finirai, tu finiras, etc.**	**je finirais, tu finirais, etc.**
vendre	**je vendrai, tu vendras, etc.**	**je vendrais, tu vendrais, etc.**

2. The irregular present conditional

Those verbs that have an irregular base for the future have the same irregular base for the conditional.

Infinitive	*Future*	*Pres. Cond.*	*Infinitive*	*Future*	*Pres. Cond.*
to	*shall, will*	*would*	*to*	*shall, will*	*would*
avoir	**j'aurai**	**j'aurais**	**pouvoir**	**je pourrai**	**je pourrais**
être	**je serai**	**je serais**	**devoir**	**je devrai**	**je devrais**
aller	**j'irai**	**j'irais**	**recevoir**	**je recevrai**	**je recevrais**
envoyer	**j'enverrai**	**j'enverrais**	**vouloir**	**je voudrai**	**je voudrais**
venir	**je viendrai**	**je viendrais**	**valoir**	**je vaudrai**	**je vaudrais**
tenir	**je tiendrai**	**je tiendrais**	**voir**	**je verrai**	**je verrais**
courir	**je courrai**	**je courrais**	**savoir**	**je saurai**	**je saurais**
faire	**je ferai**	**je ferais**	**falloir**	**il faudra**	**il faudrait**

Exercise No. 205. Change these sentences from the future to the present conditional. Translate each sentence in the present conditional.

Exemple: 1. Je voyagerais partout en Europe. I would travel everywhere in Europe.

1. **Je voyagerai partout en Europe.**
2. **Il visitera la France et l'Italie.**
3. **Nous apprendrons le français**
4. **Ma famille ne m'accompagnera pas.**

5. Elle pourra acheter beaucoup de belles choses.
6. Aura-t-il assez d'argent?
7. Ils achèteront des objets d'art.
8. Serez-vous content de rester ici?
9. Elle ne vous connaîtra pas.
10. Ils ne feront pas leurs devoirs.
11. Je vous enverrai les revues.
12. Ils ne viendront pas la semaine prochaine.

CHAPITRE 40 (QUARANTE)

M. POTTER S'EN VA
MR. POTTER GOES AWAY

Cher ami,

Quand je suis parti de New-York j'étais assez bien renseigné sur la France. J'avais lu quelques livres sur son histoire et sur les coutumes du pays. Je savais parler français passablement.

Maintenant que je suis sur le point de partir de France il me semble que je parle avec beaucoup plus de facilité. J'ai visité beaucoup de ces endroits dont nous avons parlé dans nos conversations. Dans mes lettres je ne pouvais décrire que très peu de tout ce que j'ai vu et appris. Le reste, je dois laisser pour notre prochaine rencontre.

J'aime tant de choses en France: Paris, les monuments historiques, le paysage, la peinture, et la cuisine. Mais j'aime surtout les Français. J'aime leur sentiment marqué de la dignité de l'homme, leur sens vif du comique, leur politesse et leur passion pour la discussion.

La vie en France est vraiment plus tranquille qu'à New-York, malgré mes premières impressions dans le taxi qui me conduisait à vitesse vertigineuse de l'aéroport à l'hôtel.

Comme vous savez c'était un voyage d'agrément aussi bien qu'un voyage d'affaires. Heureusement j'ai bientôt terminé mes affaires et je pouvais me dévouer complètement aux distractions.

Je n'avais pas le temps d'aller ni au Maroc ni en Corse. Dommage! Mais j'ai préferé passer mon temps à mieux connaître la France. Il y a tant à voir, à faire et à apprendre. Tout m'a enchanté.

J'aurai beaucoup à vous dire au sujet des personnes que j'ai rencontrées, des endroits que j'ai visités, et de tout ce que j'ai appris des coutumes, de la vie, de la langue, et des arts de la France.

Certainement je reviendrai en France. Je voudrais revenir l'année prochaine. Mais cette fois-ci toute la famille m'accompagnerait. Je suis sûr que je pourrais faire le guide sans difficulté. Je n'ai pas gagné le gros lot dans la loterie, mais tout de même, je reviendrai.

Celle-ci est la dernière lettre que je vous écrirai avant de partir pour New-York le premier août. Je me donnerai le plaisir de vous téléphoner dès mon arrivée pour vous inviter à dîner en famille.

Sans doute nous passerons des heures en parlant de la France et de notre Paris bien aimé.

À bientôt,
Votre ami,
John Potter

Vocabulaire

le comique comic(al)
la facilité facility
la marque mark, symbol
le reste remainder, rest
la rencontre meeting
le sens sense
s'en aller to go away
conduire to drive
renseigné informed
dès as early as, from

French Expressions

1. **je m'en vais** I go away
   tu t'en vas you go away
   il, elle s'en va he, she goes away
   nous nous en allons we go away
   vous vous en allez you go away
   ils, elles s'en vont they go away
2. **être sur le point de partir** to be about to leave
3. **tant à voir** so much to see
4. **faire le guide** to act as guide
5. **dès mon arrivée** immediately on my arrival
6. **combien de choses** how many things
7. **beaucoup de choses** many things
8. **tant de choses** so many things

Exercise No. 206—Test of Reading Comprehension

1. Before leaving for France, how had Mr. Potter obtained knowledge of that country?
2. How much was he able to describe in his letters?
3. What does he like best in France?
4. What does he like about the French people?
5. How does he compare life in France with life in the United States?
6. When had he gotten a different impression?
7. Who would accompany him on his next trip to France?
8. What is he sure of?
9. When is he leaving for New York?
10. What will he be glad to do immediately upon his arrival home?
11. What does he think he and Mr. Picard will do when they are together again?

Grammar Notes

1. The past conditional. What *would have happened.* **parler, aller**

I would have spoken
you would have spoken, etc.

I would have gone
you would have gone, etc.

j'aurais parlé	**nous aurions parlé**	**je serais allé(e)**	**nous serions allés, allées**
tu aurais parlé	**vous auriez parlé**	**tu serais allé(e)**	**vous seriez allé(s), allée(s)**
il aurait parlé	**ils auraient parlé**	**il serait allé**	**ils seraient allés**
elle aurait parlé	**elles auraient parlé**	**elle serait allée**	**elles seraient allées**

The past conditional is formed by the auxiliary **j'aurais, etc.,** plus the past participle, for all **avoir**-verbs; and by the auxiliary **je serais, etc.,** plus the past participle, for all **être**-verbs (including reflexive verbs).

2. Conditional sentences. **si** (*if*)-clauses.

A conditional sentence is one that includes a **si** (*if*)-clause. Compare the tenses of the verbs used in the following French conditional sentences with those used in the corresponding English sentences:

1. Si je le vois, je lui parlerai.	1. If I see him, I shall speak to him.
2. S'il gagne le prix, il ira en Europe.	2. If he wins the prize, he will go to Europe.
3. Si je le voyais, je lui parlerais.	3. If I saw him, I would speak to him.
4. S'il gagnait le prix, il irait en Europe.	4. If he won the prize, he would go to Europe.
5. Si je l'avais vu, je lui aurais parlé.	5. If I had seen him, I would have spoken to him.
6. S'il avait gagné le prix, il serait allé en Europe.	6. If he had won the prize, he would have gone to Europe.

The tenses of conditional sentences in French are often the same as the tenses in the corresponding English conditional sentences. Note however these differences:

As in English, French uses the present tense to imply future action in the **si**-clause. It *never* uses a future tense in the **si**-clause. See sentences 1 and 2.

French uses the imperfect tense in the **si**-clause where English can use either the past or *should* or *were to*. See sentences 3 and 4.

3. **Si** (*whether*)

When **si** means *whether,* it is followed by the same tenses as in English.

Je ne sais pas s'il fera un voyage en Europe l'été prochain.	I don't know whether he will take a trip to Europe next summer.

Exercise No. 207. Practice the French sentences aloud:

1. Si j'ai le temps, je vous accompagnerai jusqu'à la gare.	1. If I have time, I shall accompany you as far as the station.
2. Si vous la voyez, faites-lui mes amitiés.	2. If you see her, give her my regards.
3. Si vous revenez à Paris, j'espère avoir le plaisir de vous revoir.	3. If you return to Paris, I hope to meet you again.

4. Si nous pouvons vous aider, nous le ferons.	4. If we are able to help you, we shall do so.
5. Si les affaires ne retiennent M. Potter à Paris, il visitera la Côte d'Azur.	5. If business does not detain Mr. Potter in Paris, he will visit the Riviera.
6. Si nous vivions en France, les enfants iraient à l'école pour apprendre le français.	6. If we were living in France, the children would go to school to learn French.
7. Si vous parliez plus lentement, je vous comprendrais mieux.	7. If you spoke more slowly, I would understand you better.
8. Seriez-vous surpris si je vous disais que j'étudie le français?	8. Would you be surprised if I told (were to tell) you that I am studying French?
9. Si j'allais à Paris, je rendrais visite à la famille de M. Parmentier.	9. If I went to Paris, I would pay a visit to the family of Mr. Parmentier.
10. Si j'avais assez d'argent, je ferais un voyage autour du monde.	10. If I had enough money, I would take a trip around the world.
11. Ils auraient réussi dans l'examen s'ils avaient travaillé dur.	11. They would have passed (succeeded in) the examination if they had worked hard.
12. Si elle avait cherché un peu plus longtemps, elle l'aurait trouvé.	12. If she had looked a little longer, she would have found it.
13. Nous serions allés au cinéma si nous avions fini nos devoirs plus tôt.	13. We would have gone to the movies if we had finished our homework sooner.
14. Si M. Potter n'avait pas lu les guides, il n'aurait pas su se tirer d'affaire en France.	14. If Mr. Potter had not read the guide books, he would not have known how to get along in France.

RÉVISION 9
CHAPITRES 37–40 PREMIÈRE PARTIE

NOUNS

1. l'annonce	**8. l'herbe (*f*)**	**15. le panier**	1. advertisement	8. grass	15. basket
2. le bijou	**9. l'huile (*f*)**	**16. le reste**	2. jewel	9. oil	16. remainder
3. le bonheur	**10. le jambon**	**17. le sentiment**	3. happiness	10. ham	17. feeling
4. la boutique	**11. la lune**	**18. la serviette**	4. shop	11. moon	18. napkin
5. le coq	**12. lendemain, le lendemain**	**19. le son**	5. rooster	12. tomorrow, the next day	19. sound
6. l'essence	**13. le métro**	**20. le trottoir**	6. gasoline	13. subway	20. sidewalk
7. l'église	**14. la nappe**	**21. la vitrine**	7. church	14. tablecloth	21. shop window

VERBS

1. ajouter	**7. il nous ennuie**	**13. respirer**	1. to add	7. he bores us	13. to breathe
2. battre	**8. gagner**	**14. réveiller**	2. to beat	8. to earn, win	14. to awake
3. cacher	**9. louer**	**15. rire de**	3. to hide	9. to rent	15. to laugh at
4. conduire	**10. négliger**	**16. rêver**	4. to drive	10. to neglect	16. to dream
5. couper	**11. oser**	**17. se souvenir (de)**	5. to cut	11. to dare	17. to remember
6. ennuyer	**12. reprendre**	**18. Je me souviens.**	6. to bore, annoy	12. to take again	18. I remember.

ADJECTIVES

1. ne–aucun aucune (*f*)[1]	**3. gros grosse (*f*)**	**5. entouré**	1. no, no one, none	3. big, large stout	5. surrounded
2. délicieux délicieuse (*f*)	**4. sage**	**6. renseigné**	2. delicious	4. well-behaved	6. informed

NOTE 1. **Aucun** may be used as a pronoun or as an adjective. Thus:

Aucun de ses amis n'ètait à la station. None of his friends was at the station.
Il n'a eu aucune intention de l'acheter. He had no intention of buying it.

ADVERBS

1. soudain	**2. tant**	**3. vraiment**	1. suddenly	2. so much, so many	3. truly

FRENCH EXPRESSIONS

1. être de service	1. to be on duty
2. être à plat	2. to have a flat
3. faire le compte	3. to add up the bill
4. faire le plein d'essence	4. to fill up the tank
5. faire le guide	5. to act as guide
6. se mettre à la besogne	6. to set to work
7. il sort de l'ordinaire	7. it's out of the ordinary
8. tant pis	8. too bad
9. c'est toujours ça	9. that's all to the good

DEUXIÈME PARTIE

Exercise No. 208. Translate the following sentences accurately. All the tenses you have learned are illustrated here.

1. **Elles sont allées au marché pour faire des achats.**
2. **Les Français ont fait une forte impression sur M. Potter.**
3. **Il est allé à la gare pour demander des renseignements.**
4. **Je pourrai me tirer d'affaire en France parce que je parle bien le français.**
5. **Après demain nous rendrons visite à M. Duval.**
6. **Le jeune homme avait déjà fait le plein d'essence et vérifié l'huile.**
7. **L'été prochain M. Potter pourra faire le guide pour toute la famille.**
8. **Si M. Potter avait eu plus de temps, il aurait fait un voyage au Maroc.**
9. **À l'Hôtel du Quai Voltaire nous n'avons manqué de rien.**
10. **Après avoir terminé ses affaires, M. Potter s'est dévoué complètement aux distractions.**
11. **Je vais écrire une lettre à mon représentant pour lui faire savoir la date de mon arrivée.**
12. **Après avoir fait nos adieux, nous sommes montés dans l'avion.**
13. **Je pensais aux conseils de mon professeur pendant que le taxi filait à toute vitesse par les rues de Paris.**
14. **Autrefois M. Potter faisait traduire sa correspondance française, mais à l'avenir** (in the future) **il la traduira lui-même.**
15. **Les enfants s'amusaient à jeter des pierres dans l'eau.**
16. **Si vous trouvez les caoutchoucs que j'ai laissés chez vous, rendez-les-moi s'il vous plaît.**
17. **Je n'oublierai pas de vous les rendre.**
18. **Je n'avais jamais vu un spectacle pareil.**
19. **Lorsque M. Potter voyageait en Europe, Mme. Potter s'occupait des enfants.**
20. **Je n'ai jamais été en France mais je compte y aller l'été prochain.**

Exercise No. 209. Complete the following sentences in French.

1. **M. Potter** (is a businessman from New York).
2. **Il a fait** (a trip to Paris in order to visit his agent).
3. **Il voulait** (to get acquainted with him).
4. **Avant de partir pour la France** (he had learned to speak French well).
5. (He had also read many books) **sur la France.**
6. **Il a écrit** (many letters to his friend and teacher).
7. **Il a décrit** (many of the interesting places of which they had spoken in their conversations).
8. **Malgré ses premières impressions** (he had found life in France more tranquil than in the United States).
9. **Il pensait au taxi** (which had taken him to his hotel).
10. (The dizzying speed of the taxi) **ne lui avait pas fait plaisir.**
11. **Heureusement** (he soon finished his business matters).
12. **Il aime surtout les Français,** (their politeness and their marked feeling for the dignity of man).
13. **Tout de même** (he did not have time to go to Morocco or Corsica).
14. **Il y avait** (so much to see, so much to do, so much to learn).
15. **Il avait beaucoup appris** (about the customs, the life, the language and the arts of France).
16. **L'année prochaine** (he will return to France).
17. **Toute la famille** (would accompany him).
18. (He has not won the first prize in the lottery) **mais il aura** (enough money).
19. **Celle-ci est la dernière lettre** (which Mr. Potter will write before leaving France).
20. **Sans aucune doute** (he will invite Mr. Picard to dinner with his family) **quand il sera de retour**[1] **à New-York.**

NOTE 1. **être de retour,** *to be back*

Exercise No. 210—Lecture
Nice, La Capitale De La Côte D'Azur

Il y a vraiment deux villes dans Nice: la ville italienne et la ville française, la vieille ville et la ville moderne. On peut se promener dans les vieux quartiers où on entend rien que l'italien, car il n'y a qu'en 1860 que Nice est devenue française. Dans ce quartier, on vend des macaronis, des raviolis, des olives et des saucisses. L'air est parfumé d'ail et de sauce tomate. On crie, on chante, on marchande. C'est un quartier tout à fait italien.

Mais à deux pas,[1] en traversant la Place Masséna, on se trouve dans la ville française. On monte le Boulevard Victor Hugo sous une allée de superbes arbres et on admire les boutiques magnifiques. On voit des voitures longues comme des trains. C'est la ville de luxe.

Nice est aussi un centre sportif. Il y a un club de tennis magnifique; il y a l'hippodrome de Cagnes, tout près; les célèbres sports d'hiver à Beuil, dans les montagnes; le yachting et les bains de mer. Il est vrai que la plage est pierreuse,[2] mais ça ne fait rien;[3] on y va tout de même pour adorer le soleil.

La ville où on est né, où on va à l'école, où on gagne son pain, cette ville-là existe aussi. Cette ville a son commerce: le tourisme, les fleurs, les parfums, les olives, la pêche. Elle a sa vie culturelle: la musique, qu'elle prend très au sérieux, l'opéra, le théâtre, les conférences, les librairies. Comme dans les autres villes de la France il y a le goût de[4] la science, et le gout de l'art.

Mais après tout, la vraie gloire de Nice est sa situation. Elle se lève de la mer bleue aux collines ornées de villas fleuries[5] jusqu'aux pieds des montagnes couvertes de neige. Le ciel est d'un bleu intense comme la mer. L'air est doux, embaumé.

Tout y est pour rendre le monde heureux.

NOTE 1. close by 2. **pierreux (pierreuse** *f*) rocky 3. that does not matter 4. **le goût de** an interest in *or* taste for 5. flower-covered

DICTIONARY—ENGLISH-FRENCH

A

a (an) un, une
able capable
able (to be) pouvoir
aboard: all aboard! en voiture!
about de; sur; autour de (*around*); **What's it about?** De quoi s'agit-il?
above au dessus de; en haut
absolutely absolument
accept *v* accepter
accident l'accident *m*
accompany *v* accompagner
accomplish *v* accomplir
according to selon
accurate juste, exact
accustomed: to get accustomed to s'habituer à
acquaintance la connaissance; **to make the acquaintance of** faire la connaissance de
acquainted with (to be) connaître
across en travers, à travers
active actif, active
actor l'acteur *m,* l'actrice *f;* le comédien, la comédienne
actually réelement
add *v* ajouter, additionner
address l'adresse *f*
address *v* adresser
admire *v* admirer
admission l'entrée *f*
admit *v* admettre
adore *v* adorer
adorned orné
advance *v* avancer
advantage l'avantage *m*
advertise *v* annoncer
advertisement l'annonce *f*
advice le conseil
advise *v* conseiller
affair l'affaire *f*
afraid (to be) avoir peur
after ensuite, après
afternoon l'après-midi *m,* **in the afternoon** (p.m.) de l'après-midi
afterward après
again encore
against contre
age l'âge *m*
agent l'agent *m,* le représentant
ago il y a; **ten years ago** il y a dix ans
agree to *v* consentir à; être d'accord
agreeable agréable
agreed entendu, d'accord
aid *v* aider
air l'air *m;* **in the open air** en plein air
airmail par avion
airplane l'avion *m*
airport l'aéroport *m*
alike pareil, pareille; semblable
all tout, toute, tous, toutes; **not at all** pas du tout; **all right** parfait, entendu
allow *v* permettre
allowed permis
almost presque
alone seul
along le long de
already déjà
also aussi
although bien que; quoique
always toujours
ambassador l'ambassadeur *m*
ambitious ambitieux, ambi-/tieuse
American américain; l'Américain (the American)
among parmi
amount la somme
amuse *v* amuser
and et; **and so on** ainsi de suite
angry fâché **to get angry** se fâcher
animal l'animal *m*
announce *v* annoncer
annoy *v* ennuyer
another un autre, une autre; **one more** encore un (une)
answer la réponse
answer *v* répondre
any quelque; de (*partitive*); **anybody, anyone** quelqu'un
anything quelque chose
apartment l'appartement *m*
appear *v* apparaître; paraître (*to seem*)
appetite l'appétit *m*
apple la pomme
appointment le rendez-vous
appreciate *v* apprécier
approach *v* s'approcher de
April l'avril *m*
arise *v* se lever
arm le bras
around autour de
arrange *v* arranger
arrival l'arrivée *f*
arrive *v* arriver
art l'art *m*
article l'article *m*
artist l'artiste *m/f*
artistic artistique
as . . . as aussi . . . que; **as well as** aussi bien que; **as little as** aussi peu que; **as much as** autant que; **as long as** tant que; **as if** comme si
ashtray le cendrier
ask (for) *v* demander
ask (questions) *v* poser des questions
asleep endormi
assist *v* aider à
assortment l'assortiment *m*
assure *v* assurer
astonish *v* étonner
at à; **at first** d'abord; **at last** enfin; **at once** tout de suite; **at home** chez moi, chez soi, etc.
attention l'attention *f;* **pay attention to** *v* faire attention à
August août *m*
aunt la tante
author l'auteur *m*
automobile l'automobile *f,* l'auto *f;* la voiture
autumn l'automne *m*
avenue l'avenue *f*
awake éveillé
awaken *v* réveiller
away absent; **to go away** s'en aller

B

baby le bébé, l'enfant *m/f*
back le dos (*body*); **to be back** être de retour; **in back of** derrière
backwards en arrière
bad mauvais
badly mal
baggage les bagages
baker le boulanger
bakery la boulangerie
ball la balle, le ballon
banana la banane
bank la banque, la rive (*river*)
banknote le billet de banque
bar la buvette (*drinking*)
barber le barbier
bargain *v* marchander
basket le panier
bath le bain; **bathroom** la salle de bain
bathe *v* se baigner
be *v* être; **be hungry** avoir faim; **be right** avoir raison; **be wrong** avoir tort; **be sleepy** avoir sommeil; **be thirsty** avoir soif; **be in the act of** être en train de
beautiful beau, bel, belle
because parce que
become *v* devenir
bed le lit; **bedcover** la couverture de lit
bedroom la chambre à coucher
beef le boeuf; **beefsteak** le biftek
beer la bière
before avant (*time*) devant (*place*)
begin *v* commencer; se mettre à
beginning le commencement
behind derrière
believe *v* croire
bell la cloche; **housebell** la sonnette
below en bas
belt la ceinture
bench le banc
besides d'ailleurs
best le meilleur *adj;* le mieux *adv*
better meilleur *adj;* mieux *adv;* **so much the better** tant mieux
between entre
bicycle la bicyclette, le vélo
big grand
bill la note (*at hotels*); le compte, l'addition (*at restaurants*); **bill of fare** le menu
birthday l'anniversaire *m*
bit (a) un peu
black noir
blanket la couverture
blouse la blouse
blow le coup
blue bleu
boat le bateau
body le corps
book le livre
bookstore la librairie
born (to be) *v* naître; **born** né(e)
borrow *v* emprunter
both les deux
bottle la bouteille
bottom le bas; le fond
box la boîte
boy le garçon
bracelet le bracelet
brake *n* le frein; *v* freiner
brandy le cognac, l'eau de vie *f*
brave courageux, courageuse
bread le pain
break *v* casser; rompre
breakfast le petit déjeuner; **to have breakfast** prendre le petit déjeuner
breathe *v* respirer
brief bref, brève
bright clair
bring *v* apporter; **bring back** rapporter
broad large
broken cassé
brother le frère
brown brun
brush *n* la brosse; *v* brosser
build construire; bâtir
building l'immeuble *m,* le bâtiment
burn *v* brûler
bus l'autobus *m*
business l'affaire *f;* **in business** dans les affaires; **to do business in** faire le commerce de
businessman l'homme d'affaires
busy occupé
but mais
butcher le boucher
butcher shop la boucherie
butter le beurre
buy *v* acheter
buyer l'acheteur *m*
by par

C

cab le taxi
cake le gâteau
calendar le calendrier
call *v* appeler; **to be called** s'appeler
calm calme
camera l'appareil photographique *m*
can la boîte de conserve
can (to be able) *v* pouvoir
candy store la confiserie
capital city la capitale
car la voiture (*auto*); le wagon (*railroad*); le tram (*streetcar*); **by car** en voiture
card la carte; **postcard** la carte postale
care le soin; **take care of** s'occuper de, soigner
carry *v* porter; **carry away** emporter
case le cas; la caisse (*box*); **in any case** en tout cas
cashier le caissier
castle le château, les châteaux
cat le chat
catch *v* attraper; **catch cold** attraper un rhume

cause la cause; la raison
cease *v* cesser
ceiling le plafond
celebrate *v* célébrer, fêter
center le centre
ceramics la céramique
certain certain; sûr
certificate le certificat
chair la chaise
chance la chance; **Good luck!** Bonne chance!
change *v* changer; **change money** changer de l'argent; **change (coins)** la monnaie
charm *v* enchanter; charmer
charming charmant; ravissant
chat *v* causer
cheap bon marché
cheaper meilleur marché
check le chèque
check *v* vérifier; contrôler
cheerful gai
cheese le fromage
chicken le poulet
child l'enfant *m/f*
chocolate le chocolat
choose *v* choisir
Christmas la Noël
church l'église *f*
cigar le cigare
circle le cercle
city la ville; **to the city (downtown)** en ville
city hall l'hôtel de ville *m*
class la classe; la sorte
clean propre
clear clair
clerk l'employé de bureau *m*
clever astucieux, astucieuse
climate le climat
clock l'horloge *f*
close *v* fermer
closed fermé
cloth l'étoffe *f;* le drap
clothe *v* habiller
clothes les vêtements; les habits *m*
club le cercle; le club
coast la côte
coat le manteau; **overcoat** le pardessus; **raincoat** l'imperméable *m*
coffee le café
cold froid; **It (weather) is cold.** Il fait froid; **I am cold.** J'ai froid; **I have a cold.** Je suis enrhumé.
color la couleur; **What is the color of . . . ?** De quelle couleur est . . . ?
comb *n* le peigne; *v* peigner
come *v* venir; **come back** revenir; **come in** entrer
comfortable comfortable, commode
commerce le commerce
common courant; ordinaire
companion le copain, la copine
compare *v* comparer
complete complet, complète
compliment le compliment
computer l'ordinateur *m*
concern la maison (*business*); **That does not concern me** Cela ne me regarde pas.
concert le concert
conduct *v* conduire
conductor le receveur (*on train, bus, etc.*)
confess *v* avouer
confidentially entre nous
congratulate *v* féliciter
congratulation la félicitation
consent *v* consentir
consequently par conséquent
considerable considérable
consist of *v* consister de
contain *v* contenir
content (to be) être content; être satisfait
continue *v* continuer
contrary le contraire; **on the contrary** au contraire
contribute *v* contribuer
conversation la conversation
cook *n* la cuisinière; *v* cuire; faire la cuisine
cookbook le livre de recettes
cool frais; **It (weather) is cool.** Il fait frais.
corner le coin
correct correct; exact; **That's right.** C'est correct.
correspondence la correspondance
cost *n* le prix; **cost** *v* coûter
costume le costume
cotton le coton
count *v* compter
country la campagne (*opposite of city*); le pays (*nation*)
course le cours; le plat (*of meal*); **Of course!** Bien entendu! Mais oui!
cousin le cousin, la cousine
cover *n* la couverture; *v* couvrir
covered couvert
cream la crème
cross *v* traverser
crowd la foule
cry *v* crier, s'écrier (*shout*); pleurer (*weep*)
cup la tasse
curiosity la curiosité
custom l'usage *m;* la coutume
customary habituel
customer le client
customhouse la douane
customs official le douanier
cut *v* couper

D

daily quotidien, quotidienne
dairy la laiterie
dance *n* la dance; *v* danser
dangerous dangereux, dangereuse
darling (my) mon chéri; ma chérie
date la date
daughter la fille
day le jour, la journée; **day after tomorrow** après-demain; **day before yesterday** avant-hier
dead mort
dear cher, chère
death la mort
December décembre *m*
decide *v* décider
declare *v* déclarer
deed le fait; l'action *f*
delay *v* tarder
delicious déliceux, délicieuse
delighted ravi, enchanté
delightful ravissant
deliver *v* livrer
demand *v* exiger
dentist le dentiste
department le département
department store le grand magasin
departure le départ
descend *v* descendre
describe *v* décrire
description la description
design le dessin
desire le désir; l'envie *f;* **to have a desire to (a mind to)** avoir envie de
desk le bureau
dessert le dessert
detain *v* retenir
develop *v* développer
devoted dévoué
dictionary le dictionnaire
die *v* mourir
difference la différence
different différent
difficult difficile
difficulty la difficulté
dine *v* dîner
dining room la salle à manger
dinner le dîner
direction la direction
dirty sale
disagreeable désagréable
disappear *v* disparaître
discontented with mécontent de
discover *v* découvrir
discuss *v* discuter
dish le plat; l'assiette *f* (plate)
distance la distance
distribute *v* distribuer
district le quartier
divide *v* diviser
do *v* faire
doctor le médecin, le docteur
dog le chien
door la porte
doubt le doute
downstairs en bas
downtown le centre, en ville
dozen la douzaine
drama le drame
dream *v* rêver; **dream of** *v* songer à
dress *n* la robe; *v* habiller; s'habiller
dress designer le couturier
dressmaker la couturière
dressmaking le couture
drink *n* la boisson; **drink** *v* boire
drive *v* conduire (*a car*)
driver le chauffeur
drop *v* laisser tomber (Lit. *let fall*)
drugstore la pharmacie
dry sec, sèche
duck le canard
during pendant; durant
duty le devoir
dwell *v* demeurer
dye *v* teindre

E

each chaque *adj;* chacun, chacune *pron*
ear l'oreille *f*
early de bonne heure; tôt
earn *v* gagner
earth la terre
easily facilement
east l'est *m*
Easter Pâques *f pl;* **Happy Easter** Joyeuses Pâques
easy facile
eat *v* manger
edge le bord; **at the edge of** au bord de
effect l'effet *m*
effort l'effort *m*
egg l'oeuf *m*
either l'un ou l'autre; **either . . . or** ou . . . ou
electric(al) électrique
elegant élégant
elevator l'ascenseur *m*
else: someone else quelqu'un d'autre
embassy l'ambassade *f*
embroidered brodé
employee l'employé *m;* l'employée *f*
empty vide
end la fin
end *v* terminer
England l'Angleterre
English anglais; l'anglais (*language*); l'Anglais (*Englishman*)
enjoy *v* jouir de; **enjoy oneself** s'amuser
enough assez
enter *v* entrer (dans)
entirely tout à fait
envelope l'enveloppe *f*
equal égal
erase *v* effacer
especially surtout
essential essentiel, essentielle
estimate *v* estimer
etc. et cetera
European européen; l'Européen (*the European*)
even même; **even though** quand même
evening le soir; **Good evening!** Bonsoir; **yesterday evening** hier soir; **tomorrow evening** demain soir; **this evening** ce soir
ever jamais; toujours
every chaque; **every day** tous les jours
everybody tout le monde
everyone chacun, chacune
everything tout
everywhere partout
exact précis, exact
examine *v* examiner
exceed *v* dépasser
excellent excellent
except sauf, excepté
excite *v* exciter; agiter
exclaim *v* s'écrier
excursion l'excursion *f*
excuse *v* excuser; **Excuse me!** Excusez-moi! Pardonnez-moi!
exit la sortie
expect *v* espérer; attendre
explain *v* expliquer
express l'express (*train*)
exquisite exquis
extra en plus, supplémentaire
eye l'oeil *m;* les yeux *pl*
eyeglasses les lunettes *f pl*

F

face la figure; le visage
fact le fait; **in fact** en effet
factory la fabrique; l'usine *f*
fail *v* manquer; **Do not fail to write me.** Ne manquez pas de m'écrire; **without fail** sans faute
fall *n* la chute; *v* tomber
false faux, fausse
family la famille
famous célèbre
far loin; **as far as** jusqu'à
fare le prix de la place; le prix du voyage
farther plus loin
farthest le plus éloigné
fashion la mode
fashionable à la mode
fast *adj* vite, rapide; *adv* vite, rapidement
fasten *v* attacher
fat gros, grosse; gras, grasse
father le père
fault la faute
favor *n* le service; **do a favor** rendre un service
fear *n* le peur; *v* avoir peur; craindre
feather la plume
February février *m*
feel *v* sentir; **He feels at home.** Il se sent chez lui. **How do you feel? (health)** Comment vous portez-vous?
feeling le sentiment
fetch *v* apporter; aller chercher
few peu; **few people** peu de gens
field le champ
figure *v* calculer
fill *v* remplir; **fill the tank with gas** faire le plein d'essence.
film le film
finally enfin; finalement
find *v* trouver
fine *adj* fin; *n* l'amende (*money*)
finger le doigt
finish *v* finir; terminer
fire le feu
firm *adj* firm; *n* la maison (*business*)
first le premier, la première; **at first** d'abord
fish le poisson
fit convenable (*suitable*)
fit *v* aller à; **This dress fits me well.** Cette robe me va bien.
flat plat; **I have a flat tire.** Je suis à plat.
flatter *v* flatter; **You flatter me.** Vous êtes trop aimable.
flavor le goût; la saveur
flight le vol
floor le plancher; l'étage *m* (*story*)
flour la farine
flower la fleur
fly *v* voler
follow *v* suivre
following suivant
fond of (to be) aimer; être friand de (*foods*)
food la nourriture; les vivres *m pl*, les victuailles *f pl*
foot le pied; **on foot** à pied
for pour; **for me** pour moi; car (*since, because*)
force *n* la force; *v* forcer
foreigner l'étranger, l'etrangère
forest la forêt
forget *v* oublier
forgive *v* pardonner
fork la fourchette
form la forme
form *v* former
formality la formalité
former (the) celui-là, celle-là, ceux-là, celles-là
formerly autrefois
fortunate heureux, heureuse
fortunately heureusement
forward en avant
found trouvé
fountain la fontaine, le jet d'eau
fountain pen le stylo
fragrant parfumé
frame *n* le cadre; *v* encadrer
franc le franc
free libre, gratis
French français, le français (*language*); le Français (Frenchman)
frequently souvent, fréquemment
fresh frais, fraîche
Friday le vendredi
friend l'ami, l'amie
friendly aimable
frighten *v* effrayer
from de
front le devant; **in front of** devant
fruit le fruit
full plein
fun l'amusement *m;* **have fun** s'amuser
funny drôle
fur la fourrure
furious furieux, furieuse
furnish *v* meubler (*a room*)
furnished meublé
furniture les meubles
further plus loin
future l'avenir *m;* **in the future** à l'avenir

G

gaiety la gaieté
gain *v* gagner
gamble *v* jouer
gambler le joueur
game le jeu; la partie
garage le garage
garden le jardin
gasoline l'essence *f;* **gasoline station** le poste d'essence
gate la porte
gay gai
gem la pierre précieuse
general général; **in general** en général; **general delivery** poste restante
generous généreux, généreuse
gentle doux, douce
gentleman le monsieur; **gentlemen** les messieurs; **ladies and gentlemen** mesdames et messieurs
genuine authentique
geography la géographie
German allemand; l'allemand (*language*); l'Allemand (*the German*)
Germany l'Allemagne
get *v* obtenir; recevoir
get up *v* se lever
get into *v* monter en voiture (*car*)
gift le cadeau
girl la jeune fille
give *v* donner
give back *v* rendre
glad content; heureux
gladly volontiers
glass le verre; **fine glass** le cristal
glitter *v* briller
glove le gant
go *v* aller
go away *v* s'en aller
go back *v* retourner
go down *v* descendre
go home *v* rentrer
go out *v* sortir
go to bed *v* se coucher
go to sleep *v* s'endormir
go up *v* monter
God Dieu *m*
gold l'or *m*
good *adj* bon, bonne; *adv* bien; **Good morning!** Bonjour! **Good afternoon!** Bonjour! **Good evening!** Bonsoir! **Good night!** Bonne nuit! Bonsoir!
goodbye au revoir; adieu; **bid goodbye to** faire ses adieux à
goodness la bonté
goods la marchandise
grand magnifique
granddaughter la petite-fille
grandfather le grand-pêre
grandmother la grand'mère
grandson le petit-fils
grant *v* accorder; **Granted!** D'accord!
grape le raisin
grasp *v* saisir
grateful reconnaissant
gray gris
great grand
green vert
greet *v* saluer
greeting la salutation
grocer l'épicier *m*
grocery store l'épicerie *f*
ground la terre
group le groupe
guard le garde
guard *v* guarder
guess *v* deviner
guide *n* le guide; *v* guider

H

hair les cheveux
hairdo la coiffure
hairdresser le coiffeur
half *adj* demi; *n* la moitié
ham le jambon
hand la main; **shake hands** se serrer la main
handbag le sac à main
handkerchief le mouchoir
handsome beau, bel, belle
happen *v* arriver; se passer; **What is happening?** Qu'est-ce qui se passe?
happy heureux, heureuse
hard difficile (*difficult*); dur (*not soft*)
hat le chapeau
have *v* avoir; **have to** (*must*) devoir; **have something done** faire faire
he il
head la tête
headache mal à la tête; **I have a headache** J'ai mal à la tête
health la santé; **Here's to your health!** À votre santé!
hear *v* entendre
heart le coeur
heaven le ciel; **Good Heavens!** Mon Dieu!
heavy lourd
help *v* aider
her la; lui; son, sa, ses
here ici; **here is (are)** voici
herself se; elle-même
high haut
him le; lui
himself se; lui-même
hire *v* louer
his son, sa, ses; à lui; le sien, la sienne, les siens, les siennes
history l'histoire *f*
hold *v* tenir
holiday le jour de fête; **vacation holidays** les vacances *m*
home la maison; **at home** à la maison; chez moi, chez lui, etc.
hope *v* espérer
horse le cheval, les chevaux
horseback *v* à cheval
hospital l'hôpital *m,* la clinique
hot chaud; **It (weather) is hot.** It fait chaud. **I am hot.** J'ai chaud.
hotel l'hôtel *m*
hour l'heure
house la maison
how comment; combien; **How are you?** Comment allez-vous? **How much does that cost?** Combien cela coûte-t-il? **How much money?** Combien d'argent? **How many books?** Combien de livres? **How often?** Combien de fois? **How pretty!** Que c'est joli!
however cependant; pourtant
hundred cent
hunger la faim
hungry (to be) avoir faim
hurry *v* se dépêcher, se hâter; **I am in a hurry.** Je suis pressé.
hurt *v* faire mal à
husband le mari

I

I je; moi
ice cream la glace
if si; **if not** sinon
ill malade
illustration l'illustration *f*

imagine *v* s'imaginer
immediately tout de suite; immédiatement
imperfect défectueux, défectueuse
import *v* importer
important important
importer l'importateur *m*
impossible impossible
in dans; en
inch le pouce
included compris
incorrect inexact
increase *v* augmenter
incredible incroyable
indeed en effet; vraiment; **Yes, indeed!** Mais oui!
indicate *v* indiquer
indispensable indispensable
industrious diligent
industry l'industrie *f*
infant le petit enfant; le bébé
influence l'influence *f*
inform *v* informer; faire savoir
information les renseignements *f pl;* **He asks for information.** Il demande des renseignements.
inhabit *v* habiter
ink l'encre *f*
inn l'auberge *f*
inquire *v* prendre des renseignements
inside dedans
insist *v* insister
instantly à l'instant
instead of au lieu de
instruct *v* enseigner
instrument l'instrument *m*
intelligent intelligent
intend *v* avoir l'intention de; compter fair quelque chose
interest l'intérêt *m;* **to be interested in** s'intéresser à
interesting intéressant
into dans; en
introduce *v* présenter
invitation l'invitation *f*
invite *v* inviter
irritate *v* irriter; agacer
it il, elle, ce; **It's late.** Il est tard. **It's five o'clock.** Il est cinq heures. **It's true.** C'est vrai.
Italian italien; l'italien (*language*); l'Italien, l'Italienne (*the Italian*)
Italy l'Italie
its son, sa, ses
itself se; lui-même; elle-même

J

jacket la veste; le veston
January janvier *m*
jewel le bijou, les bijoux
joke la plaisanterie
joke *v* plaisanter
journey le voyage
joyous joyeux
judge le juge
juice le jus; **orange juice** le jus d'orange
July juillet *m*
jump *v* sauter
June juin *m*
just juste; **I have just eaten.** Je viens de manger.

K

keep *v* garder
key la clef
kill *v* tuer
kind *adj* gentil, aimable; *n* la sorte
kindly: Will you kindly . . . ? Voulez-vous bien . . . ?
kindness la bonté
kiss *n* le baiser; *v* embrasser
kitchen la cuisine
knife le couteau
knock *v* frapper
know *v* savoir (*to have knowledge of, to know how*); connaître (*to be acquainted with*)

L

lack *v* manquer; **I lack nothing.** Je ne manque de rien.
lady la dame; **ladies and gentlemen** mesdames et messieurs
lamb l'agneau *m;* **leg of lamb** le gigot
lamp la lampe
land *v* aterrir (*airplane*); débarquer (*ship*)
landscape le paysage
language la langue; le langage
large grand; gros, grosse
last le dernier, la dernière; **last night** hier soir
late tard; en retard
laugh *v* rire; **They laugh at him.** Ils se rient de lui.
laundry la blanchisserie
lay *v* poser
lazy paresseux, paresseuse
lead *v* conduire
leap *v* sauter
learn *v* apprendre
least le moins; **at least** au moins
leather le cuir
leave *v* partir (*depart*); quitter (*quit*)
left gauche; **to the left** à gauche
leg la jambe
lemon le citron
lemonade la limonade
lend *v* prêter
length la longueur
less moins; **less than five** moins de cinq
lesson la leçon
let *v* permettre (*permit*)
letter la lettre
library la bibliothèque
lie *v* mentir (*tell a lie*)
lie down *v* se coucher
life la vie
lift *v* lever
light la lumière
like *adv* comme; *adj* pareil, pareille; *v* aimer; vouloir; **I would like** je voudrais
likewise également; aussi
linen le lin; le linge
liner le paquebôt
lip le lèvre
list *n* la liste
listen *v* écouter
little petit; peu de; **little money** peu d'argent
live *v* vivre; demeurer (*dwell*)
lively gai; vif, vive
living room le salon
long long, longue; **He left a long time ago.** Il est parti il y a longtemps.
look *v* regarder; chercher (*look for*); **Look out!** Attention!
lose *v* perdre
lost perdu
lot beaucoup; **a lot of people** beaucoup de monde
loud haut; **in a loud voice, aloud** à haute voix
love *n* l'amour *f; v* aimer; **in love** amoureux, amoureuse
lovely charmant
low bas, basse *f*
luck la chance
lucky heureux, heureuse
luggage les bagages
lunch le déjeuner; **I have lunch.** Je prends le déjeuner

M

madam madame
magazine la revue
magnificent magnifique
maid la bonne
mail le courrier
majority la majorité, la plupart
make *v* faire
man l'homme *m*
manner la manière
manufacture *v* fabriquer
many beaucoup; **many others** beaucoup d'autres
map la carte
March mars *m*
market le marché
marvelous merveilleux, merveilleuse
match *n* l'allumette *f*
matter l'affaire; la chose; **in the matter of** au sujet de, quant à; **It does not matter.** N'importe.
mattress le matelas
May mai *m*
may pouvoir (*be able*)
me me; moi
meal le repas
mean *v* vouloir dire
meanwhile (in the) en attendant
measure la mesure
measure *v* mesurer
meat la viande
mechanic le mécanicien
medicine la médicine
meet *v* rencontrer
meeting la rencontre; le rendez-vous; la réunion (*many people*)
memory la mémoire; le souvenir
mend *v* raccommoder, réparer
merchandise la marchandise
merchant le marchand, le commerçant
message le message
metal le métal
middle le milieu; **in the middle of** au milieu de
midnight minuit *m*
mild doux, douce
milk le lait
million le million
mind l'esprit *m;* **I have a mind to** j'ai envie de
mine à moi; le mien, la mienne, les miens, les miennes
minute la minute; **Wait a minute!** Attendez un instant!
mirror le miroir
miscellaneous divers
misfortune le malheur
Miss mademoiselle
miss *v* manquer; **I shall miss you.** Vous me manquerez.
mistake la faute
mistaken (to be) *v* se tromper
Mister monsieur
mode la mode
model le modèle
modern moderne
moment le moment; **Just a moment!** Un instant!
Monday le lundi
money l'argent; la monnaie (*coins*)
money order le mandat-poste
month le mois
moon la lune
more plus; **more than** plus que, plus de (*before a number*); **not any more** ne . . . plus
morning le matin; la matinée; **in the morning (a.m.)** du matin
most le (la) plus; **most of the people** la plupart des gens; **for the most part** pour la plupart
mother la mère; la maman
motor *n* le moteur; *v* aller en auto
mountain la montagne
mouth la bouche
move *v* bouger; déménager (*to new home*)
movies le ciné; le cinéma
much beaucoup; **much more** beaucoup plus
museum le musée
music la musique
musician le musicien
must *v* devoir; falloir; **I must (ought to) do it.** Je dois le faire. **I must (have to) go.** Il me faut aller.
my mon, ma, mes
myself me; moi-même

N

name le nom; **What is your name?** Comment vous appelez-vous?
namely c'est à dire
napkin la serviette
narrow étroit
nation la nation
naturally naturellement
nature la nature
near près de; proche
nearly presque; à peu près
neat propre
necessary nécessaire; **it is necessary** il faut
neck le cou
necklace le collier

necktie la cravate
need *v* avoir besoin de
neglect *v* négliger
neighbor le voisin
neither non plus; **neither . . . nor** ne . . . ni . . . ni
never ne . . . jamais
nevertheless tout de même
new nouveau, nouvel, nouvelle; neuf, neuve
news les nouvelles; **What's the news?** Quelles sont les nouvelles? **What's new?** Quoi de neuf? **news program or newsreel** les actualités *f pl*
nice gentil, gentille
night la nuit; le soir
no non; **No parking!** Défense de stationner! **No Smoking!** Défense de fumer!
nobody personne; ne . . . personne
noise le bruit
none ne . . . aucun
noon le midi
nor, neither . . . nor ne . . . ni . . . ni
north le nord
nose le nez
not ne . . . pas; ne . . . point
notebook le cahier
nothing ne . . . rien
notice *v* remarquer
notify *v* avertir
November novembre *m*
now maintenant; **now and then** de temps en temps
nowhere nulle part
number le nombre; le numéro

O

obey *v* obéir
object l'objet *m*
oblige *v* obliger
observe *v* observer
obtain *v* obtenir
occupation le métier; l'occupation *f*
October octobre *m*
of de; **of it, of them** en; **I have some** (*of it, of them*). J'en ai.
offer *v* offrir
office le bureau
officer l'officier *m*
often souvent; **quite often** assez souvent
oil l'huile *f*
old ancien, ancienne; vieux, viel, vielle; **How old are you?** Quel âge avez-vous?
once une fois; **at once** tout de suite; **all at once** tout à coup; **once more** encore une fois
one un, une; on (*people, you*) **How does one say?** Comment dit-on?
only seul; seulement; ne . . . que
open *adj* ouvert; *v* ouvrir
opera l'opéra *m*
opposite en face de, vis à vis
or ou; **either . . . or** ou . . . ou
order *n* l'ordre *m*, la commande; **in order to** afin de; *v* commander
ordinary ordinaire, banal
other autre
otherwise sinon
our notre, nos
out dehors
outside dehors; hors de
over dessus; au dessus de
overcoat le pardessus
owe *v* devoir
own *adj* propre; *v* posséder

P

pack *v* emballer; **He packs his bags.** Il fait ses valises.
pain *n* mal; *v* faire mal à
painting la peinture
pair la paire
pale pâle
pancake la crêpe
pants le pantalon
paper le papier
parcel le paquet
parcel post le colis postal
pardon *v* pardonner
park le parc
park *v* stationner (*a car*)
part la partie
pass *v* passer
passenger le voyageur
passport le passeport
past passé; **the past week** la semaine passée
pastry shop la pâtisserie
pause *n* la pause; *v* faire une pause
pay *v* payer
pea le petit pois
pear la poire
pearl la perle
pedestrian le piéton
pen la plume
pencil le crayon
people le peuple; les gens; on
perceive *v* apercevoir
percent pour-cent
perfect parfait; **Perfect!** Parfait! Très bien!
performance la représentation; la séance
perfume le parfum
perhaps peut-être
permit *v* permettre
permitted permis
person la personne
pharmacy la pharmacie
photograph *n* la photo; **take a photograph** prendre une photo
physician le médecin
pick up *v* ramasser
picture *n* le tableau, l'image *f*
piece le morceau; la pièce
pillow l'oreiller *m*
pin l'épingle *f*
pitcher (*milk*) le pot au lait
pity la pïtié **What a pity!** Quel dommage!
place l'endroit *m;* le lieu; **to take place** avoir lieu; **in place of** au lieu de
plane (*air*) l'avion *m*
plate l'assiette *f*
play *n* la pièce de théatre; *v* jouer
pleasant agréable
please *v* plaire; *(If you)* **please.** S'il vous plaît. **That pleases me.** Cela me plaît.
pleasure le plaisir
pocket la poche
point le point; **on the point of departure** sur le point de partir
police la police
policeman l'agent de police *m*
politely poliment
poor pauvre
porter le porteur
portrait le portrait
possess *v* posséder
possible possible
poster l'affiche *f*
postman le facteur
post office la poste; le bureau de poste
potato la pomme de terre
pottery la poterie
pound la livre
powder la poudre
practice *v* pratiquer
praise *v* louer
pray *v* prier
precede *v* précéder
precious précieux, précieuse
prefer *v* préférer; aimer mieux
prepare *v* préparer
present *n* le cadeau; *adv* présent; **at present** actuellement; **to be present at** assister à; *v* offrir, présenter
press *v* presser; **press clothes** repasser des vêtements
pretty joli
price le prix
prize le prix
probably probablement; sans doute
produce *v* produire
profession la profession
professor le professeur
profit le profit
program le programme
prohibit *v* défendre
promise *v* promettre
pronounce *v* prononcer
propose *v* proposer
protect *v* protéger
provided that pourvu que
publish *v* éditer, faire paraître
publisher l'éditeur
pull *v* tirer
punish *v* punir
pupil l'élève *m/f*
purchase *n* l'achat *m;* l'emplette *f;* *v* acheter
purchaser l'acheteur, acheteuse
purse le porte-monnaie
push *v* pousser
put *v* mettre; poser; **to put on** mettre

Q

quality la qualité
quantity la quantité
quarter le quart; le quartier
question *n* la question; *v* poser des questions
quick rapide
quickly rapidement; vite
quiet *adj* tranquille; calme **Keep quiet!** Restez tranquille! *v* calmer
quit *v* quitter
quite tout à fait; **quite often** assez souvent
quote *v* citer

R

radio la radio
railroad le chemin de fer
rain la pluie
rain *v* pleuvoir; **It is raining.** Il pleut.
raincoat l'imperméable *m*
raise *v* lever; élever
rapid rapide
rapidly rapidement
rate le tarif
rather plûtot; **rather than** plûtot que; **I would rather** j'aimerais mieux
razor le rasoir
reach *v* arriver
read *v* lire
ready prêt
realize *v* comprendre; se rendre compte de
really vraiment; en vérité
rear le fond; **in the rear** au fond
reason la raison
recall *v* se rappeler (*remember*)
receipt la quittance
receive recevoir
recognize *v* reconnaître
recommend *v* recommander
recommendation la recommendation
record le disque (*phonograph*)
recover *v* se remettre (*health*)
red rouge
reference la référence; **in reference to** à propos de
reflect *v* réfléchir
refreshment le rafraîchissement
refund *v* rembourser
refuse *v* refuser
regards: give my regards to faites mes amitiés à
regret *v* regretter
relate *v* raconter
relative le parent
rely upon *v* compter sur
remainder le reste
remarkable remarquable
remember *v* se rappeler; se souvenir de
remembrance le souvenir
remove *v* enlever
rent *v* louer
repair *v* réparer
repeat *v* répéter
reply *n* la réponse; *v* répondre
represent *v* représenter
representative le représentant
request *v* demander
require *v* avoir besoin de
resemble *v* ressembler à
reserve *v* retenir; réserver
reside *v* demeurer
residence la résidence; la maison
respect *n* le respect; *v* respecter
responsible responsable
rest le reste (*remainder*); le repos (*repose*); *v* se reposer
rested délassé
restless agité
result le résultat
retail en détail
retain *v* retenir
retire *v* se retirer

return *n* le retour; *v* revenir (*come back*); rendre (*give back*); retourner (*go back*)
review la révision
rum le rhum
rice le riz
rich riche
ride *v* se promener; **in a car, on a bicycle, on horseback** en voiture, à bicyclette, à cheval
right droit; **to the right** à droite
right juste, exact; **That's right.** C'est exact (juste); **You are right.** Vous avez raison.
ring *n* l'anneau *m,* la bague, l'alliance *f* (*wedding ring*); *v* sonner
river le fleuve, la rivière
road le chemin; la route
room la chambre
rough rude
round rond
route la route
row le rang
rubbers les caoutchoucs
ruler la règle (*measuring*)
run *v* courir

S

sad triste
sadly tristement
safe sauf; **safe and sound** sain et sauf
sailor le marin
salad la salade
sale la vente
salesgirl la vendeuse
salesman le vendeur
salt le sel
same même; **all the same** tout de même
sample l'échantillon *m*
satisfactory satisfaisant
satisfy *v* contenter; satisfaire
Saturday le samedi
sauce la sauce
saucer la soucoupe
sausage la saucisse, le saucisson
say *v* dire
scarcely à peine
scarf l'écharpe *f,* le foulard, le fichu
scene la scène
schedule l'horaire *m*
school l'école *f;* **to school** à l'école
scissors les ciseaux *m*
sea la mer; **at sea** en mer
seaport le port de mer
seashore la plage
season la saison
seat la place
seated assis
second le (la) deuxième
see *v* voir
seek *v* chercher
seem *v* sembler; paraître
seize *v* saisir
seldom rarement
sell *v* vendre
send *v* envoyer
sense le sens; **common sense** le bon sens
sentiment le sentiment
separate *v* séparer
September septembre *m*
serious sérieux, sérieuse
servant la bonne; le (la) domestique
serve *v* servir
set *v* mettre, placer; **set out** se mettre en route
several plusieurs
sew *v* coudre; **sewing** la couture
shake *v* secouer; **shake hands** se serrer la main
shape la forme
shave *v* se raser
shawl le châle
shine *v* briller
ship *v* expédier
shipment l'envoi *m*
shirt la chemise
shoe la chaussure, le soulier
shoemaker le cordonnier
shop la boutique
shop window la vitrine
shopping (to go) faire des achats
short court
shoulder l'épaule *f*
shout *v* crier
show *v* montrer
shut *adj* fermé; *v* fermer
sick malade
sickness la maladie
side le côté; **at the side of** à côté de
sidewalk le trottoir
signify *v* signifier
silence le silence
silk la soie; **a silk dress** une robe de soie
silken, silky soyeux, soyeuse
silver l'argent
similar semblable
simple simple
since depuis (*time*); puisque (*because*)
sincerely sincèrement; **Yours sincerely.** Votre tout dévoué.
sing *v* chanter
singer le chanteur, la chanteuse
single seul; célibataire (*unmarried*)
sir monsieur
sister la soeur
sit *v* être assis; **sit down** s'asseoir; **Sit down.** Asseyez-vous.
size la taille; la grandeur
skin la peau
skirt la jupe
sky le ciel
sleep le sommeil
sleep *v* dormir; **fall asleep** s'endormir; **I am sleepy** J'ai sommeil.
slowly lentement
small petit
smell *n* l'odeur *f; v* sentir
smile *n* le sourire; *v* sourire
smoke *n* la fumée; *v* fumer **No smoking!** Défense de fumer!
snapshot la photo
snow *n* la neige; *v* neiger
so (thus) ainsi; **and so forth** ainsi de suite
soap le savon
sock la chaussette
soft doux, douce *f*
software le logiciel
soldier le soldat
solid solide
some quelque, quelques; des
somebody quelqu'un
someone quelqu'un
something quelque chose
sometimes parfois
somewhere quelque part
son le fils
song la chanson
soon bientôt; **sooner** plus tôt; **as soon as possible** aussitôt que possible
sorry (to be) regretter
sort la sorte
sound le son
soup la soupe; le potage
south le sud; le Midi
southern du sud
Spain l'Espagne *f*
Spanish espagnol; l'espagnol (*language*); l'Espagnol (*Spaniard*)
speak *v* parler
special delivery exprès
spectator le spectateur
speed la vitesse; **at full speed** à toute vitesse
spend *v* dépenser, verser (*money*); passer (*time*)
spinach les épinards *m pl*
spirit l'esprit *m*
spit *v* cracher
splendid splendide
spoil *v* gâter
spoon la cuiller; la cuillère
sport le sport
spring le printemps; **in spring** au printemps
stairs l'escalier *m*
stamp le timbre (*postage*)
stand *v* être debout; **Stand up!** Levez-vous!
starch l'amidon *m;* **No starch!** Sans amidon
start *v* commencer
station la gare (*railroad*)
stay *n* le séjour (*visit*); *v* rester
steak le bifteck
steamer le paquebôt
steel l'acier *m*
stenographer la sténographe
step le pas
stick le bâton
still *adj* calme, tranquille; *adv* encore; toujours; **It is still raining.** Il pleut toujours.
stocking le bas; le collant (*panty-hose*)
stop *v* s'arrêter, cesser; **The taxi stops.** Le taxi s'arrête.
store le magasin; la boutique
story l'histoire *f;* l'étage *m* (*of house*)
straight droit
strange curieux, curieuse
stranger l'étranger, l'etrangère
strawberry la fraise
street la rue
strike *v* battre; frapper
stroll *v* faire une promenade (un tour)
strong fort
student l'étudiant *m,* l'étudiante *f*
studious diligent
study l'étude *f; v* étudier
stupid stupide
style le style; **in style** à la mode
subject le sujet; **change the subject** parlant d'autre chose
suburbs la banlieue
succeed *v* réussir
success le succès; la réussite
such tel, telle, tels, telles; **such a man** un tel homme
suddenly tout à coup
suffer *v* souffrir
sufficient suffisant; **That's sufficient.** Cela suffit.
sugar le sucre
suggest *v* proposer
suit le costume; le complet; l'ensemble *m*
suitable convenable
sum la somme
summary le résumé
summer l'été *m,* **in summer** en été
sun le soleil
Sunday le dimanche
supermarket le supermarché, le magasin à grande surface
supper le souper
suppose *v* supposer
sure sûr
surname nom de famille *m*
surprise *v* surprendre
surprised surpris
surroundings les environs *m*
sweater le chandail; le pullover
sweet doux, douce
swift rapide
swim *v* nager
sympathetic sympathique

T

table la table; **to set the table** mettre la table
tablecloth la nappe
tailor le tailleur
take *v* prendre; **take away** emporter
talk *v* parler; causer
tall grand
tank le réservoir; **fill the tank with gas** faire le plein d'essence
taste *n* le goût; *v* goûter
tax l'impôt *m*
taxi le taxi
tea le thé
telegram le télégramme
telegraph *v* télégraphier
telephone *n* le téléphone; *v* téléphoner, appeler; donner un coup de fil
television la télévision
tell *v* dire; raconter
temperature la température
text le texte
than que
thank *v* remercier
thanks merci; les remerciements
that ce, cet, cette; celui, celle; cela; qui, que
the le, la, les
theater le théâtre
their leur, leurs
theirs le leur, la leur, les leurs; à eux, à elles
them les, leur; eux, elles
then alors; puis; ensuite
there là; y; violà; **There he is!** Le voila! **there is (are)** il y a; **over there** là bas

therefore donc
these ces; ceux, celles
they ils, elles
thick épais, épaisse
thing la chose; l'objet
think *v* penser; croire; **I think so.** Je crois que oui.
thirst la soif; **I'm thirsty.** J'ai soif.
this ce, cet, cette; **this one** celui-ci, celle-ci; ceci
thoroughly à fond
those ces; ceux, celles
though quoique
thought la pensée; l'idée *f*
thousand mille; mil (*dates*)
throat la gorge; **have a sore throat** avoir mal à la gorge
throw *v* jeter
thumb le pouce
Thursday le jeudi
thus ainsi
ticket le billet; **one way ticket** le billet simple, le billet d'aller; **round trip ticket** le billet d'aller-retour
ticket-window le guichet
time le temps; l'heure *f* (*hour*); **from time to time** de temps en temps; **What time is it?** Quelle heure est-il? **to have a good time** s'amuser
time le temps; la fois **one time** une fois; **How many times?** Combien de fois? **At times** parfois; **sometimes** quelquefois
timetable l'horaire *f*
tip *n* le pourboire (*gratuity*); *v* donner un pourboire
tire le pneu (*car*); **spare tire** le pneu de rechange
tired fatigué
tiresome ennuyeux, ennuyeuse
to à, en, vers, pour
tobacco le tabac
today aujourd'hui
together ensemble
tomato la tomate
tomorrow demain; **till tomorrow** à demain
tone le ton
tongue la langue
tonight ce soir
too aussi (*also*); trop (*too much*)
tooth la dent
toothache mal aux dents
toothbrush la brosse à dents
toothpaste la pâte dentifrice
total *n* le total; le montant
touch *v* toucher
tour le tour; le voyage
tourist le (la) touriste
toward vers; envers
towel la serviette; **bath towel** la serviette de bain; **dish-towel** le torchon
town la ville
toy le jouet
traffic la circulation
train *n* le train
tranquil tranquille
translate *v* traduire
travel *v* voyager
traveler le voyageur
tray le plateau
treat *v* traiter
tree l'arbre *m*
tremendous énorme
trip le voyage; **to take a trip** faire un voyage
trouble *n* la difficulté; *v* déranger; inquiéter; **Don't trouble yourself!** Ne vous dérangez pas!
trousers le pantalon
true vrai
truly vraiment; **Yours truly,** Agréez, Monsieur, l'assurance de ma considération distinguée.
trunk la malle
truth la vérité
truthful sincère
try *v* essayer; tâcher
turn *v* tourner; **Turn left!** Prenez la première à gauche!
twice deux fois
typewriter la machine à écrire

U

ultimately à la fin
umbrella le parapluie
unbelievable incroyable
uncle l'oncle *m*
uncover *v* découvrir
under sous; au-dessous de
undergo *v* subir
understand *v* comprendre
undertake *v* entreprendre
undertaking l'entreprise *f*
undress (to) se déshabiller
unequal inégal
unexpected inattendu
unfair injuste
unfamiliar peu connu
unfortunately malheureusement
unheard of inoui
unite *v* unir
united uni
United States les États-Unis
university l'université *f*
unknown inconnu
unless à moins que
unoccupied inoccupé; libre
unpack *v* déballer
unpleasant désagréable
unsatisfied mécontent
until jusqu'à; **until now** jusqu'à présent
up to jusqu'à
upon sur
upstairs en haut
us nous
use *v* se servir de
useful utile
useless inutile
usher *n* l'ouvreuse *f*
usual ordinaire; **usually** d'ordinaire
utensil l'ustensile *m*

V

vacation les vacances
vain: in vain en vain
valise la valise
valley la vallée
valuable de valeur
varied varié
variety la variété
various divers
vase le vase
veal le veau; **veal stew** la blanquette de veau
vegetable le légume
verify *v* vérifier
very très
vicinity les environs
view *n* la vue; *v* voir
village le village
vinegar le vinaigre
visit *n* la visite; *v* visiter; rendre visite à
visitor le visiteur, la visiteuse
visa le visa
voice la voix; **in a loud voice** à haute voix; **in a low voice** à demi-voix
voyage le voyage

W

wages le salaire
wait *v* attendre; **wait for** attendre
waiter le garçon
wake *v* réveiller; se réveiller
walk *n* la promenade; *v* aller à pied; **go for a walk** se promener
wallet le portefeuille
wardrobe la garde-robe; l'armoire *f*
warm chaud; **It (weather) is warm.** Il fait chaud. **I am warm.** J'ai chaud.
wash *v* laver; **I wash (myself).** Je me lave.
washroom le cabinet de toilette
watch la montre
water l'eau *f*
way la manière; **by the way** à propos
we nous
weak faible
wear *v* porter
weather le temps **What's the weather?** Quel temps fait-il? **The weather is nice (bad).** Il fait beau (mauvais).
week la semaine; **twice a week** deux fois par semaine
weep *v* pleurer
weigh *v* peser
welcome bienvenu; **Welcome!** Soyez le bienvenu (la bienvenue)! **You're welcome (Don't mention it).** Il n'y a pas de quoi.
well bien; **Well!** Eh bien!
west l'ouest *m*
what *adj* quel, quelle, quels, quelles
what? *subject of verb* qu'est-ce qui?
what? *object of verb* que? qu'est-ce que?
what? *object of preposition* quoi?
when quand; lorsque
where où
whether si
which *adj* quel, quelle, quels, quelles
which *relative pronoun* qui, que
which (*that which*) ce qui, ce que
which one lequel, laquelle
which ones lesquels, lesquelles
while pendant que
who? *interrogative pronoun* qui? qui est-ce qui? *relative pronoun* qui
whom? *interrogative pronoun* qui? qui est-ce que? *relative pronoun* que
width la largeur
wife la femme
willingly volontiers
win *v* gagner
wind le vent; **It's windy.** Il fait du vent.
window la fenêtre
wine le vin
winter l'hiver *m*
wipe *v* essuyer
wise sage
wish *v* desirer; vouloir
with avec
withdraw se retirer
without sans; **do without** se passer de
woman la femme
wonder la merveille
wonderful merveilleux; **wonderfully** à merveille
wood(s) le bois
wool la laine; **a woolen shirt** une chemise de laine
word le mot
work *n* le travail; l'oeuvre *f*; *v* travailler
worker l'ouvrier, l'ouvrière
work of art l'objet d'art *m*
world le monde
worry *v* s'inquiéter; **Don't worry!** Ne vous inquiétez pas!
worst le mauvais; le pire
worth la valeur
worthy digne
wrap *v* emballer
wrist-watch la montre-bracelet
write écrire
writer l'écrivain
written écrit
wrong faux, fausse
wrong (to be) avoir tort; **He is wrong.** Il a tort.

Y

year l'an *m*, l'année *f*
yellow jaune
yes oui; si; **Yes, indeed!** Mais oui!
yesterday hier; **day before yesterday** avant-hier
yet encore; **not yet** pas encore
you vous; tu, te, toi
young jeune
your votre, vos; ton, ta, tes
yours à vous, à toi
yourself vous-même, toi-même

Z

zero le zéro
zoo le jardin zoologique

DICTIONNAIRE—FRANÇAIS-ANGLAIS

A

à to, at, on, in, until
abord: d'abord at first
l'accord *m* harmony; **d'accord** agreed, granted
l'achat *m* purchase; **aller faire des achats** to go shopping
acheter to buy
les actualités newsreel
actuellement now, at present
l'addition *f* bill
l'affaire *f* business, affair; **M. Potter est dans les affaires.** Mr. Potter is in business.
l'affiche *f* poster
l'âge *m* age; **Quel âge avez-vous?** How old are you?
l'agent *m* agent; **l'agent de police** policeman
aider to help
l'ail *m* garlic
ailleurs elsewhere; **d'ailleurs** besides
aimer to like, love; **aimer mieux** to prefer
l'aîné *m*, **l'aînée** *f* oldest or older son or daughter
ainsi thus, so; **ainsi de suite** and so forth
l'air *m* air, look, expression; **à l'air libre** in the open air
ajouter to add, join
aller to go; **s'en aller** to go away; **Comment allez-vous** How are you? **ça va bien.** I am well. **Cette robe me va bien.** This dress fits me.
l'allumette *f* match
alors well, then, in that case, and so
l'amateur *m* lover (*of things*), fancier
l'ambassade *f* embassy
l'ami *m*, **l'amie** *f* friend
l'amour *m* love
amoureux *m*, **amoureuse** *f* in love
s'amuser to enjoy oneself, have fun; **amusons-nous** let's have some fun
l'an *m* year
ancien *m*, **ancienne** *f* old, ancient; former
anglais English; **l'anglais** English *(language);* **l'Anglais** *(Englishman)*
L'Angleterre *f* England; **en Angleterre** in England
l'anneau *m* ring
l'année *f* year; **l'année scolaire** school year
l'anniversaire *f* birthday, anniversary
annoncer to announce; advertise
apercevoir to perceive, observe
l'appartement *m* apartment
apparaître to appear
appeler to call; **s'appeler** to be called (named); **Comment vous appelez-vous?** What is your name? **Je m'appelle** my name is
l'appétit *m* appetite
apporter to bring
apprécier to appreciate
apprendre to learn, teach
s'approcher de to approach, get near, go up to; **Je me suis approché de la voiture.** I approached the car.
après after, afterward; **après-demain** after tomorrow
l'après-midi *m* afternoon; **de l'après-midi** in the afternoon, p.m.
l'arbre *m* tree
l'argent *m* money, silver
l'arrêt *m* stop, halt
s'arrêter to stop; **L'autobus s'arrête là-bas.** The bus stops over there.
arrière behind, backwards
l'arrivée *f* arrival
arriver (à) to arrive (at), reach, happen. **Qu'est-ce qui est arrivé?** What has happened?
l'art *m* art
l'ascenseur *m* elevator
l'aspect *m* appearance, look
s'asseoir to sit down; **Asseyez-vous.** Sit down.
l'assiette *f* dish, plate
assez enough; **c'est assez** that's enough; **assez souvent** quite often
assis *m*, **assise** *f* seated
l'assortiment *m* assortment
astucieux *m*, **astucieuse** *f* clever
s'attabler to sit down at table; **attablé** seated at table
attendant waiting; **en attendant** in the meantime
attendre to wait (for); await
s'atterrir to land; **L'avion s'atterre.** The plane is landing.
attraper to catch; **attraper un rhume** to catch cold
l'auberge *f* inn
aucun *m*, **aucune** *f* none, no one, not any
au dessous de below, under
au dessus de above, over
aujourd'hui today
aussi also, as; **moi aussi** I/me too; **aussi bien que** as well as
aussitôt soon, immediately; **aussitôt que possible** as soon as possible.
autant que as much (many) as; **Je travaille autant que jamais.** I am working as much as ever.
autour de around
autre other, another, different; **quelque chose d'autre** something else
autrefois formerly
l'avance *f* advance; **d'avance** beforehand, in advance; **en avance** ahead of; early
avancer to advance, progress
avant before; **avant-hier** day before yesterday
avec with
avide eager
l'avion *m* airplane; **en avion** by airplane
l'avocat *m* lawyer
avoir to have; **avoir peur de** to be afraid of; **avoir raison (tort)** to be right (wrong); **avoir envie de** to have a mind to; **avoir besoin de** to have need of; **avoir l'intention de** to intend to; **avoir mal de tête (mal aux dents, mal à la gorge)** to have a headache (toothache, sore throat); **Quel âge avez vous? J'ai dix ans.** How old are you? I am ten years old.
avouer to confess
l'annonce *f* advertisement, announcement

B

les bagages baggage
la baguette wand; long loaf of bread
le bain bath; **la salle de bain** bathroom
le banc bench
la banlieue suburbs
la barbe beard
le bas stocking; **le bas collant** pantyhose
bas *m*, **basse** *f* low; **en bas** downstairs; **tout bas** in a low voice; **là-bas** over there
le bateau boat
le bâtiment building
bâtir to build
battre to beat
bavard talkative
beau *m*, **bel** *m* (before a vowel or sometimes h), **belle** *f* beautiful
beaucoup (de) much, very much, many; **beaucoup d'autres** many others; **beaucoup plus** much more; **merci beaucoup** many thanks
la besogne work, job; **se mettre à la besogne** to set to work
le besoin need; **avoir besoin de** to need **Nous en avons besoin tout de suite.** We need it (have need of it) at once.
le beurre butter
la bibliothèque library; book case
bien well, fine, very; **bien sûr** surely; **assez bien** quite well; **bien de fois** many times
bientôt soon; **à bientôt** see you soon
bienvenu welcome; **soyez le bienvenu** (be) welcome!
le bijou *s*, **les bijoux** *pl* jewel
le billet bill, ticket, note; **le billet d'aller-retour** round trip ticket; **le billet d'aller (le billet simple)** one-way ticket
blanc *m*, **blanche** *f* white
la blanchisserie laundry
bleu blue
la blouse blouse
le boeuf beef; **le boeuf bourgignon** beef stew Burgundy-style
boire to drink; **boire dans la bouteille** to drink from the bottle
le bois wood
la boisson beverage, drink
la boîte box; **la boîte aux lettres** letter box
bon *m*, **bonne** *f* good; **bon marché** cheap; **c'est bon** that's fine
le bonheur happiness
la bonne the maid
le bord edge; **au bord de la mer** at the edge of the sea
la bouche mouth
le boucher butcher
la boucherie butcher shop
bouger to move, budge
la boulangerie bakery
bousculé pushed around, jostled
le bout bit, tip, end; **faire un bout de toilette** wash up a bit
la bouteille bottle
la boutique shop
le bras arm
briller to shine
la brise breeze
le bruit noise
brun brown
le bureau office; **le bureau de poste** post office
la buvette bar

C

ça (cela) that, it
cacher to conceal, hide
le cadeau gift
le cadet, la cadette the younger, youngest one (*in a family*)
le cahier notebook; **le cahier de musique** music book

la caisse case, box; cashier's desk; cash register
calculer to figure
le calvados brandy of Brittany
le camarade comrade
le camion truck
le camionneur truckdriver
la campagne the country, countryside; **à la campagne** in the country
le canif penknife
les caoutchoucs rubbers
car for, because, since
la carte menu, map, card; **la carte postale** postcard
le cas case; **en tout cas** in any case
casser to break
la cause cause, case; **à cause de** because of
causer to chat, to talk
ce, cet, cette, ces this, that, those
ceci this
la ceinture belt
cela (ça) that
célèbre famous
célébrer to celebrate
celui *m*, **celle** *f* this one, that one
le cendrier ashtray
une centaine about a hundred, a hundred or so
le centimètre (cm) centimeter (2.5 cms equal 1 inch)
cependant however
certain certain, sure
cesser to cease, stop
la cesse stoppage; **sans cesse** continually
ceux *m*, **celles** *f* these, those
chacun *m*, **chacune** *f* each, each one
la chaise chair
la chaleur heat
la chambre room; **la chambre à coucher** bedroom
le champ field
changer to change, revise; **changer de l'argent** to change money; **changer de place** to change one's seat
la chanson song
chanter to sing
le chanteur *m*, **la chanteuse** *f* singer
le chapeau hat
chaque each, every
le château *s*, **les châteaux** *pl* chateau, castle
chaud hot, warm; **le chaud** heat, warmth; **il fait chaud** it (weather) is warm (hot); **j'ai chaud** I am (feel) warm
la chaussette sock
la chaussure shoe, footwear; **une paire de chaussures** a pair of shoes
le chemin road; **le chemin de fer** railroad
la chemise shirt
cher *m*, **chère** *f* dear; expensive **plus cher** dearer
chercher to look for, to seek
le chéri *m*, **la chérie** *f* dear one, darling; **mon chéri, ma chérie** my dear, my darling
le cheval *s*, **les chevaux** *pl* horse
les cheveux *m pl* hair
chez at the house (home) of; **chez moi** at my house; **chez M. Brown** at Mr. Brown's house
le chien dog
choisir to choose
la chose thing; **quelque chose** something
le ciel sky
le cinéma cinema, movies; movie house
citer to cite, to mention; to quote
clair clear
la classe class; **en classe** in school
la clef key
le coeur heart; **par coeur** by heart
le coin corner
le colis postal *s*, **les colis postaux** *pl* parcel post package
la colline hill
combien (de) how much, how many; **Combien cela coute-il?** How much does this cost?
comique comic
comme like, as, for, how; **comme ci comme ça** so so; **Comme il est tard!** How late it is!
commencer to begin
comment how **Comment ça va?** How are you?
commode comfortable
la compagnie company
complet complete; **le complet** suit of clothes
comprendre to understand
compris understood, included
le compte the bill; **faire le compte** to add up the bill
compter to count; to intend, to count on
conduire to drive, to conduct, lead
la conférence lecture
la connaissance knowledge, acquaintance; **faire la connaissance de** to make the acquaintance of, to meet
connaître to know, to be acquainted with
connu known
le conseil advice
conséquent following; **par conséquent** consequently
construire to construct, to build
content happy
continuer to continue, keep on
contre against; **par contre** on the other hand
contrôler to control, to check
le coq rooster
le corps body; group of people acting together
corriger to correct
le costume costume; **le costume tailleur** suit (woman's)
le côté side; **à côté de** at the side of
se coucher to lie down, go to bed
la couleur color; **De quelle couleur est . . . ?** What is the color of . . . ?
le coup blow, stroke; **tout à coup** all of a sudden; **un coup de main** a helping hand; **donner un coup de pied** to kick
couper to cut
courant common, current; **au courant** well informed
courir to run
le courrier mail
le cours course
court short
le couteau knife
coûter to cost
la coutume custom, habit
la couture dress designing; dressmaking; sewing
le couturier dress designer
la couturière dressmaker
couvert covered; **le couvert** place setting (*at table*)
la couverture cover; **la couverture de lit** bed cover
couvrir to cover
la cravate necktie
le crayon pencil
la crème cream
la crêpe pancake
crever to break, to puncture; **crever un pneu** to have a blowout
crier to cry out
croire to believe, to think; **je crois que oui (non)** I think so (not)
la croix cross
la cuisine kitchen, cooking
la cuisinière cook; stove
la cuiller spoon
curieux *m*, **curieuse** *f* curious

D

la dame lady
dans in, into
la date date
de of, from, by, with
debout standing; **il est (il reste) debout** he is standing
débrouillard resourceful
découvrir to discover, uncover
décrire to describe
la défense prohibition, defense; **Defense de fumer!** No smoking. **Defense de stationner!** No parking.
dehors outside, out of doors
déjà already
le déjeuner lunch; **le petit déjeuner** breakfast
délassé refreshed; rested
demain tomorrow; **à demain** until tomorrow; **demain matin** tomorrow morning
demander to ask, ask for; **se demander** to wonder
déménager to move
demeurer to reside, to live
demi half; **le demi** glass of draft beer
la dent tooth; **mal aux dents** toothache
le départ departure
dépasser to exceed **Le poids des bagages dépasse cent livres.** The weight of the baggage exceeds 100 lbs.
se dépêcher to hurry
depuis since, for (duration)
dernier *m*, **dernière** *f* last, final
derrière behind
dès since, from, as early as; **dès mon arrivé** immediately upon my arrival
descendre to descend, go down
désespérer to despair, to be without hope
désirer to desire, want, wish
le dessert dessert
le dessin design, drawing
dessous under, underneath; **au-dessous de** under
dessus over, above **au-dessus de** on, upon
la dette debt
devant in front of, before
devenir to become
deviner to guess
le devoir duty; **les devoirs** homework; **faire ses devoirs** to do his (her) homework
devoir to owe; to be obliged to; to have to; to be supposed to
difficile difficult
la difficulté difficulty
digne worthy
dîner to dine; **le dîner** dinner
le diplôme diploma
dire to say, tell; **c'est à dire** that is to say; **dites-moi** tell me
distingué distinguished
la distraction recreation
divers various, several
le doigt finger
domestique *m/f* servant
dominer to reign, to dominate
le dommage injury; **Quel dommage!** What a pity!
donc therefore
donner to give
dont of which, of whom, whose
dormir to sleep
la douane the customs, custom-house

le doute doubt; **sans doute** of course, without doubt
la douzaine dozen
doux *m,* **douce** *f* gentle, sweet, mild
le drap cloth, sheet
le droit law; right; **droit** right, straight; **à droite** to the right; **tout droit** straight ahead; **la main droite** the right hand
durant during

E

l'eau *f* water; **l'eau de vie** brandy
l'échantillon *m* sample
l'écharpe *f* long scarf
l'éclat *m* brightness, glitter; **de tout son éclat** in all its brilliance
éclater to burst out, to resound
l'école *f* school
écouter to listen to; **Nous écoutons le professeur.** We listen to the teacher.
l'écran *m* screen
s'écrier to cry out
écrire to write
l'écrivain *m* writer
l'effet *m* effect; **en effet** in fact
égaler to equal
égayer to cheer up
l'église *f* church
l'élève *m/f* pupil
elle she, it; her; **elle-même** herself; **elles** they
l'embouchure *f* mouth (of river)
embrasser to kiss
l'employé *m* employee, clerk
employer to employ
emporter to carry away, to take away
emprunter to borrow
en in, into, while, on to; of it, of them
encadré framed
enchanté delighted; charmed
encore still, yet, again; **encore une fois** once more; **encore un (une)** one more, another; **pas encore** not yet
l'encre *f* ink
l'endroit *m* place
l'enfant *m/f* child
enfin finally
ennuyer to bore, annoy; **s'ennuyer** to be bored
ennuyeux *m,* **ennuyeuse** *f* boring
ensemble together, whole
enseigner to teach
ensuite then, afterwards
entendre to hear, understand; **entendu** agreed, all right; **bien entendu** of course
entouré surrounded
entre between; **entre nous** confidentially
l'entrecôte *m* small steak
l'entrée *f* entrance; main dish
entreprendre to undertake
entrer (dans) to enter, come in
l'envie *f* wish, desire, longing; **J'ai envie de dormir.** I feel like sleeping.
environ about, nearly
les environs *m* vicinity, neighborhood; suburbs
s'envoler to fly away
envoyer to send
l'épicier *m* grocer
l'épicerie *f* grocery store
épuisé worn out
equivaloir to equal
l'escalier *m* staircase
l'Espagne Spain
espagnol Spanish; **l'espagnol** *(language)* **l'Espagnol** *(Spaniard)*
espérer to hope, hope for, expect
essayer to try, to try on
l'essence *f* gasoline; **faire le plein d'essence** to fill the tank with gasoline
l'est *m* east
l'estomac *m* stomach; **mal à l'estomac** stomach-ache
et and
l'étage *m* story or floor (of house)
l'étalage *m* display
l'état *m* state; **coup d'état** political takeover; **dans tous ses états** terribly excited
l'été *m* summer; **en été** in summer
l'étoffe *f* cloth
l'étoile *f* star (of heavens)
étonner to astonish
être to be; **être en train de** to be in the act of
les étrennes New Year's presents
l'étude *f* study; **ils font leurs études** they are carrying on their studies
l'étudiant *m* student
étudier to study
évoquer to evoke
excepté except
excuser to excuse; **Excusez-moi.** Excuse me.
l'exemple *m* example; **par exemple** for example
exiger to demand
expliquer to explain
exprimer to express
extra extra; **c'est de l'extra** it's especially good

F

la fabrique factory
facile easy
faché annoyed
la facilité facility
le facteur postman
la faim hunger; **avoir faim** to be hungry
faire to make, to do
Il fait ses adieux à son ami. He is saying goodbye to his friend.
Faites mes amitiés à Mme. Picard. Give my regards to Mrs. Picard.
Il fait beau (mauvais). The weather is nice (bad).
Il fait le compte. He adds up the bill.
Je veux faire sa connaissance. I want to meet him.
Ils font leurs devoirs. They are doing their homework.
Elle fait ses achats. She is shopping.
Ils font des progrès. They are making progress.
Il fait peser ses valises. He is having his bags weighed.
Il fait le plein d'essence. He is filling up the tank with gasoline.
Cela nous fait plaisir. That pleases us.
Ça ne fait rien. That doesn't matter.
Nous allons faire un voyage. We are going to take a trip.
Nous allons rendre visite à mon oncle. We are going to visit my uncle.
le fait act, deed, fact; **tout à fait** entirely, quite
fait done (*past participle of* **faire)**
falloir to be necessary; **il faut** it is necessary; **il faudra** it will be necessary
la famille family; **en famille** together with the family
fatigué tired
faut: il faut it is necessary
la faute mistake
faux *m,* **fausse** *f* false
féliciter to congratulate
la femme woman, wife
la fenêtre window
fermer to close
le fermier farmer
la fête holiday, festival
le feu fire, light; **le feu d'artifice** fireworks
le fichu scarf
fier *m,* **fière** *f* proud
la figure face
le fil thread
filer to spin; **en filant à toute vitesse** running at full speed
la fille daughter; **la jeune fille** girl
le film film; **le film policier** detective film; **le film de reportage** documentary film
le fils son
la fin end; **à la fin de** at the end of
finir to finish
flatté flattered
la fleur flower; **Marché aux Fleurs** Flower Market
le fleuve river
la fois time; **deux fois** two times; **combien de fois** how many times; **encore une fois** one more time; **quelquefois** sometimes
la folie madness; **à la folie** madly
le fond bottom; **au fond** basically; in the rear; **à fond** thoroughly
la force strength
forcer to force
la forêt forest
le foulard square scarf
la fourchette fork
fort strong, strongly
fournir to furnish
la fourrure fur
le frais coolness, freshness; **frais** *m,* **fraîche** *f* cool; fresh; **il fait frais** it is cool
la fraise strawberry
français French; **le français** French *(language);* **le Français** *(Frenchman);* **la Française** *(Frenchwoman)*
frapper to knock, strike
les freins *m* brakes
le frère brother
friand de fond of
la friandise treat
froid cold; **le froid** the cold, coldness; **il fait froid** it (the weather) is cold; **j'ai froid** I am cold
fumer to smoke; **Defense de fumer!** No smoking.

G

gagner to gain, win, earn
gai gay
le garçon boy, waiter; **le garçon à tout faire** office boy
garder to guard, to keep; **il garde sa chambre** he keeps to his room
la gare railroad station
le gâteau cake
gauche left; awkward; **la main gauche** the left hand
les gens people, persons, folk, men
gentil *m,* **gentile** *f* nice, kind
le gigot leg of lamb
le gilet cardigan sweater
la glace ice cream
le goût taste, flavor
la grâce grace; **grâce à vous** thanks to you
grand big, large, great, tall
la grand'mère grandmother
le grand-père grandfather
gras *m,* **grasse** *f* fat
le gratte-ciel skyscraper
gris gray

gros *m*, **grosse** *f* big, large, stout, thick; **en gros** wholesale; all together
le guichet ticket window
le Guignol Punch and Judy, puppet show

H

s'habiller to dress oneself, to get dressed
habiter to live in, to inhabit
l'habitude *f* habit, custom; **d'habitude** usually
s'habituer à to get accustomed to; to get used to
haut high, loud; **à haute voix** in a loud voice
la hauteur height
l'herbe *f* grass
l'heure *f* hour; **de bonne heure** early; **Quelle heure est-il?** What time is it?
heureux *m*, **heureuse** *f* happy
hier yesterday; **hier soir** last night; **hier matin** yesterday morning
l'hiver *m* winter; **en hiver** in winter
l'homme *m* man; **l'homme d'affaires** businessman
les hors d'oeuvre appetizers
l'huile *f* oil, cooking oil

I

ici here
l'idée *f* idea; **Quelle bonne idée!** What a fine idea!
l'imperméable *m* raincoat
importer to matter; **n'importe (pas)** it doesn't matter
l'ingénieur *m* engineer
intéresser to interest; **s'intéresser à** to be interested in
l'intérêt *m* interest
isolé isolated
l'itinéraire *m* itinerary, route

J

jamais ever; **ne . . . jamais** never; **Mieux vaut tard que jamais.** Better late than never.
la jambe leg
le jambon ham
le jardin garden
jaune yellow
jeter to throw
le jeu game
jeune young; **la jeune fille** girl
la joie joy
joli pretty
jouer to play; **jouer à** to play (a game); **jouer de** to play (an instrument)
le joueur gambler
jouir de to enjoy
le jour day; **tous les jours** everyday; **le jour de l'an** New Year's Day; **de jour en jour** from day to day
le journal newspaper
la journée the day; **toute la journée** all day
la jupe skirt
le jus juice; **le jus d'orange** orange juice
jusque up to, until, as far as; **jusqu'à présent** up to now; **jusqu'ici** as far as here

K

le kilogramme (kg) kilogram *(2.2 pounds)*
le kilomètre (km) kilometer *(5/8 of a mile)*

L

la *f* the (See Chapter 13 Grammar Note 1)
la *f* her, it (See Chapter 15 Grammar Note 2)
là there; **là-bas** over there
la laine wool; **un fichu de laine** a woolen scarf
laisser to let, to leave
le lait milk
la langue language, tongue
large wide
la largeur width
le lavabo washroom, sink
laver to wash; **se laver** to wash oneself
la leçon lesson
le légume vegetable
lendemain the next day
lent slow
le *m* the (See Chapter 3 Grammar Note 1)
le *m* him, it (See Chapter 15 Grammar Note 2)
lequel *m*, **laquelle** *f*, **lesquels** *m pl*, **lesquelles** *f pl* who, whom, which (See Chapter 34 Grammar Notes); which one? which ones?
les *pl* the (See Chapter 3 Grammar Note 1)
les them (See Chapter 15 Grammar Note 2)
la lettre letter; **les belles lettres** literature
leur, leurs *possessive adjective* (See Chapter 13 Grammar Note 2)
leur *indirect object pronoun* (to) them (See Chapter 20 Grammar Note 2)
lever to raise, to lift; **se lever** to get up, to stand up; to rise; **levez-vous** stand up
libre free; **à l'air libre** in the open air
le lieu place; **au lieu de** instead of; **avoir lieu** to take place
la librairie bookstore
le lin linen (cloth)
le linge linen (bed linen, clothing)
lire to read
le lit bed; **au lit** in bed
le livre book
la livre pound
la loi law
loin far; **loin d'ici** far from here
long *m*, **longue** *f* long; **le long du chemin** along the way
la longueur length
longtemps a long time; **plus longtemps** longer
lorsque when; **lorsqu'il est arrivé** when he arrived
louer to rent
le loup wolf
lourd heavy
lui *indirect object pronoun* (to) him, (to) her (See Chapter 20 Grammar Note 2)
lui *independent pronoun* him (See Chapter 23 Grammar Notes 2, 3)
la lumière the light
la lune moon
le luxe luxury; **les articles de luxe** luxury articles
le lycée French secondary school

M

ma *f* my (See Chapter 13 Grammar Note 2)
madame madame, Mrs.
mademoiselle young lady, Miss
le magasin store; **le magasin à grande surface** supermarket; **les grands magasins** department stores
la main hand; **la main gauche** left hand; **la main droite** right hand; **à la main gauche (droite)** on the left (right); **ils se donnent (serrent) la main** they shake hands
maintenant now
mais but; **mais oui** of course, yes indeed
la maison house, home; **à la maison** at home
la maître master, teacher
la maîtresse teacher, mistress
mal badly; **le mal** pain; **j'ai mal à la tête, (mal aux dents, à l'estomac)** I have a headache (toothache, stomach-ache); **ça fait mal aux yeux** it hurts the eyes
malade sick; **malade** *m/f* sick person
malgré in spite of
le malheur misfortune
malheureux *m*, **malheureuse** *f* unhappy, unfortunate
malheureusement unfortunately
manger to eat
la manière manner
manquer to lack, to need; **je ne manque de rien** I lack nothing; **manquer** to fail, to miss; **Ne manquez pas de faire vos devoirs.** Don't fail to do your homework. **Vous me manquerez.** I shall miss you.
le manteau coat, cloak
le marchand merchant, storekeeper; **marchand de vin** wine merchant
marchander to bargain
la marchandise merchandise
le marché the market; **faire son marché** to do one's marketing
marcher to walk, to march
le mari husband
marier to marry; **se marier** to get married
le marin sailor, seaman
le matin morning; **du matin** in the morning, a.m.
matinal early-rising
la matinée morning
le médecin medical doctor, physician
meilleur better; **le meilleur** best; **meilleur marché** cheaper
même same, even, self; **la même chose** the same thing; **tout de même** all the same; **moi-même** myself; **même les plus riches** even the wealthiest
mener to lead
la mer sea; **en mer** at sea
merci thanks; **merci beaucoup** many thanks
la mère mother
la merveille marvel; **à merveille** wonderfully
merveilleux *m*, **merveilleuse** *f* wonderful
mes my (See Chapter 15 Grammar Note 2)
le métier trade, business; **C'est mon métier.** That's my trade.
le mètre meter (about 39 inches)
mettre to put, to put on; **se mettre à table** to sit down at the table; **se mettre en route** to set out; **se mettre à + *infinitive*** to begin to; **Il se met à écrire.** He is beginning to write.
meubler to furnish
les meubles furniture
le midi noon; **le Midi** south of France
mieux *adv* better; **tant mieux** so much the better; **Ça va mieux.** I feel better. **Mieux vaut tard que jamais.** Better late than never.
le milieu middle; **au milieu de** in the middle of

le miroir mirror
la mode fashion; **à la mode** in style
moi me, to me, I (See Chapter 23 Grammar Notes 2, 3)
le mois month
moins less, minus; **moins de cinq** fewer than five
mon, ma, mes *possessive adjective* my
le monde world; **tout le monde** everybody
la monnaie coin, money, change; **en monnaie** in change
le monsieur gentleman, sir, Mr.; **les messieurs** gentlemen
la montagne mountain
le montant total
monter to go up, to ascend, to carry up; **monter en voiture** to get into the car
la montre watch; **la montre-bracelet** wrist watch
montrer to show
le morceau piece, morsel
mort dead; **la mort** death
le mot word
le mouchoir handkerchief
mourir to die; **ennuyer à mourir** to bore to death
les moyens *m* means
le mur wall; **au mur** on the wall

N

naître to be born; **né** born
nager to swim
la nappe tablecloth
ne; ne . . . pas not; **ne . . . jamais** never; **ne . . . rien** nothing; **ne . . . plus** no longer; **ne . . . ni . . . ni** neither nor; **ne . . . que** only; **je n'ai qu'un professeur** I have only one teacher
nécessaire necessary
la neige snow
neiger to snow
neuf (neuve *f***)** new
le nez nose
ni . . . ni neither . . . nor; **ni moi non plus** neither do I
la Noël Christmas
noir black
le nom name
le nombre number
non no; **non plus** neither
le nord north
la note bill; grade (school); **la note d'hôtel** hotel bill
notre, nos our *possessive adjective* (See Chapter 15 Grammar Note 2)
nouveau *m*, **nouvel** *m (before vowel or h)*, **nouvelle** *f* new
les nouvelles news; **Point de nouvelles bonnes nouvelles.** No news is good news. **Quelles sont les nouvelles?** What is the news?
la nuit night

O

obéir to obey
l'objet d'art *m* art object
obtenir to obtain
l'occasion opportunity, occasion, chance
s'occuper de to busy oneself with, to take care of; **Mme. Davis s'occupe des enfants.** Mrs. Davis takes care of the children.
l'oeuf *m* egg
l'oeil *m* eye; **les yeux** eyes
l'oeuvre *f* work; **le chef d'oeuvre** masterpiece
offrir to offer
on one, people, you, we, they; **on dit** one says; people (they, you, we) say; it is said
l'or *m* gold; **la montre d'or** the gold watch
l'oreille *f* ear
original original; creative
oser to dare
ou or
où where
oublier to forget
l'outillage *m* tool kit
ouvert open
l'ouvreuse *f* usher
l'ouvrier *m*, **l'ouvrière** *f* worker
ouvrir to open

P

le pain bread, loaf of bread; **les petits pains** rolls
pâle pale
le panier the basket
le pantalon trousers
le paquebot steamship, liner
Pâques *f pl* Easter; **Joyeuse Pâques!** Happy Easter!
par by, through; **par-ici** this way; **par-ci par-là** here and there
le parapluie umbrella
paraître to seem, to appear
parce que because
parcourir to glance through
le pardessus overcoat
pardonner to pardon; **pardonnez-moi** pardon me
pareil (pareille *f***)** like, equal, similar, such
parfait perfect
parfois at times
parler to speak; **parlant d'autre chose** speaking of something else, to change the subject
parmi among
la part share, part; **de ma part** for my part; **quelque part** somewhere; **nulle part** nowhere
la partie the part (first, second, etc.); the game
partir (de) to leave; **partir en voyage** to leave on a trip
partout everywhere
pas, ne . . . pas not; **pas du tout** not at all; **pas encore** not yet
le pas step; **un faux pas** slip, social error
le passeport passport
passer to spend, to pass; **se passer de** to do without; **Qu'est-ce qui se passe?** What is happening?
passionnant fascinating
pauvre poor
payer to pay; **payer ses repas** to pay for one's meals
le pays country
le paysage landscape, scenery
le paysan peasant, farmer
la pêche peach; fishing
le pêcheur fisherman
la peinture painting
pendant during; **pendant que** while
penser (à) to think (of); **je pense que oui** I think so; **Il pense à son ami.** He is thinking of his friend.
perdre to lose
le père father; **tel père tel fils** like father like son
permettre to permit
personne person, nobody
peser to weigh; **faire peser** to have weighed
petit small, little; **petit à petit** little by little
peu little, few; **un peu plus** a little while longer; **peu de choses** few things; **beaucoup de choses** many things
la peur fear; **avoir peur** to be afraid
peut-être perhaps
la phrase sentence
la pièce room; piece; play (theater)
le pied foot; **à pied** on foot
la pierre stone
pierreux *m*, **pierreuse** *f* rocky
pire *adj* worse
pis *adv* worse
la place place; seat; square
plaire to please; **il plaît** it pleases; **s'il vous plaît** please (if it pleases you)
le plaisir pleasure; **le plaisir est à moi** the pleasure is mine
le plat dish, plate, course
plat flat; **être à plat** to have a flat (tire)
le plateau tray
plein full; **faire le plein (d'essence)** to fill the tank
pleurer to weep
pleuvoir to rain; **Il pleut à verse.** It's raining buckets.
le plomb lead; **soleil de plomb** sun beating down
la pluie rain
la plupart (de) most (of), the majority; **la plupart des places** most of the places; **pour la plupart** for the most part
plus more; **plus de cinq** more than five; **non plus** either; **en plus** in addition; **plus tôt** sooner; **de plus en plus** more and more; **plus ou moins** more or less
plusieurs several
plutôt rather
le pneu tire; **pneu de rechange** spare tire
la poche pocket
le poids weight
le point point; **Il est sur le point de partir** He is about to leave **ne . . . point** not at all; **Il ne parle point.** He doesn't speak at all.
les petits pois *m* peas
le poisson fish
politique political
la pomme apple; **la pomme cuite** baked apple; **la pomme de terre** potato
le pont bridge
le port de mer seaport
la porte door
le porte-parapluie umbrella stand
porter to bear; to carry; to wear; **se porter** to feel (health); **Comment vous portez-vous?** How do you feel?
le porteur porter
poser to pose; to put; **poser des questions** to ask questions
la poste post office; **le mandat-poste** money order; **poste-restante** general delivery
le poste post, station; **le poste d'essence** gasoline station
le pot au lait milk pitcher
la poterie pottery
la poularde fatted chicken
le poulet chicken
pour for, to, in order to, for the sake of
le pourboire tip, gratuity
le pourcentage percentage
pourquoi why
pourtant however
pouvoir to be able, can, may
précise precise, sharp; **à cinq heures précises** at five o'clock sharp
préférer to prefer
premier *m*, **première** *f* first
prendre to take; **prendre des renseignements** to get information; **prendre le petit déjeuner** to have breakfast

près (de) near, close to; **à peu près** pretty near, more or less
presque almost, nearly
prêt ready
prêter to lend
prier to pray; to beg
le prix price, prize; **à prix fixe** at a fixed price
le problème problem
prochain next
proche near
produire to produce
le produit product
profond profound, deep
le programme program
le progrès progress; **faire des progrès** to make progress
le projet project
la promenade walk, stroll; **faire une promenade** to take a walk; **une promenade à bicyclette** a bicycle ride
se promener to go for a walk; **se promener en voiture** to go for a drive
promettre to promise
la propagande propaganda
propos: à propos by the way; **à propos du film** with reference to the film
propre own; clean, neat; **leur propre langue** their own language
la puce flea; **le Marché aux Puces** the Flea Market
puis then
puisque since
punir to punish

Q

la qualité quality
quand when
quant à as for, as to; **quant à moi** as for me
la quantité quantity
le quartier quarter; neighborhood
que, qu'est-ce que *interrogative pronoun object* what? **Que voulez-vous? Qu'est que vous voulez?** What do you want?
que *relative pronoun object* whom, that, which; (See Chapter 34 Grammar Note 1) **Voilà les clefs que vous cherchiez.** There are the keys (that) you were looking for.
que *conjunction* that; than; **Je sais qu'il a raison.** I know that he is right. **Il est plus grand que moi.** He is taller than I.
quel *m,* **quelle** *f adj* what, which; **Quelle cravate avez-vous choisie?** Which necktie have you chosen? *interrogative pronoun* what? which? **Quel est le prix?** What's the price?
quelconque any, whatsoever; **un dessert quelconque** some sort of dessert
quelque some, any; **quelque chose d'autre** something else; **quelques films** some films; **quelque part** somewhere; **quelque peu** somewhat; **quelquefois** sometimes
quelqu'un *m,* **'une** *f* someone, somebody; **quelques-uns** *n,* **-unes** *f* some, several
qu'est-ce qui *interrogative pronoun subject* what? **Qu'est-ce qui est arrivé?** What has happened?
qui *interrogative pronoun subject or object* who? whom? **Qui est-ce?** Who is it? **Qui cherchez-vous?** Whom are you looking for? **De qui parlez-vous?** Of whom are you speaking?
qui *relative pronoun subject* who (See Chapter 34 Grammar Note 1); **Connaissez-vous l'homme qui demeure ici?** Do you know the man who lives here?
la question question; **poser des questions** to ask questions
une quinzaine two weeks; **dans une quinzaine** in two weeks (*fifteen days*)
quitter to leave; **Il quitte la chambre.** He leaves the room.
quoi *pronoun used with prepositions* what **À quoi pensez-vous?** What are you thinking of? **Il n'y a pas de quoi.** Don't mention it. You're welcome.
quoique although
quotidien *m,* **quotidienne** *f* daily; everyday

R

raconter to tell (a story)
la radio radio
la raison reason; **il a raison** he is right
ramasser to pick up
le rang row
se rappeler to recall, to remember; **Je ne me rappelle pas son adresse.** I don't recall his address.
rapporter to bring back
rapprocher to bring nearer
le rasoir razor; **le rasoir de sûreté** safety razor; **le rasoir électrique** electric razor
recevoir to receive
réchauffer to warm up, to warm up again
recommencer to begin again
recommender to recommend
refuser to refuse
regarder to look at; to concern **dans tout ce qui regarde les en-têtes** in everything that concerns the headings
la règle rule
regretter to regret, to be sorry; **Je le regrette beaucoup.** I'm very sorry.
remarquer to notice
remercier to thank
remplir to fill; **rempli de** filled with
remporter to carry back
la rencontre meeting; **Je vais à la rencontre de Mme. D.** I am going to meet Mrs. D.
se rencontrer to meet each other
rendre to give back; to render; **rendre visite à** to pay a visit to (somebody); **rendre service à** to do a service to, to aid; **se rendre compte de** to realize
le renseignement information; **prendre des renseignements** to ask for information, to make inquiries
rentrer to come home
renvoyer to send back
répéter to repeat
répondre to answer, to reply
la réponse answer
le repas meal
le repos rest, repose
se reposer to rest
réserver to reserve
respirer to breathe
ressembler to resemble, to be alike; **ils se ressemblent** they resemble each other
le reste remainder, rest
rester to remain; **rester (être) debout** to stand
le retard delay; **en retard** late; **Nous sommes en retard.** We are late.
retenir to hold back, to retain; to reserve; **retenir une place** to reserve a seat
se retirer to withdraw
le retour return; **M. Black est de retour.** Mr. Black is back.
retourner to return, to go back
réussir to succeed
réveiller to awaken; **se réveiller** to wake up
revenir to come back, to return
rêver to dream
revoir to see again; **au revoir** good-bye
la revue magazine
le rhum rum
le rhume cold; **Je suis enrhumée.** I have a cold.
riche rich
le rideau curtain
le rien nothing; **ne . . . rien** nothing; **rien de plus facile** nothing easier; **de rien** or **il n'y a pas de quoi** you're welcome
rire to laugh; **se rire de** to laugh at
la rive bank (of river)
la rivière stream, river, branch of a river
la robe dress
le rôle role, part
le roman novel
rond round, plump
la roue wheel
rouge red
la rue street

S

sage good, well behaved; wise
sain healthy
la saison season
saisir to seize, to grasp
sale dirty; nasty
la salle room; **salle de classe** classroom; **salle à manger** dining room **salle d'attente** waiting room
le salon living room, parlor
saluer to greet
sans without
la santé healthy; **À votre santé!** Here's to you! Your health!
la saucisse sausage
sauf except; **sauf** *m,* **sauve** *f* safe; **sain et sauf** safe and sound
sauter to jump; to hop
savoir to know; **savoir-faire** tact, know-how; **savoir-vivre** good manners
le savon soap
la séance performance
le séjour sojourn
selon according to
la semaine week; **deux fois par semaine** twice a week
sembler to seem, to appear
le sens sense, opinion, direction; **le bon sens** common sense; **sens unique** one-way (street)
le sentiment feeling, sentiment
sentir to feel; to perceive; to smell; **Il se sent chez lui.** He feels at home.
la serviette napkin; **serviette de bain** bath towel
servir to serve
seul alone
seulement only; **non seulement . . . mais aussi** not only . . . but also
si if; whether; **sinon** otherwise
le siècle century
la soeur sister
la soie silk; **une robe de soie** a silk dress
la soif thirst; **il a soif** he is thirsty
soigner to take care of
le soir evening; **ce soir** this evening, tonight
le soleil sun

la somme sum
le sommeil sleep; **j'ai sommeil** I am sleepy
le son sound
son, sa, ses *possessive adj* his, her, its
songer (à) to dream (of)
sonner to sound, to ring
la sorte sort, kind
la sortie departure, exit
sortir to go out, to leave; **il sort de l'ordinaire** it's out of the ordinary
la soucoupe saucer
soudain suddenly
souffrir to suffer
souhaiter to wish for, to desire
le soulier shoe, pump
le souper supper
sourire to smile
sous under
se souvenir de to remember; **Nous ne nous souvenons pas de tous les circumstances.** We do not remember all the circumstances.
souvent often; **assez souvent** quite often; **plus souvent** more often
stationner to park; **Defense de stationner!** No parking allowed.
la sténo stenographer
le style style
le stylo fountain pen
le sucre sugar
le sucrier sugar bowl
le sud south
suffire to be sufficient; **cela suffit** that's enough
la suite sequence, result, continuation; **tout de suite** immediately; **et ainsi de suite** and so forth
suivre to follow
le sujet subject; **au sujet de** about, in the matter of
le supplément supplement, extra; **en supplément** in addition, extra
sur on, upon, over, above, about
sûr sure; **bien sûr** surely
surprendre to surprise
surtout above all, especially
sympathique nice, pleasant

T

le tabac tobacco
tâcher to try
tant so much, so many; **tant mieux!** good! so much the better! **tant pis!** so much the worse! **tant d'exercises** so many exercises
tantôt soon
tard late
la tarte tart, pie
la tasse cup
tel *m,* **telle** *f,* **tels** *m pl,* **telles** *f pl* such, like; **Tel père tel fils.** Like father, like son. **un tel homme** such a man
téléphoner to telephone
le temps time; weather; **de temps en temps** from time to time; **Quel temps fait-il?** How is the weather? **à temps** in time
tenir to hold, to keep; **tenir table ouverte** to keep open house
terminer to finish
la tête head; **mal de tête** *or* **mal à la tête** headache
tiens! well!
le timbre stamp; **le timbre-poste** postage stamp
tirer to draw, to pull; **se tirer d'affaire** to get along
le toit roof
tomber to fall
le ton tone
ton, ta, tes *possessive adj* your
le tort wrong; **Vous avez tort.** You are wrong.
tôt soon, early; **plus tôt** sooner, earlier; **le plus tôt possible** as soon as possible
toucher to touch
toujours always, still; **Comme toujours.** As ever. **Il pleut toujours.** It is still raining.
tourner to turn
tout *m,* **(toute** *f,* **tous** *m pl,* **toutes** *f pl)* all, whole, every; **tout le monde** everybody; **en tout cas** in any case; **pas du tout** not at all; **tout à fait** quite, entirely **tout à coup** all of a sudden
traduire to translate
le trajet flight, trip
le travail work
travailler to work
très very
tremper to soak
triste sad
se tromper to be mistaken
trop too, too much, too many; **trop tard** too late; **trop de livres** too many books; **trop d'argent** too much money
le trottoir sidewalk
trouver to find; **se trouver** to be (somewhere); **Où se trouve mon chapeau?** Where is my hat?

U

l'unité *f* unity
unir to unite; **uni** united; **les États Unis** the United States
l'usage *m* custom, usage; **L'usage rend maître.** Practice makes perfect.
l'usine *f* factory
l'ustensile *m* utensil
utile useful

V

la valeur value
valoir to be worth; **Cela ne vaut rien.** That isn't worth anything.
varier to vary, to change
le veau veal; **la blanquette de veau** veal stew
la vedette star (theater or film)
le velours velvet
le vendeur (vendeuse *f***)** seller, salesman, saleswoman
vendre to sell
venir to come; **venir de** to have just; **La caisse vient d'arriver.** The case has just arrived.
le vent wind; **Il fait du vent.** It is windy.
la vente sale; **en vente** on sale
le ventre stomach
la vérité truth
le verre glass (for drinking)
vers about, toward
verser to pour; to spend (money)
vert green
les vêtements clothes
(il) veut dire it means **Que veut dire ce mot?** What does this word mean?
la viande meat
vide empty
la vie life; **l'eau de vie** *f* brandy
vieux *m,* **vieil** *m* (before a vowel or h), **vieille** *f* old; **le vieux portrait** the old portrait; **le vieil arbre** the old tree; **les vieux quartiers** the old sections
vif *m,* **vive** *f* alive, living, lively
la ville city, town; **en ville** to the city, downtown; **Mme. Morelle va en ville pour faire ses achats.** Mrs. Morelle goes downtown to shop.
le vin wine
le visage face
la visite visit; **Nous allons lui rendre visite.** We are going to pay him a visit.
visiter to visit (places); **Nous visiterons tous les musées.** We shall visit all the museums.
vite rapidly, quickly, fast
la vitesse speed; **à toute vitesse** at full speed
la vitrine shop window
vivre to live
voici here is, here are; **le voici** here he is; **me voici** here I am; **les voici** here they are
la voie way, thoroughfare; **voie publique** public thoroughfare
voilà there is, are (*pointing*); there now! behold! that's that! **la voilà** there she is
voir to see
la voiture car, carriage; **en voiture** by car; **En voiture!** All aboard!
la voix voice; **à haute voix** in a loud voice
le vol flight; **L'avion prend son vol.** The airplane takes off.
volontiers gladly, with pleasure
votre, vos *possessive adj* your
vouloir to want, wish; **Voulez vous bien me dire . . . ?** Will you kindly tell me . . . ? **Je voudrais l'acheter.** I should like to buy it.
le voyage voyage, trip; **Bon voyage!** Pleasant journey! **M. Potter est en voyage.** Mr. Potter is on a trip. **le voyage de commerce** the business trip; **le voyage d'agrément** pleasure trip
voyager to travel
le voyageur *m,* **voyageuse** *f* traveler, passenger
vrai true; **C'est vrai.** It's true.
vraiment really, truly; **Vraiment!** Really!
la vue sight, view; **Je le connaît de vue.** I know him by sight.

W

le wagon-lit sleeping car (train); **le wagon-restaurant** dining-car

Y

y there

Z

le zéro zero

ANSWERS

Exercise No. 1

1. qui	6. mère	11. bureau
2. homme d'affaires	7. fils; et	12. Il est
3. dans	8. s'appellent; et	13. vingtième
4. il y a	9. cinq pièces	14. toute la journée
5. père	10. cuisine; salle de bain	

Exercise No. 2

1. la	5. la	9. la; une
2. une	6. une	10. l'; le
3. le, la	7. un	11. l'; le
4. le	8. la	12. une; un

Exercise No. 3

1. les chambres	6. les salons	11. les oncles
2. les mères	7. les Américains	12. les enfants
3. les pièces	8. les étages	13. les cuisines
4. les fils	9. les bureaux	14. les rues
5. les hommes	10. les personnes	15. les avenues

Exercise No. 4

1. M. Potter est un homme d'affaires Américain.
2. Il demeure à New-York.
3. Il y a six personnes dans la famille.
4. Il demeure dans une maison particulière.
5. Il y a cinq pièces dans la maison.
6. M. Potter est le père.
7. Mme. Potter est la mère.
8. Le bureau est dans la rue Whitehall.
9. M. Potter prend le train.
10. Il travaille au bureau.

Exercise No. 6

1. qui	9. c'est pourquoi
2. importateur	10. le professeur
3. objets d'art	11. un ami de M. Potter
4. au printemps	12. rendez-vous
5. il désire	13. Ils parlent
6. parler	14. rapidement
7. aussi	15. très intelligent
8. mais	16. un bon professeur

Exercise No. 7

1. est	5. il apprend	9. Ont-ils
2. est-il	6. il désire	10. Il compte
3. il ne parle pas	7. il n'étudie pas	11. faire
4. parle-t-il	8. il sait	12. parler

Exercise No. 8

(1 d)	(3 g)	(5 c)	(7 a)	(9 b)
(2 f)	(4 b)	(6 e)	(8 j)	(10 i)

Exercise No. 9

1. le français	9. très bien	17. où
2. le Français	10. rapidement	18. bon
3. merci	11. un peu	19. mauvais
4. aussi	12. là	20. avec
5. peut-être	13. de	21. des articles
6. le bureau	14. ici	22. des endroits
7. presque	15. grand	23. C'est pourquoi
8. toujours	16. mais	24. Comment allez-vous?

Exercise No. 11

1. est assis	6. au dessus de
2. beaucoup de choses	7. entre
3. Il faut savoir	8. des lettres
4. qu'est-ce que c'est que ça?	9. c'est assez
5. joue; chante	10. à jeudi

Exercise No. 12

2. au	4. du	6. à la	8. au	10. de la
3. des	5. à l'	7. aux	9. à l'	

Exercise No. 13

2. près de la	5. entre les	8. devant
3. sur le	6. autour de la	9. dans la
4. au dessus du	7. derrière la	10. avec, dans le

Exercise No. 14

1. M. Potter est assis dans le salon.
2. M. Picard est assis près de lui.
3. Il y a beaucoup de choses autour de nous.
4. Oui, elle chante bien.
5. Madame Potter joue bien du piano.
6. Il est sur le piano.
7. Il est au mur au dessus du piano.
8. La bibliothèque est près d'une fenêtre.
9. Le miroir est entre les fenêtres.
10. Le bureau est près de la porte.
11. Une chaise est devant le bureau.
12. Il y a des livres sur la petite table.

Exercise No. 15

(1 g)	(3 i)	(5 j)	(7 l)	(9 d)	(11 b)
(2 e)	(4 h)	(6 k)	(8 a)	(10 c)	(12 f)

Exercise No. 16

1. toute la journée	7. Comment allez-vous?
2. s'il vous plaît	8. Où
3. peut-être	9. Qu'est-ce que c'est que ça?
4. Bonsoir	10. Qui
5. en ville	11. Qu'est-ce qui
6. C'est pourquoi	12. Quand

Exercise No. 17

(1 d)	(3 i)	(5 h)	(7 c)	(9 j)	(11 e)
(2 f)	(4 k)	(6 g)	(8 a)	(10 b)	

Exercise No. 18

1. devant la maison	6. Les livres du garçon
2. autour de la table	7. La mère de la jeune fille
3. près de la porte	8. Le maitre des enfants
4. derrière le bureau	9. au mur
5. sur le piano	10. À qui

Exercise No. 19

1. Qui est M. Potter?
2. Il est un homme d'affaires américain.
3. Où demeure-t-il?
4. Il demeure dans les environs de New-York.
5. Pourquoi apprend-il le français?
6. Il désire faire un voyage en France.
7. Qui est son maître?
8. Son maître est M. Picard.
9. Pourquoi apprend-il rapidement?
10. Il apprend rapidement parce qu'il est intelligent.
11. Combien d'enfants y a-t-il dans la famille Potter (*or* dans la famille de M. Potter)?
12. Il y a quatre enfants.
13. Combien de pièces y a-t-il dans la maison de M. Potter?
14. Il y a cinq pièces, une salle de bain et une cuisine.

Exercise No. 20

Mr. Potter Is Learning French

Mr. Potter is an American businessman who imports art objects from France. That is why he wants to make a trip to France in the spring. He wants to talk with his agent. He also wants to visit some interesting places in France. But he does not know how to speak French.

Mr. Potter has a good teacher. He is a Frenchman who lives in New York and who is called Mr. Picard. Every Tuesday and Thursday the teacher takes the train to go to the home of his pupil. There the two gentlemen talk a little in French. Mr. Potter is very intelligent and he learns rapidly. During the first lesson, for example, he learns the greetings and farewells by heart. He already knows how to say, "Good day. How are you? See you soon," and "Until tomorrow." He already knows how to say in French the names of many things that are in his living room, and he knows how to answer correctly to the questions, "What is that?" and "Where is . . .?" Mr. Picard is very satisfied with his pupil's progress and he says, "Very good. That's enough for today. So long."

Exercise No. 21

1. sont importants
2. des verbs
3. Pourquoi
4. Parce que
5. avec lui
6. d'autres pays
7. en bateau ou en avion
8. Combien
9. très rapidement
10. Ça suffit (*or* c'est assez) pour aujourd'hui

Exercise No. 22

2. ils ne parlent pas
3. nous comptons
4. elles désirent
5. je travaille
6. demeurez-vous?
7. il écoute
8. il ne coûte pas
9. nous causons
10. vous étudiez
11. elles demeurent
12. elle ne visite pas
13. vous commencez
14. importe-t-il
15. Qui parle?
16. Les enfants jouent

Exercise No. 23

2. Paul n'étudie pas . . .
3. Nous ne parlons pas . . .
4. Ils n'écoutent pas . . .
5. ne jouez pas . . .
6. Elle ne désire pas . . .
7. Qui n'étudie pas . . .?
8. Nous ne travaillons pas . . .
9. Elle ne compte pas . . .
10. Vous ne travaillez pas . . .

Exercise No. 25

1. Les messieurs sont assis dans le salon chez M. Potter.
2. M. Picard commence à parler.
3. M. Potter écoute avec attention.
4. M. Picard pose les questions.
5. M. Potter répond aux questions.
6. Oui, monsieur, les verbes sont importants.
7. Oui, il importe des objets d'art.
8. Il désire faire un voyage en France.
9. Il compte visiter la France, le Maroc, et peut-être la Corse.
10. Il va voyager en avion.
11. M. Potter apprend rapidement.

Exercise No. 26

1. ouvre
2. Entrez, monsieur
3. Passez au salon s'il vous plaît
4. Ma fille
5. Avez-vous
6. j'ai
7. Nous sommes
8. l'ainé
9. dix ans
10. la plus jeune
11. Ils causent
12. accepte

Exercise No. 27

1. avez-vous
2. J'ai
3. a-t-elle
4. Elle a
5. Avez-vous
6. Nous n'avons pas
7. as-tu
8. Je n'ai pas
9. ont-elles
10. Elles n'ont pas
11. a
12. a
13. avez-vous
14. J'ai

Exercise No. 28

1. va-t-il
2. Il va
3. Allez-vous
4. nous allons
5. vont-il
6. va
7. vas-tu
8. va
9. Allez-vous
10. Nous n'allons pas
11. allez-vous
12. Nous allons
13. Comment allez-vous? *or* Comment ça va?
14. Ça va bien

Exercise No. 29

1. est
2. est
3. est
4. est
5. est-il
6. il n'est pas
7. Êtes-vous
8. je suis
9. sont
10. Ils sont
11. sont-ils
12. Ils sont
13. Êtes-vous

Exercise No. 30

1. M. Picard sonne à la porte.
2. La bonne ouvre la porte.
3. M. Potter attend M. Picard dans le salon.
4. Anne est malade.
5. Oui, elle est enrhumée.
6. Il a quatre enfants.
7. Il y a six personnes dans sa famille.
8. Ils s'appellent Charles, Thomas, Elizabeth et Anne.
9. Charles a dix ans.
10. Oui, ils vont à l'école.
11. Il invite M. Picard à visiter son bureau.
12. Oui, il accepte l'invitation.

Exercise No. 31

1. grandes
2. On peut
3. journaux
4. est assis
5. de vous voir
6. J'aime bien
7. Je vois
8. De quelle couleur
9. bleu
10. Mon Dieu!
11. Pas loin d'ici
12. Tant mieux! Allons y!

Exercise No. 32

1. assise
2. petits
3. intelligente
4. jolies
5. commode
6. haute
7. gris
8. intelligents
9. bon
10. jolies
11. grands
12. illustrées
13. grande
14. rouge; bleu
15. noires
16. vieux

Exercise No. 33

1. belle
2. bonne
3. belles
4. bonnes
5. blanches
6. longue
7. quel
8. quelles
9. quelle
10. quels
11. toute
12. tous

Exercise No. 34

1. Le bureau de M. Potter est très commode.
2. Les fenêtres du bureau sont grandes.
3. Il y a des affiches illustrées aux murs.
4. Il y a des journaux français sur la table.
5. Le ciel sur l'affiche est bleu.
6. Le soleil est jaune.
7. Comment allez-vous, M. Potter?
8. Très bien, merci.
9. J'ai faim.
10. Moi aussi.

Exercise No. 35

1. Il est au vingtième étage d'un gratte-ciel.
2. Il n'est pas grand.
3. Oui, il est commode.
4. Il y a des affiches illustrées aux murs.
5. Il y a beaucoup de papiers sur le bureau de M. Potter.
6. Près de la porte il y a un petit bureau.
7. Entre les fenêtres il y a une longue table.
8. Le soleil est jaune.
9. Les cheminées sont noires.

10. La colline est verte.
11. Oui, madame, le ciel est bleu.
12. Le château est blanc.
13. Le toit est rouge.
14. Oui, il a faim.

Exercise No. 36

1. Ses parents
2. Son ami
3. Voici
4. n'est-ce pas
5. J'apprends
6. n'est pas difficile
7. Je l'étudie
8. Le français me plaît
9. à merveille
10. Je comprends M. Picard.
11. Vous êtes
12. Pas du tout; la vérité

Exercise No. 37

1. Are you learning French? Yes, I am learning French. —Is Charles learning French? No, he is not learning French.
2. Are you writing a letter? I am not writing a letter. —What are you writing? I am writing the French lesson.
3. What are you reading? I am reading a French newspaper. —What is Anne reading? She is reading a French magazine.
4. Do you understand your teacher when he speaks fast? No, but we understand him well when he speaks slowly.
5. What does Mr. Potter sell? He sells art objects. —Does he sell wholesale or retail? He only sells wholesale.
6. Whom is Mr. Potter waiting for? He is waiting for Mr. Picard. —Where is he waiting for him? He is waiting for him in the living room.

Exercise No. 38

2. Nous apprenons
3. Je comprends
4. Ils lisent
5. Écrivez-vous
6. Je prends
7. Ils ne prennent pas
8. Nous répondons
9. Qui apprend
10. Ils ne comprennent pas
11. nous n'écrivons pas
12. Écrivons
13. vendent-ils
14. Lisez
15. Nous attendons
16. Entendez-vous

Exercise No. 39

1. M. Dupont demeure à New-York.
2. Oui. Il parle bien le français.
3. Non, monsieur, ses parents ne sont pas Américains. Ils sont Canadiens.
4. Il sait que M. Potter apprend le français.
5. Il entre un jour dans le bureau de M. Potter.
6. Il salue M. Potter en français.
7. M. Potter apprend à parler, à lire et à écrire le français.
8. Il étudie diligemment.
9. M. Picard est son professeur de français.
10. C'est un bon professeur.
11. Il comprend bien quand M. Picard parle français.
12. Il apprend les mots et les expressions de la vie quotidienne.
13. M. Potter va faire un voyage en France.
14. Il espère partir au printemps.

Exercise No. 40

(1 c)	(3 a)	(5 i)	(7 j)	(9 h)
(2 e)	(4 g)	(6 b)	(8 d)	(10 f)

Exercise No. 41

1. Je parle français.
2. Ils demeurent aux États-Unis.
3. Nous avons faim.
4. La revue est blanche et noire.
5. Les maisons sont rouges.
6. J'ai quinze ans.
7. Les professeurs posent des questions.
8. Nous répondons aux questions.
9. Il attend son ami.
10. J'écris des lettres.

Exercise No. 42

1. travaillons
2. apprennent
3. ne savez pas
4. écris
5. lisent
6. ne comprends pas
7. étudie
8. prenez
9. attendent
10. ne répondez pas
11. lisez
12. n'attendez pas

Exercise No. 43

1. j'ai faim; je n'ai pas faim.
2. je suis enrhumé; je ne suis pas . . .
3. j'étudie la leçon; je n'étudie pas . . .
4. j'attends le professeur; je n'attends pas . . .
5. je compte voyager; je ne compte pas . . .
6. j'apprends à écrire le français; je n'apprends pas . . .
7. je lis la revue; je ne lis pas . . .
8. j'écris la lettre; je n'écris pas . . .
9. je comprends les questions; je ne comprends pas . . .
10. j'accepte l'invitation; je n'accepte pas . . .
11. je commence à lire; je ne commence pas . . .
12. je réponds à la question; je ne réponds pas . . .

Exercise No. 44

1. Qui
2. Qui
3. Qui est-ce que
4. qui est-ce que
5. qui
6. qu'est-ce que
7. Qu'
8. Qui
9. Qu'est-ce qui
10. Que
11. Qu'est-ce que
12. Qu'est-ce qui

Exercise No. 45

Mr. Potter already knows the names of all the objects in his house. Now he is beginning to study the verbs because he wants to learn to read, write, and speak in French. He also wants to learn the numbers in French. Since he wants to visit his agent in Paris, who does not speak English, he wants to learn to speak French as soon as possible. Therefore he needs much practice with people who speak French well. Luckily he has two French friends who are in business near his office in Whitehall Street.

One day Mr. Potter goes to visit these French gentlemen. The two gentlemen listen with attention while Mr. Potter talks with them in French. After ten minutes of conversation, the gentlemen ask their friend many questions, and they are well satisfied with his progress.

Exercise No. 46

Thursday, April twenty-second, at nine o'clock in the evening, Mr. Picard arrives at the house of his pupil, Mr. Potter. The oldest son, a ten-year-old boy, opens the door, and greets the teacher politely. They go into the living room where Mr. Potter is usually waiting for his teacher.

But this evening he is not there. Mrs. Potter is not there either. Mr. Picard is very much surprised, and he asks the boy, "Where is your dad?" The son answers sadly, "My dad is sick. He is in bed because he has a bad cold."

The teacher is a bit annoyed but he only says, "What a pity! Well, next week we shall study for two hours. Until next Tuesday, then. Goodbye, little one." The boy answers "Goodbye, sir."

Exercise No. 47

1. Ils prennent
2. ces tasses
3. fleurs bleues
4. célèbre
5. chaque région
6. très jolie
7. presqu'aussi jolie
8. vous connaissez
9. C'est vrai
10. beaucoup de
11. Comme vous dites
12. C'est un plat simple
13. encore une tasse
14. Tout

Exercise No. 49

1. nous disons
2. je vois
3. il ne dit pas
4. il dit
5. dit-il?
6. Que dites-vous?
7. Que voyez-vous?
8. ils voient
9. vois-tu?
10. je ne vois pas
11. ils disent
12. Que disent-ils?
13. elle ne voit pas
14. Voyons
15. Dites-moi

Exercise No. 50

1. ce	3. ce	5. cette	7. ce	9. ces	11. ces
2. ces	4. ces	6. cet	8. cette	10. cet	12. cet

Exercise No. 52

1. Ils sont assis dans la salle à manger.
2. Ils prennent du café avec des gâteaux.
3. M. Potter dit, —Comment trouvez-vous ces tasses et ces soucoupes?
4. La tasse blanche est de Limoges.
5. La porcelaine de Limoges est célèbre.
6. Il est de Vallauris.
7. Elle est célèbre pour sa poterie.
8. Elle est en Provence.
9. Elle est très jolie.
10. M. Potter connaît bien son métier.
11. Il a des échantillons de poterie ordinaire.
12. Elle est simple.
13. Il accepte encore une tasse de café.
14. Il dit, —Merci bien. Tout est délicieux.

Exercise No. 53

1. Vous savez
2. aussi importante que
3. à quoi
4. Je crois que oui; voulez dire
5. Vous avez raison; sont indispensables
6. Nous avons besoin
7. Sans l'argent; grand' chose
8. En attendant; vous avancez rapidement
9. C'est
10. A jeudi prochain

Exercise No. 54

1. Je veux
2. Je peux (puis)
3. Voulez-vous
4. Pouvez-vous
5. Nous voulons
6. Nous ne pouvons pas
7. Ils ne veulent pas
8. Pouvez-vous
9. Veut-il
10. Peut-elle

Exercise No. 55

a) trente	e) seize	i) soixante-deux
b) dix	f) trente-huit	j) soixante-huit
c) cinquante	g) dix-sept	k) vingt-quatre
d) quarante-neuf	h) quinze	l) treize

Exercise No. 56

a) deux et six font huit
b) dix et sept font dix-sept
c) sept fois huit font cinquante-six
d) neuf fois sept font soixante-trois
e) dix-neuf moins huit font onze
f) dix-huit moins six font douze
g) soixante divisé par dix font six
h) soixante-neuf divisé par trois font vingt-trois

Exercise No. 57

2. Il y a douze mois dans une année.
3. Il y a vingt-quatre heures dans une journée.
4. Il y a soixante minutes dans une heure.
5. Il y a soixante secondes dans une minute.
6. Il y a trente jours dans le mois de septembre.
7. Il y a trente-six étudiants dans la classe.
8. J'ai dix-sept ans.
9. Il a dix-neuf ans.
10. Il y a quinze automobiles dans le garage.

Exercise No. 58

1. Il sait déjà que les noms des choses et des personnes sont importants.
2. Les nombres sont aussi importants que les noms et les verbes.
3. Nous avons besoin de nombres pour le commerce.
4. Il pense tout de suite au commerce.
5. Nous avons besoin de nombres pour téléphoner.
6. M. Potter veut comprendre et employer les nombres correctement.
7. Il avance rapidement.
8. dix, vingt, trente, quarante, cinquante, soixante

Exercise No. 59

1. Combien de fois; en voyage
2. On; pour acheter des billets
3. dans les grands magasins
4. Connaissez-vous
5. Je le connais
6. vaut
7. à peu près
8. Vous voulez acheter
9. Vous donnez
10. Il me rend

Exercise No. 60

1. What are you doing? I am writing a letter.
2. What is Jean doing? He is playing piano.
3. What is Marie doing? She is studying the French lesson.
4. What are the girls doing? They are shopping.
5. What are you doing, child? I am playing ball.
6. What is Mr. Martin doing? He is having the baggage weighed.
7. Do you believe this story? I do not believe it.
8. Does your friend believe it? He doesn't believe it either.

Exercise No. 61

a) quatre cents
b) mille
c) sept cent cinquante-trois
d) mille neuf cent soixante-quatorze
e) quatre-vingt-quinze
f) soixante-dix-sept
g) quatre-vingt-six
h) soixante et onze
i) six cent soixante-dix
j) quatorze mille cinq cent quatre-vingt-six

Exercise No. 63

1. Je reçois 600 (six cents) francs.
2. Je paye 1.500 (quinze cents *or* mille cinq cents) francs.
3. Je paye 20 (vingt) francs.
4. Je reçois 88 (quatre-vingt-huit) francs.
5. J'ai en poche 3.250 (trois mille deux cent cinquante) francs.
6. Oui, monsieur, il est millionaire.
7. Un billet de mille francs a plus de valeur qu'un (*than a*) billet de cinq dollars.
8. Pas moi, monsieur (*not I*). *or* Je ne sais pas (*I don't know*).

Exercise No. 64

1. Savez-vous
2. Nous connaissons
3. Nous ne savons pas
4. Il sait (comment)
5. Je sais
6. Ils ne connaissent pas
7. Je connais
8. Savez-vous (comment)
9. Connaissent-ils
10. savoir

Exercise No. 65

1. Nos	5. ses	9. sa	13. ton; mon
2. ma	6. vos	10. leurs	14. son
3. notre	7. votre	11. notre	15. leur
4. leurs	8. son	12. son	

Exercise No. 66

10 dix	22 vingt-deux	16 seize
20 vingt	44 quarante-quatre	32 trente-deux
30 trente	66 soixante-six	48 quarante-huit
40 quarante	88 quatre-vingt-huit	64 soixante-quatre
50 cinquante	110 cent dix	80 quatre-vingts
100 cent	220 deux cent vingt	160 cent soixante

Exercise No. 67

1. Nous dînons au restaurant.
2. L'addition pour tout le monde monte à 270 (deux cent soixante-dix) francs.
3. Nous laissons 27 (vingt-sept) francs.
4. Je porte une valise très lourde à la gare.
5. Elle pèse 30 (trente) kilos ou 66 (soixante-six) livres.
6. En France on compte les distances en kilomètres.
7. M. Potter sait changer les kilomètres en milles.
8. M. Potter achète trois paires de chaussures.
9. Le sujet de la prochaine conversation est les heures de la journée.
10. M. Potter dit, "Mieux vaut tard que jamais."

Exercise No. 68

1. A quelle heure
2. La première séance; quatre heures et demie de l'après-midi
3. d'autres questions
4. la gare
5. demande des renseignements
6. un billet d'aller et retour
7. est-ce que le train part
8. Arrive-t-il
9. de bonne heure
10. Les voici
11. Merci bien *or* Merci beaucoup
12. A votre service

Exercise No. 69

1. part
2. partez-vous
3. Nous dormons
4. ne dort pas
5. sert
6. sentez-vous
7. Je ne sens pas
8. sortent-ils
9. Je sors
10. Ne dormez pas

Exercise No. 70

2. dix heures et quart du soir
3. six heures et demie du matin
4. midi
5. quatre heures et demie de l'après-midi
6. sept heures moins vingt du soir
7. à neuf heures du soir
8. quatre heures dix de l'après-midi
9. huit heures moins le quart du matin
10. neuf heures moins vingt du matin

Exercise No. 71

1. Tout le monde veut savoir quelle heure il est.
2. M. Potter joue le rôle du voyageur.
3. M. Picard joue le rôle de l'employé du guichet.
4. Il désire un billet de première classe.
5. Un billet d'aller et retour coûte 154 (cent cinquante-quatre) francs.
6. M. Picard joue le rôle d'un employé au cinéma.
7. M. Potter demande des renseignements.
8. Il y a trois séances à ce ciné.
9. Il achète deux billets pour la troisième séance.
10. Il paye quarante francs pour ces deux billets.

Exercise No. 72

(1 f) (2 h) (3 a) (4 j) (5 b) (6 i) (7 c) (8 d) (9 e) (10 g)

Exercise No. 73

2. Nous avons besoin d'
3. connait son métier
4. changer de l'argent
5. pensez-vous
6. Aimez-vous
7. j'ai faim
8. voulez-vous dire
9. nous payons nos repas
10. Vous avez raison
11. vous avez tort
12. avez-vous besoin

Exercise No. 74

(1 c) (2 h) (3 a) (4 d) (5 g) (6 k) (7 b) (8 e) (9 l) (10 f) (11 i) (12 j)

Exercise No. 75

2. je veux faire . . .
3. je peux acheter . . .
4. je porte . . .
5. je pars . . .
6. je compte . . .
7. je dis . . .
8. je connais . . .
9. je donne . . .
10. je sais . . .

Exercise No. 76

2. nous ne calculons pas . . .
3. nous ne trouvons pas . . .
4. nous ne lisons pas . . .
5. nous n'écrivons pas . . .
6. nous ne dinons pas . . .
7. nous ne connaissons pas . . .
8. nous n'achetons pas . . .
9. nous n'avons pas . . .
10. nous ne savons pas . . .

Exercise No. 77

The Potter Family Drops In On Daddy
(*Lit*. Makes A Little Visit To Daddy)

It is the first time that the Potter family comes to see Mr. Potter at his office. Mrs. Potter and her four children enter a skyscraper and go up to the twentieth floor in the elevator. Anne, the youngest, who is only five years old, is very curious. She asks her mother many questions about the office.

When they arrive at the office the father gets up and says, "What a pleasant surprise! How glad I am to see you!"

The children admire all the objects they see in the office: the typewriter, the computer, the things from Paris, the samples of French pottery, the French magazines and especially the colored posters on the walls. Everybody is very happy.

Charles, the oldest, looks out the large window and sees the blue sky and the sun, which is shining. Below, he sees the automobiles, which are going through the street. From the twentieth floor they seem very small.

The visit over, the whole family goes into a restaurant that is not far from the office. They all eat heartily, especially the boys, because they are very hungry.

Exercise No. 78

The Draft-Horse And The Automobile
A Modern Fable

Anne, the youngest of Mr. Potter's children, likes the old fables of Aesop very much. She also likes this modern fable which Mr. Picard has written for her. Here is the fable: "The Draft-horse and the Automobile."

An automobile is moving along the road and sees a Percheron. The Percheron is a French draft-horse, big and strong. However this Percheron seems very tired. He is harnessed to a heavy cart.

The automobile stops and says to the Percheron, "Good morning. You are going along very slowly. Don't you want to go fast like me?"

"Oh yes, madam. But tell me how is it possible?"

"It is not difficult," says the automobile. "My gasoline tank is full. Drink some and you'll see something!"

So the Percheron drinks some gasoline. Now he does not go along slowly any more. He does not go fast either. In fact, he does not go at all. He has a stomach ache.

Poor horse! He is not very intelligent, is he? He does not know that gasoline is good for automobiles but that it is not worth anything to horses.

Exercise No. 79

1. J'aime beaucoup voir
2. ne m'intéressent pas
3. Ils adorent
4. tous les vedettes de l'écran
5. Ils les connaissent
6. près de chez vous
7. à pied
8. Nous préférons
9. Donc; de bonne heure

Exercise No. 80

1. Je viens
2. Ils ne viennent pas
3. vient
4. viennent
5. venez
6. Venez-vous
7. Nous revenons
8. revient-il
9. Elle ne vient pas
10. venez-vous
11. devenir
12. Je veux devenir

Exercise No. 81

1. les
2. la
3. l'
4. les
5. le
6. la
7. le
8. vous
9. nous
10. nous
11. y
12. y
13. vous
14. m'
15. t'

Exercise No. 82

1. M. Potter sait demander des renseignements.
2. Ils préfèrent le théâtre.
3. Ils préfèrent le ciné.
4. Oui, monsieur, ils les connaissent bien.
5. Il est près de la maison de M. Potter.
6. Ils préfèrent les places du quatorzième ou du quinzième rang.
7. De là il est possible de bien voir et entendre.
8. Ils arrivent de bonne heure.

Exercise No. 83

1. Vous savez (comment)
2. un événement important
3. Commençons
4. Comme
5. une date triste
6. une date victorieuse
7. Finissons
8. aussi bien que
9. D'ailleurs
10. Il m'apprend
12. Pas du tout

Exercise No. 84

1. finissez-vous
2. Nous finissons
3. choisissez-vous
4. Je choisis
5. punit
6. il n'obéit pas
7. bâtissent
8. Remplissez
9. Ils ne finissent pas
10. remplit
11. Choisissons

Exercise No. 85

1. première
2. troisième
3. quatorzième
4. cinquième
5. douzième
6. premier
7. dernière
8. neuvième
9. derniers

Exercise No. 86

1. le dix-huit avril mil sept cent (*or* dix-sept cent) soixante-quinze
2. le douze octobre mil quatre cent (*or* quatorze cent) quatre-vingt douze
3. le vingt-deux fevrier mil huit cent (*or* dix-huit cent) neuf
4. le premier mai mil neuf cent (*or* dix-neuf cent) cinquante-six

Exercise No. 87

1. Il apprend vite parce qui'il aime les questionnaires en français.
2. M. Picard va citer quelques dates de l'histoire de France.
3. M. Potter va citer un événement important pour chacune.
4. Il cite la prise de la Bastille.
5. Il cite la bataille de Waterloo.
6. C'est une date triste.
7. Il cite la victoire des Alliés à la fin de la première guerre mondiale.
8. C'est une date glorieuse pour les Parisiens.

Exercise No. 88

1. Voyons; la géographie de France.
2. que je vous pose
3. recevoir un prix
4. est situé
5. de café, coton, et sucre
6. le fleuve le plus long
7. beaucoup plus long que
8. plus petit que
9. la montagne la plus haute
10. plus haut que
11. que vous avez raison
12. est terminé

Exercise No. 89

1. Je mets
2. Qui met?
3. Pourquoi mettez-vous?
4. Que mets-tu? *or* Qu'est-ce que tu mets?
5. Nous mettons
6. Ils ne mettent pas
7. Je ne permets pas
8. Permet-il?
9. Pourquoi permettez-vous?
10. Nous permettons
11. Ne permet-il pas?
12. Permettez-moi

Exercise No. 90

1. Are French films better than American films?
2. Some are better, some are worse. In France and in the United States one can see the best and also the worst films. In general I like the French films better.
3. Robert sings badly. Richard sings worse than Robert. But Bernard sings worst of all.
4. Herbert writes well. But you write better than he. Renée writes best of all.
5. Where do they make the best porcelain? They make it in Limoges.
6. Better late than never.

Exercise No. 91

2. plus aimable que
3. la meilleure plume
4. si bonne que
5. plus grande que
6. le plus diligent
7. la plus jeune
8. plus intéressant que
9. le plus long
10. la plus grande ville
11. plus long et plus large que
12. si mal
13. les meilleurs films
14. la pire (la plus mauvaise)
15. plus de

Exercise No. 92

1. La question est: Sur quel grand fleuve est-ce que la ville de Paris est située?
2. Il est situé à l'embouchure de la Seine.
3. Il est un grand marché de café, coton et sucre.
4. Le Mississippi est plus long et plus large que la Loire.
5. Le Mount McKinley est plus haut que le Mont Blanc.
6. a. M. Dupont est le plus jeune des trois.
   b. M. Arnaud est le plus âgé des trois.
   c. M. Millet est plus âgé que M. Dupont.
   d. M. Dupont est le plus riche.
   e. M. Arnaud est le moins riche.
   f. M. Millet n'est pas si riche que M. Dupont. *or* Il est moins riche que M. Dupont.

Exercise No. 93

1. une journée typique
2. à six heures et demie
3. matinal
4. de bonne heure
5. Que mangez-vous
6. du café, des petits pains et des oeufs
7. Parfois
8. au bureau
9. mon courrier; les réponses
10. Que faites-vous
11. me voir
12. finissez-vous
13. Je quitte
14. Nous nous mettons

Exercise No. 94

2. se
3. se, s'
4. vous
5. vous
6. se
7. se
8. nous
9. vous
10. s'
11. m'
12. toi
13. vous
14. me
15. se

Exercise No. 95

1. What is your name? My name is Albert.
2. At what time do you get up? I get up at 7 A.M.
3. At what time do you go to bed? I go to bed at 11 P.M.
4. Do you dress quickly? Yes, I dress very quickly.
5. How are you? I'm feeling well, thank you.
6. How is your father? He is not well. He has a cold.
7. At what time does Mr. Potter sit down at the table? He sits down at the table at 7 P.M.
8. Are the boys having a good time playing basketball? Yes, they are having a very good time.

Exercise No. 96

1. Il se lève à six heures et demie.
2. Il se lave et il s'habille.
3. Il s'habille dans une demi-heure plus ou moins.

4. A sept heures à peu près il se met à table dans la salle à manger.
5. Elle se lève de bonne heure.
6. Ils déjeunent ensemble.
7. Il prend du jus d'orange, du café, des petits pains, et des oeufs.
8. Parfois il mange des crêpes au lieu des oeufs.
9. Il est prêt à partir à sept heures et demie.
10. Il arrive à son bureau à neuf heures.
11. Il prend son déjeuner à une heure.
12. Il mange un sandwich, un café et un dessert quelconque.
13. Des clients viennent le voir dans l'après-midi.
14. Il finit sa journée à cinq heures.

Exercise No. 97

1. bien renseigné
2. tout de même
3. Nous restons
4. son marché
5. des fruits, des légumes, du lait, du beurre, du fromage, et du café
6. des bas et des casseroles
7. stationner
8. à son aise
9. de bons camarades
10. J'ai envie de déménager

Exercise No. 98

1. du, du
2. du; du; des
3. de
4. des
5. des
6. d'
7. de la; de la; des
8. de
9. de l'
10. de

Exercise No. 99

2. Oui, elle en achète.
3. Non, je n'en ai pas.
4. Prenez-en
5. N'en mangez pas.
6. Il en a trente.
7. Merci. Je n'en veux pas.
8. Oui, ils en ont assez.

Exercise No. 100

1. M. Picard est toujours curieux.
2. Il sait déjà que M. Potter rentre assez tard.
3. La famille Potter ne termine pas son dîner beaucoup avant huit heures et demie.
4. Parce que les enfants ne veulent pas se coucher.
5. Elle les fait au supermarché.
6. On achète des fruits, des légumes, du lait, du café, des conserves, toutes sortes de viande, et ainsi de suite (*and so on*).
7. On n'y trouve pas de pardessus.
8. Plusieurs des grands magasins ont des succursales.
9. Ils aiment leurs maîtres d'école.
10. M. Picard a envie de déménager à la banlieue.

Exercise No. 101

(1 i) (2 e) (3 f) (4 h) (5 g) (6 a) (7 c) (8 j) (9 b) (10 d)

Exercise No. 102

1. le fleuve le plus long
2. plus grande que
3. plus fatigué que
4. si grand que
5. plus haut que
6. la plus haute montagne
7. le premier jour
8. le 30 janvier 1988 (mil neuf cent quatre-vingt-huit)
9. de la famille
10. mon meilleur ami

Exercise No. 103

1. Do you take coffee or chocolate for your breakfast? I take neither one nor the other. I drink a glass of water.
2. Do you want cream and sugar in your coffee? I want some cream but I do not want any sugar.
3. What do they eat for breakfast in France? They eat very little; generally rolls and coffee.
4. What do they eat for breakfast in the United States? Usually they begin with orange juice. Sometimes they eat some cereal or other, a piece of toast or eggs. Americans are also very fond of pancakes with syrup. Of course there is also coffee, tea, or milk to drink.

Exercise No. 104

2. Non, je ne le préfère pas.
3. Oui, ils les connaissent bien.
4. Oui, nous vous attendons.
5. Je me lève tard.
6. Nous nous couchons à onze heures.
7. Oui, ils s'habillent très vite.
8. Je m'appelle Albert Martin.
9. Nous les finissons à quatre heures de l'après-midi.
10. Oui, ils le finissent maintenant.

Exercise No. 105

1. fatiguée; pareille
2. Ils se mettent à table
3. Ils sont (*or* restent) debout
4. sont assis
5. de temps en temps; au lieu de
6. attraper un rhume
7. la plupart de
8. à l'heure
9. les bienvenus
10. de bonne heure; tard

Exercise No. 106

A Visit to the Liner Queen Elizabeth 2

It is Saturday. Mr. Potter gets up at eight o'clock and looks out the window. The sky is blue. The sun is shining. He says to his wife, "Today let's visit the liner Queen Elizabeth 2, which arrived this morning. I have some goods on board. We'll have a good opportunity to visit the ship."

"Fine," says Mrs. Potter.

At nine o'clock, they leave in the car and in about one hour they arrive at the pier. At the entrance they see a group of boys eating ice cream and talking French.

Mr. Potter greets the boys and he chats a bit with the nearest one. Here is the conversation.

"Good morning, young man. Are you French?"

"No sir, I am American."

"But you speak French very well."

"Well these boys who work on the liner are my friends and they are teaching me how to speak correctly. They are my teachers. Besides, I study French in high school and every day I read a few pages of French. By the way, are you French?"

"Thank you for the compliment. No, young man, I am American like you and like you I am studying French. But I have only one teacher."

"I see. But you speak very well."

"Thanks again. Goodbye and good luck."

"Goodbye, sir. It's a pleasure (meeting you)."

Mr. Potter goes back to his wife who is waiting for him smiling and they continue on their way for the visit to the steamship.

"Il est sympathique, ce garçon," Mr. Potter says to his wife. Then he translates the sentence because she doesn't understand French.

Exercise No. 107

1. Quel sale temps!
2. Entrez, entrez; trempé
3. votre imperméable
4. Mettez
5. Ça va mieux
6. attraper un rhume
7. on ne doit pas sortir
8. Venez
9. leur apporte
10. Prenez
11. Permettez-mois
12. il pleut toujours

Exercise No. 108

2. nous
3. lui
4. leur
5. leur
6. lui
7. m'
8. lui
9. lui
10. nous
11. nous
12. moi
13. leur
14. lui
15. lui

Exercise No. 109

1. Il pleut à verse.
2. La bonne ouvre la porte.
3. Il le met dans le porte-parapluies.
4. Il les laisse à l'entrée.

5. Ils entrent dans la salle à manger.
6. Ils prennent du thé au rhum.
7. Elle met sur la table des tasses, des soucoupes, une théière pleine de thé, un sucrier, des cuillers à thé et une bouteille de rhum.
8. Après elle sort de la salle à manger.

Exercise No. 110

1. en prenant
2. à pleuvoir
3. il fait chaud
4. il fait très froid
5. il pleut souvent
6. Je préfère (*or* J'aime mieux)
7. préférez-vous (*or* aimez-vous mieux)
8. parlons plutôt
9. de chaleur et de froid
10. doit
11. il fait beau

Exercise No. 112

2. n'—pas encore
3. ne—jamais
4. n'—pas—non plus
5. ne—rien; ne—rien
6. ne—pas
7. n'—plus
8. ne—pas non plus
9. n'—rien
10. n'—qu'
11. rien
12. pas encore
13. ne—jamais
14. ne—ni—ni

Exercise No. 113

1. Ils parlent du climat.
2. Le climat de la France est quelque peu différent de celui des États-Unis.
3. Il fait chaud. Des fois il fait très chaud.
4. Il préfère l'automne.
5. Il préfère le printemps.
6. Il y a une différence assez marquée entre les saisons en France.
7. Il pleut beaucoup, il fait du vent, le ciel est gris.
8. Le ciel est bleu clair et l'air est doux, embaumé.

Exercise No. 114

1. nous allons continuer
2. très désagréable
3. qui ont les moyens
4. Est-ce qu'il n'y a pas d'hiver
5. Il ne fait jamais froid
6. Il fait mettre
7. nager le matin
8. On peut voir
9. doit être
10. Si vous avez le temps

Exercise No. 115

1. Which pottery do you prefer, that of Vallauris or that of Biot? I prefer that of Biot.
2. Which hat do you like better? This one or that one? I prefer that one.
3. Which climate is milder, that of France or that of Canada? That of France is milder.
4. How do you like these dresses? I like this one but I find the colors of that one too loud (*Lit*. brilliant).
5. Which seats do you prefer, those in the first rows or those in the rear? We prefer those in the first rows.
6. What kind of handkerchiefs are you going to buy? I am going to buy those which are cheapest.

Exercise No. 116

2. ceux
3. celui-là
4. celles-là
5. celles-là
6. ceux-là
7. celui-ci; celui-là
8. celle-ci; celle-là
9. celui
10. cela

Exercise No. 117

1. Ils quittent Paris en hiver parce que l'hiver est désagréable.
2. Ils vont en Suisse ou à la Côte d'Azur.
3. L'hiver est doux. Le soleil brille prèsque tous les jours.
4. En été il fait plus chaud, mais il y a toujours une jolie brise de mer.
5. Sur la Côte d'Azur on peut nager le matin et faire du ski l'après-midi.
6. On peut voir les montagnes couvertes de neige.
7. Il fait frais pendant la nuit.
8. Il fait très froid dans les montagnes.
9. Les montagnes sont à une distance d'à peu près quatre-vingts kilomètres.
10. M. Potter va tâcher de faire ce petit voyage au mois de juin.

Exercise No. 118

1. la bonne cuisine français
2. un des plus grands plaisirs
3. à déjeuner
4. Cela arrive
5. nous fait cadeau
6. Envoyez à votre femme
7. Je vais vous dire
8. Tout ce qui; de bonne qualité
9. Il faut avoir
10. du beurre, du beurre, et encore du beurre

Exercise No. 119

1. avec moi
2. pour toi
3. chez moi
4. chez nous
5. chez elle
6. sans eux
7. près d'elle
8. autour de nous
9. à nous
10. à elles

Exercise No. 120

1. Lui; Elle
2. Moi
3. moi; nous; eux
4. toi
5. moi
6. lui
7. elle et moi
8. Moi
9. à vous
10. à lui

Exercise No. 121

1. La bonne cuisine française est un des plus grands plaisirs du touriste en France.
2. Oui. Il connaît un peu la cuisine française.
3. Elle nous fait cadeau de beaucoup d'expressions d'usage courant.
4. Il doit faire une liste de ses plats préférés.
5. Vraiment, non. La cuisine française n'est pas compliquée.
6. Le troisième secret est: du beurre, du beurre et encore du beurre.
7. Oui. Il va tout de suite les raconter à sa femme.
8. M. Potter est un mari modèle.
9. M. Potter a un appétit de loup.
10. M. Picard va casser la croûte avec lui.

Exercise No. 122

(1 c) (2 f) (3 a) (4 e) (5 g) (6 i) (7 k) (8 b) (9 d) (10 l) (11 h) (12 j)

Exercise No. 123

1. j'ai froid
2. j'ai chaud
3. il fait chaud
4. il pleut beaucoup
5. il fait frais
6. il fait froid
7. un imperméable
8. je porte un pardessus
9. tombe
10. toutes les saisons

Exercise No. 124

(1 d) (2 f) (3 a) (4 g) (5 i) (6 h) (7 e) (8 b) (9 j) (10 c)

Exercise No. 125

1. lui
2. lui
3. l'
4. le
5. la; se
6. moi; vous
7. les
8. la
9. m'
10. leur

Exercise No. 126

1. Je ne connais personne.
2. Nous ne mangeons jamais de viande.
3. Je n'ai qu'un professeur.
4. Elle ne veut plus ce chapeau-là.
5. Jeanne ne va pas encore à l'école.
6. Je ne suis pas fatiguée non plus.
7. Nous n'avons plus de temps.
8. Pourquoi ne dites-vous rien?
9. Nous n'avons ni temps ni argent.

Exercise No. 127

Gerard Does Not Like To Study Arithmetic

One day upon returning home from school Gerard says to his mother, "I don't like to study arithmetic. It's so difficult. Why do we need so many exercises and so many problems? We have calculators, don't we? Well, then!"

Mrs. Martin looks at her son and says, "You are wrong, my dear (*Lit.* my little one). We cannot do without numbers. For example, one always needs to spend money, go shopping, estimate distances and . . . and . . ." The mother stops speaking on seeing that Gerard is not paying attention to what she says.

"By the way, dear," she continues, smiling, "baseball doesn't interest you either?"

"What an idea! You're joking."

"Well then if the Dodgers have won eighty games and they have lost twenty do you know what percentage of games they have won?"

On hearing this Gerard exclaims, "You're right, mother. Numbers, arithmetic and mathematics are very important. I think that now I'm going to study much more."

Exercise No. 128

1. quelques
2. les allumettes; le cendrier
3. très à mon aise
4. Ils se ressemblent
5. partout
6. comme vous dites
7. quelques-unes de ces
8. Les pêcheurs et les marins
9. Les fermiers
10. Les ouvriers des mines
11. Nous n'avons pas besoin
12. ne ressemble pas
13. discuter

Exercise No. 129

1. étudions, étudiant
2. venons, venant
3. lisons, lisant
4. achetons, achetant
5. voulons, voulant
6. disons, disant
7. choisissons, choisissant
8. finissons, finissant
9. bâtissons, bâtissant
10. connaissons, connaissant
11. apprenons, apprenant
12. appelons, appelant
13. comptons, comptant
14. dormons, dormant
15. mettons, mettant
16. faisons, faisant
17. avons, ayant
18. sommes, étant

Exercise No. 130

1. quelqu'un
2. quelques
3. Quelques-uns
4. Quelques-unes
5. quelques-unes
6. quelques
7. quelques
8. quelques
9. quelques-unes
10. quelqu'un

Exercise No. 131

1. Il va poser quelques questions à M. Picard sur les Français.
2. Il demande si les Français se ressemblent plus ou moins.
3. Oui. Il est vrai qu'il y a de très grandes différences entre tous les Français.
4. Il y a des différences entre les Français à cause de la géographie et aussi à cause de leurs métiers.
5. Les pêcheurs de la Bretagne sont très dévots et très dévoués au Calvados.
6. L'homme du Midi est bavard et blagueur.
7. Non. Il ne ressemble pas trop au montagnard de l'Auvergne.
8. Oui. Les Français aiment beaucoup discuter.
9. Ils sont fiers de leur tradition de démocratie, de philosophie de belles lettres et de science.
10. Ils aiment tous la bonne cuisine et le bon vin.

Exercise No. 132

1. vient de recevoir
2. est en train d'admirer
3. non seulement . . . mais aussi
4. que vous n'aimez pas
5. n'est-ce pas?
6. les beaux arts
7. la peinture, la sculpture et l'architecture
8. Je compte sur le plaisir
9. tout à fait exceptionnel
10. Je vous admire

Exercise No. 133

1. Elle achète
2. Préférez-vous
3. je préfère
4. Répétons
5. J'espère
6. vous levez-vous
7. Je me lève
8. célèbre
9. s'appelle
10. jettent
11. appelle
12. Je lève

Exercise No. 134

1. Il vient de recevoir une grande caisse de marchandise.
2. M. Picard est en train de regarder et d'admirer.
3. Il y a des échantillons de riches étoffes de soie.
4. La belle étoffe de laine est de la maison Dior.
5. M. Picard croit que M. Potter n'aime pas la mode.
6. M. Potter est amateur des arts.
7. Il va voir l'art des grands maîtres.
8. Il éspère visiter aussi les musées de l'art moderne.
9. M. Potter s'intéresse à l'art, à l'histoire et aux belles lettres.
10. Ils vont former une société d'estime mutuelle.

Exercise No. 135

1. la grande fête nationale
2. On célèbre
3. Tout le monde
4. toute la journée; toute la nuit
5. les Guignols
6. célébrée
7. en dormant
8. Le jour de l'An
9. les étrennes
10. table ouverte
11. doit être
12. tout le monde quitte Paris
13. par-ci ou par là

Exercise No. 136

1. Il tient
2. Nous obtenons
3. Je ne retiens pas
4. tient table ouverte
5. Nous commençons à travailler
6. changeons-nous
7. prononcez-vous
8. Nous le prononçons
9. Nous ne mangeons pas
10. nous nageons
11. Nous corrigeons
12. Recommençons

Exercise No. 137

1. on
2. personne ne
3. On
4. rien
5. personne
6. rien
7. Rien
8. Personne
9. personne
10. Personne ne

Exercise No. 138

1. Ils vont parler des jours de fêtes en France.
2. On célèbre le quatorze juillet dans les rues.
3. On danse dans les rues.
4. On vend des crêpes, des gauffres, des glaces et toutes sortes de friandises.
5. Il y a les petits chevaux de bois et les Guignols pour les enfants.
6. Il faut dire *la Noël.*
7. On dort parce qu'on a réveillonné toute la nuit.
8. Les enfants reçoivent leurs cadeaux le jour de l'An.
9. On les appelle les étrennes.
10. La ville est morte.

Exercise No. 139

1. Je voyagerai
2. Je visiterai
3. Il vous faudra
4. Je ferai
5. J'irai
6. Je passerai
7. Je prendrai
8. Je reviendrai
9. mieux que moi
10. sera
11. qui arrive à tout le monde
12. chez soi

Exercise No. 140

1. Where will you go next summer? I shall go to France. When will you leave N.Y.? I shall leave May 31.
2. How much time will you spend in France? I shall spend three months there. Will you travel by plane or by boat? I shall travel by plane.

3. Will you take a trip to Morocco? I shall take a trip to Morocco. Will Mr. Picard be able to go with you? Unfortunately, he will not be able to go with me.
4. Will you see your agent in Paris? Yes indeed. He will be waiting for me at the airport. How long will you stay in Paris? I shall stay there two weeks.
5. Will you visit the Riviera? Of course I shall visit it. When will you return to the U.S.? I shall return September 1.

Exercise No. 141

1. il visitera
2. je voyagerai
3. nous irons
4. ils n'écriront pas
5. il faudra
6. verrez-vous?
7. ils ne partiront pas
8. nous vendrons
9. ne finira-t-il pas?
10. elle n'apprendra pas
11. il sera
12. viendrez-vous?
13. j'aurai
14. tu n'écouteras pas
15. nous étudierons
16. je ne ferai pas
17. pourrez-vous?
18. irez-vous?

Exercise No. 142

1. Il voyagera en avion.
2. Il verra la Vénus de Milo, la Mona Lisa et la salle de céramique grecque.
3. Il passera par le jardin des Tuileries.
4. Il prendra un taxi à la Place de l'Étoile.
5. Il visitera la Tour Eiffel.
6. Il se promènera en taxi au Bois de Boulogne.
7. M. Potter connaît le Paris des guides.
8. On se sent chez soi à Paris.
9. Le soir du quatorze juillet on voit jouer les grandes fontaines à Versailles.
10. Il se trempera dans la mer et dans le soleil à la Côte d'Azur.
11. Il reviendra à Paris par la route des Alpes.

Exercise No. 143

(1 e)	(4 n)	(7 i)	(10 j)	(13 d)
(2 g)	(5 b)	(8 o)	(11 h)	(14 a)
(3 l)	(6 c)	(9 m)	(12 k)	(15 f)

Exercise No. 144

1. la ceinture de cuir leather belt
2. la robe de soie silk dress
3. la montre d'or gold watch
4. la salle de bain bathroom
5. la chemise de laine woolen shirt
6. le bureau de poste post office
7. le voyage d'affaires business trip
8. le cahier de musique music book
9. le tissu de coton cotton cloth
10. le bracelet d'argent silver bracelet
11. l'objet d'art art object
12. le chapeau de paille straw hat

Exercise No. 145

2. Elle coûtera cent francs.
3. J'irai en France.
4. Je reviendrai aux États-Unis le 31 décembre.
5. Je me coucherai à minuit.
6. Je me lèverai à six heures du matin.
7. Je ne lui dirai rien.
8. Personne n'ira avec moi.
9. Je travaillerai toute la journée.
10. Nous nous rencontrerons à l'entrée du théâtre.

Exercise No. 146

2. Nous n'avons pas besoin de continuer.
3. Elle a l'intention de porter son manteau neuf.
4. Avez-vous envie de m'accompagner?
5. Il fera son possible pour vous aider.
6. Allez-vous faire des achats au Marché aux Puces?
7. M. Potter est en train d'ouvrir la caisse.
8. Avez-vous peur de dire la vérité?
9. Allez-vous vous promener en voiture au Bois de Boulogne?
10. Vous savez que M. Potter ne s'intéresse pas à la mode.

Exercise No. 147

1. mon chapeau
2. ton manteau
3. sa chemise de laine
4. sa robe de soie
5. notre ceinture de cuir
6. vos gants rouges
7. leur pardessus
8. leur fichu
9. cette robe
10. cette cravate
11. ces gants
12. cette jupe

Exercise No. 148

Mrs. Potter's Birthday

It is March 22, Mrs. Potter's birthday. She is thirty-five years old today. To celebrate this festive day the Potter family is going to dine in an elegant restaurant on Madison Avenue in New York.

When they enter the restaurant they see a beautiful basket full of white roses on the table reserved for the Potters. Naturally Mrs. Potter is very much surprised. She thanks and kisses her dear husband warmly.

At the end of a delicious dinner Anne, the youngest, says in a low voice to the other children, "Now!" And each of the four children takes a pretty little box from under the table. These are presents for their mother.

Anne gives her a silk handkerchief; Elizabeth, a linen blouse; Thomas, a pair of gloves; and Charles, a woolen scarf.

The following week, Mr. Potter figures out the bill for that day, which follows:

Dinner	$160
Tip	24
Flowers	40
Gifts	126
Total	$350

"What a coincidence," says Mr. Potter. "Three hundred fifty dollars, ten times thirty-five years."

Exercise No. 149

1. à la main
2. vient d'arriver
3. qui suit
4. Je partirai
5. J'ai l'intention
6. très occupé
7. Par conséquent
8. Depuis quelque temps; deux fois par semaine
9. une seule faute
10. Voulez-vous bien

Exercise No. 150

2. recevra
3. Ils sauront
4. Il ne voudra pas
5. courront
6. ne vaudront pas
7. Ils nous devront
8. Ils tiendront
9. Traduirez-vous
10. Nous ne suivrons pas
11. Je ferai
12. Nous pourrons

Exercise No. 151

2. pendant les mois
3. Depuis quand
4. depuis dix ans
5. depuis deux ans
6. depuis trois heures
7. Combien de temps
8. Il y a trois jours
9. Depuis quand demeurez-vous
10. Nous y demeurons

Exercise No. 152

1. Ils sont assis dans le salon chez M. Potter.
2. Il tient deux lettres à la main.
3. Il va lire sa lettre à M. Parmentier.
4. Il partira de New-York le 31 mai.
5. Il passera deux mois en France. *or* Il y passera deux mois.
6. Il restera à Paris trois semaines.
7. Il espère voyager au Maroc en avion, et peut-être en Corse.
8. M. Parmentier est très occupé.
9. Il veut faire la connaissance de M. Parmentier.
10. Il écrit d'avance dans l'espoir de pouvoir arranger un rendez-vous.
11. Il y a cinq mois que M. Potter prend des leçons de français

Exercise No. 153

1. Il est en train de lire
2. J'ai reçu
3. pendant les mois
4. Je compte sur le plaisir
5. que je causerai en français
6. vous feliciter
7. Vous avez connu
8. si je suis fier
9. vous verrez
10. Je pourrai

Exercise No. 154

1. Did Mr. Picard ask Mr. Potter some difficult questions? Yes, he asked some difficult questions. Did Mr. Potter answer well? Yes, he answered all the questions well.
2. When did Mr. Potter write the letter to his agent? He wrote the letter two weeks ago today. To whom did he read a copy of the letter? He read the copy to Mr. Picard.
3. Did Mr. Picard find many mistakes in the letter? He did not find a single mistake. What book helped Mr. Potter a great deal? The book, "Commercial Correspondence," helped him a great deal.
4. Did Mr. Potter appreciate the services of Mr. Parmentier? Yes, he always appreciated his loyal services. What did Mr. Picard say when Mr. Potter finished reading the letter? He said, "It is a nice letter."

Exercise No. 155

2. décidé
3. apprécié
4. contribué
5. vendu
6. écrit
7. lu
8. rendu
9. fait
10. entendu; dit
11. fini
12. servi

Exercise No. 156

1. M. Potter écrit une lettre à son représentant.
2. Il a lu la copie de cette lettre à son professeur.
3. Il n'a pas trouvé une seule faute.
4. M. Parmentier sera à Paris pendant les mois de juin et juillet.
5. Il va rencontrer M. Potter (*or* Il va le rencontrer) à l'aéroport Charles de Gaulle.
6. Il va causer en français avec lui.
7. Il l'a connu comme représentant sérieux.
8. M. Potter est certain qu'il sera content parmi les Français.
9. Les deux messieurs auront leur dernier rendez-vous mardi prochain.
10. Ils se rencontreront au bureau de M. Potter.
11. M. Picard lui donnera quelques derniers conseils.

Exercise No. 157

1. Par la fenêtre ouverte
2. J'ai envie
3. Voulez-vous bien me donner
4. avec plus de formalité
5. Chaque homme est digne
6. se connaître l'un l'autre
7. est plus tranquille
8. Avez-vous lu
9. J'ai parcouru
10. Je passerai
11. Vous allez me manquer *or* Vous me manquerez
12. Je serai content

Exercise No. 158

1. parcouru
2. compris; dit
3. mis
4. promis
5. entendu; compris
6. vu
7. couru
8. appris
9. pris
10. pris

Exercise No. 159

1. Have you recommended these guides? I have recommended them.
2. Did he write the answer? He wrote it.
3. Where did he find the money? He found it on the desk.
4. Did you understand the question? I did not understand it.
5. Has she learned the proverb? She hasn't learned it.
6. Who reserved the two seats? My father reserved them yesterday.
7. When did you see your friend? I saw her yesterday evening.
8. When did they finish the examination? They finished it at two o'clock.
9. When did the postman bring the letters? He brought them this morning.
10. Did you hear the bell? I did not hear it.
11. Has Mr. Potter scanned all the guide books? He has scanned them all.
12. What letter did he read to Mr. Picard? He read the letter which he received from Mr. Parmentier.

Exercise No. 160

1. Ils se trouvent dans le bureau de M. Potter.
2. Il fait chaud.
3. On entend les bruits de la rue.
4. M. Potter est content de quitter la ville.
5. M. Picard a envie d'accompagner M. Potter. (*or* de l'accompagner.)
6. Il répond, —Malheureusement, ce n'est pas possible.
7. On fait les choses avec plus de formalité en France.
8. Il a remarqué que les affaires se traitent en France avec plus de formalité qu'ici.
9. M. Potter est las d'être bousculé.
10. M. Potter a lu des livres sur la France.
11. M. Picard les a recommandés.
12. M. Picard passera l'été à New-York.
13. M. Potter pensera souvent à M. Picard.

Exercise No. 161

1. Il y a cinq mois
2. Il a appris
3. Il a vraiment travaillé
4. Il a obtenu
5. Il a écrit
6. a promis
7. il doit être
8. ne l'accompagne pas
9. doivent finir
10. a fait
11. Ils montent tous
12. a fait peser ses bagages
13. Il doit payer
14. fait ses adieux à
15. en route

Exercise No. 162

1. il a voulu
2. vous avez ouvert
3. j'ai su
4. a-t-il ouvert?
5. nous avons eu
6. ils ont été
7. je n'ai pas couvert
8. ont-ils su?
9. nous n'avons pas ouvert
10. elle a été
11. a-t-il voulu?
12. j'ai offert

Exercise No. 163

2. illustrées
3. fermées
4. connu
5. cassées
6. levés
7. habillé
8. envoyées
9. reservée
10. perdus

Exercise No. 164

1. Il y a cinq ans qu'il étudie le français.
2. Il a passé beaucoup de temps en conversation avec son professeur M. Picard.
3. Il a appris les règles essentielles de la grammaire.
4. Il a vraiment travaillé beaucoup.
5. Il parle bien le français maintenant.
6. M. Potter obtenu son billet, son passeport et ses chèques de voyage.
7. Il a écrit à son représentant.
8. Son représentant lui a promis de le recontrer à l'aéroport.
9. Ils se sont levés à sept heures du matin.
10. Il part à sept heures précises.
11. Chaque voyageur doit faire contrôler son billet et son passeport.
12. Sa famille n'accompagne pas M. Potter (*or* ne l'accompagne pas) en France.
13. Ils doivent finir l'année scolaire.
14. Elle doit rester à New-York pour s'occuper des enfants.

Exercise No. 165

1. obtained obtenir
2. left laisser
3. been être
4. said dire
5. finished finir
6. wanted vouloir
7. received recevoir
8. written écrire

9. read lire
10. learned apprendre
11. known savoir
12. given back rendre
13. put mettre
14. obeyed obéir
15. seen voir
16. eaten manger
17. done, made faire
18. taken prendre
19. listened écouter
20. covered couvrir
21. understood comprendre
22. opened ouvrir
23. had avoir
24. permitted permettre
25. been able pouvoir

Exercise No. 166

(1 g) (2 e) (3 a) (4 h) (5 c) (6 i) (7 d) (8 j) (9 b) (10 f)

Exercise No. 167

1. Avez-vous fait
2. Faites mes amitiés
3. de ma part
4. dans votre propre langue
5. Pardonnez-moi
6. me tirer d'affaires
7. de faire votre connaissance
8. Ils montent en voiture
9. Ils descendent de la voiture
10. a fait ses adieux

Exercise No. 168

2. Il l'a écrite à M. Parmentier.
3. Oui, monsieur, il les a appreciés.
4. M. Potter l'a faite.
5. Oui, monsieur, ils m'ont rendu grand service.
6. Elle a servi du thé au rhum.
7. Non, monsieur, je ne l'ai pas comprise.
8. Philippe ne les a pas faites.
9. Non, madame, nous ne l'avons pas vu.
10. Il a apporté un colis postal.

Exercise No. 169

An Unusual Program At The Movies

This evening Mr. and Mrs. Potter are going to the movies. They don't like the majority of Hollywood films, especially the Westerns in which the cowboys fire shots at everybody and are constantly galloping. Detective stories don't interest them either.

But this evening there is an unusual program in a theater very near their home. The picture is called "A Voyage in France." This is a documentary film on the country which Mr. Potter is going to visit in a few months. There are scenes portraying the history of France, others which show its countryside, its rivers, its mountains, its large cities, etc. That is to say that it is a most interesting film for tourists.

The Potters arrive at the theatre at 8:30. Almost all the seats are taken and so they have to sit in the third row. Mr. Potter does not like this because the movements on the screen hurt his eyes. Fortunately they are able to change their seats after a quarter of an hour, and they take seats in the thirteenth row.

The Potters enjoy this picture very much. They find it fascinating.

On leaving the theatre Mr. Potter says to his wife, "Do you know Alice, I think that I'll get along well in France. I understood almost all that they said."

Exercise No. 170

1. à la salle d'attente
2. Tout de suite
3. Il m'a demandé
4. J'ai repondu
5. de faire votre connaissance
6. Le plaisir est à moi
7. J'ai pensé à moi-même
8. Nous avons pris un taxi
9. à vitesse vertigineuse
10. Pas si vite!
11. Je ne suis pas pressé
12. Ni moi non plus
13. reservée pour Potter
14. Quel est le prix
15. quatre cent francs par jour

Exercise No. 171

1. Did Philippe go to the station to meet his father? Yes, he left the house 20 minutes ago. Did his sister Marie go with him? His sister Marie and also his brother Henri went with him.
2. Has Mrs. Potter returned from the city? She has not returned but she will return soon. Why did she go to the city? She went there to do her shopping.
3. Why did Mr. Potter return so late this evening? Many clients came to see him in the afternoon. At what time does he usually leave his office? Usually he leaves at five o'clock sharp, but today he did not leave until a quarter to six.
4. At what time did Mr. Potter leave for the airport? He left at six o'clock in the morning. At what time did he get on the plane? He got on the plane at a quarter to eight.

Exercise No. 172

2. allées
3. né
4. mort
5. devenus; monté
6. retournée
7. partie
8. entrés
9. resté
10. partis; arrivés

Exercise No. 173

1. Il a passé par la douane et il est allé à la salle d'attente.
2. Un bel homme s'est approché.
3. Il a dit, —Pardon monsieur, êtes-vous M. Potter?
4. Il a répondu, —À votre service.
5. Le taxi est allé en ville à toute vitesse.
6. A la fin il a crié, —Je ne suis pas pressé!
7. Le chauffeur a répondu, —Ni moi non plus.
8. Il a dit, —Bonjour, monsieur. Avez-vous une chambre réservée pour M. Potter?
9. Il a répondu, —Bienvenu à Paris, Monsieur Potter.

Exercise No. 174

1. m'a appelé
2. prendre le thé
3. Nous nous sommes arretés
4. Je suis monté
5. Jai sonné; m'a invité
6. s'est approché pour me saluer
7. Je suis content de vous voir
8. Il y a beaucoup de maisons
9. Nous sommes entrés
10. m'a presenté
11. veut être
12. se sont retirés; leurs devoirs
13. Nous nous sommes mis
14. Nous avons parlé (causé)
15. Je suis revenu
16. par les vieux quartiers

Exercise No. 175

1. I got up
2. you went to bed, you lay down
3. he got dressed
4. she enjoyed herself
5. we stopped
6. you approached
7. they met each other
8. they knew each other
9. I did not take a walk
10. he was not mistaken
11. did they not withdraw?
12. did they not sit down?

Exercise No. 176

1. Did the children go to bed early? They went to bed early.
2. Did Jean get up late? No, he did not get up late.
3. Did Marie dress quickly? Yes, she dressed quickly.
4. Were you mistaken, Charles? No, I was not mistaken.
5. Did you have a good time, Anne? No, I did not have a good time.
6. Where did you meet, gentlemen? We met at the office.
7. Where did the bus stop? It stopped on the corner over there.
8. Did Mrs. Potter take care of the children? She took care of the children.
9. Did the tourist feel at home in Paris? Like all tourists he felt at home.

Exercise No. 177

1. M. Parmentier a appelé M. Potter par téléphone.
2. Il s'est arrêté à cinq heures.
3. Une petite bonne fraîche a ouvert la porte.
4. M. Parmentier s'est approché pour le saluer.
5. Elle a l'air du dix-huitième siècle.
6. Les messieurs sont entrés dans un grand salon.
7. Ils sont les fils de M. Parmentier.
8. Ils font leurs études au Lycée Henri IV.
9. L'aîné veut être docteur.
10. Ils se sont retirés pour aller faire leurs devoirs.
11. On a parlé de la vie en France.

12. M. Parmentier a recommandé le Marché aux Puces.
13. Mme. Parmentier l'a invité à l'accompagner au Marché aux Fleurs.
14. Il a passé une heure agréable en parlent d'une chose et d'une autre.
15. Il est revenu à pied.

Exercise No. 178

1. me chercher	9. On y joue
2. Nous sommes restés	10. On y écrit
3. sans rien attraper	11. Les passants
4. à jeter des pierres	12. Ensuite; notre route
5. Nous avons continué	13. m'a quitté
6. la plus belle place	14. J'ai suivi
7. Quelle belle avenue!	15. dans la chaise la plus proche
8. m'a frappé	

Exercise No. 179

1. Did you understand all that the teacher said? I did not understand all (of it).
2. Did you read the guides that I lent you? I read them with much interest.
3. What is the first secret of good cooking? All that enters into a dish must be of good quality.
4. Can one ski in the mountains? Those who are young and strong do it all the time.
5. What café did you visit today? I visited the Royale-Concorde of which we have often spoken.
6. Where are the valises in which I have put my clothes? They are in your room.

Exercise No. 180

1. que	5. qui	8. que
2. ce qu'il	6. laquelle	9. tout ce qui
3. qui	7. dont	10. que
4. ce qui		

Exercise No. 181

1. Il écrit sa lettre (*or* Il l'écrit) attablé dans le café Royale-Concorde.
2. Il est venu le chercher à l'hôtel.
3. Ils sont restés très longtemps sur le Pont Neuf.
4. Ils ont vu des pêcheurs, des bateaux-mouches, et des enfants.
5. Il pense que cela doit être la plus belle place du monde.
6. Ils se sont attablés pour prendre un café, mais surtout pour se reposer.
7. L'importance du café dans la vie quotidienne l'a frappé.
8. Dans un café on joue aux échecs.
9. Le café est un deuxième bureau pour les hommes d'affaires.
10. Ils ont contemplé l'immense Arc de Triomphe.
11. Il a quitté M. Potter à la Place de l'Alma.
12. Il a admiré la Seine.
13. Il est tombé fatigué, épuisé, et enchanté dans la chaise du café.

Exercise No. 182

1. Vous avez raison	8. Presque tout de suite
2. me voilà	9. Par ici
3. Je prends (Je bois)	10. les oreilles
4. les champs et les forêts	11. a duré
5. par la fenêtre	12. rester pour contempler
6. Les fermiers; les champs	13. est poussé; on est tiré
7. J'ai pris un taxi	14. On doit suivre

Exercise No. 183

1. What was Mr. Potter doing when you entered the room? He was reading aloud a letter which he had just received from his agent. What was Mr. Picard doing? He was listening to him.
2. What were you doing while the train was crossing the fields and the forests? I was looking out of the window. What did you see? I saw the peasants who were working in the fields.
3. Were there many vendors at Mont Saint Michel? There was an army of them. What were they selling? They were selling souvenirs of the Mont.
4. Do you often play tennis? Formerly I played (used to play) almost every day, but this year I have played only once.

Exercise No. 184

1. **(criaient et hurlaient)** The vendors were calling and yelling when I arrived at the market.
2. **(j'écoutais)** While I was listening to the radio somebody telephoned me.
3. **(nous faisions)** When we were doing our homework, they entered our room.
4. **(elle descendait)** She fell when she was getting out of the car.
5. **(allait)** When the taxi was going at full speed, I cried, "Not so fast."
6. **(il était)** We visited him when he was ill.
7. **(Il y avait)** There were many people at the airport when our plane arrived.
8. **(nous attendions)** While we were waiting for the bus, it began to rain.
9. **(nous venions)** We met them when we were coming from the movies.
10. **(dormaient)** Mr. Potter returned while the children were sleeping.

Exercise No. 185

1. Il écrit attablé dans un café.
2. Le métier de touriste demande beaucoup de repos.
3. Le café est dans la ville de Perros-Guirec.
4. Il prend un Calvados.
5. Il regardait par la fenêtre.
6. Il voyait les paysans qui travaillaient dans les champs.
7. Il pouvait voir les femmes qui lavaient le linge.
8. Il a entendu un bruit terrifiant.
9. La tête lui tournait comme une toupie.
10. Il voulait rester pour contempler la sculpture.
11. Il a reçu une impression imposante.
12. Il se tourne vers la Bretagne.

Exercise No. 186

1. Je suis revenu	7. il y a deux heures	12. Ils riaient
2. de plus en plus	8. J'étais	13. ne bougeait
3. je suis allé	9. Je marchais	14. Ils ne disait rien
4. Je ne peux	10. Je me suis approché	15. n'étaient pas du tout
5. la tête		
6. Je me suis dit	11. étaient	16. J'ai dit

Exercise No. 187

2. vivait	12. j'étais
3. lavaient	13. s'approchait
4. étaient-ils	14. commençaient
5. venait	15. mangeait
6. rendions visite à	16. se rencontraient
7. pensait-il	17. n'avions pas
8. descendait	18. ne voulaient pas
9. revenais	19. Pouviez-vous
10. montions	20. savait; devait
11. souriait	

Exercise No. 188

1. M. Potter est allé au Louvre pour le visiter à fond.
2. Il s'est dit, —Imbécile.
3. Il s'est tourné vers le Jardin des Tuileries.
4. Il a entendu des rires immodérés.
5. Il a vu un petit, joli théâtre.
6. Guignol ne bougeait pas.
7. Les enfants éclataient de rire.
8. Il a pris une place à côté d'une toute petite fille.
9. Elle a crié, —Papa.
10. La petit Gringalet était en train de donner de grands coups de tête dans le ventre de Guignol.
11. Non, monsieur les enfants n'étaient pas fâchés.
12. L'enfant a répondu gentiment, —Au revoir, papa.

Exercise No. 189

1. Mr. Potter has left for Paris.
2. His wife remained at home.
3. Mrs. Picard went out one hour ago.
4. She hasn't returned yet.
5. We went up in the elevator.
6. They went down on foot.
7. Why did you return so late, Marie?
8. I went to the market to do my shopping.
9. His grandfather died this morning.
10. My grandmother was born June 5, 1927.

Exercise No. 190

2. rencontrés	7. descendu	12. fait
3. pris	8. reservé	13. demandé
4. sortis	9. née	14. ouvertes; ouvertes
5. arrêté	10. mis	
6. arrivée	11. dit	

Exercise No. 191

1. **(rendrons)** Tomorrow we shall pay a visit to the Potter family.
2. **(sont allés)** Yesterday evening the children went to the movies.
3. **(parlait)** The pupils were not listening while the teacher was talking.
4. **(avez-vous passé)** Where did you spend last winter?
5. **(verrai)** I shall not see them until tomorrow.
6. **(jouaient)** We were doing our homework while they were playing cards.
7. **(pleuvait)** They remained at home, because it was raining buckets.
8. **(ferez-vous)** Will you take a trip to Europe next summer?
9. **(a prêté)** He lent us five dollars yesterday.
10. **(vous vous êtes levé)** At what time did you get up this morning?

Exercise No. 192

1. Il pleuvait à verse
2. J'étais très content
3. quand M. Potter a reçu
4. quand mon représentant m'a téléphoné
5. nous allions
6. Je ne savais pas
7. Nous ne pouvions pas
8. Voulaient-ils voyager *or* Est-ce qu'ils voulaient voyager
9. Elle n'avait pas le temps
10. Elle devait

Exercise No. 193

An Excursion To Versailles

One day Mr. Potter invited Mr. Parmentier's sons to accompany him on an excursion to Versailles.

It is not very far from Paris and they arrived without any difficulty. On the way to the palace, Mr. Potter had a novel idea.

"Let's lunch on the grass in the big park at the edge of the lake. I'm told that it's allowed."

"Wonderful! Let's go."

They entered a grocery to buy some ham, a Camembert cheese and a bottle of red wine. In a bakery next door they bought two loaves of French bread and three eclairs.

"I'm as hungry as a wolf," said the older one as they left the bakery.

"Let's eat right away," said Mr. Potter. "But what to do about utensils?"

"Let's see what there is in our pockets," said the younger one. The two boys found two penknives.

"Here! And we'll drink out of the bottle."

They entered the palace through the great iron gate but instead of taking the tour they went out, crossing the immense garden. The garden with its statues, fountains and groves of trees made a strong impression on Mr. Potter. The two boys were in agreement. The younger one said: "I assure you that the garden is the jewel of Versailles. But the palace bores us to death."

Mr. Potter answered laughing, "We're not obliged to go there."

When they arrived at the lake they sat down on the grass to eat. They talked of one thing and another while eating and Mr. Potter was struck once more by their intelligence. The boys ate like two wolves and they had a wonderful time. All three of them will remember this excursion to Versailles for a long time.

Exercise No. 194

Avenue De L'Opéra

We are strolling along the Avenue de l'Opéra. It is a fine wide avenue, which leads from the Palais Royal to the Opera.

There are many people on the avenue. All the tourists meet there. The sidewalks are lined with luxury shops where one can buy all sorts of beautiful things, if one has money: jewels, fine lingerie, gloves, china, blouses, leather goods and also books, for we are in France where people like to read. There is even a small shop and bookstore inside the Opera house.

There is also a well-known café-restaurant on the Place de l'Opéra: the Café de la Paix. Let's go have a beer, shall we? With pleasure.

Exercise No. 195

1. Mr. Potter has noticed that although French villages differ, they all have a Main Street.
2. The street often leads to a square surrounded by trees.
3. Behind the trees are the well-arranged shops of the village.
4. The dry-cleaner's shop is painted violet.
5. One can see delicious cakes in the window of the pastry shop. In the grocery window. In the laundry window.
6. The flies are walking tranquilly on the legs of lamb hanging in front of the butcher shop.
7. The city hall, the church and the school are all on the square.
8. The children are well-behaved in France.
9. Mr. Potter gets up early not to miss anything of the street spectacle.
10. First he hears a rooster crowing.
11. A small boy rushes into the street.
12. He suddenly stops to examine something which catches his eye.
13. Our hero returns with a loaf of bread almost as long as he is.
14. It is seven-thirty and Mr. Potter has an appointment with the Parmentier boys to go to Chartres.
15. He will describe the adventures of that afternoon.

Exercise No. 196

1. à une place entourée d'arbres
2. bien rangées
3. est peinte
4. est remplie de gâteaux délicieux
5. a pendu ses gigots
6. s'y promènent
7. Au milieu du village
8. des rires et des chansons
9. Pour ne rien manquer du spectacle
10. On dort
11. à se saluer
12. se réveille
13. Ce que les Français mangent
14. revient avec un pain
15. Je dois tout de même

Exercise No. 197

1. Did you send the pottery to Mr. Potter? We sent it to him.
2. Do many people meet each other on the Avenue de l'Opéra? All tourists meet each other there.
3. Please send me the French newspapers. We shall send them to you tomorrow.
4. Has the waiter given you the bill? He hasn't given it to me yet.
5. Did you ask the employee for the tickets? I haven't asked him for them yet because he is very busy.
6. How many dishes are there in this case? There are 25 dozen (of them).
7. Did you return the money (to him), which you borrowed from him? I shall return it to him this evening.
8. Has the maid put on the desk the porcelain which Mr. Potter has just received from Limoges? Yes, she has put it there.
9. Will you lend me your umbrella? I'll lend it to you; but please return it to me tomorrow. Many thanks. I'll return it to you tomorrow.
10. Please show me the new dress you have bought. I cannot show it to you, because it has not yet arrived from the store.

Exercise No. 198

1. Mr. Potter wanted to be back in time to go to the opera.
2. They had prepared a good lunch.
3. The car was waiting downstairs.
4. He heard a sound that he recognized immediately.
5. They had a flat tire.
6. The young men wanted to help change the tire.
7. There was no jack in the tool kit of the car.
8. The truckdriver offered to give them a hand.
9. The truckdriver had so much natural dignity.
10. The boys invited him to share their lunch.
11. They ate their chicken and the truckdriver's ham, and drank the bottle of wine.
12. They said, "This ham is delicious."
13. He said, "My wife does not neglect me."
14. They had a nap, then they all said goodbye.
15. Mr. Potter has to dress to go to the opera.

Exercise No. 199

1. me chercher
2. Ils avaient préparé
3. une nappe, des serviettes, des couteaux, des fourchettes
4. Et nous voilà
5. Tout à coup
6. Nous avons crevé un pneu
7. Il n'y avait pas de cric
8. Personne ne
9. Nous nous sommes assis
10. Bientôt un grand camion
11. un coup de main
12. En tout cas
13. s'est mis à la besogne
14. lui offrir un pourboire
15. déjeuner avec nous

Exercise No. 200

2. **Nous avions vraiment travaillé** . . . We had really worked hard.
3 **Ils n'avaient pas encore obtenu** . . . They had not yet obtained their tickets.
4. **Avait-il écrit** . . .? Had he written a letter to his friend?
5. **Qui avait promis** . . .? Who had promised to meet him at the airport?
6. **J'avais oublié** . . . I had forgotten my umbrella.
7. **Avaient-ils reservé** . . .? Had they reserved a room for Mr. Potter?
8. **Aviez-vous lu** . . .? Had you read many guide books?
9. **Ses jeunes amis avaient préparé** . . . His young friends had prepared a good lunch.
10. **N'avait-il pas loue** . . .? Had he not rented a car?

Exercise No. 201

2. **Un grand camion s'était approché** . . . A large truck had approached rapidly.
3. **Nous nous étions assis** . . . We had sat down under a large tree.
4. **J'étais allé** . . . I had gone to the waiting room.
5. **Nous n'étions par sortis** . . . We had not gone out together.
6. **Ils étaient arrivés** . . . They had arrived safe and sound.
7. **Le taxi s'était arrêté** . . . The taxi had stopped before the hotel.
8. **Étiez-vous allé** . . .? Had you gone to the customs office?
9. **Nous nous étions dit** . . . We had said good-bye to each other.
10. **Elles n'étaient pas restées** . . . They had not stayed in Paris two weeks.

Exercise No. 202

1. We have good teachers. How do you find yours?
2. Let's go to the post office in your car. Ours has a flat tire.
3. Please lend me your pen. Mine does not write.
4. I have forgotten my umbrella. Will you lend me yours?
5. You have no jack. Do you want to borrow mine?
6. Paul's bicycle costs more than mine, but mine is better than his.
7. Louise and I bought theatre tickets yesterday. I have mine, but unfortunately she has lost hers.
8. Here are our hats. This one is mine and that one is yours.

Exercise No. 203

1. He had never been a gambler.
2. He had noticed that people were taken up greatly with the National Lottery.
3. He dreamed of winning the first prize.
4. He would have sufficient money to travel all over Europe.
5. His wife would go with him.
6. The children would go to school somewhere in France.
7. Mr. Potter bought a lottery ticket from a young girl at a ticket booth.
8. The next morning he rang for coffee, croissants, and the newspaper.
9. Only the newspaper interested him.
10. He stopped breathing and began to look for his ticket.
11. He was making trips to the moon.
12. Mr. Potter had the number 25,000.
13. The prize-winning number was 26,000.
14. Mr. Potter decided that the emotions of the gambler were not for him.
15. He likes a quiet life.

Exercise No. 204

1. Je n'avais jamais été
2. des postes de vente de billets de loterie
3. qu'on s'occupait beaucoup de
4. Je voyais des affiches illustrées
5. Si je gagnais le premier prix
6. Je pourrais acheter
7. l'homme le plus heureux du monde
8. Et voilà comment
9. de bonne heure
10. Je ne m'intéressais qu'au journal
11. Je cherche
12. à peine le tenir
13. C'est un cinq, pas un six
14. en riant de moi-même

Exercise No. 205

2. **Il visiterait** . . . He would visit France and Italy
3. **Nous apprendrions** . . . We would learn French.
4. **Ma famille ne m'accompagnerait pas.** My family would not accompany me.
5. **Elle pourrait acheter** . . . She would be able to buy many beautiful things.
6. **Aurait-il** . . .? Would he have enough money?
7. **Ils achèteraient** . . . They would buy some art objects.
8. **Seriez-vous** . . .? Would you be satisfied to remain here?
9. **Elle ne vous connaîtrait pas** . . . She would not know you.
10. **Ils ne feraient pas** . . . They would not do their homework.
11. **Je vous enverrais** . . . I would send you the magazines.
12. **Ils ne viendraient pas** . . . They would not come the next week.

Exercise No. 206

1. Mr. Potter had read a few books on the history of France and on its customs.
2. He was able to describe only a little of what he had seen and learned.
3. He likes the French people especially.
4. He likes their politeness, their feeling for the dignity of man, and their keen sense of humor.
5. He thinks life is more quiet in France.
6. He had gotten a different impression in the taxi when he first arrived.
7. His whole family would accompany him.
8. He is sure he could be a guide to them without any trouble.
9. He is leaving on August 1.
10. He will be glad to telephone Mr. Picard when he returns.
11. He thinks they will spend hours talking about France, and the Paris they love.

Exercise No. 208

1. They went to the market to shop.
2. The French people made a strong impression on Mr. Potter.
3. He went to the railroad station to ask for information.
4. I shall be able to get along in France because I speak French well.

5. After tomorrow we shall visit Mr. Duval.
6. The young man had already filled the tank and checked the oil.
7. Next summer Mr. Potter will be able to act as guide for his whole family.
8. If Mr. Potter had had more time, he would have taken a trip to Morocco.
9. At the Hotel Quai Voltaire we lacked nothing.
10. After having finished his business matters, Mr. Potter devoted himself completely to recreation.
11. I'm going to write a letter to my agent to let him know the date of my arrival.
12. After saying goodbye we got into the plane.
13. I was thinking of my teacher's advice while the taxi was racing at full speed through the streets of Paris.
14. Formerly Mr. Potter had his French correspondence translated, but in the future he will translate it himself.
15. The children were amusing themselves by throwing stones into the water.
16. If you find the rubbers which I left at your home, return them to me please.
17. I shall not forget to return them to you.
18. I had never seen such a sight.
19. When Mr. Potter was traveling in Europe, Mrs. Potter was taking care of the children.
20. I have never been in France, but I intend to go there next summer.

Exercise No. 209

1. est un homme d'affaires de New-York.
2. un voyage à Paris pour rendre visite à son représentant.
3. faire sa connaissance.
4. il avait appris à bien parler le français.
5. Il avait aussi lu beaucoup de livres sur la France.
6. beaucoup de lettres à son ami, le professeur.
7. beaucoup des endroits intéressants dont ils avaient parlé dans leurs conversations.
8. il avait trouvé la vie en France plus tranquille qu'aux Etats-Unis.
9. qui l'avait conduit à son hôtel.
10. La vitesse vertigineuse du taxi
11. il a bientôt terminé ses affaires.
12. leur politesse et leur sentiment marqué de la dignité de l'homme.
13. il n'a pas eu le temps d'aller ni au Maroc ni en Corse.
14. tant à voir, à faire et à apprendre.
15. des coutumes, de la vie, de la langue et des arts de la France.
16. il reviendra en France.
17. l'accompagnerait.
18. Il n'a pas gagné le gros lot dans la loterie mais il aura assez d'argent.
19. que M. Potter écrira avant de quitter la France.
20. il invitera M. Picard à dîner en famille.

Exercise No. 210

Nice, Capital of the Riviera

There are really two cities in Nice: the Italian city and the French city; the old city and the new city. One can walk in the old districts where one hears nothing but Italian, for Nice became French only in 1860. In this district they sell macaroni, ravioli, olives, and sausage. The air is perfumed with garlic and tomato sauce. People shout, sing, bargain. This part of the city is entirely Italian.

But close by, crossing the Place Massena, you are in the French city. You walk up Boulevard Victor Hugo under a row of splendid trees and you admire the magnificent shops. You see cars as long as trains. It is a city of luxury.

Nice is also a sports center. There is a magnificent tennis club; there is the race track at Cagnes, nearby; the famous winter sports at Beuil in the mountains; yachting, and sea bathing. It is true that the beach is stony but that does not matter. You go there anyway to worship the sun.

The city where people are born, where they go to school, where they earn a living, this city exists too. This city has its commerce: tourism, flowers, perfume, olives, fishing. It has its cultural life: music, which it takes very seriously, opera, theater, lectures and book stores. As in other cities of France there is an interest in science and an interest in art.

But after all the real glory of Nice is its location. It rises from the blue sea to the hills adorned with flower-covered villas up to the foothills of the mountains covered with snow. The sky is intensely blue like the sea. The air is mild and balmy.

Everything is there to make people happy.

REGULAR VERBS

Infinitive Present Participle	Present Tense			Future Pres. Conditional	Imperfect Convers. Past
parler to speak	**je parle**	**tu parles**	**il parle**	**je parlerai**	**je parlais**
parlant	**nous parlons**	**vous parlez**	**ils parlent**	**je parlerais**	**j'ai parlé**
finir to finish	**je finis**	**tu finis**	**il finit**	**je finirai**	**je finissais**
finissant	**nous finissons**	**vous finissez**	**ils finissent**	**je finirais**	**j'ai fini**
vendre to sell	**je vends**	**tu vends**	**il vend**	**je vendrai**	**je vendais**
vendant	**nous vendons**	**vous vendez**	**ils vendent**	**je vendrais**	**j'ai vendu**

AUXILIARY VERBS

Infinitive Present Participle	Present Tense			Future Pres. Conditional	Imperfect Convers. Past
avoir to have	**j'ai**	**tu as**	**il a**	**j'aurai**	**j'avais**
ayant	**nous avons**	**vous avez**	**ils ont**	**j'aurais**	**j'ai eu**
être to be	**je suis**	**tu es**	**il est**	**je serai**	**j'étais**
étant	**nous sommes**	**vous êtes**	**ils sont**	**je serais**	**j'ai été**

COMMON IRREGULAR VERBS

Infinitive Present Participle	Present Tense			Future Pres. Conditional	Imperfect Convers. Past
aller to go	**je vais**	**tu vas**	**il va**	**j'irai**	**j'allais**
allant	**nous allons**	**vous allez**	**ils vont**	**j'irais**	**je suis allé**
s'asseoir to sit down	**je m'assieds (assois)**	**tu t'assieds (assois)**	**il s'assied (assoit)**	**je m'assoirai**	**je m'asseyais**
s'asseyant	**nous nous asseyons**	**vous vous asseyez**	**ils s'assoient**	**je m'assoirais**	**je me suis assis**
battre to beat	**je bats**	**tu bats**	**il bat**	**je battrai**	**je battais**
battant	**nous battons**	**vous battez**	**ils battent**	**je battrais**	**j'ai battu**
boire to drink	**je bois**	**tu bois**	**il boit**	**je boirai**	**je buvais**
buvant	**nous buvons**	**vous buvez**	**ils boivent**	**je boirais**	**j'ai bu**
conduire to conduct	**je conduis**	**tu conduis**	**il conduit**	**je conduirai**	**je conduisais**
conduisant	**nous conduisons**	**vous conduisez**	**ils conduisent**	**je conduirais**	**j'ai conduit**
connaître to know	**je connais**	**tu connais**	**il connaît**	**je connaîtrai**	**je connaissais**
connaissant	**nous connaissons**	**vous connaissez**	**ils connaissent**	**je connaîtrais**	**j'ai connu**
courir to run	**je cours**	**tu cours**	**il court**	**je courrai**	**je courais**
courant	**nous courons**	**vous courez**	**ils courent**	**je courrais**	**j'ai couru**
couvrir to cover	**je couvre**	**tu couvres**	**il couvre**	**je couvrirai**	**je couvrais**
couvrant	**nous couvrons**	**vous couvrez**	**ils couvrent**	**je couvrirais**	**j'ai couvert**
croire to believe	**je crois**	**tu crois**	**il croit**	**je croirai**	**je croyais**
croyant	**nous croyons**	**vous croyez**	**ils croient**	**je croirais**	**j'ai cru**
devoir to owe, must	**je dois**	**tu dois**	**il doit**	**je devrai**	**je devais**
devant	**nous devons**	**vous devez**	**ils doivent**	**je devrais**	**j'ai dû**
dire to say	**je dis**	**tu dis**	**il dit**	**je dirai**	**je disais**
disant	**nous disons**	**vous dites**	**its disent**	**je dirais**	**j'ai dit**
dormir to sleep	**je dors**	**tu dors**	**il dort**	**je dormirai**	**je dormais**
dormant	**nous dormons**	**vous dormez**	**ils dorment**	**je dormirais**	**j'ai dormi**
écrire to write	**j'écris**	**tu écris**	**il écrit**	**j'écrirai**	**j'écrivais**
écrivant	**nous écrivons**	**vous écrivez**	**ils écrivent**	**j'écrirais**	**j'ai écrit**
envoyer to send	**j'envoie**	**tu envoies**	**il envoie**	**j'enverrai**	**j'envoyais**
envoyant	**nous envoyons**	**vous envoyez**	**ils envoient**	**j'enverrais**	**j'ai envoyé**
faire to do, make	**je fais**	**tu fais**	**il fait**	**je ferai**	**je faisais**
faisant	**nous faisons**	**vous faites**	**ils font**	**je ferais**	**j'ai fait**
falloir to be necessary			**il faut**	**il faudra**	**il fallait**
				il faudrait	**il a fallu**

Infinitive Present Participle	Present Tense			Future Pres. Conditional	Imperfect Convers. Past
lire to read **lisant**	**je lis** **nous lisons**	**tu lis** **vous lisez**	**il lit** **ils lisent**	**je lirai** **je lirais**	**je lisais** **j'ai lu**
mentir to lie **mentant**	**je mens** **nous mentons**	**tu mens** **vous mentez**	**il ment** **ils mentent**	**je mentirai** **je mentirais**	**je mentais** **j'ai menti**
mettre to put **mettant**	**je mets** **nous mettons**	**tu mets** **vous mettez**	**il met** **ils mettent**	**je mettrai** **je mettrais**	**je mettais** **j'ai mis**
mourir to die **mourant**	**je meurs** **nous mourons**	**tu meurs** **vous mourez**	**il meurt** **ils meurent**	**je mourrai** **je mourrais**	**je mourais** **je suis mort**
naître to be born **naissant**	**je nais** **nous naissons**	**tu nais** **vous naissez**	**il naît** **ils naissent**	**je naîtrai** **je naîtrais**	**je naissais** **je suis né**
offrir to offer **offrant**	**j'offre** **nous offrons**	**tu offres** **vous offrez**	**il offre** **ils offrent**	**j'offrirai** **j'offrirais**	**j'offrais** **j'ai offert**
ouvrir to open **ouvrant**	**j'ouvre** **nous ouvrons**	**tu ouvres** **vous ouvrez**	**il ouvre** **ils ouvrent**	**j'ouvrirai** **j'ouvrirais**	**j'ouvrais** **j'ai ouvert**
paraître to appear **paraissant**	**je parais** **nous paraissons**	**tu parais** **vous paraissez**	**il paraît** **ils paraissent**	**je paraîtrai** **je paraîtrais**	**je paraissais** **j'ai paru**
partir to set out, leave **partant**	**je pars** **nous partons**	**tu pars** **vous partez**	**il part** **ils partent**	**je partirai** **je partirais**	**je partais** **je suis parti**
plaire to please **plaisant**	**je plais** **nous plaisons**	**tu plais** **vous plaisez**	**il plaît** **ils plaisent**	**je plaîrai** **je plaîrait**	**je plaisais** **j'ai plu**
pleuvoir to rain **pleuvant**			**il pleut**	**il pleuvrai** **il pleuvrais**	**il pleuvais** **il a plu**
pouvoir to be able **pouvant**	**je peux (puis)** **nous pouvons**	**tu peux** **vous pouvez**	**il peut** **ils peuvent**	**je pourrai** **je pourrais**	**je pouvais** **j'ai pu**
prendre to take **prenant**	**je prends** **nous prenons**	**tu prends** **vous prenez**	**il prend** **ils prennent**	**je prendrai** **je prendrais**	**je prenais** **j'ai pris**
recevoir to receive **recevant**	**je reçois** **nous recevons**	**tu reçois** **vous recevez**	**il reçoit** **ils reçoivent**	**je recevrai** **je recevrais**	**je recevais** **j'ai reçu**
rire to laugh **riant**	**je ris** **nous rions**	**tu ris** **vous riez**	**il rit** **ils rient**	**je rirai** **je rirais**	**je riais** **j'ai ri**
savoir to know **sachant**	**je sais** **nous savons**	**tu sais** **vous savez**	**il saît** **ils savent**	**je saurai** **je saurais**	**je savais** **j'ai su**
sentir to feel **sentant**	**je sens** **nous sentons**	**tu sens** **vous sentez**	**il sent** **ils sentent**	**je sentirai** **je sentirais**	**je sentais** **j'ai senti**
servir to serve **servant**	**je sers** **nous servons**	**tu sers** **vous servez**	**il sert** **ils servent**	**je servirai** **je servirais**	**je servais** **j'ai servi**
sortir to go out **sortant**	**je sors** **nous sortons**	**tu sors** **vous sortez**	**il sort** **ils sortent**	**je sortirai** **je sortirais**	**je sortais** **je suis sorti**
suivre to follow **suivant**	**je suis** **nous suivons**	**tu suis** **vous suivez**	**il suit** **ils suivent**	**je suivrai** **je suivrais**	**je suivais** **j'ai suivi**
tenir to hold **tenant**	**je tiens** **nous tenons**	**tu tiens** **vous tenez**	**il tient** **ils tiennent**	**je tiendrai** **je tiendrais**	**je tenais** **j'ai tenu**
valoir to be worth **valant**	**je vaux** **nous valons**	**tu vaux** **vous valez**	**il vaut** **ils valent**	**je vaudrai** **je vaudrais**	**je valais** **j'ai valu**
venir to come **venant**	**je viens** **nous venons**	**tu viens** **vous venez**	**il vient** **ils viennent**	**je viendrai** **je viendrais**	**je venais** **je suis venu**
vivre to live **vivant**	**je vis** **nous vivons**	**tu vis** **vous vivez**	**il vit** **ils vivent**	**je vivrai** **je vivrais**	**je vivais** **j'ai vécu**
voir to see **voyant**	**je vois** **nous voyons**	**tu vois** **vous voyez**	**il voit** **ils voient**	**je verrai** **je verrais**	**je voyais** **j'ai vu**
vouloir to want **voulant**	**je veux** **nous voulons**	**tu veux** **vous voulez**	**il veut** **ils veulent**	**je voudrai** **je voudrais**	**je voulais** **j'ai voulu**